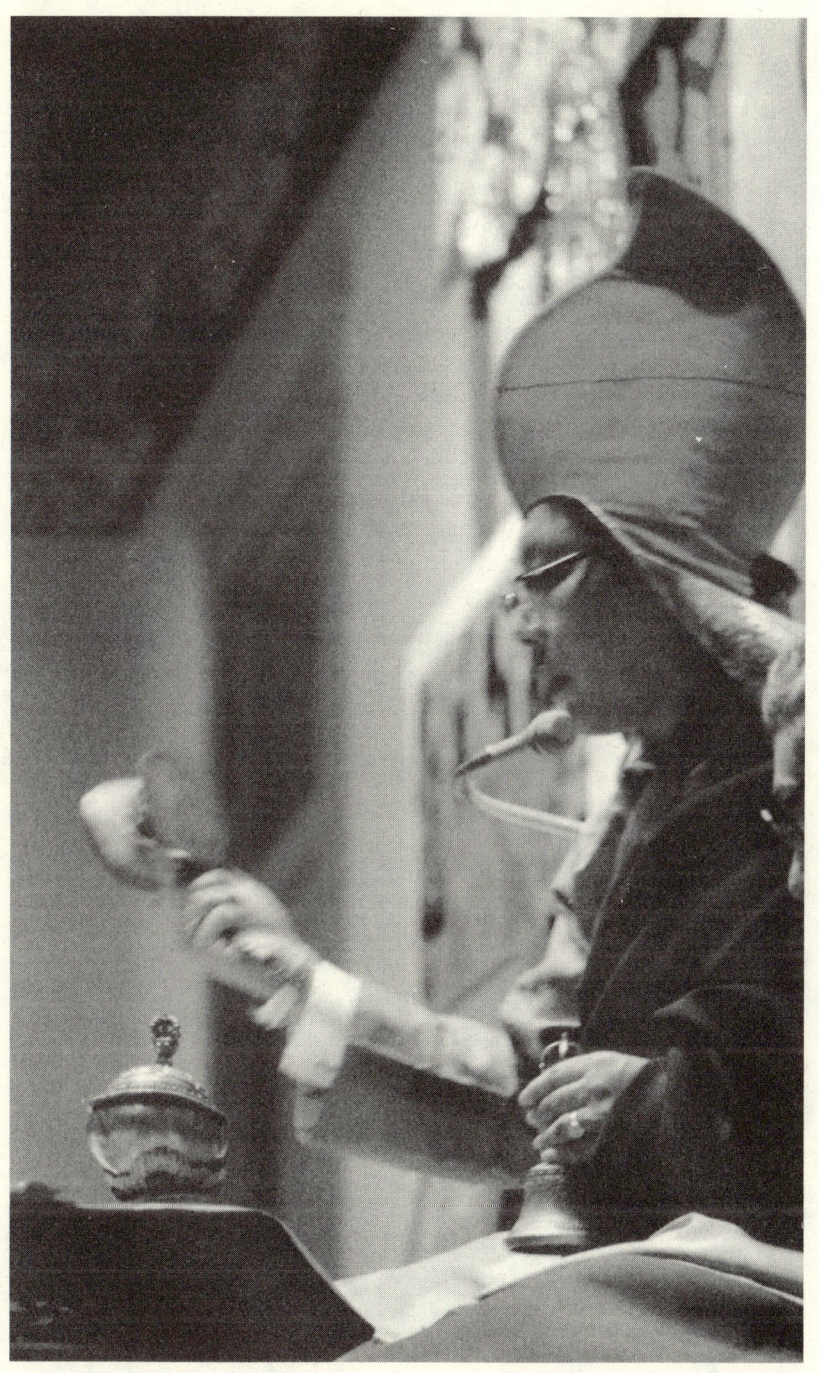

The Collected Works of Chögyam Trungpa

VOLUME ONE

Born in Tibet • *Meditation in Action* • *Mudra* • Selected Writings

VOLUME TWO

Glimpses of Abhidharma • *Glimpses of Mahayana* • *Glimpses of Shunyata* • *The Path Is the Goal* • *Training the Mind and Cultivating Loving-Kindness* • Selected Writings

VOLUME THREE

Cutting Through Spiritual Materialism • *The Heart of the Buddha* • *The Myth of Freedom* • Selected Writings

VOLUME FOUR

The Dawn of Tantra • *Journey without Goal* • *The Lion's Roar* • An Interview with Chögyam Trungpa

VOLUME FIVE

Crazy Wisdom • *Illusion's Game* • *The Life of Marpa the Translator* (Excerpts) • *The Rain of Wisdom* (Excerpts) • *The Sadhana of Mahamudra* (Excerpts) • Selected Writings

VOLUME SIX

Glimpses of Space • *Orderly Chaos* • *Secret Beyond Thought* • *The Tibetan Book of the Dead*: Commentary • *Transcending Madness* • Selected Writings

VOLUME SEVEN

The Art of Calligraphy (Excerpts) • *Dharma Art* • *Visual Dharma* (Excerpts) • Selected Poems • Selected Writings

VOLUME EIGHT

Great Eastern Sun: The Wisdom of Shambhala • *Shambhala: The Sacred Path of the Warrior* • Selected Writings

THE COLLECTED WORKS OF
CHÖGYAM TRUNGPA

VOLUME FIVE

Crazy Wisdom

Illusion's Game: The Life and Teachings of Naropa

The Life of Marpa the Translator (Excerpts)

The Rain of Wisdom (Excerpts)

The Sadhana of Mahamudra (Excerpts)

Selected Writings

EDITED BY
Carolyn Rose Gimian

SHAMBHALA · *Boston & London* · 2004

Shambhala Publications, Inc.
Horticultural Hall
300 Massachusetts Avenue
Boston, Massachusetts 02115
www.shambhala.com

Page i: Chögyam Trungpa performing the abhishekha of Vajrayogini, an advanced tantric empowerment. Boulder, Colorado, ca. 1979. Photograph by Paul Kloppenburg. Used by permission.

See pages 383–384 for a continuation of the copyright page.

9 8 7 6 5 4 3 2 1

First Edition
Printed in the United States of America

♾ This edition is printed on acid-free paper that meets
the American National Standards Institute Z39.48 Standard.
Distributed in the United States by Random House, Inc.,
and in Canada by Random House of Canada Ltd

Library of Congress Cataloging-in-Publication Data

Trunpga, Chögyam, 1939–
[Works. 2003]
The collected works of Chögyam Trungpa / edited by Carolyn Rose Gimian; forewords
by Diana J. Mukpo and Samuel Bercholz.—1st ed.
p.   cm.
Includes bibliographical references and index.
ISBN 1-59030-025-4 (v. 1: alk. paper)—ISBN 1-59030-026-2 (v.2: alk. paper)—
ISBN 1-59030-027-0 (v.3: alk. paper)—ISBN 1-59030-028-9 (v.4: alk. paper)—
ISBN 1-59030-029-7 (v.5: alk. paper)—ISBN 1-59030-030-0 (v.6: alk. paper)—
ISBN 1-59030-031-9 (v.7: alk. paper)—ISBN 1-59030-032-7 (v.8: alk. paper)—
1. Spiritual life—Buddhism.   2. Buddhism—Doctrines.   I. Gimian, Carolyn Rose.   II. Title.

BQ4302.T7823   2003
294.3′420423—dc22   2003058963

CONTENTS

CONTENTS

ILLUSION'S GAME: THE LIFE AND TEACHING OF NAROPA

CONTENTS

Selected Writings

INTRODUCTION
TO VOLUME FIVE

V OLUME FIVE BRINGS US to a series of writings that concern themselves with the themes of lineage and devotion in the context of
vajrayana Buddhism and Chögyam Trungpa's transmission of dharma to
America. The first two offerings in this volume, *Crazy Wisdom* and *Illusion's Game: The Life and Teaching of Naropa*, are commentaries by Chögyam Trungpa on the significance of the lives of two great lineage
holders: Padmasambhava, or Guru Rinpoche, who introduced Buddhism
to Tibet in the eighth century; and Naropa, the Indian guru who gave
the root teachings of the Kagyü lineage to his Tibetan disciple Marpa in
the eleventh century. Marpa is known as the father of the Kagyü lineage
in Tibet, and it is his life and teachings that are the subject of the next
two selections in Volume Five. In this case, *The Collected Works* includes
Chögyam Trungpa's preface and his translator's colophon to *The Life of
Marpa the Translator*, which was translated by Trungpa Rinpoche and the
Nālandā Translation Committee (NTC) and first published in 1982. Since
translations in general are beyond the scope of *The Collected Works*, only
the preface and the colophon are included. Likewise, *The Collected Works*
includes Chögyam Trungpa's foreword and colophon to *The Rain of Wisdom*, another translation undertaken by the NTC under Rinpoche's direction. Rinpoche's own songs, or religious poetry, that are part of the
English edition of *The Rain of Wisdom* are also presented.

The next selection is an excerpt from *The Sadhana of Mahamudra*, the
tantric text that Chögyam Trungpa received as terma in Bhutan in 1968.
This is followed by "Joining Energy and Space," an article based on some
of the teachings that he subsequently gave to his students about the

significance of the sadhana. *The Sadhana of Mahamudra* brings together the ultimate teachings from two great Tibetan spiritual lineages: the dzogchen, or maha ati, teachings of the Nyingma and the mahamudra teachings of the Kagyü.

Next are two short articles that present the vajrayana practice of mantra, which uses the repetition of sacred syllables to invoke the wisdom and energy of egolessness in the form of various herukas,[1] or nontheistic deities. The first article, "HUM: An Approach to Mantra," is a general explanation of the basic usage of mantra as well as a specific discussion of the mantra HUM, which is the seed, or root, syllable for all of the herukas. The next article, "Explanation of the Vajra Guru Mantra," also presents general guidelines for understanding the practice of mantra. However, the main body of this piece is an explanation of this mantra and its association with invoking the power and presence of Padmasambhava.

Next is an interview with Chögyam Trungpa on the ngöndro practices, or the four foundations, which are the entrance into the formal practice of vajrayana. This interview was part of the introduction to the English translation of *The Torch of Certainty*, a classic Tibetan text on ngöndro composed by Jamgön Kongtrül the Great and translated by Judith Hanson. Trungpa Rinpoche's foreword from this book is also included.

"The Practicing Lineage" and "The Mishap Lineage" discuss the origins of Trungpa Rinpoche's own spiritual lineage, the line of the Trungpas. Then there is the short piece "Teachings on the Tulku Principle" and finally three articles on Milarepa, Tibet's most famous Buddhist yogi.

Lineage, one of the main topics of this volume, means the continuity and transmission of the awakened state of mind, which is passed down in an unbroken, direct line from teacher to disciple, beginning with the Buddha—or *a* buddha—and continuing up to the present day. There are many branches of transmission. Some of them trace back directly to Gautama Buddha, the buddha of this age or world realm who appeared in human form. Other lineages trace back to a transmission from one or more of the buddhas who exist on a celestial plane, such as Vajradhara or Samantabhadra, who manifest in a transcendental or dharmakaya aspect. This is often the case in the Tibetan lineages.

---

1. *Heruka* is the Sanskrit term. *Yidam* is the Tibetan for a vajrayana deity.

As mentioned earlier, the teachings presented here concern themselves with two major branches within Tibetan Buddhism, both of which were part of Chögyam Trungpa's direct heritage: the teachings of the Nyingma, or "ancient," lineage of Padmasambhava; and those of the Kagyü, the "oral" or "command" lineage, which originated with the Indian guru Tilopa, who received the ultimate teachings directly from the dharmakaya buddha Vajradhara.

Chögyam Trungpa's primary intent was not to present a historical or scholarly approach to these lineages of transmission. As he says in *Crazy Wisdom*, "Our approach here, as far as chronology and such things are unconcerned, is entirely unscholastic. For those of you who are concerned with dates and other such historical facts and figures, I am afraid I will be unable to furnish accurate data. Nevertheless, the inspiration of Padmasambhava, however old or young he may be, goes on" (page 65). In his talks on the forefathers of the Tibetan Buddhist teachings, he drew on events from their spiritual biographies, which are stories of complete liberation, or *namthars*, composed in order to bring to life the journey that each of these great practitioners made. He shows us the enormous commitment to sanity that they made and the extraordinary difficulties that they endured in order to become holders of the wisdom of buddhadharma and to transmit that wisdom to others. Above all, he presents their lives as examples to guide us in awakening our own sanity as we tread on the path of dharma.

Devotion, the other main theme of this volume, is the emotional attitude and experience of the student that make transmission and realization possible. Devotion is the water that flows through the teachings and maintains them as a living transmission. Devotion is the human element of lineage, the bond between teacher and student that brings vajrayana to life. If one approaches the vajrayana teachings purely with the intellect, it is like trying to use physics to fathom outer space. The physics of space may be extremely subtle and profound, but studying those principles and equations does not bring any genuine *experience* of space. In fact, it may make it seem that direct personal experience of something so far-reaching and profound would be impossible.

What makes the impossible possible is, first, meeting a genuine teacher, someone who is the embodiment of what one is seeking. Second, one has to make friends with outer space as presented in this human form. That is the role of devotion in one's relationship with the

teacher. It involves surrendering one's egotism and selfishness uncondi-
tionally in order to gain a vast perspective. It seems that there is really
only one thing that allows us to sacrifice ourselves completely, and that
is love. We have to begin with love—completely giving ourselves to one
person, the teacher, before we can surrender properly to the whole
world. Without a personal connection, devotion is too abstract and, par-
adoxically, too limited. You might say that it's not important to surrender to a teacher per se: you could give yourself to anyone. However,
devotion is about unconditional surrender, not about creating further
ego-oriented entanglements. In the student's "love affair" with the
teacher, you give yourself to space; you give yourself to someone who
speaks for space. That someone is the teacher, and that surrender, or
abandonment of oneself, is the experience of devotion.

In many respects, this is even more difficult to talk about now than
it was when Chögyam Trungpa first gave these talks and translated the
devotional texts that are excerpted or referred to here. Throughout his
years of teaching in America, Chögyam Trungpa warned against the
dangers of charlatan gurus. As he said in *Cutting Through Spiritual Materialism*, "Because America is so fertile, seeking spirituality, it is possible for
America to inspire charlatans. . . . Because America is looking so hard
for spirituality, religion becomes an easy way to make money and
achieve fame."[2] He advised people to be careful, to think twice, and to
use their intelligence to seek out and connect with a genuine teacher.
However, there is an entirely different approach that has become more
popular in the last few years, which is to do away with the absolute
nature of the student-teacher relationship altogether, so that the student
goes it on his or her own, accepting advice where it is helpful but never
surrendering beyond a certain point.

That is certainly one way to avoid a disastrous relationship with a
fraudulent teacher. Rather than accepting a "pseudo" guru, it is prefera-
ble to keep one's own counsel. There is much that can be accomplished
on one's own or with a teacher as adviser rather than as the ultimate
reference point. To learn to meditate and practice loving-kindness—one
could do far worse than that! For most of us, to accomplish just that is a
lifetime's work.

But to deny the possibility of attaining stainless, pure enlightenment

---

2. *Cutting Through Spiritual Materialism*, Shambhala Classics edition (2002), p. 18.

and to deny the possibility of the means—to deny the value of genuine devotion and the existence of genuine teachers—seems to be closing off one of the greatest opportunities that human beings have: the opportunity to be fully awake. Awakening is not achieved easily or comfortably, and the journey is not without dangers and extremes, but that makes it no less real or precious. In this volume are the wonderful stories of some of the outrageous and fully awakened gurus of the Buddhist lineage. What an inspiration they are! At the same time, it is almost unthinkable that these are stories about real people, not just mythical figures in the past. Yet part of Chögyam Trungpa's genius was his ability to personally introduce you to this cast of characters, as though they were sitting in front of you, as though they might walk in the front door anytime. As though one of them might be your teacher . . .

In *Crazy Wisdom*—which is made up of talks edited from two seminars that Chögyam Trungpa gave in December 1972—we are introduced to some of the main themes in the life of Padmasambhava. An Indian teacher, he brought the Buddhist teachings to Tibet in the eighth century at the invitation of King Trisong Detsen. Thus, he is regarded as the father of Buddhism in Tibet and is revered by all Tibetan lineages and by the Tibetan people. Often, biographies of a teacher present the story of how that person became a student of the buddhadharma, met his or her guru, underwent extensive trials and training, and finally became enlightened, or realized. Such stories provide inspiration and many helpful lessons to students entering the path. In this case, however, Padmasambhava is considered to have been primordially enlightened. That is, he was born fully enlightened, it is said, as an eight-year-old child seated on a lotus flower in the middle of a lake. It is a highly improbable story. As Chögyam Trungpa says, "For an infant to be born in such a wild, desolate place in the middle of a lake on a lotus is beyond the grasp of conceptual mind. . . . Such a birth is impossible. But, then, impossible things happen, things beyond our imagination" (p. 27). Rather than trying to explain or defend this tale, Trungpa Rinpoche accepts the story of Padmasambhava's birth as the ground to discuss primordial innocence. As he says, "It is possible for us to discover our own innocence and childlike beauty, the princelike quality in us . . . it is a fresh discovery of perception, a new discovery of a sense of things as they are" (p. 28). Throughout this book, he is describing not so much the life of a Buddhist saint who lived over a thousand years ago, but the aspects of our own journey and our own lives that might connect with this timeless and extraordinary energy.

Sherab Chödzin Kohn, the editor of *Crazy Wisdom*, has rendered this material artfully, with love and fidelity to the original talks. In reading this book, one has the opportunity to plumb the depths of what crazy wisdom actually is—which is both crazier and wiser than one could possibly imagine!

"Crazy wisdom" was one of a number of terms that Chögyam Trungpa coined in English. It has caught on and has come to be used to describe a variety of styles of behavior, some of them more crazy than wise. In his original meaning of the term, which is a translation of the Tibetan *yeshe chölwa*, it describes the state of being of someone who has gone beyond the limitations of conventional mind and is thus "crazy" from the limited reference point of conceptual thinking; yet such a person is also existing or dwelling in a state of spontaneous wisdom, free from thought in the conventional sense, free from the preoccupations of hope and fear. Crazy wisdom is sometimes referred to as "wisdom gone beyond." The outrageousness of crazy wisdom is that it will do whatever needs to be done to help sentient beings: it subdues whatever needs to be subdued and cares for whatever needs its care. It will also destroy what needs to be destroyed. Padmasambhava was the embodiment of crazy wisdom; hence the title of the book. This topic is particularly alive and juicy in the hands of Chögyam Trungpa because he was a guru in the lineage of crazy wisdom. It is in part his own fearless wisdom that he communicates in this book.

Sherab Chödzin Kohn also edited the next book in Volume Five, *Illusion's Game: The Life and Teaching of Naropa*, a commentary on the biography of the great Indian teacher. Naropa's biography takes the more traditional approach of Tibetan spiritual biography: it is the inspired tale of Naropa's arduous search for his guru and his experiences while studying with the Indian master Tilopa. *Illusion's Game* is based on two seminars in which Trungpa Rinpoche reflected on the meaning of events in Naropa's life, using the biography translated by Herbert V. Guenther as his main reference point. Most of the students who attended the seminars had read Dr. Guenther's book. In *Illusion's Game*, excerpts from Dr. Guenther's translation are included to help readers understand the context of the discussion, and in his editor's introduction, Sherab Chödzin also provides an excellent summary of the salient events in the biography.

Naropa was the abbot of Nalanda University. One day while he was studying, an ugly old woman suddenly appeared and asked him if he understood the words or the sense of the Buddhist teachings he was reading. She was very happy when he told her that he understood the words, but she became very angry when he said that he also understood the sense. He asked her to tell him who, then, knew the real meaning, and she answered that he should seek her brother Tilopa. Inspired by this encounter, Naropa left the university, much to the dismay of his colleagues and students, and set out to find his guru Tilopa.

On the way, he encountered one horrific illusion after another. Each situation was a test by Tilopa of his prospective disciple's understanding, and on each occasion Naropa missed the point, so that he had to keep searching on and on. Eventually, he found Tilopa eating fish entrails by the side of a lake. This was just the beginning. Naropa had to undergo many trials, over many years, until finally he became fully realized. As Sherab Chödzin Kohn tells us in the introduction of the book, "Tilopa required him [Naropa] to leap from the roof of a tall temple building. Naropa's body was crushed. He suffered immense pain. Tilopa healed him with a touch of his hand, then gave him instructions. This pattern was repeated eleven more times. Eleven more times Tilopa remained either motionless or aloof for a year; then Naropa prostrated and asked for teaching. Tilopa caused him to throw himself into a fire, . . . be beaten nearly to death, have his blood sucked out by leeches, be pricked with flaming splinters . . . ," and on the story goes. It is difficult to know what to make of such a tale. We could dismiss it as craziness or treat it as symbolism. But could we imagine that such things actually took place and that such people could actually exist?

Trungpa Rinpoche published a poem in *First Thought Best Thought* titled "Meetings with Remarkable People." After describing encounters with three very strange beings, who are actually vajrayana deities, he says:

> Can you imagine seeing such people and receiving and
>   talking to them?
> Ordinarily, if you told such stories to anybody, they would
>   think you were a nut case;

But, in this case, I have to insist that I am not a nut case;

. . . .

Don't you think meeting such sweet friends is worthwhile
    and rewarding?

. . . .

I would say meeting them is meeting with remarkable men
    and women:
Let us believe that such things do exist.[3]

In that spirit, it may be valuable to explore the life of Naropa and
how it might apply personally to oneself. Not only does Trungpa Rinpoche present the outrageous qualities of Naropa's life, but he also draws
analogies to our own experience. Of Naropa's trials, he writes, "these
twelve experiences that Naropa went through were a continuous unlearning process. To begin with, he had to unlearn, to undo the cultural
facade. Then he had to undo the philosophical and emotional facade.
Then he had to step out and become free altogether. This whole process
was a very painful and very deliberate operation. This does not apply to
Naropa and his time alone. This could also be something very up-to-
date. This operation is applicable as long as we have conflicting emotions
and erroneous beliefs about reality" (p. 186). From that point of view, the
story makes good sense. However, on another level, it remains utterly
outrageous. If we look at most of the stories about the lives of the Tibetan lineage holders—Padmasambhava, Tilopa, Naropa, Marpa, Milarepa, and others—we see that these were people who did not exclude
anything from their experience. They could, in fact, be quite terrifying in
their fearlessness.

In the article "Milarepa: A Warrior's Life," which appears in Volume
Five, Trungpa Rinpoche includes the last instructions given by the yogi
Milarepa to his students, as he lay on his deathbed: "Reject all that increases ego-clinging, or inner poison, even if it appears good. Practice all
that benefits others, even if it appears bad. This is the true way of
dharma. . . . Act wisely and courageously according to your innate insight, even at the cost of your life." The great forefathers of the lineage
were willing to work with whatever might come up. In fact, they delighted in embodying the most extreme aspects of human experience, if

---

3. *First Thought Best Thought* (1983), p. 125.

in doing so they could help others. From their point of view, they were not striving to be outrageous or even helpful; their behavior was just the natural expression of what is.

This is the training that Chögyam Trungpa had himself received. A story from his early life illustrates how he put this training into effect, in extreme as well as ordinary circumstances. When Tibet was invaded by the communist Chinese, he had to flee the country over the Himalayas to avoid imprisonment and probable death. Before he set out on his journey to India, he heard of people being tortured and killed; his monastery was sacked; there was a price on his head. The journey out of Tibet lasted ten months—an almost unimaginably long time to be trekking on foot over the Himalayas (without modern mountain gear, jeeps, or thermal underwear, one might add), constantly in fear of being discovered by the Chinese, while facing extraordinary physical difficulties, crossing one high pass after another, fording roaring rivers in the dead of winter, reduced in the end to boiling saddlebags for food.[4] When Trungpa Rinpoche and his party reached the Brahmaputra River, close to the end of the journey, they had to make their crossing at night in somewhat unstable boats made of leather. Someone in a nearby town had alerted the Chinese that a group of Tibetans was going across that night, and the Chinese ambushed Rinpoche's party. Out of more than two hundred traveling together, fewer than two dozen made it across. Trungpa Rinpoche luckily was one of those who did. Reaching the other side while hearing gunshots in the background, he and most of the remaining band hid in some holly trees until the next night. In *Born in Tibet*, he wrote, "We dared not open our food pack and there was no water. We could only moisten our lips with the hoar frost."[5] While they were hiding, hoping to reconnect with some of the rest of the party who they thought had escaped capture, they could hear and sometimes see the Chinese searching for them. Their clothes had been soaked during the crossing, and the weather was so cold that their clothing became frozen to their skin, so it crackled when they moved. Later that day, as it became dark, they climbed for five hours to reach shelter in some fir trees above the village. Hiding in the cover of the trees, after everything they had been

---

4. The story of Chögyam Trungpa's voyage out of Tibet is told in his autobiography, *Born in Tibet*, which appears in Volume One.

5. *Born in Tibet* (1976), p. 233.

through, Rinpoche and his attendant quietly discussed whether or not their experiences were a test of their meditation and how their meditative equanimity would fare if they were captured the next day by the Chinese. Several members of the party made jokes about doing the yoga of inner heat to try to keep warm. Rinpoche and others found quite a lot of humor in this dire situation.

This is not exactly a crazy wisdom story, except that it is almost inconceivable that, faced with the loss of family and friends, with the prospect of capture and possible torture or death, Chögyam Trungpa and his companions—many of whom were also highly trained practitioners—approached their experience with evenhandedness and humor and seemingly very little fear. That in itself is rather crazy but also seems quite wise, and it does remind one of the lineage forefathers and their outrageous journeys to freedom.

When the going gets tough, these are people you might want to have on your team. In that vein, it is worth looking twice at what Chögyam Trungpa has to say about the life of these great Buddhist adepts. It is indeed applicable to things we may face today—or tomorrow. Their compassion was compassion for the toughest times. It may be just what the world needs now.

Both *Crazy Wisdom* and *Illusion's Game* are the work of a great storyteller. In his first five or six years in North America, Chögyam Trungpa taught more than forty seminars on the life and teachings of the Kagyü forefathers. (The life of Padmasambhava was a less common topic. In addition to the two seminars that were edited for *Crazy Wisdom*, he presented one other seminar specifically on the life and teachings of Padmasambhava.) He also gave several seminars on his own teacher, Jamgön Kongtrül, and on the lineage of the Trungpa tulkus. In seminars on other topics, Rinpoche often would bring up a story about Tilopa, Naropa, Marpa, Milarepa, or Gampopa to illustrate a point he was making. These stories are included in *Cutting Through Spiritual Materialism* and other popular books. When he told these tales, you felt that he knew these people; he definitely seemed to be on a first-name basis with them. And like any good father telling his children about their grandparents and great-grandparents, one point of his storytelling was to make the younger generation feel close to the ancestors and the ancestral wisdom. He never failed to make those in the audience feel that they were part of or just about to join this lineage of awakened mind.

The Life of Marpa the Translator continues the theme of perilous journeys and extreme trials on the path to realization. Marpa was the chief disciple of the Indian guru Naropa, whose search for enlightenment is the subject of *Illusion's Game*. Marpa was born and lived in southeastern Tibet. He made three journeys to India, filled with obstacles and difficult tests of his understanding and devotion. In India, Marpa obtained the teachings that form the core of the Kagyü tradition, and he translated many of these Indian teachings into the Tibetan language. Marpa's lifestyle has some parallels to those of modern students, in that he was a married householder with a number of children. He owned and operated a farm and outwardly led a rather ordinary and quite secular life. Superficially, at least, it may be easier to connect with Marpa's approach than with the more austere lifestyles of some of the other lineage holders. Nevertheless, his understanding of and dedication to the dharma were anything but ordinary.

In his preface and colophon to *The Life of Marpa*, Trungpa Rinpoche pays homage to Marpa as the founder of the Kagyü lineage in Tibet. Rinpoche also talks about the process of translating this book and the kinship that he feels with Marpa as one translator to another. Indeed, the translation process that Chögyam Trungpa organized and which continues to this day, more than fifteen years after his death, has proven very successful in furthering the translation of many Tibetan texts into English. The Nālandā Translation Committee, the group of Rinpoche's students who collaborated with him on the translation of *The Life of Marpa the Translator*, as well as on *The Rain of Wisdom*, is to be congratulated for its excellent work on these and many other projects.

The Nālandā Translation Committee's first major project for general publication was *The Rain of Wisdom*, a translation of the *Kagyü Gurtso*, songs of the forefathers and lineage holders of the Karma Kagyü lineage. Chögyam Trungpa very much wanted to bring these wonderful songs of devotion and spiritual liberation into the English language. First compiled and edited in the sixteenth century by the eighth Karmapa, Mikyö Dorje, the *Kagyü Gurtso* (literally "The Ocean of Songs of the Kagyü") was intended to be "the liturgy for a chanting service that would invoke the blessings of the entire Karma Kagyü lineage. With the same aim in mind, successive editions of the *Kagyü Gurtso* have added songs by holders of the Karma Kagyü lineage born after the time of Mikyö Dorje."[6]

---

6. *The Rain of Wisdom* (1980), afterword by the NTC, p. 304.

(In keeping with tradition, the English edition of *The Rain of Wisdom* includes songs by a current lineage holder, Chögyam Trungpa himself.)

In the foreword, Rinpoche talks about how he read the *Kagyü Gurtso* as a child and how it made him weep with longing and devotion. This magnificent collection of poetry, with many accompanying stories, still has the power to evoke joy and sadness and the inspiration to practice the heart teachings of the buddhadharma. Trungpa Rinpoche advises readers of this book to "reflect on the value and wisdom which exist in these songs of the lineage in the following ways. First there are the life examples of our forefathers to inspire our devotion. There are songs which help us understand the cause and effect of karma and so illuminate the path to liberation. There are songs which give instruction in relative bodhichitta, so that we can realize the immediacy of our connection to the dharma. Some are songs of mahamudra and transmit how we can actually join together bliss and emptiness through the profound methods of coemergence, melting, and bliss. Other songs show the realization of Buddha in the palm of our hand. . . . Reading these songs or even glancing at a paragraph of this literature always brings timely messages of how to conduct oneself, how to discipline oneself" (p. 287).

Once again, the stories and wisdom of past teachers are not just of historical interest but are presented to inspire our own journey on the path. The courage, majesty, and conviction of the Kagyü gurus are overwhelming. Just reading Trungpa Rinpoche's introduction and his few songs, one gains a sense of the grandeur and the heartfelt depth of realization contained in *The Rain of Wisdom*.

In what may have been purely a fortuitous coincidence, the translation of the *Kagyü Gurtso* was published in 1980, when students of Chögyam Trungpa were celebrating the tenth anniversary of his arrival in North America. The publication of this important text in the English language seems a fitting testament to all that he had accomplished in ten short years. In addition to having produced a brilliant translation, the members of the Nālandā Translation Committee must be acknowledged for the excellent afterword they contributed to the text, as well as for the extensive notes and glossary.

In 1976, one of Chögyam Trungpa's teachers from Tibet, an elder statesman and revered guru of the Nyingma lineage, His Holiness Dilgo Khyentse Rinpoche, made his first visit to America, at Trungpa Rinpoche's invitation. He was accompanied by two attendants, Lama Yönten Gyamtso (who had been an attendant of Trungpa Rinpoche's at Surmang Monastery, accompanying him on his escape from Tibet) and Lama Ugyen Shenpen, a student of Khyentse Rinpoche's for many years. With Khyentse Rinpoche's blessing, Lama Ugyen stayed on in America to work with the Nālandā Translation Committee after His Holiness departed. His extensive understanding of Tibetan literature and vajrayana teachings, as well as his growing grasp of English, made it possible for the NTC to make great strides in their translation work. His input was instrumental to the successful translation of both *The Rain of Wisdom* and *The Life of Marpa*. Lama Ugyen worked with the NTC until his death in 1994.[7]

Next in Volume Five are the excerpt from *The Sadhana of Mahamudra* and an article about the meaning of the text. The sadhana, which Trungpa Rinpoche "discovered" in Bhutan in 1968, is a particular kind of text or teaching called terma. In Tibet, Chögyam Trungpa had already been recognized as a tertön, a teacher who "finds" or reveals terma, which are the teachings that Padmasambhava concealed in physical locations throughout Tibet and in the realm of mind and space. As Trungpa Rinpoche describes in *Crazy Wisdom*, "He [Padmasambhava] had various writings of his put in gold and silver containers like capsules and buried in certain appropriate places in the different parts of Tibet so that people of the future would rediscover them. . . . This process of rediscovering the treasures has been happening all along, and a lot of sacred teachings have been revealed. One example is the *Tibetan Book of the Dead*. Another approach to preserving treasures of wisdom is the style of the thought lineage. Teachings have been rediscovered by certain appropriate teachers who have had memories of them and written them down from

---

7. The translation committee has quite a large number of other members, and it is not feasible to name all of them here. However, in the acknowledgments to *The Rain of Wisdom*, a central translation committee for this project is identified, "consisting of Robin Kornman, John Rockwell, Jr., and Scott Wellenbach in collaboration with Lama Ugyen Shenpen, Loppön Lodrö Dorje Holm, and Larry Mermelstein [the Executive Director of the NTC]." In *The Life of Marpa*, the core group is identified as David Cox, Dana Dudley, John Rockwell, Jr., Ives Waldo, and Gerry Weiner, in collaboration with Loppön Lodrö Dorje and Larry Mermelstein—with much guidance from Trungpa Rinpoche and Lama Ugyen. These are just some of the members of the NTC who worked on these translations. The large membership of the translation group points out how quickly and to what extent Rinpoche was able to share the wealth of his tradition, including so many bright minds and dedicated students in his work.

memory. This is another kind of hidden treasure" (pp. 142–43). *The Sadhana of Mahamudra* is such a mind terma.[8]

This text is particularly important to our discussion here because of how it joins together the teachings of both the Nyingma and Kagyü lineages. As Chögyam Trungpa says in the accompanying article, "Joining Energy and Space," "The lineage of *The Sadhana of Mahamudra* is the two traditions of immense crazy wisdom and immense dedication and devotion put together. The Kagyü, or mahamudra tradition, is the devotion lineage. The Nyingma, or ati tradition, is the lineage of crazy wisdom. The sadhana brings these two traditions together as a prototype of how emotion and wisdom, energy and space, can work together" (p. 312). Additionally, the sadhana contains a vivid description of the obstacles presented by physical, psychological, and spiritual materialism in the modern age and prescribes unwavering devotion to wakefulness as the antidote to the materialistic outlook.

While in England, Chögyam Trungpa had been tutoring the crown prince (now the king) of Bhutan, Jigme Singye Wangchuk, while the prince was studying at Ascot. At the invitation of the queen of Bhutan, Trungpa Rinpoche journeyed to Bhutan in 1968. Rinpoche was accompanied to Asia by one of his young English students, Richard Arthure (who worked with Rinpoche on the translation of the sadhana and was also the editor of *Meditation in Action*).[9] In preparation for the publication of *The Collected Works*, Richard kindly contributed information about their journey and the circumstances under which the sadhana was received:

It would be a sad thing if *The Collected Works* were published without including at least an excerpt from *The Sadhana of Mahamudra*. Along with the Shambhala teachings, it seems to be the quintessential expression of his [Trungpa Rinpoche's] enlightened mind and was openly recognized as such by both Tulku Urgyen Rinpoche and H. H. Dilgo Khyentse. The Vidyadhara [Chögyam Trungpa] himself wanted it to be propagated and practiced widely and without restric-

8. Traditionally, when a terma text is written out, a special mark or sign is placed at the end of each line of text. The terma marks have been omitted from the excerpt from *The Sadhana of Mahamudra* that appears in Volume Five.

9. See the introduction to Volume One for Richard Arthure's comments on the editing of *Meditation in Action*.

tion, and he gladly shared it even with acquaintances, such as Thomas Merton, who were not Buddhist.[10]

Before going into retreat at Taktsang, Trungpa Rinpoche and I traveled with Khyentse Rinpoche by jeep from Bhutan to Sikkim in order to spend some time with H. H. the sixteenth Karmapa. At [Trungpa] Rinpoche's request, the Karmapa performed the Karma Pakshi empowerment for us. Immediately, the Vidyadhara, with my assistance, set to work to prepare an English language translation of the Karma Pakshi sadhana.[11] (There exists a photograph—tactfully suppressed for general purposes—of the two of us sitting side by side in the guest house at Rumtek smoking cigarettes and working on this translation.) It was to be my daily practice at Taktsang. It is unlikely that this translation has survived.

On our return to Bhutan, we received the Dorje Trolö [the wrathful aspect of Guru Rinpoche, in which he manifested at Taktsang before entering Tibet] empowerment from Dilgo Khyentse in a very informal setting, with just a handful of people present in Khyentse Rinpoche's tiny bedroom. Then we went up to Taktsang, traveling on horseback and then on foot up the steep trail, to begin our retreat. Once there, my morning practice was the Karma Pakshi sadhana. At noon I would go to Trungpa Rinpoche's room and we would have lunch together. In the afternoon I would sit with Rinpoche in the main shrine room while he performed a Dorje Trolö feast practice, tormas and butter lamps having been prepared by a Bhutanese monk and a Tibetan yogi who were students of Dilgo Khyentse. We would share a light meal in the early evening and generally stay up late talking. A principal topic of our wide-ranging discussions was how to create an enlightened society, what form it would take, etc., Rinpoche favoring a combination of democracy and enlightened monarchy. The idea of the delek[12] system was first proposed during these

---

10. It was during the 1968 visit to Asia that Rinpoche met Thomas Merton, shortly before Merton's untimely death.

11. Karma Pakshi (1203–1282) was the second Karmapa. He was invited to China by Prince Kublai Khan and by his rival and older brother, Mongka Khan. When His Holiness the sixteenth Karmapa made his second visit to the United States in 1976, Trungpa Rinpoche asked him to perform the Karma Pakshi abhisheka as a blessing for all of Rinpoche's students, which he did.

12. *Delek* is a Tibetan word that means "auspicious happiness." Chögyam Trungpa used it to refer to creating a system of governance that fosters peace and good communication within the meditation centers he established. The discussion here is of the genesis of the

discussions. A young Australian woman traveler, Lorraine, showed up with a copy of Erich Fromm's *The Sane Society* in her backpack. We devoured it. Rinpoche had me write a synopsis of the main ideas in it to add fuel to our discussions.

Towards the end of our retreat, *The Sadhana of Mahamudra* arose in Rinpoche's mind, and the main part of it was written down very quickly, in one or two days. Several more days were spent in refining and polishing. We began translating it into English almost immediately, although most of the work was done after we had come down the mountain from Taktsang and were staying in a guest house belonging to the Queen's mother on the outskirts of Thimphu. Here's how the process worked, more or less (and you should understand that I don't speak or read Tibetan): Word by word and phrase by phrase Rinpoche would explain the meaning to me, as far as his vocabulary allowed. From those basic building blocks of meaning, it became possible to construct the English language version of the sadhana. I tried to create something that would transmit the dharma in a powerful and poetic way, utilizing the natural cadences and rhythms of spoken English. For example, Rinpoche would say something like: "All . . . *namthok* is thoughts . . . disappear. . . . Shunyata . . . like a bird in the sky, doesn't make, how would you say, footprints?—not like a horse or man walking in snow, but same idea." And this, after a few tries, would give rise to: "All thoughts vanish into emptiness, like the imprint of a bird in the sky."[13] Later, I saw that same simile translated as "like the traceless path of a bird in the sky," which I think is pretty good. I chose the word *imprint* because it gives the echo or faint suggestion of *footprint*, so carries the resonance of that image into the dimension of space.

Perhaps the Dakinis inspired our work together. Rinpoche

idea of the delek system in 1968. Trungpa Rinpoche did not actually introduce deleks until 1981. At that time, he suggested that people in the Buddhist communities he worked with should organize themselves into deleks, or groups, consisting of about twenty or thirty families, based on the neighborhoods in which they lived. Each neighborhood or small group was a delek and its members, the delekpas. Each delek would elect a leader, the dekyong—the "protector of happiness"—by a process of consensus for which Rinpoche coined the phrase "spontaneous insight." The dekyongs were then organized into the Dekyong Council, which would meet and make decisions affecting their deleks and make recommendations to the administration of Vajradhatu, the international organization he founded, about larger issues.

13. This line is not part of the excerpt printed in Volume Five.

seemed to think they were taking an active interest, at least. While we were staying in that guest house, tremendous rainstorms and floods caused landslides and destroyed roads and bridges so that we were unable to travel. Rinpoche commented: "This is the action of the Dakinis, making sure we don't leave until the translation is finished."[14]

Richard's commentary provides quite a lot of new information about the circumstances surrounding the "discovery" of *The Sadhana of Mahamudra*. It has previously not been widely known that Chögyam Trungpa received both the Karma Pakshi and Dorje Trolö empowerments prior to entering retreat at Taktsang. He undoubtedly would have received these abhishekas earlier, while studying in Tibet, but having them "refreshed" in his mind may have had some influence on what occurred at Taktsang. These two gurus, visualized as yidams or vajrayana nontheistic deities, are combined as one central figure in *The Sadhana of Mahamudra*, thus unifying the energies of their respective lineages, the Kagyü and the Nyingma. We also see in Richard's reminiscences that Trungpa Rinpoche's facility with the English language was still limited in 1968. It is, therefore, remarkable both how accurately the translation of the sadhana captured the spirit and meaning of the original Tibetan (the translation used today is virtually the same as the original)[15] and also how fast Rinpoche's grasp of the language developed after 1968. We have recordings of him teaching in America as early as 1970, and his sentence structure and vocabulary are nothing like the fragmentary approach that Richard reports less than two years earlier. His remarks complement Trungpa Rinpoche's own description of the retreat, which appears in "Joining Energy and Space." Richard sets the outer scene for us; Rinpoche describes more of the inner experiences he had, empty at the beginning, charged with energy and power at the end.

Although this article and the attendant excerpt are brief, they deserve significant commentary, because *The Sadhana of Mahamudra* had *such* a

---

14. Letter from Richard Arthure to Carolyn Rose Gimian, December 2001.

15. The Nālandā Translation Committee did prepare a more literal translation of *The Sadhana of Mahamudra* in 1990, for students' use in studying the text. The beginning sections of this translation were done with Chögyam Trungpa. He himself felt that the original translation captured something that would be lost by making extensive changes. The NTC's work is available to interested students.

huge impact on Trungpa Rinpoche's development as a teacher and on the whole thrust of his teaching in the West. In a sense, the most articulate presentation of spiritual materialism and the most profound understanding of how to vanquish it are presented in this sadhana. In this, as well as other areas of his teaching, Trungpa Rinpoche first had the main realization, full and complete within itself, received almost in an instant. He then spent years sharing that understanding with others. This was also true with his propagation of the Shambhala teachings, which were heralded by his receiving another terma text, *The Golden Sun of the Great East*, well before he began to lecture publicly on the Shambhala path of warriorship. This approach is, in fact, quite orthodox. The Buddha first became enlightened; only some weeks later did he begin to teach. Similarly, Chögyam Trungpa discovered the heart teachings of his lineage—the ecumenical tradition of Ri-me—in Taktsang in 1968. He spent the next two decades sharing that realization with sentient beings.

As Richard also points out in his letter, after discovering and translating *The Sadhana of Mahamudra*, Trungpa Rinpoche was delighted to share this practice with anyone who might be interested. When he returned to England, his students there took up the practice of the sadhana immediately. In an unpublished memoir, Rinpoche's wife, Diana Mukpo, describes the practice of the sadhana at Samye Ling, Rinpoche's meditation center in Scotland: "When I was visiting Samye Ling with my mother in 1969, Rinpoche had only recently returned from this trip to Bhutan. Now, in addition to traditional Tibetan practices, students at Samye Ling chanted an English translation of *The Sadhana of Mahamudra*, crudely printed on coloured paper."

Once he arrived in America in 1970, in spite of his insistence on the sitting practice of meditation as the main discipline, Trungpa Rinpoche encouraged students to gather together and read the sadhana on the new and full moon. This practice continues to the present day. During Trungpa Rinpoche's lifetime, he conferred the formal empowerment, or abhisheka, for this sadhana twice that we know of: in India in 1968 and slightly later in England. In 1982, His Holiness Khyentse Rinpoche requested that Trungpa Rinpoche write down the abhisheka text, which he had spontaneously composed when he gave the transmissions years before. He did not accomplish this before he died, but Khyentse Rinpoche, who had a very close connection to Trungpa Rinpoche and to his students, completed both the abhisheka and the feast liturgy in 1990. Rinpoche's eldest son, Sakyong Mipham Rinpoche, who inherited the leadership of the Shambhala Buddhist community in 1990, has conferred this abhisheka in a number of ceremonies, beginning in 1993. Several thousand students, both senior students and recent meditators, have taken part in these events. Carried out of a lonely retreat in a cave in Bhutan, the lineage of transmission has traveled far and grown quite large in less than three decades.

In *The Sadhana of Mahamudra*, the seed syllable HUM plays a major role in invoking the power of sanity to overcome the forces of materialism in the world. The next offering in Volume Five is "HUM: An Approach to Mantra," a short article on the mantra HUM, which was originally published in 1972 in *Garuda II: Working with Negativity*. As he so often does, Chögyam Trungpa begins his discussion by dispelling preconceptions. That is, he first tells the reader what mantra practice is *not*. It is not, he informs us, "a magical spell used in order to gain psychic powers for selfish purposes, such as accumulation of wealth, power over others, and destruction of enemies." He explains that the genuine usage of mantra arises from an understanding of the teachings of the Buddha on the four marks of existence: impermanence, suffering, emptiness, and egolessness. Mantra is the invocation of egoless or nontheistic energies of wisdom and insight. He also distinguishes the Buddhist understanding of mantra from its usage in Hindu tantra, explaining that the divinities invoked in Buddhist tantra are not external but rather represent "aspects of the awakened state of mind." Trungpa Rinpoche then describes a number of ways in which the mantra HUM has been used. It was employed by Guru Padmasambhava "to subdue the force of the negative environment created by minds poisoned with passion, aggression, and ignorance." For beginning meditators, he suggests that chanting the sacred music of HUM can quiet the mind and ease the force of irritating thoughts. For advanced meditators, he states that the syllable HUM is a means of developing the wisdom of the five buddha families, innate wisdoms arising from emptiness, which one finds within oneself, not somewhere in the external world. He also describes HUM as the "sonorous sound of silence" and as "that state of meditation when awareness breaks out of the limits of ego." Finally, he describes the relationship of the mantra HUM to the Vajrakilaya Mandala, in which the power of egolessness is visualized as a dagger that pierces through the seductions of ego.

When this article was reviewed for inclusion in *The Collected Works*, an early, unpublished version was uncovered. In most respects, it was very similar to the final form in which the article appeared in *Garuda II*. However, the closing paragraph of the original was omitted when it was published. Here, Trungpa Rinpoche suggests that those who practice *The Sadhana of Mahamudra* would benefit from studying this essay on the mantra HUM. This paragraph has been restored in the version that appears here.

Next in Volume Five we have "Explanation of the Vajra Guru Mantra," an article never before published, which deals with the mantra that invokes Guru Rinpoche, or Padmasambhava. Here, Chögyam Trungpa describes mantra as creating "a living environment of energy." This article was probably written while Chögyam Trungpa was still in England or shortly after he arrived in the United States. He translates each syllable of the mantra (if it is translatable) and then discusses the meaning of each syllable in some detail. There is a very pithy but penetrating discussion of the guru principle, which presents three aspects of one's devotion and relationship to the teacher. First, one sees the guru as the superior teacher to whom one opens and surrenders oneself completely. Second, the guru manifests as the spiritual friend, because—as Rinpoche points out—"you must be able not only to surrender but to communicate." Trungpa Rinpoche relates this aspect of devotion to the meeting of two minds: "Your mind is open to the open space and the guru's mind is open to the open space. In this way, your mind becomes one with that of the teacher—both are inseparable from unconditioned space." Finally, Rinpoche talks about the guru as environment, which is seeing occurrences in life as the manifestation of the energy of the teacher. One learns to appreciate the wisdom of the phenomenal world and to see life situations as messages that embody wisdom. If the practitioner ignores the meaning of experiences, then a stronger message, in the form of chaos, will provide the feedback that one has lost touch with "the life situation as teacher." Recognizing this affords the student an opportunity for further opening and communication. The result is that one develops compassion, the genuine ability to communicate with and help others, as well as the power of *siddhi*, which is sometimes translated as "magical power" or the ability to perform miracles. Here, Trungpa Rinpoche suggests that siddhi is a situation that develops unexpectedly, a sudden unforeseen coming together of circumstances. He ends the article with the suggestion that the real miracle is the "power of compassion, ultimate communication."

The next offering is Rinpoche's foreword to *The Torch of Certainty* and the interview with Chögyam Trungpa that appeared in the introduction to the book. The foundation practices that are discussed here are often referred to as the four extraordinary or special preliminaries. They are a practitioner's first formal introduction to visualization practice and other distinctly tantric aspects of Buddhist yoga and are prerequisites for more advanced meditation practices in the vajrayana. The foundations include 108,000 repetitions of the refuge formula combined with 108,000 prostrations, 108,000 repetitions of the Vajrasattva mantra, and 108,000 mandala offerings, concluding with a guru yoga recitation. These ngöndro practices are a process of surrendering, purifying, offering, and identifying with the lineage by developing longing for the teacher and the teachings.

For a student who has connected with the preceding teachings on lineage and devotion, the ngöndro practices offer the way to actually embark on the path. Although sometimes they are given to students with no other formal background, Trungpa Rinpoche makes it clear that, from his point of view, these practices are only appropriate or helpful for students who have experience in taming and training the mind, which are accomplished through the sitting practice of meditation.

The next two articles, "The Practicing Lineage" and "The Mishap Lineage" are edited versions of the first two talks in "The Line of the Trungpas," a seminar taught by Chögyam Trungpa at Karmê Chöling meditation center in Vermont in 1975. Both of these talks present an introduction to the Kagyü lineage. It was only in the later talks from the seminar, which remain unpublished, that Rinpoche talked more specifically about the teachers in his particular lineage. In "The Practicing Lineage" he talks about the literal meaning of *Kagyü* as "the lineage of the sacred word," but he focuses on the lineage as *drubgyü*, or "the practicing lineage," as it became known during the time of Milarepa. The importance of having a teacher and the necessity of transcending spiritual materialism and ego-clinging are stressed: "The practicing lineage teaches us that we have to get rid of those ego-centered conceptualized notions of the grandiosity of our development. If we are truly involved with spirituality, we are willing to let go of trying to witness our own enlightenment." In "The Mishap Lineage," Trungpa Rinpoche talks about how the Kagyü have always loved desolate mountain peaks and practicing in wild and sometimes haunted places. This, he suggests, has made them adept at conquering extreme, foreign territory of all kinds, and thus they have long been known for spreading the dharma in foreign lands. That love of harsh extremes is combined in the Kagyü lineage with profound gentleness and devotion. He also describes how constant mishaps are welcomed by the Kagyü practitioner as further fuel to spark awareness. This also harks back to the story of Rinpoche's escape from the Chinese at the Brahmaputra River.

"Teachings on the Tulku Principle" is a brief article on the history and meaning of reincarnation and the Tibetan practice of realized teachers taking rebirth in successive incarnations. Such a teacher is called a *tulku*, which literally means "emanation body." The first Karmapa, the head of the Karma Kagyü lineage to which Chögyam Trungpa belonged, was in fact the first tulku to be recognized in Tibet. "Teachings on the Tulku Principle" clarifies that a tulku does not represent the continuation of ego or self, but rather expresses the continuity of awake mind, generated by compassion, from one incarnation to the next.

The final group of articles in Volume Five presents three quite distinct discussions of the life of Milarepa. As is the case with his lectures on the life and teachings of Marpa, Trungpa Rinpoche's seminars on Milarepa have not yet been edited for publication. One of the first teachings he gave in America was a sixteen-talk seminar on the significance of Milarepa's life. Over the next ten years, he gave many other teachings on Milarepa, including a long seminar titled "The Yogic Songs of Milarepa" at the Naropa Institute in the mid-1970s. We can hope that this material will eventually be made available. For now, the three articles included in *The Collected Works* give us a good indication of the richness of Rinpoche's insights into Jetsun Milarepa's teachings.

Milarepa is undoubtedly the most famous and beloved yogi of Tibet. Students from all lineages study his spiritual songs. Trungpa Rinpoche pays tribute to both the rugged quality of Milarepa's realization and its simplicity. Milarepa's austere life in mountain caves and his deep devotion to his guru, Marpa, epitomize the qualities that Trungpa Rinpoche points to in "The Mishap Lineage" as the core of the Kagyü sensibility.

"Milarepa: A Warrior's Life" is a previously unpublished article that was prepared in 1978 as a text to accompany a calendar of reproductions of Tibetan thangkas, or scroll paintings, that depicted scenes from Milarepa's life. The calendar was never published, so the article was filed away. It was one of the first articles that I worked on with Rinpoche. I uncovered it tucked away in some files in the Shambhala Archives while I was in the process of searching for material for inclusion in *The Collected Works*. It presents the basic events in Milarepa's life story, with commentary on their significance, making the other two articles easier to follow for readers unfamiliar with the story. The careful reader will notice that each of the three articles differs in some small respects in presenting the details of Milarepa's life. There are a number of versions of his namthar, or spiritual biography, and quite probably Chögyam Trungpa consulted different texts at different times. In working with me on "Milarepa: A Warrior's Life," Rinpoche suggested that I consult Lobsang Lhalungpa's translation of *The Life of Milarepa*.

The second article is simply called "Milarepa: A Synopsis." It too emerged from the files when I was searching for material for *The Collected Works* and has never been published before. It presents a series of scenes from Milarepa's life, with little commentary on their significance. The writing is quite vivid, however. Excerpts from a number of Milarepa's songs are included, based on the translation of *The Hundred Thousand Songs of Milarepa* by Garma C. C. Chang. Although it was impossible to definitively confirm this, it is likely that this article is actually an early treatment prepared by Chögyam Trungpa for a movie on the life of Milarepa, which he began filming in the early 1970s. He and several of his students, including two filmmakers from Los Angeles—Johanna Demetrakas and Baird Bryant—traveled to Sweden to film some exquisite thangkas of the life of Milarepa, which were to be featured in the movie. More information about the film itself—which was also to be an exploration of the qualities of the five buddha families—appears in the introduction to Volume Seven, which presents Rinpoche's teachings on art and the artistic process.

Volume Five closes with "The Art of Milarepa," which originally appeared in *Garuda II*. The title is somewhat misleading in that the article has little to do with Milarepa's artistic expression—his songs—in and of themselves and more to do with his art of life. The opening part of the article is a discussion of how the secret practice of Buddhist yoga evolved in India, especially in the ninth century in the great universities of Nalanda and Vikramashila. The connection that Marpa (Milarepa's main teacher) had to this tradition is also discussed. In this article, one sees Trungpa Rinpoche's brilliant insight into Milarepa's journey through life, the obstacles he encountered, and his final attainment. Throughout, Rinpoche brings together immense appreciation for Milarepa as a highly developed person on the one hand, with a down-to-earth insight into the humanness and ordinary quality of his practice on the other.

After he met his guru, Milarepa lived an austere, ascetic life and spent many years in solitary retreat in caves in the wilderness of Tibet. His lifestyle might seem distant from that of most people, especially in this modern age. Yet Trungpa Rinpoche makes Milarepa's experience accessible by demystifying it, while maintaining his tremendous appreciation for the attainment of his forefather. He tells us that Milarepa remained an ascetic simply because "that physical situation had become part of his makeup. Since he was true to himself, he had no relative concept of other living styles and did not compare himself to others. Although he taught people with many different lifestyles, he had no desire to convert them." Milarepa's asceticism is treated here as an ordinary but very sacred experience, one that really does not have much to do with embracing austerity per se. As Rinpoche concludes, "Simplicity is applicable to the situation of transcending neurotic mind by using domestic language. It becomes profound without pretense, and this naturally provokes the actual practice of meditation."

It seems fitting that Volume Five should end with these three articles celebrating the life of Milarepa. Although outwardly his was a life marked by the trappings of a secular existence, Chögyam Trungpa, like Milarepa, gave up everything familiar and cozy to bring the dharma of his lineage from Tibet to North America. He, like his forefathers, was rugged and direct, yet supremely sweet and gentle, and marked by an almost unbearable sadness, which became the expression of bliss. As he says in "The Dohā of Sadness," one of his songs in *The Rain of Wisdom:*

> You, my only father guru, have gone far away,
> My vajra brothers and sisters have wandered to the ends of
> the earth.
> Only I, Chögyam, the little child, am left.
> Still, for the teachings of the profound and brilliant practice
> lineage,
> I am willing to surrender my life in sadness.

In many thangkas, Milarepa is shown holding his hand up to his right ear. It is often said that he is listening to himself singing his own songs of realization. But I wonder if he is not listening to hear who will pick up the song of dharma that Trungpa Rinpoche sang in the West. Who will carry forward that melody? The Kagyü gurus are waiting to hear that song sung completely in a foreign tongue, echoing the same wisdom they have guarded with their lives for so many, many years. Let us aspire to join them in their song!

CAROLYN ROSE GIMIAN
February 6, 2002
Trident Mountain House
Tatamagouche Mountain, Nova Scotia

CRAZY WISDOM

EDITED BY
SHERAB CHÖDZIN KOHN

Editor's Foreword

THE VENERABLE CHÖGYAM TRUNGPA RINPOCHE gave two seminars on "crazy wisdom" in December 1972. Each lasted about a week. The first took place in an otherwise unoccupied resort hotel in the Tetons near Jackson Hole, Wyoming. The other happened in an old town hall cum gymnasium in the Vermont village of Barnet, just down the road from the meditation center founded by Trungpa Rinpoche now called Karmê Chöling, then known as Tail of the Tiger.

Rinpoche had arrived on this continent about two and a half years previously, in the spring of 1970. He had found an America bubbling with social change, animated by factors like hippyism, LSD, and the spiritual supermarket. In response to his ceaseless outpouring of teachings in a very direct, lucid, and down-to-earth style, a body of committed students had gathered, and more were arriving all the time. In the fall of 1972, he made his first tactical pause, taking a three-month retreat in a secluded house in the Massachusetts woods.

This was a visionary three months. Rinpoche seemed to contemplate the direction his work in America would take and the means at hand for its fulfillment. Important new plans were formulated. The last night of the retreat, he did not sleep. He told the few students present to use whatever was on hand and prepare a formal banquet. He himself spent hours in preparation for the banquet and did not appear until two in the morning—very beautifully groomed and dressed and buzzing with extraordinary energy. Conversation went on into the night. At one point, Rinpoche talked for two hours without stopping, giving an extremely vivid and detailed account of a dream he had had the night before. He left the retreat with the dawn light and traveled all that day. That evening, still not having slept, he gave the first talk of the "Crazy Wisdom" seminar at Jackson Hole. It is possible that he went off that morning with a sense of beginning a new phase in his work. Certainly elements of such a new phase are described in the last talk of the seminar at Jackson Hole.

After the first Vajradhatu Seminary in 1973 (planned during the 1972 retreat), Trungpa Rinpoche's teaching style would change. His presentation would become much more methodical, geared toward guiding his students through the successive stages of the path. The "Crazy Wisdom" seminars thus belonged to the end of the introductory period of Rinpoche's teaching in North America, during which, by contrast, he showed a spectacular ability to convey all levels of the teachings at once. During this introductory phase, there was a powerful fruitional atmosphere, bursting with the possibilities of the sudden path. Such an atmosphere prevailed as he made the basic teachings and advanced teachings into a single flow of profound instruction, while at the same time fiercely lopping away the omnipresent tentacles of spiritual materialism.

It might be helpful to look at these two seminars for a moment in the context of the battle against spiritual materialism. Though they had been planned in response to a request for teaching on the eight aspects of Padmasambhava, Trungpa Rinpoche had slightly shifted the emphasis and given the headline to crazy wisdom. His "experienced" students, as well as the ones newly arriving, had a relentless appetite for definite spiritual techniques or principles they could latch onto and identify with. The exotic iconography of the eight aspects of Padmasambhava, if presented too definitely, would have been bloody meat in the water for spiritually materialistic sharks. This may partly explain why a tidy hagiography of the eight aspects, with complete and consistent detail, was avoided, and the raw, ungarnished insight of crazy wisdom was delivered instead.

Some editing of this material from the original spoken presentation has been necessary for the sake of basic readability. However, nothing has been changed in the order of presentation, and nothing has been left out in the body of the talks. A great effort has been made not to cosmeticize Trungpa Rinpoche's language or alter his diction purely for the sake of achieving a conventionally presentable tone. Hopefully, the reader will enjoy those sentences of his that run between our mental raindrops and touch us where ordinary conceptual clarity could not. The reader will also hopefully appreciate that passages that remain dark on one reading may become luminously clear on another.

Here, we have the mighty roaring of a great lion of dharma. May it put to flight the heretics and bandits of hope and fear. For the benefit of all beings, may his wishes continue to be fulfilled.

CRAZY WISDOM SEMINAR I

Jackson Hole, 1972

Pema Gyalpo (Padmasambhava).

ONE

Padmasambhava and Spiritual Materialism

THE SUBJECT that we are going to deal with is an extraordinarily difficult one. It is possible that some people might get extraordinarily confused. Or people might very well get something out of it. We will be discussing Guru Rinpoche, or as he is often called in the West, Padmasambhava; we will be considering his nature and the various lifestyles he developed in the process of working with students. This subject is very subtle, and some aspects of it are very difficult to put into words. I hope nobody will regard this humble attempt of mine as a definitive portrayal of Padmasambhava.

To begin with, we probably need some basic introduction to who Padmasambhava was; to how he fits into the context of the buddhadharma (the Buddhist teachings), in general; and to how he came to be so admired by Tibetans in particular.

Padmasambhava was an Indian teacher who brought the complete teachings of the buddhadharma to Tibet. He remains our source of inspiration even now, here in the West. We have inherited his teachings, and from that point of view, I think we could say that Padmasambhava is alive and well.

I suppose the best way to characterize Padmasambhava for people with a Western or Christian cultural outlook is to say that he was a saint. We are going to discuss the depth of his wisdom and his lifestyle, his skillful way of relating with students. The students he had to deal with were Tibetans, who were extraordinarily savage and uncultured. He was invited to come to Tibet, but the Tibetans showed very little under-standing of how to receive and welcome a great guru from another part of the world. They were very stubborn and very matter-of-fact—very earthy. They presented all kinds of obstacles to Padmasambhava's activ-ity in Tibet. However, the obstacles did not come from the Tibetan peo-ple alone, but also from differences in climate, landscape, and the social situation as a whole. In some ways, Padmasambhava's situation was very similar to our situation here. Americans are hospitable, but on the other hand, there is a very savage and rugged side to American culture. Spiritually, American culture is not conducive to just bringing out the brilliant light and expecting it to be accepted.

So there is an analogy here. In terms of that analogy, the Tibetans are the Americans and Padmasambhava is himself.

Before getting into details concerning Padmasambhava's life and teachings, I think it would be helpful to discuss the idea of a saint in the Buddhist tradition. The idea of a saint in the Christian tradition and the idea of a saint in the Buddhist tradition are somewhat conflicting. In the Christian tradition, a saint is generally considered someone who has direct communication with God, who perhaps is completely intoxicated with the Godhead and because of this is able to give out certain reassur-ances to people. People can look to the saint as an example of higher consciousness or higher development.

The Buddhist approach to spirituality is quite different. It is nontheis-tic. It does not have the principle of an external divinity. Thus, there is no possibility of getting promises from the divinity and bringing them from there down to here. The Buddhist approach to spirituality is con-nected with awakening within oneself rather than with relating to some-thing external. So the idea of a saint as someone who is able to expand himself to relate to an external principle, get something out of it, and then share that with others is difficult or nonexistent from the Buddhist point of view.

A saint in the Buddhist context—for example, Padmasambhava or a great being like the Buddha himself—is someone who provides an exam-ple of the fact that completely ordinary, confused human beings can wake themselves up; they can put themselves together and wake them-selves up through an accident of life of one kind or another. The pain, the suffering of all kinds, the misery, and the chaos that are part of life begins to wake them, shake them. Having been shaken, they begin to question: "Who am I? What am I? How is it that all these things are happening?" Then they go further and realize that there is something in them that is asking these questions, something that is, in fact, intelligent and not exactly confused.

This happens in our own lives. We feel a sense of confusion—it seems to be confusion—but that confusion brings out something that is worth exploring. The questions that we ask in the midst of our confusion are potent questions, questions that we really have. We ask, "Who am I? What am I? What is this? What is life?" and so forth. Then we explore further and ask, "In fact, who on earth asked that question? Who is that person who asked the question, 'Who am I?' Who is the person who asked, 'What is?' or even 'What is what is?'" We go on and on with this questioning, further and further inward. In some way, this is nontheistic spirituality in its fullest sense. External inspirations do not stimulate us to model ourselves on further external situations. Rather the external situations that exist speak to us of our confusion, and this makes us think more, think further. Once we have begun to do that, then of course there is the other problem: once we have found out who and what we are, how do we apply what we have learned to our living situation? How do we put it into practice?

There seem to be two possible approaches here. One is trying to live up to what we would *like* to be. The other is trying to live what we are. Trying to live up to what we would like to be is like pretending we are a divine being or a realized person, or whatever we might like to call the model. When we realize what is wrong with us, what our weakness is, what our problems and neuroses are, the automatic temptation is to try to act just the opposite, as though we have never heard of such a thing as our being wrong or confused. We tell ourselves, "Think positive! Act as though you're okay." Although we know that something is wrong with us on the level of the actual living situation, on the kitchen-sink level, we regard that as unimportant. "Let's forget those 'evil vibrations,'" we say. "Let's think the other way. Let's pretend to be good."

This approach is known in the Buddhist tradition as *spiritual materialism*, which means not being realistic, or to use hippie jargon, spacing out. "Let's forget the bad and pretend to be good." We could classify as spiritual materialism any approach—such as Buddhist, Hindu, Jewish, or Christian—that provides us with techniques to try to associate with the good, the better, the best—or the ultimately good, the divine.

When we begin associating ourselves with the good, it makes us happy. We feel full of delight. We think, "At last I've found an answer!" That answer is that the only thing to do is regard ourselves as free already. Then, having established the position that we are free already, we just have to let all things flow.

Then we add a further touch to reinforce our spiritual materialism: everything that we do not know or did not understand in connection with our spiritual quest we connect with descriptions in various scriptures about that which is beyond mind, beyond words, ineffable—the ineffable Self, or whatever. We associate our own lack of understanding about what is going on with us with those unspoken, inexpressible things. This way our ignorance is made into the greatest discovery of all. We can connect this "great discovery" with a doctrinal supposition; for example, "the savior" or some interpretation of the scriptures.

Whereas before, we didn't know anything at all, now we "know" something that we actually don't know. There is something ahead of us now. We cannot describe it in terms of words, concepts, and ideas, but we have discovered that, to begin with, it is a matter of twisting ourselves into the good. So we have this one thing to start with: we can directly and deliberately translate our confusion as being something that is not confused. We do this just because we are seeking pleasure, spiritual pleasure. In doing it, we affirm that the pleasure we are seeking is of an unknowable nature, because we actually have no idea what kind of spiritual pleasure we are going to get out of this maneuver. And all the spiritual interpretations of the scriptures referring to the unknowable can be applied to the fact that we do not know what to do spiritually. Nevertheless, we are definitely involved in spiritual conviction now, because we have suppressed our original doubts about who we are and what we are—our feeling that perhaps we might not be anything. We have suppressed that; we may not even know about it anymore.

Having suppressed this embarrassment of ego that provided us with stepping-stones to the unknown, the nature of which we did not understand, we end up with two games of confusion going on: a game of the unknown and a game of the transcendental unknown. Both of these are part of spiritual materialism. We do not know who or what we are, but we do know that we would like to be someone or something. We decide to go ahead with what we would like to be even though we do not know what that is. That is the first game. Then on top of that, in connection with being something, we would also like to know that there is something about the world or the cosmos that corresponds to this "something" that we are. We have a sense of finding this something that we want to know, but we actually can't understand it, so that becomes the transcendental unknown. Since we can't understand it, we say, "Let's make that bigger and more gigantic confusion into the spirituality of the infiniteness of the Godhead," or something like that.

This should give us some understanding of spiritual materialism. The danger of spiritual materialism is that under its influence we make all kinds of assumptions. First, there are the domestic or personal-level assumptions, which we make because we want to be happy. Second, there are the spiritual assumptions that are made because that transcendental, gigantic, greater discovery is left mysterious. This brings further great assumptions: we do not know what we are actually going to achieve by achieving that unknown thing, but nevertheless, we give it some vague description, such as "being absorbed into the cosmos." And since nobody has yet gone that far, if anybody questions this discovery of "absorption into the cosmos," then we just make up further logic or look for reinforcement from the scriptures or other authorities.

The result of all this is that we end up confirming ourselves and confirming that the experience we are proclaiming is a true experience. Nobody can question it. At some stage, there's no room left for questioning at all. Our whole outlook becomes completely established with no room left at all for questioning. This is what we could call achieving egohood, as opposed to achieving enlightenment. At that point, if I would like to practice my aggression and passion on you and you don't accept that, then that's your fault. You do not understand the ineffable spirituality, so you are at fault. The only way left for me to help you is to reduce you to a shrunken head, to take out your brain and heart. You become a mere puppet under my command.

That is a rough portrait of spiritual materialism. It is the first of the two possible approaches: trying to live up to what you would *like* to be. Now let's talk about the second possible approach, that of trying to live what you are.

This possibility is connected with seeing our confusion, or misery and pain, but not making those discoveries into an answer. Instead, we explore further and further and further without looking for an answer. It is a process of working with ourselves, with our lives, with our psychology, without looking for an answer but seeing things as they are—seeing what goes on in our heads directly and simply, absolutely literally. If we can undertake a process like that, then there is a tremendous possibility that our confusion—the chaos and neurosis that go on in our minds—might become a further basis for investigation. Then we look further and further and further. We don't make a big point or an answer out of any one thing. For example, we might think that because we have discovered one particular thing that is wrong with us, that must be *it*, that must be the problem, that must be the answer. No. We don't fixate on that, we go further. "Why is that the case?" We look further and further. We ask, "Why is this so? Why is there spirituality? Why is there awakening? Why is there this moment of relief? Why is there such a thing as discovering the pleasure of spirituality? Why, why, why?" We go on deeper and deeper and deeper and deeper, until we reach the point where there is no answer. There is not even a question. Both question and answer die simultaneously at some point. They begin to rub each other too closely and they short-circuit each other in some way. At that point, we tend to give up hope of an answer, or of anything whatsoever, for that matter. We have no more hope, none whatsoever. We are purely hopeless. We could call this transcending hope, if you would like to put it in more genteel terms.

The hopelessness is the essence of crazy wisdom. It is hopeless, utterly hopeless. It is beyond hopelessness. (Of course, it would be possible, if we tried to turn that hopelessness itself into some kind of solution, to become confused again, to say the least.)

The process is one of going further in and in and in without any reference point of spirituality, without any reference point of a savior, without any reference point of goodness or badness—without any reference points whatsoever! Finally, we might reach the basic level of hopelessness, of transcending hope. This does not mean we end up as zombies. We still have all the energies; we have all the fascination of discovery, of seeing this process unfolding and unfolding and unfolding, going on and on. This process of discovery automatically recharges itself so that we keep going deeper and deeper and deeper. This process of going deeper and deeper is the process of crazy wisdom, and it is what characterizes a saint in the Buddhist tradition.

The eight aspects of Padmasambhava that we are going to discuss are connected with such a process of psychological penetration, of cutting through the surface of the psychological realm and then cutting through a further surface and infinitely further surfaces down through ever further depths of further surfaces, deeper and deeper. This is the process we involve ourselves in by discussing Padmasambhava's life, the eight aspects of Padmasambhava, and crazy wisdom.

In this context, we see that the Buddhist approach to spirituality is one of ruthlessly cutting through any chance we might have of confirming ourselves at any particular stage of development on the spiritual path. When we discover that we have made some progress on the spiritual path, that discovery of progress is regarded as a hindrance to further progress. So we don't get a chance to rest, to relax, or to congratulate ourselves at all. It is a one-shot, ongoingly ruthless spiritual journey. And that is the essence of Padmasambhava's spirituality.

Padmasambhava had to work with the Tibetan people of those days. You can imagine it. A great Indian magician and pandit, a great vidyadhara, or tantric master, comes to the Land of Snow, Tibet. The Tibetans think he is going to teach them some beautiful spiritual teaching about how to know the essence of the mind. The expectations built up by the Tibetans are enormous. Padmasambhava's work is to cut through the Tibetans' layers and layers of expectations, through all their assumptions as to what spirituality might be. Finally, at the end of Padmasambhava's mission in Tibet, when he manifested as Dorje Trolö, all those layers of expectation were completely cut through. The Tibetans began to realize that spirituality is cutting through hope and fear as well as being the sudden discovery of intelligence that goes along with this process.

Student: What is the difference between crazy wisdom and just being crazy? Some people might want to just go on being crazy and confused and excuse themselves by saying this is crazy wisdom. So what is the difference?

Trungpa Rinpoche: Well, that is what I have been trying to explain through my whole talk, but let's try again. In the case of ordinary craziness, we are constantly trying to win the game. We might even try to turn craziness into a credential of some kind so we can come out ahead. We might try to magnetize people with passion or destroy them with aggression or whatever. There's a constant game going on in the mind. Mind's game—constant strategies going on—might bring us a moment of relief occasionally, but that relief has to be maintained by further aggression. That kind of craziness has to maintain itself constantly, on and on.

In the case of the primordial craziness of crazy wisdom, we do not permit ourselves to get seduced by passion or aroused by aggression at all. We relate with these experiences as they are, and if anything comes up in the midst of that complete ordinariness and begins to make itself into a big deal, then we cut it down—without any special reference to what is good and what is bad. Crazy wisdom is just the action of truth. It cuts everything down. It does not even try to translate falseness into truthfulness, because that in itself is corruption. It is ruthless, because if you want the complete truth, if you want to be completely, wholely wholesome, then any suggestion that comes up of translating whatever arises into your terms, interpreting it in your terms, is not worth looking into. On the other hand, the usual crazy approach is completely up for that kind of thing—for making whatever comes up fit into your thing. You make it suit what you want to be, suit what you want to see. But crazy wisdom becomes completely accurate out of the moment of things as they are. This is the style of action of Padmasambhava.

Student: How does discipline relate to being what you really are? I thought discipline meant imposing something on yourself.

Trungpa Rinpoche: The most difficult discipline is to be what you are. Constantly trying to be what you are *not* is much easier, because we are trained to con either ourselves or others, to fit things into appropriate categories. Whereas if you take all of that away, the whole thing becomes too irritating, too boring. There's no room for talking yourself into anything. Everything is quite simple.

Student: You often make use of your sense of humor in explaining things. Is sense of humor, the way you use it, the same as crazy wisdom?

Trungpa Rinpoche: Not quite. Sense of humor is still too much slanted toward the other side, toward hope and fear. It's a dialectic mentality, whereas crazy wisdom is an overall approach.

Student: Do we relate to hope and fear through the discipline of spiritual practice?

Trungpa Rinpoche: That's a good point, actually. From this point of view, anything that is ruthless—anything that knows nothing of hope and fear—is related to spiritual practice.

TWO

The Trikaya

WE HAVE DISCUSSED two possible approaches to spirituality: spiritual materialism and transcending spiritual materialism. Padmasambhava's way is that of transcending spiritual materialism, of developing basic sanity. Developing basic sanity is a process of working on ourselves in which the path itself rather than the attainment of a goal becomes the working basis. The path itself is what constantly inspires us, rather than, in the style of the carrot and the donkey, promises about certain achievements that lie ahead of us. In other words, to make this perfectly clear, the difference between spiritual materialism and transcending spiritual materialism is that in spiritual materialism promises are used like a carrot held up in front of a donkey, luring him into all kinds of journeys; in transcending spiritual materialism, there is no goal. The goal exists in every moment of our life situation, in every moment of our spiritual journey.

In this way, the spiritual journey becomes as exciting and as beautiful as if we were buddha already. There are constant new discoveries, constant messages, and constant warnings. There is also constant cutting down, constant painful lessons—as well as pleasurable ones. The spiritual journey of transcending spiritual materialism is a complete journey rather than one that is dependent on an external goal.

It is this completeness of the journey that we are going to discuss in relation to Padmasambhava's life. This completeness can be described in terms of certain aspects: it contains basic space, or totality; it contains energy and play; and it also contains pragmatic application, or dealing

Padmasambhava as a young bhikshu.

with life situations as they are. We have three principles there: the totality as the whole sense of environment on the path, the sense of play on the path, and the sense of practicality on the path. These are the three categories that develop.

Before getting into the details of Padmasambhava's eight aspects, it would be good to discuss these three principles in terms of how Padmasambhava manifests them to us as path.

First, we have to look more closely at the nature of the path itself. The path is our effort, the energy that we put into the daily living situation; it consists of our trying to work with the daily living situation as a learning process—whether that situation is creative or destructive or whatever. If you spill a cup of coffee on your neighbor's table or if you just pass someone the salt, it's the same thing. These are the happenings that occur all the time in our life situations. We are constantly doing things, constantly relating with things or rejecting things. There is constant play. I am not particularly talking about spirituality at this point, but just daily existence: those events that happen all the time in our life situations. That is the path.

The path does not particularly have to be labeled as spiritual. It is just a simple journey, the journey that contains exchange with the reality of this and that—or with the unreality of it, if you prefer. Relating with these exchanges—the living process, the being process—is the path. We may be thinking of our path in terms of attaining enlightenment or of attaining egohood or whatever. In any case, we never get stuck in any way at all. We might think we get stuck. We might feel bored with life and so forth; but we never really get bored or really get stuck. The repetitiousness of life is not really repetition. It is composed of constant happenings, situations constantly evolving, all the time. That is the path.

From this point of view, the path is neutral. It is not biased one way or the other. There is a constant journey happening, which began at the time of the basic split. We began to relate in terms of "the other," "me," "mine," "our," and so on. We began to relate with things as separate entities. The other is called "them" and this thing is called "I" or "me." The journey began right from there. That was the first creation of samsara and nirvana. Right at the beginning, when we decided to connect in some way with the energy of situations, we involved ourselves in a journey, in the path.

After that, we develop a certain way of relating with the path, and the path becomes conditioned toward either worldliness or spirituality. In other words, spirituality is not really the path, but spirituality is a way of conditioning our path, our energy.

Conditioning our path happens in terms of the three categories I have already mentioned. It happens, for example, in terms of the totality of experience, the first category. That is one aspect of *how* we relate to our path—in terms of the totality of our experience. The path is happening anyway, then we relate to it in a certain way, we take a certain attitude toward it. The path then becomes either a spiritual path or a mundane path. This is the way we relate to the path; this is how our motivation begins. And our motivation has the threefold pattern.

In the Buddhist tradition, these three aspects of the path are called *dharmakaya, sambhogakaya,* and *nirmanakaya.* The conditioning of the path happens in terms of those three aspects. The ongoing process of the path has a certain total attitude. The journey takes on a pattern that has an element of total basic sanity in it. This total sanity, or enlightened quality, is not particularly attractive in the ordinary sense. It is the sense of complete openness that we discussed earlier. It is this complete total openness that makes us able to transcend hope and fear. With this openness, we relate to things as they are rather than as we would like them to be. That basic sanity, that approach transcending hope and fear, is the attitude of enlightenment.

This attitude is very practical. It does not reject what comes up on the path, and it does not become attached to what comes up on the path. It just sees things as they are. So this is total, complete openness—complete willingness to look into whatever arises, to work with it, and to relate to it as part of the overall process. This is the dharmakaya mentality of all-encompassing space, of including everything without bias. It is a larger way of thinking, a greater way of viewing things, as opposed to being petty, finicky.

We are taking the dharmakaya approach as long as we do not relate to the world as our enemy. The world is our opportune situation; it is what we have to work with. Nothing that arises makes us have to fight with the world. The world is the extraordinarily rich situation that is there; it is full of resources for us. This basic approach of generosity and richness is the dharmakaya's approach. It is total positive thinking. This greater vision is the first attitude in relation to the path.

Then we have the second attitude, connected with the sambhogakaya. Things are open and spacious and workable as we have said, but there is something more. We also need to relate to the sparkiness, the energy, the flashes and aliveness that take place within that openness. That energy, which includes aggression, passion, ignorance, pride, jealousy, and so forth, also has to be acknowledged. Anything that goes on in the realm of the mind can be accepted as the glittering light that shines through the massiveness of the spiritual path. It shines constantly, surprises us constantly. There is another corner of our being that is so alive, so energetic and powerful. There are discoveries happening all the time. That is the sambhogakaya's way of relating with the path.

Thus, the path contains the larger sense of total acceptance of things as they are; and the path also contains what we might call fascination with the exciting discoveries within situations. It is worth repeating here that we are not putting our experiences into pigeonholes of "virtuous" or "religious" or "worldly." We are just relating with the things that happen in our life situations. Those energies and passions that we encounter on our journey present us with continual discoveries of different facets of ourselves, different profiles of ourselves. At that point, things become rather interesting. After all, we are not so blank or flat as we imagined ourselves to be.

Then we have the third kind of relationship with the path, which is connected with the nirmanakaya. This is the basic practicality of existing in the world. We have the totality, we have the various energies, and then we have how to function in the world as it is, the living world. This last aspect demands tremendous awareness and effort. We cannot simply leave it to the totality and the energy to take care of everything; we have to put some discipline into our approach to our life situations. All the disciplines and techniques spoken of in spiritual traditions are connected with this nirmanakaya principle of application on the path. There is practicing meditation, working with the intellect, taking a further interest in relationships with each other, developing fundamental compassion and a sense of communication, and developing knowledge or wisdom that is capable of looking at a whole situation and seeing the ways in which things might be workable. All those are nirmanakaya disciplines.

Taken together, for three principles, or three stages—dharmakaya, sambhogakaya, nirmanakaya—provide us with a complete basis for our spiritual journey. Because of them, the journey and out attitude toward it become something workable, something we can deal with directly and intelligently, without having to relegate it to some vague category like "the mysteriousness of life."

In terms of our psychological state, these principles each have another characteristic, which it is worth mentioning here. As a psychological state, the dharmakaya is basic being. It is a totality in which confusion and ignorance have never existed; it is total existence that *never needs any reference point*. The sambhogakaya is that which continually contains spontaneous energy, because it *never depends on any cause-and-effect kind of energy*. The nirmanakaya is self-existing fulfillment in relation to which *no strategizing about how to function is necessary*. Those are the psychological aspects of buddha nature that develop.

In looking at Padmasambhava's life and his eight aspects, we will find those three principles. Seeing those psychological principles in action in Padmasambhava's life can help us to not regard Padmasambhava purely as some mythical figure that no one has ever met. Those are principles that we can work on together, and each one of you can work on them in relation to yourself.

Student: Are the eight aspects of Padmasambhava like eight stages that we can work through in trying to make a breakthrough in our own psychological development?

Trungpa Rinpoche: Actually, the eight aspects are not really linear, successive levels of development. What we have is more a single situation with eight aspects—a central principle surrounded by eight types of manifestation. There are eight aspects of all kinds of situations.

Psychologically, we could make some kind of breakthrough by relating with that. You see, as it tells us in the scriptures, when Padmasambhava manifested as the eight aspects, he was already enlightened. The eight aspects were not his spiritual journey, but he was expressing himself, dancing with situations. He was already coming out with his crazy-wisdom expressions.

What I'm trying to say is, we could find all those eight aspects within ourselves, in one working situation. We could connect with them. We could break through with all eight simultaneously.

S: So it's definitely not a linear progression like the ten *bhumis*.

TR: You see, here we are talking about the sudden path, the direct or sudden path of tantra. This is realization that does not depend on a progressive, external buildup or unmasking. It is realization eating out from the inside rather than unmasking taking place from the outside. Eating out from the inside is the tantric approach. In some sense, this supersedes the ten bhumis, or stages, of the bodhisattva path. We are discussing more the vajra-like samadhi of the Buddha and his way of relating with things, which of course is connected with buddha nature; we are approaching that here as a sudden, direct transmission, a direct way, without going through the paramitas or the bhumis. The approach here is to regard oneself as being a buddha already. Buddha is the path rather than the goal. We are working from the inside outward. The mask is falling off by itself.

Student: Was Padmasambhava already buddha when he was born?

Trungpa Rinpoche: He was more an awake person than a fully realized buddha. He was the dharmakaya principle trying to manifest itself on the sambhogakaya level and then beginning to relate to the world outside. Thus, he could be regarded as a person who was a potential buddha at birth and who then broke the barriers to the fulfillment of that potential ruthlessly and without fear. He attained instantaneous enlightenment on one spot, and it seems that we could do the same.

Student: Is this connected with the idea of our having to take a leap that you have spoken about so often?

Trungpa Rinpoche: This has more to do with the *attitude* of taking a leap than actually taking the leap. You are willing to leap, so then there is the situation of leaping. The important thing here is the basic spirit or outlook you have, rather than just the particular application of how you handle things. It is something much bigger than that.

Student: You've talked a lot about ruthlessness and fearlessness. What are you ruthless toward? Do you just ruthlessly assume a particular psychological attitude?

Trungpa Rinpoche: The whole point of ruthlessness is that when you are ruthless, no one can con you. No one can seduce you in an unhealthy direction. It is ruthlessness in that sense rather than in the conventional sense of illogical aggression—such as in the case of Mussolini or Hitler or someone like that. You cannot be conned or seduced; you would not accept that. Even attempts to seduce you arouse energy that is destructive toward that attempted seduction. If you are completely open and completely aroused in terms of crazy wisdom, no one can lure you into their territory.

S: You can maintain the ruthlessness—

TR: You don't maintain the ruthlessness. Your ruthlessness is maintained by others. You don't maintain anything at all. You just *be* there, and whatever situation comes to you, you just project back. Take the example of fire. It does not possess its destructiveness. That just happens. When you put something in the fire or try to kill the fire, its offensive power just comes out. It is the organic or chemical nature of fire.

S: When these things come at you, then you have to be ruthless in order to repel them, right? Then it seems that a judgment has to be made as to right and wrong, as to whether what is coming at you is positive or negative, and whether to be compassionate or ruthless.

TR: I don't think so. That's the whole point of the transcendental type of ruthlessness. It does not need judgment. The situation brings the action. You simply react, because the elements contain aggression. If the elements are interfered with or dealt with in an irreverent or unskillful way, they hit you back.

Ruthlessness may seem to survive on a sense of relativity, of "this" versus "that," but in fact it actually does not. It is absolute. The others present a relative notion, which you cut through. This state of being is not on a relative level at all. In other words, this absoluteness cuts through the relative notion that comes to it, but still it remains self-contained.

S: That would make it very isolated, very lonely.

TR: No, I don't think so, because absolute means *everything*. So you have more than you need, so to speak.

S: Are you saying that hopelessness and fearlessness are the same thing?

TR: Yes. They are the ultimate thing, if you are able to work with that. They are the ultimate thing.

Student: How does ruthlessness apply to the destruction of ego? Ruthlessness seems so uncompassionate, almost ego-like itself.

Trungpa Rinpoche: Well, it is ego's intensity that brings forth "uncompassionate" measures. In other words, when neurosis and confusion reach an extreme point, the only way to correct the confusion is by destroying it. You have to completely shatter the whole thing. That process of destruction is demanded by the confusion itself rather than it being a question of somebody thinking it is a good idea to destroy the confusion by force. No other thinking is involved. The intensity of confusion itself demands its own destruction. Ruthlessness is just putting that energy into action. It is just letting that energy burn itself out rather than your killing something. You just let ego's neurosis commit suicide rather than killing it. That's the ruthlessness. Ego is killing itself ruthlessly, and you are providing the accommodation for that.

This is not warfare. You are there, and therefore it happens. On the other hand, if you are not there, there is the possibility of scapegoats and sidetracks of all kinds. But if you are there, you don't even actually have to be ruthless. Just be there; from the point of view of ego, that is ruthless.

THREE

Primordial Innocence

THE DISCOVERY OF THE PATH and the appropriate attitude toward it have a certain function spiritually. The path can make it possible to connect with basic, primordial, innocent being.

We put so much emphasis on pain and confusion that we forget basic innocence. The usual approach that we take toward spirituality is to look for some experience that might enable us to rediscover our adulthood rather than go back to our innocent childlike quality. We have been fooled into looking for a way to become completely grown-up and respectable, as it were, or psychologically sound.

This seems to correspond to the basic idea we have of enlightenment. An enlightened person is supposed to be more or less an old-wise-man type: not quite like an old professor, but perhaps an old father who can supply sound advice on how to handle all of life's problems or an old grandmother who knows all the recipes and all the cures. That seems to be the current fantasy that exists in our culture concerning enlightened beings. They are old and wise, grown-up and solid.

Tantra has a different notion of enlightenment, which is connected with youth and innocence. We can see this pattern in Padmasambhava's life story, where the awakened state of mind is portrayed not as old and adult but as young and free. Youth and freedom in this case are connected with the birth of the awakened state of mind. The awakened state of mind has the quality of morning, of dawn—fresh and sparkling, completely awake. This is the quality of the birth of Padmasambhava.

Having identified ourselves with the path and the proper attitude toward the path, we suddenly discover that there is something beautiful about it. The path has a freshness to it that contrasts sharply with the monotony of going through a program of various practices. New discoveries are being made. New discovery is the birth of Padmasambhava.

Padmasambhava was born in a lotus flower on a lake in Uddiyana. He had the appearance of an eight-year-old. He was inquisitive, bright, youthful, untouched by anything. Since he had never been touched by anything, he was not afraid to touch anything. He was surrounded by dakinis making offerings to him and playing music. There were even beasts, wild animals, all around paying homage to him on this fresh, unpolluted lake—Lake Dhanakosha in Uddiyana, somewhere in the Himalayan region of Afghanistan. The landscape was similar to that of Kashmir, with very fresh mountain air and snow-capped mountains all around. There was a sense of freshness and at the same time some sense of wildness.

For an infant to be born in such a wild, desolate place in the middle of a lake on a lotus is beyond the grasp of conceptual mind. For one thing, a child cannot be born from a lotus. For another, such a wild mountain region is too hostile to accommodate the birth of a child, and a healthy one at that. Such a birth is impossible. But then, impossible things happen, things beyond our imagination. In fact, impossible things happen before our imagination even occurs, so we could appropriately describe them as unimaginable—even "out of sight" or "far out."

Padmasambhava was born in a lotus on this lake. He was born a prince, young and cute, but also bright, terrifyingly bright. His bright eyes look at you. He is not afraid to touch anything at all. Sometimes it is embarrassing to be around him, this good and beautiful eight-year-old infant.

The awakened state of mind could as well be infantlike as grown-up, the way we usually imagine grown-up. Life batters us, confuses us, but somebody manages to cross the turbulent river of life and find the answer; somebody works very, very hard and finally achieves peace of mind. That is our usual idea, but that is not how it is with Padmasambhava. He is inexperienced. Life has not battered him at all. He was just born out of a lotus in the middle of a lake in Afghanistan somewhere. That is a very exciting message, extraordinarily exciting. One can be enlightened and be infantlike. That is in accord with things as they are: if we are awake, we are only an infant. At the first stage of our experience, we are just an infant. We are innocent, because we have gone back to our original state of being.

Padmasambhava was invited to the court of King Indrabhuti. The king had asked his gardeners to collect fresh flowers—lotuses and mountain flowers—in the region of the lake. To one of the gardeners' surprise, he discovered a gigantic lotus with a child sitting on it—very happily. He did not want to touch the child; he was afraid of the mysteriousness of it. He reported back to the king, who told him to bring the child as well as the flower. Padmasambhava was enthroned and crowned as the Prince of Uddiyana. He was called Padma Raja, or Pema Gyalpo in Tibetan, "the Lotus King."

It is possible for us to discover our own innocence and childlike beauty, the princelike quality in us. Having discovered all our confusions and neuroses, we begin to realize that they are harmless or helpless. Then gradually we find the innocent-child quality in us. Of course, this is quite different from the primal-scream type of idea. And it does not mean that we are being *reduced* to a child. Rather, we discover the child-*like* quality in us. We become fresh, inquisitive, sparkling; we want to know more about the world, more about life. All of our preconceptions have been stripped away. We begin to realize ourselves—it is like a second birth. We discover our innocence, our primordial quality, our eternal youth.

The first breakthrough presents us with our childlike quality, but we are still somewhat apprehensive about how to deal with life, though we are not terrified by it. There is a sense of reaching out our hand and beginning to explore all the unknown areas for the first time. Our experience of duality, what we thought we knew, our preconceptions—all that has become false, has fallen apart. Now, for the first time, we recognize the real quality of the path. We give up our ego reservations, or at least realize them.

The more we realize ego and ego's neurosis, the closer we are to that infantlike state of mind of not knowing how to handle the next step in life. Often people ask, "Suppose I do meditate, then what am I going to do? If I attain a peaceful state of mind, how am I going to deal with my enemies and my superiors?" We actually ask very infantlike questions. "If thus-and-such happens as we progress along the path, then what's going to happen next?" It is very childlike, infantlike; it is a fresh discovery of perception, a new discovery of a sense of things as they are.

So Padmasambhava lived in the palace; he was taken care of and entertained. At a certain point, he was asked to marry. Because of his innocence, he had great reservations about this, but he finally decided to go ahead. The young prince grew up. He explored sexuality and the marriage system and related with a wife. Gradually he came to realize that the world around him was not all that delicate anymore, not as delicate as lotus petals. The world was exciting, playful. It was like being given, for the first time, a substantial toy that could be bashed about, unscrewed, taken apart, put back together again.

This is a very moving story of a journey ever further outward. Starting from the basic innocence of the dharmakaya level, which is the embryonic state of buddha nature, we have to come out, step out. We have to relate with the playfulness of the world as it is on the sambhogakaya and nirmanakaya levels.

Padmasambhava as a baby represents that complete, childlike state in which there is no duality; there is no "this" and no "that." This state is completely all-pervading. There is also a sense of freshness, because this state is total, it is all over, there is no reference point. If there is no reference point, then there is nothing to pollute one's concepts or ideas. It is one absolute ultimate thing altogether.

Starting from that, Padmasambhava, having married, became more playful. He even began to experiment with his aggression, finding that he could use his strength to throw things and things could get broken. And he carried this to an extreme, knowing that he had the potential for crazy wisdom within him. He danced holding two scepters—a vajra and a trident—on the palace roof. He dropped his vajra and trident, and they fell and hit a mother and her son who were walking below, simultaneously killing them both. They happened to be the wife and son of one of the king's ministers. The vajra hit the child's head, and the trident struck the mother's heart.

Very playful! (I am afraid this is not quite a respectable story.)

This event had serious repercussions. The ministers decided to exert their influence on the king and asked him to send Padmasambhava away, to exile him from the kingdom. Padmasambhava's crime was committed in the wildness of exploring things, which is still on the sambhogakaya level—in the realm of experiencing things and their subtleties, and of exploring birth and death as well. So the king exiled Padmasambhava. This was much to the king's own regret, but the play of the phenomenal world had to be legal. The phenomenal world is a very basic legal setup. The play of phenomena has cause and effect constantly happening within it.

This does not mean to say that Padmasambhava was subject to karma. Rather, he was exploring the legality of karma—karmic interplays with the outside world, the confused world. It was that confused world that molded him to be a teacher, rather than his proclaiming himself, saying, "I am a teacher" or "I am the savior of the world." He never claimed anything like that. But the world began to mold Padmasambhava into the shape of a teacher or savior. And one of the expressions of the world's doing that, which made this process able to proceed, was the fact that he performed this violent action and therefore had to be expelled from King Indrabhuti's kingdom and had to go to the charnel ground of Silwa Tsal ("Cool Grove"), supposedly somewhere in the region of Bodhgaya in southern India.

This infant quality and the exploratory quality that develops in our being as we begin to work on the spiritual path require working with dangers as well as working with pleasures of all kinds. That childlike quality automatically tends toward the world outside, having already realized that the sudden, instant enlightened state of mind is not the end but the beginning of the journey. The sudden awakeness happens, and then we become an infant. Then after that, we explore how to work with phenomena, how to dance with phenomena, and at the same time, how to relate with confused people. Working with confused people automatically draws us into certain shapes according to the teachings the confused people require and the situations that are required in order to relate with them.

Student: Could you say a bit more about the dharmakaya principle and the idea of totality, as well as a bit more about the sambhogakaya and nirmanakaya?

Trungpa Rinpoche: It seems that the dharmakaya principle is that which accommodates everything. It accommodates any extremes, whether the extremes are there or not—it doesn't really make any difference. It is the totality in which there is tremendous room to move about. The sambhogakaya principle is the energy that is involved with that totality and that puts further emphasis on that totality. The totality aspect of the dharmakaya is like the ocean, and the sambhogakaya aspect is like the waves of that ocean, which make the statement that that ocean does exist. The nirmanakaya aspect is like a ship on the ocean, which makes the whole situation into a pragmatic and workable one—you can sail across the ocean.

S: How does this relate to confusion?

TR: Confusion is the other partner. If there is understanding, that understanding usually has its own built-in limitation of understanding. Thus, confusion is there automatically until the absolute level is reached, where understanding does not need its own help, because the entire situation is an understood situation.

Student: How does this apply to daily life?

Trungpa Rinpoche: Well, in daily life, it's just the same. Working with the totality, there is basic room to work with life, and also there is energy and practicality involved. In other words, we are not limited to a particular thing. A lot of the frustration we have with our lives comes from the feeling that there are inadequate means to change and improvise with our life situations. But those three principles of dharmakaya, sambhogakaya, and nirmanakaya provide us with tremendous possibilities for improvisation. There are endless resources of all kinds we could work with.

Student: What was Padmasambhava's relationship with King Indrabhuti all about? How did it relate to his development from his basic innocence?

Trungpa Rinpoche: King Indrabhuti was the first audience, the first representative of samsara. Indrabhuti's bringing him to the palace was the starting point for learning how to work with students, confused people. Indrabhuti provided a strong father-figure representation of confused mind.

Student: Who were the mother and son who were killed?

Trungpa Rinpoche: There have been several interpretations of that in the scriptures and commentaries concerning Padmasambhava's life. Since the vajra is connected with skillful means, the child killed by the vajra is the opposite of skillful means, which is aggression. The trident is connected with wisdom, so the mother killed by it represents ignorance. And there area also further justifications based on the karma of previous lives: the son was so-and-so and committed thus-and-such a bad karmic act, and the same with the mother. But I don't think we have to go into those details. It gets a bit too complicated. The story of Padmasambhava at this point is in a completely different dimension—that of the psychological world. It comes down to a practical level, so to speak, when he gets to Tibet and begins dealing with the Tibetans. Before that, it is very much in the realm of mind.

Student: Is there any analogy between these two deaths and the sword of Manjushri cutting the root of ignorance? Or the Buddha's speaking about shunyata, emptiness, and some of his disciples having heart attacks?

Trungpa Rinpoche: I don't think so. The sword of Manjushri is very much oriented toward practice on the path, but the story of Padmasambhava is related with the goal. Once you have already experienced the sudden flash of enlightenment, how do you handle yourself beyond that? The Manjushri story and the story of the *Heart Sutra* and all the other stories of sutra teaching correspond to the hinayana and mahayana levels and are designed for the seeker on the path. What we are discussing here is the umbrella notion—the notion of coming down from the top: having already attained enlightenment, how do we work with further programs? The story of Padmasambhava is a manual for buddhas—and each of us is one of them.

Student: Was he experimenting with motive?

Trungpa Rinpoche: Well, in the realm of the dharmakaya, it is very difficult to say what is and what is not the motive. There isn't anything at all.

Student: I would like to know more about the contrasting metaphors of eating out from the inside and stripping away layers from the outside. If I understood correctly, stripping away is the bodhisattva path, whereas on the tantric path, you're eating out from the inside. But I really don't understand the metaphors.

Trungpa Rinpoche: The whole point is that tantra is contagious. It involves a very powerful substance, which is buddha nature eating out from the inside rather than being reached by stripping away layers from the outside. In Padmasambhava's life story, we are discussing the goal as the path, rather than the path as the path. It is a different perspective altogether; it is not the point of view of sentient beings trying to attain enlightenment, but the point of view of an enlightened person trying to relate with sentient beings. That is why the tantric approach is that of eating outward, from the inside to the outside. Padmasambhava's difficulties with his father, King Indrabhuti, and with the murder of the child and his mother are all connected with sentient beings. We are telling the story from the inside rather than looking at somebody else's newsreel taken from the outside.

Student: How does the eating away outward take place?

Trungpa Rinpoche: Through dealing with situations skillfully. The situations are already created for you, and you just go out and launch yourself along with them. It is a self-existing jigsaw puzzle that has been put together by itself.

Student: Is it the dharmakaya aspect that diffuses hope and fear?

Trungpa Rinpoche: Yes, that seems to be the basic thing. Hope and fear are all-pervading, like a haunted situation. But the dharmakaya takes away the haunt altogether.

Student: Are you saying that the story of Padmasambhava, from his birth in the lotus through his destroying all the layers of students' expectations and finally manifesting as Dorje Trolö, is moving from the dharmakaya slowly into the nirmanakaya?

Trungpa Rinpoche: Yes, that is what I have been trying to get at. So far, he has risen out of the dharmakaya and has just gotten to the fringe of the sambhogakaya. Sambhogakaya is the energy principle, or the dance principle—dharmakaya being the total background.

S: Is it that hope and fear have to fade away before the—

TR: Before the dance can take place. Yes, definitely.

Student: Is the sambhogakaya energy the energy that desire and anger are attached to?

Trungpa Rinpoche: The sambhogakaya level doesn't seem to be that. It is positive aspect that is left by the unmasking process. In other words, you get the absence of aggression and that absence is turned into energy.

S: So when the defilements are transformed into wisdom—

TR: Transmuted. It is even more than transmutation—I don't know what sort of a word there is. The defilements are being so completely related to that their function becomes useless, but their nonfunctioning becomes useful. There is another kind of energy in sambhogakaya.

Student: There seems to be some kind of cosmic joke about the whole thing. What you're saying is that you have to take the first step, but you can't take the first step until you take the first step.

Trungpa Rinpoche: Yes, you have to be pushed into it. That is where the relationship between teacher and student comes in. Somebody has to push. That is the very primitive level at the beginning.

S: Are you pushing?

TR: I think so.

FOUR

Eternity and the Charnel Ground

I WOULD LIKE TO MAKE SURE that what we have already discussed is quite clear. The birth of Padmasambhava is like a sudden experience of the awakened state. The birth of Padmasambhava cannot take place unless there is an experience of the awakened state of mind that shows us our innocence, our infantlike quality. And Padmasambhava's experiences with King Indrabhuti of Uddiyana are connected with going further after one has already had a sudden glimpse of awake. That seems to be the teaching, or message, of Padmasambhava's life so far.

Now let us go on to the next aspect of Padmasambhava. Having experienced the awakened state of mind, and having had experiences of sexuality and aggression and all the pleasures that exist in the world, there is still uncertainty about how to work with those worldly processes. Padmasambhava is uncertain not in the sense of being confused, but about how to teach, how to connect with the audience. The students themselves are apprehensive, because for one thing, they have never dealt with an enlightened person before. Working with an enlightened person is extraordinarily sensitive and pleasurable, but at the same time, it could be quite destructive. If we did the wrong thing, we might be hit or destroyed. It is like playing with fire.

So Padmasambhava's experience of relating with samsaric mind continues. He is expelled from the palace, and he goes on making further discoveries. The discovery that he makes at this point is eternity. Eternity here is the sense that the experience of awake is constantly going on without any fluctuations—and without any decisions to be made, for

Vajradhara.

that matter. At this point, in connection with the second aspect, the decisionlessness of Padmasambhava's experience of dealing with sentient beings becomes prominent.

Padmasambhava's second aspect is called Vajradhara. Vajradhara is a principle or a state of mind that possesses fearlessness. The fear of death, the fear of pain and misery—all such fears—have been transcended. Having transcended those states, the eternity of life goes on beyond them. Such eternity is not particularly dependent on life situations and whether or not we make them healthier or whether or not we achieve longevity. It is not dependent on anything of that nature.

We are discussing a sense of eternity that could apply to our own lives as well. This attitude of eternity is quite different from the conventional spiritual idea of eternity. The conventional idea is that if you attain a certain level of spiritual one-upmanship, you will be free from birth and death. You will exist forever and be able to watch the play of the world and have power over everything. It is the notion of the superman who cannot be destroyed, the good savior who helps everybody using his Superman outfit. This general notion of eternity and spirituality is somewhat distorted, somewhat cartoonlike: the spiritual superman has power over others, and therefore he can attain longevity, which is a continuity of his power over others. Of course, he does also help others at the same time.

As Vajradhara, Padmasambhava's experience of eternity—or his existence as eternity—is quite different. There is a sense of continuity, because he has transcended the fear of birth, death, illness, and any kind of pain. There is a constant living, electric experience that he is not really living and existing, but rather it is the world that lives and exists, and therefore he is the world and the world is him. He has power over the world because he does not have power over the world. He does not want to hold any kind of position as a powerful person at this point.

Vajradhara is a Sanskrit name. *Vajra* means "indestructible," *dhara* means "holder." So it is as the "holder of indestructibility" or "holder of immovability" that Padmasambhava attains the state of eternity. He attains it because he was born as an absolutely pure and completely innocent child—so pure and innocent that he had no fear of exploring the world of birth and death, of passion and aggression. That was the preparation for his existence, but his exploration continued beyond that level. Birth and death and other kinds of threats might be seen by samsaric or confused mind as solid parts of a solid world. But instead of seeing the world as a threatening situation, he began to see it as his home. In this way, he attained the primordial state of eternity, which is quite different from the state of perpetuating ego. Ego needs to maintain itself constantly; it constantly needs further reassurance. But in this case, through transcending spiritual materialism, Padmasambhava attained an ongoing, constant state based on being inspired by fellow confused people, sentient beings.

The young prince, recently turned out of his palace, roamed around the charnel ground. There were floating skeletons with floating hair. Jackals and vultures, hovering about, made their noises. The smell of rotten bodies was all over the place. The genteel young prince seemed to fit in to that scene quite well, as incongruous as it might seem. He was quite fearless, and his fearlessness became accommodation as he roamed through the jungle charnel ground of Silwa Tsal near Bodhgaya. There were awesome-looking trees and terrifying rock shapes and the ruins of a temple. The whole feeling was one of death and desolation. He'd been abandoned, he'd been kicked out of his kingdom, but still he roamed and played about as if nothing had happened. In fact, he regarded this place as another palace in spite of all its terrifying sights. Seeing the impermanence of life, he discovered the eternity of life, the constant changing process of death and birth taking place all the time.

There was a famine in the vicinity. People were continually dying. Sometimes half-dead bodies were brought to the charnel ground, because people were so exhausted with the constant play of death and sickness. There were flies, worms, maggots, and snakes. Padmasambhava, this young prince who had recently been turned out of a jewel-laden palace, made a home out of this; seeing no difference at all between this charnel ground and a palace, he took delight in it.

Our civilized world is so orderly that we do not see places like this charnel ground. Bodies are kept in their coffins and buried quite respectably. Nevertheless, there are the greater charnel grounds of birth, death, and chaos going on around us all the time. We encounter these charnel-ground situations in our lives constantly. We are surrounded by half-dead people, skeletons everywhere. But still, if we identify with Padmasambhava, we could relate with that fearlessly. We could be inspired by this chaos—so much so that chaos could become order in some sense. It could become orderly chaos rather than just confused chaos, because we would be able to relate with the world as it is.

Padmasambhava went and found the nearest cave, and he meditated on the principle of the eternity of buddha nature: buddha nature is eternally existing, without being threatened by anything at all. Realization of that principle is one of the five stages of a vidyadhara. It is the first stage, called the vidyadhara of eternity.

Vidyadhara means "he who holds the scientific knowledge" or "he who has achieved complete crazy wisdom." So the first stage of crazy wisdom is the wisdom of eternity. Nothing threatens us at all; everything is an ornament. The greater the chaos, the more everything becomes an ornament. That is the state of Vajradhara.

We might ask how a young, innocent prince came to have such training that he was able to handle those charnel-ground situations. We might ask such a question, because we generally assume that in order to handle something we need training: we have to have benefited from an educational system. We have to have read books on how to live in a charnel ground and been instructed on what is appropriate and what is not appropriate to eat there. No training was necessary for Padmasambhava, because he was enlightened at the moment of his birth. He was coming out of the dharmakaya into the sambhogakaya, and a sudden flash of enlightenment does not need training. It does not require an educational system. It is inborn nature, not dependent on any kind of training at all.

In fact, the whole concept of needing training for things is a very weak approach, because it makes us feel we cannot possess the potential in us, and that therefore we have to make ourselves better than we are, we have to try to compete with heroes or masters. So we try to imitate those heroes and masters, believing that finally, by some process of psychophysical switch, we might be able to become *them*. Although we are not actually them, we believe we could become them purely by imitating—by pretending, by deceiving ourselves constantly that we are what we are not. But when this sudden flash of enlightenment occurs, such hypocrisy doesn't exist. You do not have to pretend to be something. You *are* something. You have certain tendencies existing in you in any case. It is just a question of putting them into practice.

Still, Padmasambhava's discovery might feel somewhat desolate and slightly terrifying from our point of view if we imagine him meditating in a cave, surrounded by corpses and terrifying animals. But somehow we do have to relate with that in our personal life situations. We cannot con the existing experience of life; we cannot con our experiences or change them by having some unrealistic belief that things are going to be okay, that in the end everything is going to be beautiful. If we take that approach, then things are not going to be okay. For the very reason that we expect things to be good and beautiful, they won't be.

When we have such expectations, we are approaching things entirely from the wrong angle. Beauty is competing with ugliness, and pleasure is competing with pain. In this realm of comparison, nothing is going to be achieved at all.

We might say, "I've been practicing; I've been seeking enlightenment, nirvana, but I've been constantly pushed back. At the beginning, I got some kind of kick out of those practices. I thought I was getting somewhere. I felt beautiful, blissful, and I thought I could get even better, get beyond even that. But then nothing happened. Practice became monotonous, and then I began to look for another solution, something else. Then at the same time, I thought, 'I'm starting to be unfaithful to the practices I've been given. I shouldn't be looking for other practices. I shouldn't look elsewhere, I should have faith, I should stick with it. Okay, let's do it.' So I stick with it. But it is still uncomfortable, monotonous. In fact, it is irritating, too painful."

We go on and on this way. We repeat ourselves. We build something up and make ourselves believe in it. We say to ourselves, "Now I should have faith. If I have faith, if I believe, I'm going to be saved." We try to prefabricate faith in some way and get a momentary kick out of it. But then it ends up the same way again and again and again—we don't get anything out of it. There are always those problems with that approach to spirituality.

In Padmasambhava's approach to spirituality, we are not looking for a kick, for inspiration or bliss. Instead, we are digging into life's irritations, diving into the irritations and making a home out of that. If we are able to make a home out of those irritations, then the irritations become a source of great joy, transcendental joy, mahasukha—because there is no pain involved at all. This kind of joy is no longer related with pain or contrasted with pain at all. So the whole thing becomes precise and sharp and understandable, and we are able to relate with it.

Padmasambhava's further adaptation to the world through the attitude of eternity, the first of the five stages of a vidyadhara, plays an important part in the study of the rest of Padmasambhava's aspects. This subject comes up again and again.

Student: Why couldn't Padmasambhava's making his home in the charnel ground be considered masochism?

Trungpa Rinpoche: To begin with, there is no sense of aggression at all. He is not out to win anybody over. He is just there, relating to things as they are. In masochism, you have to have someone to blame, someone to relate to your pain: "If I commit suicide, my parents will know from that how much I hate them." There's nothing like that here. It is a non-existent world, but he is still there, existing with it.

Student: I don't understand this extrahuman quality of being born out of a lotus plant—like Christ's having a virgin mother. Isn't that presenting Padmasambhava as an ideal beyond us that we have to relate to as other-than-human?

Trungpa Rinpoche: In some way, being born from a mother and from a lotus are exactly the same situation. There is nothing all that superhuman about it: it is an expression of miracles that do exist. People who watch a birth for the first time often find that that is a miracle too. In the same way, being born from a lotus is a miracle, but there is nothing particularly divine or pure about it. Being born from a lotus is an expression of openness. The process of being in the womb for nine months does not have to be gone through. It is a free and open situation—the lotus opens and the child is there. It is a very straightforward thing. With regard to the lotus, we do not have to discuss such questions as the validity of the statement that Christ's mother was a virgin. There could only be this one lotus there at that time. Then it died. So we could say it was a free birth.

S: Birth from the lotus could also mean the negation of karmic history.

TR: That's right, yes. There is no karmic history involved at all. Just somewhere in Afghanistan a lotus happened to bear a child.

Student: Could you please say something about the relationship between the Vajradhara aspect of Padmasambhava and the dharmakaya buddha of the Kagyü lineage, also called Vajradhara?

Trungpa Rinpoche: As you say, for the Kagyü lineage, Vajradhara is the name of the primordial buddha on the dharmakaya level, who is continuously existing. Padmasambhava's Vajradhara aspect is on the sambhogakaya level of relating with life experiences; or on a secondary dharmakaya level, it is connected with the all-pervasiveness of sentient beings, there at your disposal to work with. But it is primarily a sambhogakaya principle. In this sense, the five aspects of the sambhogakaya, the five sambhogakaya buddhas, are the eight aspects of Padmasambhava.

Student: You talked about staying with the irritation; in fact, savoring it. Is the idea that pain is associated with withdrawal and avoidance, so you move into the pain or closer to the pain, and it disappears? Is there some possibility of enlightenment coming out of that?

Trungpa Rinpoche: This is actually a very delicate point. We have the problem that a sort of sadistic attitude could occur, which we find in a lot of militant attitudes toward Zen practices as well. We also have the "inspirational" approach of getting into the teachings and ignoring the pain. These attitudes lead to blind confusion. And we find our bodies being abused, not taken care of properly.

In this case, relating with the pain is not quite the sadistic approach or that of militant practice on the one hand, nor is it based on the idea of ignoring the whole thing and spacing out into your mind trip on the other hand. It is something between these two. To begin with, pain is regarded as something quite real, something actually happening. It is not regarded as a doctrinal or philosophical matter. It is simple pain or simple psychological discomfort. You don't move away from the pain, because if you do, you have no resources to work with. You don't get into the pain or inflict pain on yourself, because then you are involved in a suicidal process; you are destroying yourself. So it is somewhere between the two.

Student: How does making a home in the irritations relate to the mandala principle?

Trungpa Rinpoche: That seems to be the mandala already, in itself. Relating with the irritations has the sense of there being all kinds of irritations and infinite further possibilities of them. That *is* a mandala. You are right there. Mandala is a sense of total existence with you in the center. So here you are in the center of irritation. It is very powerful.

Student: In defining *vidyadhara*, you talked about scientific knowledge. What does scientific knowledge have to do with Padmasambhava's life?

Trungpa Rinpoche: I am using "scientific knowledge" in the sense of the most accurate knowledge on how to react to situations. The essence of crazy wisdom is that you have no strategized programs or ideals anymore at all. You are just open. Whatever students present, you just react accordingly. This is continuously scientific in the sense that it is continuously in accordance with the nature of the elements.

Let the Phenomena Play

W E MAY NOT HAVE THE TIME to go through the rest of the eight aspects of Padmasambhava at the same pace as we went through the first two. But our discussion so far has provided a basic ground for the discussion of the whole process of Padmasambhava's life and his personal expansion. What I would like to do is try to convey a sense of Padmasambhava that brings all of his aspects together. This is very hard to do, because the medium of words is limited. Words do not cover enough of the insight. But we shall do our best.

We are not talking about Padmasambhava from an external historical point of view or an external mythical one. We are trying to get at the marrow inside the bone, so to speak—the instantaneous or embryonic aspect of him and how he relates to life from that. This is a sacred or tantric way of seeing Padmasambhava's life, as opposed to accounts and interpretations that see him purely as a historical or mythical figure—like King Arthur or someone like that.

The inside story is based on the relationship of the events in Padmasambhava's life to the teachings. This is the point of view from which I have been trying to work into the story of Padmasambhava as the young prince and as the young siddha, or accomplished yogi, in the charnel ground. These two aspects are extraordinarily important for the rest of Padmasambhava's life.

Padmasambhava's next phase arose from the need for him to be accepted into the monastic life. He had to be ordained as a bhikshu, or monk. Relating with the monastic system was important because it provided a disciplinary situation. Padmasambhava was ordained by Ananda, a disciple and attendant of the Buddha. As a monk, Padmasambhava acquired the name Shakya Simha, or Shakya Senge in Tibetan, which means "lion of the Shakya Tribe." This was one of the Buddha's names (the Buddha was also sometimes known as "the Sage of the Shakyas"), and through this name Padmasambhava became identified with the tradition of the Buddha. This was very important, because one needs a tremendous sense of relationship with the lineage. So Padmasambhava associated himself with the lineage and realized what an important part it plays.

The lineage of the Buddha is a lineage of constant basic sanity, a sane approach to life. Becoming a monk means living life sanely—sanely and saintly—because it is a complete and total involvement with things as they are. As a monk, you do not miss any points. You relate with life from the point of view that the given moment actually permits a sense of a living quality, a sense of totality, a sense of not being moved by passion, aggression, or anything at all—you are just dealing with things as the monastic life permits, as they are.

As Padmasambhava developed in his monastic role, he again began to manifest in the style of a young prince, but in this case, as a young prince who had become a monk. He decided to become the savior of the world, the bringer of the message of dharma.

One day he visited a nunnery. At this particular nunnery lived a princess called Mandarava, who had just recently become a nun and had completely turned away from worldly pleasure. She lived in seclusion, guarded by five hundred women, whose task was to make sure that she maintained her monastic discipline. When Padmasambhava arrived at the monastery, everyone was quite impressed with him—naturally. He had the innocence of one born from a lotus and a pure and ideal physique. He was very beautiful. He converted all the women in the nunnery: they all became his students.

The king, Mandarava's father, soon heard something of this. A cowherd reported that he had heard an unusual male voice coming from the nunnery, preaching and shouting. The king had thought that Mandarava was an absolutely perfect nun and had no relations of any kind with men. He got quite upset at the cowherd's news and sent his ministers to find out what was happening at the nunnery. The ministers were not allowed into the nunnery compound but suspected that something funny was going on there. They reported back to the king, who decided to have the army destroy the nunnery gate, march in, and arrest this rascal posing as a teacher. This they did. They captured Padmasambhava and put him on a pyre of sandalwood and set it afire (this was the style of execution that had developed in that particular kingdom). The princess was thrown into some pitch containing thorns and lice and fleas. This was the king's idea of religion.

The fire in which Padmasambhava had been placed burned on and on for seven days. Usually when they executed someone, the fire lasted only for a day or two. In this case, however, it burned on and on. Very unusual. The king began to think that perhaps there was also something unusual about this man wandering about pretending to be a guru. He sent his men to investigate, and they found that the fire had disappeared and that the whole area where the fire had been had turned into a huge lake. In the middle of the lake was Padmasambhava, once again sitting on a lotus. When the king heard this, he decided to find out more about this person. He decided not to trust the matter to a messenger, but went himself to see Padmasambhava. When he arrived at the scene, he was overwhelmed by the presence of this person sitting on a lotus in the middle of a lake where a charnel ground and a place to burn criminals had been. The king confessed his wrongdoings and foolish actions to Padmasambhava and invited him back to the palace. Padmasambhava refused to go, saying he would not enter the palace of a sinner—the palace of a wicked king who had condemned someone who was the spiritual essence of both king and guru, who had ignored the true essence of spirituality. The king repeated his request and finally Padmasambhava accepted his invitation. The king himself pulled the car in which Padmasambhava sat. Padmasambhava became the rajguru, the king's guru, and Mandarava was rescued from the pitch.

During this phase of his life, Padmasambhava's approach to reality was one of accuracy, but within this realm of accuracy he was ready to allow people room to make mistakes on the spiritual path. He was even ready to go so far as to let the king try to burn him alive and put his student, the princess, into the pitch. He felt he should let those things happen. This is an important point that already shows the pattern of his teaching.

There had to be room for the king's realization of his neurosis—his whole way of acting and thinking—to come through by itself. His realization had to be allowed to come through by itself, rather than by Pad-masambhava's performing some miraculous act of magical power (which he was quite capable of) before he was arrested. Padmasambhava could have said, "I am the world's greatest teacher; you cannot touch me. Now you will see the greatness of my spiritual power." But he didn't do that. Instead, he let himself be arrested.

This is a very important indication of Padmasambhava's way of relating with samsaric, or confused, mind: let the confusion come through, and then let the confusion correct itself. It is like the story about a partic-ular Zen master who had a woman student. The woman became preg-nant and bore a child. Her parents came to the Zen master, bringing the child, and complained to him, saying, "This is your child; you should take care of it." The Zen master replied, "Is that so?" and he took the child and cared for it. A few years later, the woman was no longer able to bear the lie she had told—the father of the child was not the teacher but someone else altogether. She went to her parents and said, "My teacher was not the father of the child; it was someone else." Then the parents became worried and felt they had better rescue the child from the hands of the teacher, who was meditating in the mountains. They found him and said, "We have discovered that this is not your child. Now we are going to rescue it from you; we are going to take it away from you. You are not the real father." And the Zen master just said, "Is that so?"

So let the phenomena play. Let the phenomena make fools of them-selves by themselves. This is the approach. There is no point in saying, "Let me have a word with you. I would like to explain the whole situa-tion inside-out." By itself, just saying something is inadequate—not to mention the difficulty of finding the right thing to say. It simply does not work. The phenomenal world cannot be conned with words, with logic, petty logic. The phenomenal world can only be dealt with in terms of what happens within it, in terms of its own logic. This is a larger version of the logic, the totality of the logicalness of the situation. So an impor-tant feature of Padmasambhava's style is letting the phenomena play themselves through rather than trying to prove or explain something.

In the next situation, the next aspect, Padmasambhava was faced with five hundred heretics, or *tirthikas* in Sanskrit. In this case, the heretics were the theists, the Brahmanists; they could also have been Jeho-vists—or whatever you would like to call the approach that is the opposite of the nontheistic approach of the buddhadharma. A logical debate took place: A huge crowd surrounded two pandits, facing each other. The theistic pandit and the nontheistic pandit were debating each other on the nature of spirituality. Both of them were on a spiritual trip. (It does not matter whether you are a theist or a nontheist—you can still be on a spiritual trip.) Both were trying to establish their territory, to prove that they had grounds for having the spiritual path their way. In this case, the theists won and the Buddhists, who were completely overwhelmed by logical intelligence, lost. Then Padmasambhava was asked to perform a ceremony of destruction, to destroy the theists and their whole setup. He performed the ceremony and caused a huge landslide, which killed the five hundred pandits and destroyed their whole ashram.

In this aspect, Padmasambhava is known as Senge Dradrok, which is "Lion's Roar." The lion's roar destroys the dualistic psychology in which value and validity are attributed to things *because there is the other thing happening*—the Brahma, or God, or whatever you like to call it. The dualistic approach says that because "that" happened, therefore "this" also is a solid and real thing. In order to become Him or Her, whichever it may be, we should be receptive to that higher thing, that objective thing. This approach is always problematic. And the only way to destroy that dualistic setup is to arouse Padmasambhava's crazy-wisdom aspect to destroy it.

From the point of view of crazy wisdom, "that" does not exist; and the reason "that" does not exist is because "this," the self, no longer exists. In some sense, you could say that here the destruction is mutual destruction. But at the same time, this destruction is favorable from the nontheistic point of view. If Jehovah or Brahma exists, then the perceiver has to exist in order to acknowledge that existence. But the crazy-wisdom approach is that the acknowledger does not exist; it is no longer there, or at least it is questionable. And if "this" does not exist, then "that" is out of the question altogether. It is purely a phantom, imaginary. And even for an imagination to exist, you need an imaginer. So the destruction of the centralized notion of a self brings with it the nonexistence of "that."

This is the approach of Padmasambhava as Senge Dradrok, Lion's Roar. The lion's roar is heard, because the lion is not afraid of "that"; the lion is willing to go into, to overwhelm, whatever there is, because "this" does not exist to be destroyed anymore. In this sense, the lion's roar can be connected with the development of *vajra pride*.

The next aspect is Dorje Trolö, which came about when Padmasambhava went to Tibet. The Tibetans were not involved in foreign—that is, external—worship. They did not have the Hindu realm of the gods. They did not even know the word *Brahma*. What they had was *yeshen*, which is the equivalent word in the Bön tradition to "absoluteness."[1] *Ye* means "primordial"; *shen* means "ancestralness" or "great friend." In coming to Tibet, the buddhadharma was now encountering an entirely new angle, a new approach.

Up until that time, Padmasambhava had been dealing with Hindus, Brahmanists. What he encountered in Tibet was entirely different from that. The classical Tibetan word *yeshen* has a sense that is something like "ancestral" or "ancient" or even "celestial." It is similar to the Japanese word *shin*, which means "heaven," or to the Chinese word *ta*, which means "that which is above." All three terms relate to something greater, something above. There is an upward process involved, which could be associated with dragons, thunderstorms, clouds, the sun and moon, stars, and so forth. They relate to that "above" thing, to that higher, greater cosmic pattern.

This was extremely difficult for Padmasambhava to deal with. It was impossible to deal with it through logic, because the wisdom of the Bön tradition was very profound, extremely profound. If Padmasambhava had had to challenge the Bönists with logic, the only approach he could have taken would have been to say that earth and heaven are a unity, that heaven as such does not exist because heaven and earth are interdependent. But that is very shaky logic, because everyone knows that there is earth and there is heaven, that there are mountains and stars and suns and moons. You could not challenge these people by saying that there is no earth, no mountains; there is no sun, no moon, no sky, no stars.

The basic Bön philosophy is very powerful; it is much like the American Indian, Shinto, or Taoist approach to cosmic sanity. The whole thing is an extraordinarily sane approach. But there is a problem. It is also a very anthropocentric approach. The world is created for human beings; animals are human beings' next meal or their skins are human beings' next clothes. This anthropocentric approach is actually lacking in basic sanity; it is not able to respect the basic continuity of consciousness. Consequently, the Bön religion prescribes animal sacrifice to the yeshen, or great god. Here again, we find a similarity with the American Indian and Shinto outlook, with man as the center of the universe. According to that outlook, the grasses and trees, the wild animals, and the sun and the moon are there for human entertainment. The whole system is based on human existence. That is the big problem.

Buddhism is not a national religious approach. National religions tend to be theistic. Let us remember that Christianity inherited its theistic approach from Judaism; Judaism, Shintoism, Hinduism, and many other religions like them are national religions that are also theistic. They have their particular sense of the relationship between "this" and "that," earth and heaven. The nontheistic approach is extremely difficult to present in a primitive country that already has a belief in a theistic religion. The way the people of such a country relate to their basic survival already contains a sense of the earth in relation to the magnificence of heaven. Their sense of worship is already developed.

Jesuits and other Catholic missionaries have recently developed a method in which they tell primitive peoples, "Yes, your gods do exist, it is true, but my god is much wiser than your god, because it is omnipresent and so forth—ambidextrous and all the rest." But Buddhism faces an entirely different problem. There is no question of your god and my god. You have your god, but I don't have a god, so I am left just sort of suspended there. I have nothing to substitute. Where is the greatness and power of my approach? I have nothing to substitute. The only thing there is to substitute is crazy wisdom—*mind* is very powerful. We all have mind, including animals. Everybody has mind. It does not matter about Him or Them, or Them and Him, or whatever.

One's state of mind is very powerful. It can imagine destroying something, and it destroys it. It can imagine creating something, and it creates it. Whatever you intend in the realm of mind, it happens. Imagine your enemy. You want to destroy your enemy, and you have developed all kinds of tactics for doing so. You have infinite imaginations about how to handle the destruction of that enemy. Imagine your friend. You have infinite inspirations about how to relate with your friend, how to make him or her feel good or better or richer.

That is why we have built these houses and roads, manufactured these beds and blankets. That is why we have provided this food, thought up all kinds of dishes. We have done all this to prove to ourselves that we do exist. This is a kind of humanistic approach. Man does exist, his intelligence does exist. This is entirely nontheistic.

Padmasambhava's approach to magic was on this nontheistic level. Lightning happens because it does happen, rather than because there is any further why or who or what involved. It does happen. Flowers blossom because it happens, it is so. We cannot argue that there are no flowers. We cannot argue that no snow falls. It is so. It happens. It came from up there, from the sky, but so what!? What do you want to manufacture there?

Everything happens on this plane, on this really earthy plane. Everything happens on a very straight and down-to-earth level. Therefore, the crazy wisdom of Dorje Trolö begins to develop. It is extraordinarily powerful. It is powerful on the kitchen-sink level—that is what is so irritating. In fact, that is what is so powerful. It haunts everywhere—it really *is* there.

Dorje Trolö arrives in Tibet riding a pregnant tigress. The tigress is electric. She is pregnant electricity. She is somewhat domesticated, but at the same time has the potential of running wild. Dorje Trolö knows no logic. As far as Dorje Trolö is concerned, the only conventional logic there is, is relating with heaven and earth. Because the sky forms itself into its particular shape, the horizon exists. There is the vastness of space, the sky; and there is the vastness of the earth. They are vast, but okay—so what? Do you want to make a big deal out of the vastness? Who are you trying to compete with? There is this vastness, but why not consider the smallest things that are happening as well? Aren't they more threatening? The grain of sand is more threatening than the vastness of space or of the desert; because of its concentratedness, it is extremely explosive. There is a huge cosmic joke here, a gigantic cosmic joke, a very powerful one.

As Dorje Trolö's crazy wisdom expanded, he developed an approach for communicating with future generations. In relation to a lot of his writings, he thought, "These words may not be important at this point, but I am going to write them down and bury them in the mountains of Tibet." And he did so. He thought, "Someone will discover them later and find them extraordinarily mind-blowing. Let them have a good time then." This was a unique approach. Gurus nowadays think purely in terms of the effect they might have now. They do not consider trying to have a powerful effect on the future. But Dorje Trolö thought, "If I leave an example of my teaching behind, even if people of future generations do not experience my example, just hearing my words alone could cause a spiritual atomic bomb to explode in a future time." Such an idea was unheard-of. It is a very powerful thing.

The spiritual force of Padmasambhava as expressed in his manifestation as Dorje Trolö is a direct message that no longer knows any question. It just happens. There is no room for interpretations. There is no room for making a home out of this. There is just spiritual energy going on that is real dynamite. If you distort it, you are destroyed on the spot. If you are actually able to see it, then you are right there with it. It is ruthless. At the same time, it is compassionate, because it has all this energy in it. The pride of being in the state of crazy wisdom is tremendous. But there is a loving quality in it as well.

Can you imagine being hit by love and hate at the same time? In crazy wisdom, we are hit with compassion and wisdom at the same time, without a chance of analyzing them. There's no time to think; there's no time to work things out at all. It is *there*—but at the same time, it isn't there. And at the same time also, it is a big joke.

Student: Does crazy wisdom require raising your energy level?

Trungpa Rinpoche: I don't think so, because energy comes along with the situation itself. In other words, the highway is the energy, not your driving fast. The highway suggests your driving fast. The self-existing energy is there.

S: You're not worried about the car?

TR: No.

Student: Has the crazy-wisdom teaching developed in any lineages other than the Nyingma lineage?

Trungpa Rinpoche: I don't think so. There is also the mahamudra lineage, which is based on a sense of precision and accuracy. But the crazy-wisdom lineage that I received from my guru seems to have much more potency. It is somewhat illogical—some people might find the sense of not knowing how to relate with it quite threatening. It seems to be connected with the Nyingma tradition and the maha ati lineage exclusively.

Student: What was the name of the Padmasambhava aspect before Dorje Trolö?

Trungpa Rinpoche: Nyima Öser, "Holding the Sun."

S: Was that when he was with Mandarava?

TR: No. Then he was known as Loden Choksi. In the iconography, he is wearing a white turban.

Student: Are there any controls or precepts connected with crazy wisdom?

Trungpa Rinpoche: Other than itself, there doesn't seem to be anything. Just being itself.

S: There are no guidelines?

TR: There is no textbook for becoming a crazy-wisdom person. It doesn't hurt to read books, but unless you are able to have some experience of crazy wisdom yourself through contact with the crazy-wisdom lineage—with somebody who is crazy and wise at the same time—you won't get much out of books alone. A lot really depends on the lineage message, on the fact that somebody has already inherited something. Without that, the whole thing becomes purely mythical. But if you see that somebody does possess some element of crazy wisdom, that will provide a certain reassurance, which is worthwhile at this point.

Student: Could you mention one of the spiritual time bombs, other than the lineage itself, that was left behind by Padmasambhava as a legacy and as a teaching that is relevant today?

Trungpa Rinpoche: We might say this seminar is one of them. If we weren't interested in Padmasambhava, we wouldn't be here. He left his legacy, his personality, behind, and that is why we are here.

Student: You mentioned some of the difficulties Padmasambhava faced in presenting the dharma to the Tibetans, principally that the Tibetans' mental outlook was theistic while Buddhism is nontheistic. What are the difficulties in presenting the dharma to the Americans?

Trungpa Rinpoche: I think it is the same thing. The Americans worship the sun and the water gods and the mountain gods—they still do. That is a very primordial approach, and some Americans are rediscovering their heritage. We have people going on an American Indian trip, which is beautiful, but the knowledge we have of it is not all that accurate. Americans regard themselves as sophisticated and scientific, as educated experts on everything. But still we are actually on the level of ape

53

culture. Padmasambhava's approach of crazy wisdom is further education for us—we could become transcendental apes.

Student: Could you say something more about vajra pride?

Trungpa Rinpoche: Vajra pride is the sense that basic sanity does exist
in our state of being, so we don't particularly have to try to work it out
logically. We don't have to prove that something is happening or not
happening. The basic dissatisfaction that causes us to look for some spiritual understanding is an expression of vajra pride: we are not willing to
submit to the suppression of our confusion. We are willing to stick our
necks out. That seems to be a first expression of the vajra-pride instinct—
and we can go on from there!

Student: Two of the aspects of Padmasambhava seem to be contradictory. Padmasambhava allowed the confusion of the king to manifest and
then turn back on itself, yet he didn't allow the confusion of the five
hundred pandits to manifest (if you want to call dualism confusion). He
just destroyed them with a landslide. Could you comment on this?

Trungpa Rinpoche: The pandits seem to have been very simple-minded
people, because they had no connection with the kitchen-sink-level
problems of life. They were purely thriving on their projection of who
they were. So, according to the story, the only way to relate with them
was to provide them with the experience of the landslide—a sudden jerk
or shock. Anything else they could have reinterpreted into something
else. If the pandits had been in the king's situation, they would have been
much more hardened, much less enlightened, than he was. They had no
willingness to relate with anything at all, because they were so hardened
in their dogmatism. Moreover, it was necessary for them to realize the
nonexistence of themselves and Brahma. So they were provided with
the experience of a catastrophe that was caused not by Brahma but by
themselves. This left them in a nontheistic situation: they themselves
were all that there was; there was no possibility of reproaching God or
Brahma or whatever.

SIX

Cynicism and Devotion

HOPEFULLY, YOU HAVE HAD at least a glimpse of Padmasambhava and his aspects. According to tradition, there are three ways in which the life of Padmasambhava can be told: the external, factual way; the internal, psychological way; and the higher, secret way, which is the approach of crazy wisdom. We have concentrated on the secret way, with some elements of the other two.

By way of conclusion, it would be good to discuss how we can relate with Padmasambhava. Here, we are considering Padmasambhava as a cosmic principle rather than as a historical person, an Indian saint. Different manifestations of this principle appear constantly: Padmasambhava is Shakya Senge, the yogi Nyima Öser, the prince Pema Gyalpo, the mad yogi Dorje Trolö, and so forth. The Padmasambhava principle contains every element that is part of the enlightened world.

Among my students, a particular approach to the teachings seems to have developed. By way of beginning, we have adopted an attitude of distrust: distrust toward ourselves and also toward the teachings and the teacher—toward the whole situation in fact. We feel that everything should be taken with a grain of salt, that we should examine and test everything thoroughly to make sure it is good gold. In taking this approach, we have had to develop our sense of honesty—we have to cut through our own self-deceptions, which play an important part. We cannot establish spirituality without cutting through spiritual materialism.

Having already prepared the basic ground with the help of this distrust, it may be time to change gears, so to speak, and try almost the

Shakya Senge.

opposite approach. Having developed accurate and vajra-like cynicism and having cultivated vajra nature, we could begin to realize what spirituality is. And we find that spirituality is completely ordinary. It is completely ordinary ordinariness. Though we might speak of it as extraordinary, in fact it is the most ordinary thing of all.

To relate with this, we might have to change our pattern. The next step is to develop devotion and faith. We cannot relate to the Padmasambhava principle unless there is some kind of warmth. If we cut through deception completely and honestly, then a positive situation begins to develop. We gain a positive understanding of ourselves as well as of the teachings and the teacher. In order to work with the grace, or adhishthana, of Padmasambhava, with this cosmic principle of basic sanity, we have to develop a kind of romanticism. This is equally important as the cynical approach we have been taking up till now.

There are two types of this romantic, or bhakti, approach. One is based on a sense of poverty. You feel you don't have it, but the others do. You admire the richness of "that": the goal, the guru, the teachings. This is a poverty approach—you feel that these other things are so beautiful because you don't have what they have. It is a materialistic approach—that of spiritual materialism—and it is based on there not being enough sanity in the first place, not enough sense of confidence and richness.

The other type of romantic approach is based on the sense that you do have it; it is there already. You do not admire it because it is somebody else's, because it is somewhere far away, distant from you, but because it is right near—in your heart. It is a sense of appreciation of what you are. You have as much as the teacher has, and you are on the path of dharma yourself, so you do not have to look at the dharma from outside. This is a sane approach; it is fundamentally rich; there is no sense of poverty at all.

This type of romanticism is important. It is the most powerful thing of all. It cuts through cynicism, which exists purely for its own sake, for the sake of its own protection. It cuts through cynicism's ego game and develops further and greater pride—vajra pride, as it is called. There is a sense of beauty and even of love and light. Without this, relating with the Padmasambhava principle is purely a matter of seeing how deep and profound you can get in your psychological experience. It remains a myth, something that you do not have; therefore it sounds interesting but never becomes personal. Devotion or compassion is the only way of relating with the grace—the adhishthana, or blessing—of Padmasambhava.

It seems that many people find this cynical and skeptical style that we have developed so far too irritatingly cold. Particularly, people who are having their first encounter with our scene say this. There is no sense of invitation; people are constantly being scrutinized and looked down upon. Maybe that is a very honest way for you to relate with the "other," which is also you. But at some point, some warmth has to develop in addition to the coldness. You do not exactly have to change the temperature—intense coldness *is* warmth—but there is a certain twist we could accomplish. It lies only in our conceptual mind and logic. In reality, there is no twist at all, but we have to have some way of putting this into words. What we are talking about is irritatingly warm and so powerful, so magnetizing.

So our discussion of Padmasambhava seems to be a landmark in the geography of our journey together. It is time to begin with that romantic approach, if we may call it that: the sane romantic approach, not the materialistic romantic approach.

Our seminar here happened purely by accident, even though it involved a lot of organizing, working a lot of things out. But still it was worked out accidentally. It is a very precious accident that we were able to discuss such a topic as the life of Padmasambhava. The opportunity to discuss such a subject is very rare, unique, very precious. But such a rare and precious situation goes on constantly; our life as part of the teachings is extremely precious. Each person came here purely by accident, and since it was an accident, it cannot be repeated. That is why it is precious. That is why the dharma is precious. Everything becomes precious; human life becomes precious.

There is this rare preciousness of our human life: we each have our brain, our sense perceptions, our materials to work on. We have each had our problems in the past: our depressions, our moments of insanity, our struggles—all these make sense. So the journey goes on, the accident goes on—which is that we are here. This is the kind of romanticism, the kind of warmth I am talking about. It is worthwhile approaching the teaching in this way. If we do not, we cannot relate with the Padmasambhava principle.

Student: Could you tell us something about how you related to the crazy wisdom of your guru, Jamgön Kongtrül of Sechen, if he had it, and how you combined those two approaches of wealth and poverty when you studied with him?

Trungpa Rinpoche: I think my way of working with it was very similar to everyone else's. At the beginning, personally, I had a lot of fascination and admiration based on the poverty point of view. Also, it was very exciting, because seeing Jamgön Kongtrül Rinpoche rather than just having to sit and memorize texts provided quite a break. It was always fun to watch him, and to hang out with him was great.

This was still based on a poverty-stricken kind of mentality—on being entertained by that which you do not have. All I had were my books to read and my tutor to discipline me. Moreover, Jamgön Kongtrül, with his extraordinary understanding and spiritual energy, was presented as the example of what I should become when I grew up. This is what I was told over and over again, which was based on the style of poverty and materialism. Of course, the people in the monastery cared for me, but they were also concerned with public relations: fame, glory, enlightenment.

But as I became close to Jamgön Kongtrül, I gradually stopped trying to collect something for myself so that I could be enriched. I began just to enjoy his presence, just to go along with him. Then I could really feel his warmth and his richness and be part of it as well. So it seems that you start with the materialistic approach and gradually change to the sane approach, to devotion.

As far as Jamgön Kongtrül is concerned, he possessed all the qualities of Padmasambhava. Sometimes he looked just like a big baby. That was the little prince aspect. Sometimes he was kind and helpful. Sometimes he put out black air that gave you the feeling that something was wrong and made you feel extraordinarily paranoid. I used to feel like I had a huge head hanging out and was very embarrassed about it, but I didn't know what to do.

Student: Is the cynical phase that we have been going through due to our being Americans? Does it have something to do with American culture, or has it got to do with something about the teachings that is independent of culture?

Trungpa Rinpoche: I think it is both. It is because of American culture, especially because of this particular period of social change in which a spiritual supermarket has developed. So we have to be smart to beat the supermarket mentality, to not be sucked in by it.

On the other hand, it is also a very Buddhistic approach. You can imagine finding this kind of mentality at Nalanda University. Naropa and all the other pandits were cutting through everything with their super-logical minds. It was quite awesome. This approach is connected with the Buddhist idea that the teachings began with pain and suffering. This is the first noble truth. It is a realistic way of looking at things. It is not enough just to be simple-minded and malleable; some weight is needed; some cynicism. Then, by the time you get to talking about the path, which is the fourth noble truth, you have the sense of something positive coming out, which is the devotional part coming through.

So it is a combination of cultural and inherent factors. Still, that is the way it ought to begin. And it does begin that way.

Student: You used the word *accident.* In your view, does that include free will?

Trungpa Rinpoche: Well, it's both; that is, free will is the cause of the accident. Without free will, you can't have accident.

Student: We have been talking about Padmasambhava's way of relating to confused people. Do you think it's appropriate to take the viewpoint of Padmasambhava in relating to ourselves; for example, should we let the neurosis flood in and things like that?

Trungpa Rinpoche: I think that is the whole point, yes. There is a Padmasambhava aspect in us. There are certain tendencies not to accept our existing confusion and to want to cut through it. There is something in us that says we are not subject to the confusion, a revolutionary aspect.

Student: Is it important to try to avoid cynicism now in our approach to the teachings?

Trungpa Rinpoche: I think the cynicism remains continuous and becomes powerful cynicism. You cannot just switch it on and off like changing television channels. It has to continue, and it should be there. For instance, when you encounter a new or further level of teaching, you should test it out in the same way as you have been doing. Then you will have more information and your eventual trust in it will have more backbone.

Student: Does Padmasambhava's teaching remain up-to-date? Don't historical and cultural changes require changes in the teaching?

Trungpa Rinpoche: It remains up-to-date because it is based on relating with confusion. Our confusion remains up-to-date, otherwise it would not confuse us. And the realization of confusion also remains up-to-date, because confusion causes our question and prompts us to wake up. The realization of the confusion is the teaching, so it is a constantly living situation, constantly lived-in and always applicable.

Student: You spoke earlier about Padmasambhava being in a state of decisionlessness. Is that the same thing as not thinking at all? You know—the mind just functioning?

Trungpa Rinpoche: Which is thinking. But you *can* think without thinking. There is a certain kind of intelligence connected with the totality that is more precise, but it is not verbal; it is not conceptualized at all. It does think in some sense, but it is not thinking in the ordinary sense.

S: Is it thinking without scheming?

TR: Something more than that. It *is* thinking without scheming, but it is still something more than that. It is a self-existing intelligence of its own.

Student: Rinpoche, about devotion. I can become so joyous when I experience the dharma's living quality. There's such great joy; it's like being high. But then I find a fall can follow this experience, which brings me down to a sort of barren land or desolate country. I've been feeling it's better to avoid these extreme feelings, because they seem always to bring their opposite.

Trungpa Rinpoche: You see, if your approach is a poverty approach, then it is like begging for food. You're given food and you enjoy it while you're eating it. But then you have to beg again, and between the two beggings there is a very undesirable state. It's that kind of thing. It's still relating to the dharma as the "other," rather than feeling that you have it. Once you realize that the dharma is you and you are in it already, you don't feel particularly joyous. There is no extra bliss or any high of any kind at all. If you are high, then you are high all the time, so there is no reference point for comparison. And if you are not high, then you are extraordinarily ordinary.

Student: Doesn't your idea of accident contradict the law of karma, which is that everything has a cause and effect?

Trungpa Rinpoche: Accident is karma. Karmic situations take place by way of accident. It works like flint and steel coming together and causing a spark. Events come unexpectedly. Any event is always a sudden event, but it is a karmic one. The original idea of karma is the evolutionary action of the twelve nidanas, which begins with ignorance, with the potter's wheel. That evolutionary action that begins with ignorance is an accident.

S: The ignorance itself is the accident?

TR: Ignorance itself is the accident. Duality itself is the accident. It is a big misunderstanding.

CRAZY WISDOM SEMINAR II

Karmê Chöling, 1972

ONE

Padmasambhava and the
Energy of Tantra

IN THIS SEMINAR, we will be studying Tibet's great Buddhist saint Padmasambhava. Padmasambhava was the great Indian yogi and vidyadhara who introduced the complete teachings of buddhadharma to Tibet, including the vajrayana, or tantra. As to the dates and historical details, we are uncertain. Padmasambhava is supposed to have been born twelve years after the death of the Buddha. He continued to live and went to Tibet in the eighth century to propagate the buddhadharma there. Our approach here, as far as chronology and such things are concerned, is entirely unscholastic. For those of you who are concerned with dates and other such historical facts and figures, I am afraid I will be unable to furnish accurate data. Nevertheless, the inspiration of Padmasambhava, however old or young he may be, goes on.

Rather than studying the life and acts of Padmasambhava according to a chronological-historical description, we will be trying to discuss the fundamental meaning of Padmasambhava-ism, if you wish to call it that—the basic qualities of Padmasambhava's existence as they are connected with the dawn of the vajrayana teachings in Tibet. We might call this the Padmasambhava principle. The Padmasambhava principle opened the minds of millions of people in Tibet and is already opening people's minds in this country—and in the rest of the world for that matter.

Padmasambhava's function in Tibet was to bring forth the teachings of the Buddha by relating with the Tibetan barbarians. The Tibetans of

Pema Jungne (Padmasambhava).

those times believed in a self and a higher authority outside the self, which is known as God. Padmasambhava's function was to destroy those beliefs. His approach was if there is no belief in the self, then there is no belief in God—a purely nontheistic approach, I am afraid. He had to destroy those nonexistent sand castles that we build. So the significance of Padmasambhava is connected with the destruction of those delusive beliefs. His entry into Tibet meant the destruction of the delusive theistic spiritual structures that had been established in that country. Padmasambhava came to Tibet and introduced Buddhism. In the course of introducing it, he discovered that he not only had to destroy people's primitive beliefs, but he also had to raise their consciousness at the same time. So in introducing the Padmasambhava principle here, we must also relate with the same basic problems of destroying what has to be destroyed and cultivating what has to be cultivated.

To begin with, we have to destroy certain fallacious notions connected with holiness, spirituality, goodness, heaven, godhood, and so forth. What makes these fallacious is the belief in a self, ego. That belief makes it so that "I" am practicing goodness; thus, goodness is separated from "me"; or it implies some kind of a relationship in which goodness depends on "me" and "me" depends on goodness. Thus, fundamentally [since neither exists on its own], there is nothing there to build on at all. With this ego approach, a conclusion is drawn because of "other" factors that prove that the conclusion is so. From that point of view, we are building sand castles or building castles on an ice block.

According to the Buddhist outlook, ego (or self) is nonexistent. It is not founded on any definite, real factors at all. It is based purely on the belief or assumption that since I call myself so-and-so, therefore I exist. And if I do not know what I am called, what my name is, then there is no structure there on which the whole thing is based. The way this primitive belief works is that believing in "that," the other, brings "this," the self. If "that" exists, then "this" must also exist. I believe in "that" because I need a reference point for my own existence, for "this."

In the tantric, or vajrayana, approach introduced into Tibet by Padmasambhava, my existence in relationship with others who exist is based on some energy. It is founded on some sense of understanding, which could also equally well be some sense of misunderstanding.

When we ask ourselves, "Who are you, what are you?" and we answer, "I am so-and-so," our affirmation or confirmation is based on putting something into that empty question. A question is like a container that we put something into to make it an appropriate and valid container. There is some energy that is there between the two processes of giving birth to a question and producing an answer, an energy process that develops at the same time. The energy that develops between the question and the answer is connected either with complete truth or complete falsehood. Strangely enough, those two do not contradict each other. Complete truth and complete falsehood are in some sense the same thing. They make sense simultaneously. Truth is false, falsehood is true. And that kind of energy, which goes on continuously, is called tantra. Because it does not matter here about logical problems of truth or falsehood, the state of mind connected with this is called crazy wisdom.

What I am trying to say is that our minds always are completely and constantly fixed on relating to things as either "yes" or "no"; "yes" in the sense of existence, "no" in the sense of disproving that existence. Yet our framework of mind continues all the time between those two attitudes. "Yes" is based on exactly the same sense of reference point as the negation is.

So the basic framework of mind involving a sense of reference point goes on continuously, which means that there is some energy constantly happening. What this means in terms of our relating to the Padmasambhava principle is that we do not have to negate the experience of our lives. We do not have to negate our materialistic or spiritually materialistic experiences. We do not have to negate them as being bad things; nor for that matter do we have to affirm them as being good things. We could relate to the simultaneous birth into existence of things as they are.[2]

This makes sense because what we are trying to do all the time is fight on that ground or battlefield, whether the battlefield belongs to the attackers or the defenders, and so forth. But in all this, nobody has ever really discussed whether this battlefield itself actually exists or not. And what we are saying here is that that ground or battlefield does exist. Our negations or affirmations as to whether it belongs to ourselves or the others do not make any difference at all. All the time we are affirming or negating, we are standing on this ground anyway. This ground we are standing on is the place of birth as well as the place of death, simultaneously. This provides some sense of solidity as far as the principle of Padmasambhava is concerned.

We are talking about a particular energy that permits the teachings to be transmitted by the Padmasambhava principle. The Padmasambhava principle belongs neither to wickedness nor goodness; it belongs to neither yes nor no. It is a principle that accommodates everything that exists in our life situations altogether. Because that energy exists in people's life situations, the Padmasambhava principle was able to bring the buddhadharma to Tibet. In a sense, the theistic beliefs that existed in Tibet—the belief in self and God as separate and the notion of trying to reach higher realms—did have to be destroyed. Those primitive beliefs had to be destroyed, just as we are doing here. Those primitive beliefs in the separate reality of "me" and my object of worship have to be destroyed. Unless these dualistic notions are destroyed, there is no starting point for giving birth to tantra. The birth of tantra takes place from the nonexistence of belief in "this" and "that."

But Tibetans were very powerful people when Padmasambhava came. They did not believe in philosophies or any of the cunning things that pandits might say. They did not regard a pandit's cleverness as any kind of credential. The Bön tradition of Tibet was very solid and definite and sane. The Tibetans did not believe in what Padmasambhava had to say philosophically about such things as the transitoriness of ego. They would not make sense out of anything like that at all. They would regard such logical analysis as just purely a collection of riddles—Buddhist riddles.

What the Tibetans believed was that life exists and I exist and my ongoing activities of life—working with the dairy animals, working in the fields—exist. The dairy farm and the fields do exist, and my practical activities connected with them are my sacred activities, my sadhanas. The Bön outlook is that these things exist because I have to feed my child, I have to milk my cow, I have to grow my crops, I have to make butter and cheese. I believe those simple truths. Our Bön tradition is valid, because it believes in the sacredness of feeding life, bringing forth food from the earth in order to feed our offspring. These very simple things exist. This is religion, this is truth, as far as the Bön tradition is concerned.

This simplicity is similar to what we find in the American Indian tradition. Killing a buffalo is an act of creativity because it feeds the hungry; it also controls the growth of the buffalo herd and, in that way, maintains a balance. It is that kind of ecological approach.

We find all kinds of ecological approaches of this type, which are extremely sane and solid. In fact, one might have second thoughts as to whether this country is yet ripe for the presentation of Padmasambhava's wisdom, because some people believe in those ecological philosophies and some do not. Some people are very dogmatic advocates of those ecological philosophies and some have no knowledge of them at all. On account of that, one wonders a bit how to approach this culture. But on the whole, there is a certain continuity in what is happening. There is one basic general approach in this culture: we think that everything exists for our benefit.

For instance, we think the body is extremely important, because it maintains the mind. The mind feeds the body and the body feeds the mind. We feel it is important to keep this happening in a healthy manner for our benefit, and we have come to the conclusion that the easiest way to achieve this tremendous scheme of being healthy is to start with the less complicated side of it: feed the body. Then we can wait and see what happens with the mind. If we are less hungry, then we are more likely to be psychologically jolly, and then we may feel like looking into the teachings of depth psychology or other philosophies.

This is also the approach of the Bön tradition: let us kill a yak; that will make us spiritually higher. Our bodies will be healthier, so our minds will be higher. American Indians would say, let us kill one buffalo. It is the same logic. It is very sensible. We could not say that it is insane at all. It is extremely sane, extremely realistic, very reasonable and logical. There is a pattern there to be respected, and if you put the pattern into practice in a manner that is worthy of respect, then the pattern will continue and you will achieve your results.

We are involved in that kind of approach in this country as well. A lot of people in this country are into the Red American cult as opposed to the White American cult. As far as the Red American cult is concerned, you have your land, you build your tepee, you relate with your children and grandchildren and great-great-great-grandchildren. You have dignity and character. You are not afraid of any threat—you develop warriorlike qualities. Then you consider how to handle your children, how to teach them respect for the nation. You instruct your children properly and you become a solid citizen.

Philosophies of this type are to be found not only among the Red Americans, but also among the Celts, the pre-Christian Scandinavians, and the Greeks and Romans. Such a philosophy can be found in the past of any nation that had a pre-Christian or pre-Buddhist religion, a religion of fertility or ecology—such as that of the Jews, the Celts, the American Indians, whatever. That approach of venerating fertility and relating with the earth still goes on, and it is very powerful and very beautiful. I appreciate it very thoroughly, and I could become a follower of such a philosophy. In fact, I am one. I am a Bönist. I believe in Bön because I am Tibetan.

Believing so much in this makes me think of something else that lies outside this framework that is purely concerned with fertility, which is purely body-oriented, which believes that the body will feed the psychology of higher enlightenment. It makes me have questions about the whole thing. If you have such questions, this does not necessarily mean that you have to give up your previous beliefs. If you are a believer and practitioner of the Red American cult, you do not have to become a White American. The question here is, how does your philosophy relate with the reality of the psychological aspect of life? What do we really mean by "body"? What do we really mean by "mind"? What is the body? What is the mind? The body consists of that which needs to be fed; the mind is that which needs to survey whether the body is fed properly. So needing to be fed is another part of the aggregate of the structure of mind.

The whole problem comes not from having to be fed properly or from having to maintain your health properly; the problem comes from belief in the separateness of "I" and "that." I am separate from my food and my food is not me; therefore, I have to consume that particular food that is not me so that it can become part of me.

In the Bön tradition of Tibet, there was a mystical approach toward overcoming separateness, based on the advaita principle, the not-two principle, But even with this, until you became the earth itself or until you became the creator of the world, you could not solve your problem. Certain Bön ceremonies reflect a very primitive level of belief concerning overcoming the separateness. The idea is that we have to create an object of worship and then eat the object of worship—chew it, swallow it. Once we have digested it, we should believe that we are completely advaita, not-two. This is something like what happens in the Christian traditional ceremony of Holy Communion. To begin with, there is a separateness between you and God, or you and the Son or the Holy Ghost. You and they are separate entities. Until you have associated yourself with the flesh and blood of Christ, represented by certain materials into which the Holy Ghost enters, then you cannot have complete union with them. You cannot have complete union until you eat the bread and drink the wine. The fact that until you do that you cannot become one shows that this is still an act of separateness. Eating and drinking is destroying the separateness, but fundamentally the separateness is still there; when you shit and piss, you end up with the separateness again. There is a problem there.

The sense of becoming one cannot be based on a physical act of doing something—on taking part in a ceremony in this case. To become one with the reality, I have to give up hope of becoming one with the reality. In other words, in relation to "this" exists and "that" exists, I give up hope. I can't work all this out. I give up hope. I don't care if "that" exists or "this" exists; I give up hope. This hopelessness is the starting point of the process of realization.

As we were flying today from Denver to Boston, we encountered a beautiful sight, a vision if you like. Out the window of the airplane was a ring of light reflected on the clouds, a rainbow that followed us wherever we went. In the center of the rainbow ring, in the distance, there was what seemed to be a little peanut shape, a little shadow. As we began to descend and came closer to the clouds, we realized that the peanut shape was actually the shadow of the airplane surrounded by the ring of the rainbow. It was beautiful, miraculous in fact. As we descended further into the depths of the clouds, the shadow became bigger and bigger. We began to make out the complete shape of the airplane, with the tail, the head, and the wings. Then, just as we were about to land, the rainbow ring disappeared and the shadow disappeared. That was the end of our vision.

This reminded me of when we used to look at the moon on a hazy day and see a rainbow ring around the moon. At some point, you realize that it is not you looking at the moon but the moon looking at you. What we saw reflected on the clouds was our own shadow. It is mind-boggling. Who is watching who? Who is tricking who?

The approach of crazy wisdom here is to give up hope. There is no hope of understanding anything at all. There is no hope of finding out who did what or what did what or how anything worked. Give up your ambition to put the jigsaw puzzle together. Give it up altogether, absolutely; throw it up in the air, put it in the fireplace. Unless we give up this hope, this precious hope, there is no way out at all.

It is like trying to work out who is in control of the body or the mind, who has the closest link with God—or who has the closest link with the truth, as the Buddhists would say. Buddhists would say that Buddha had the truth, because he didn't believe in God. He found that the truth is free of God. But the Christians or other theists would say that the truth exists because a truth-maker exists. Fighting out those two polarities seems to be useless at this point. It is a completely hopeless situation, absolutely hopeless. We do not understand—and we have no possibility of understanding—anything at all. It is hopeless to look for something to understand, for something to discover, because there is no discovery at all at the end, unless we manufacture one. But if we did manufacture a discovery, we would not be particularly happy about that later on. Though we would thrive on it, we would know that we had cheated ourselves. We would know that there was some secret game that had gone on between "me" and "that."

So the introductory process of Padmasambhava's crazy wisdom is giving up hope, giving up hope *completely*. Nobody is going to comfort you, and nobody is going to help you. The whole idea of trying to find the root or some logic for the discovery of crazy wisdom is completely hopeless. There is no ground, so there is no hope. There is also no fear, for that matter, but we had better not talk about that too much.

Student: Is this hopelessness the same hopelessness you have talked about in connection with shunyata?

Trungpa Rinpoche: I wouldn't even like to connect it with shunyata. This hopelessness provides no security, not even as much as shunyata.

Student: I don't understand why there's no fear here. It seems there would be a possibility of quite a lot of fear.

Trungpa Rinpoche: You have no hope, how can you have fear? There's nothing to look forward to, so you have nothing to lose.

S: If you have nothing to lose and nothing to gain, why keep on studying? Why not just sit back with a bottle of beer?

TR: Well, that in itself is an act of hope and fear. If you just sit back with a beer and relax, saying to yourself, "Well, now, everything's okay—there's nothing to lose, nothing to gain," that in itself is an act of hopefulness and fearfulness. [It is trying to supply a way out,] but you have no way out.

You see, hopelessness and fearlessness is not release, but further imprisonment. You have trapped yourself into spirituality already. You have created your own spiritual trip, and you are trapped in it. That's the other way of looking at this.

S: So this is like acceptance?

TR: No, I wouldn't say it is anything so philosophical as acceptance. It is more desperate than acceptance.

S: Giving up?

TR: Giving up is desperate. In giving up, you have been squeezed into giving up hope; you haven't requested to give up hope.

Student: It seems that playing on the battlefield of your territory of "yes" and "no" is the way, since there is no way out of it.

Trungpa Rinpoche: I wouldn't say it's the way, because that provides some kind of hope.

S: But there's no other battlefield to play on.

TR: Well, that's very hopeless, yes.

Student: A minute ago, you seemed to say that even shunyata could provide a sense of security.

Trungpa Rinpoche: It depends on how you relate with it. [If we relate to shunyata as an answer, it might provide some hope.] Until we realize the true implication of hopelessness, we have no chance of understanding crazy wisdom at all, ladies and gentlemen.

S: You just have to give up hope?

TR: Hope and fear.

Student: It seems that you can't just sit back and do nothing. A certain dissatisfaction arises, and so very naturally hope arises that this dissatisfaction could somehow go away. So hope seems to be a very natural and spontaneous thing.

Trungpa Rinpoche: That's too bad. You don't get anything out of it anyway. That's too bad.

S: Yes, but it comes out of every situation, so I don't see how you can possibly avoid it.

TR: You don't have to avoid it out of being hopeful that that's the right approach. But too bad. It's very simple. The whole thing's hopeless. When we are trying to figure out who's on first and what's on second, there's no way out. Hopeless!

S: Yes, but history, Buddhism, traditions of all kinds give us hope.

TR: Well, they are based on hopelessness, which is why they give some kind of hope. When you give up hope *completely*, there are hopeful situations. But it's hopeless to try and work this out logically. Absolutely hopeless! It doesn't give us any guidelines or maps. The maps would constantly tell us, "No hope there, no hope there, no hope here, no hope there." Hopeless. That's the *whole* point.

S: Hope means the sense that I can do, I can manipulate—is that right?

TR: Yes, the sense that I can get something out of what I am trying to do.

Student: Is the achievement of hopelessness a one-shot affair, where you suddenly just flip into it—

Trungpa Rinpoche: No. It's not a sudden flash that you are saved by. Absolutely not.

S: So it's something that anybody could have some intuition of at any point.

TR: We all do, always. But even that is not *sacred*.

Student: If there are no maps and no guidelines and it's all hopelessness, is there any function for a teacher on this whole trip besides telling you that it's hopeless?

Trungpa Rinpoche: You said it!

Student: Would you advise just diving into the hopelessness or cultivating it little by little?

Trungpa Rinpoche: It's up to you. It's really up to you. I will say one thing. It's impossible to develop crazy wisdom without a sense of hopelessness, *total* hopelessness.

S: Does that mean becoming a professional pessimist?

TR: No, no. A professional pessimist is also hopeful, because he had developed his system of pessimism. It's that same old hopefulness.

Student: What does hopelessness feel like?

Trungpa Rinpoche: Just purely hopeless. No ground, absolutely no ground.

S: The moment you become conscious that you're feeling hopeless, does the hopelessness sort of lose its genuineness?

TR: That depends on whether you regard hopelessness as something sacred according to a religion or spiritual teaching, or whether you regard it as utterly hopeless. That's purely up to you.

S: I mean, we're always talking about this hopelessness, and everybody's beginning to feel that that's the key, so we want it. We feel hopeless and we say, "Well, now I'm on my way." That might eliminate some of the reality of it.

TR: Too bad. Too bad. If you regard it as the path in the sense that you feel you are going to get something out of this, that won't work. There's no way out. That approach is self-defeating. Hopelessness is not a gimmick. It means it, you know; it's the truth. It's the truth of hopelessness, rather than the doctrine of hopelessness.

Student: Rinpoche, if that's so about hopelessness, then the whole picture that we have about the hinayana, mahayana, and vajrayana, and so on seems to become just a big trip leading to giving up hope. You often talk of a kind of judo practice, using the energy of ego to let it defeat itself. Here we would somehow use the energy of hope to bring hopelessness, the energy of all this to defeat itself. Is that for real, or is this whole idea of judo practice also just part of the trip?

Trungpa Rinpoche: It is said that at the end of the journey through the nine yanas, it is clear that the journey need never have been made. So the path that is presented to us is an act of hopelessness in some sense. The journey need never be made at all. It's eating your own tail and continuing until you eat your own mouth. That's the kind of analogy we could use.

S: It seems that to proceed you have to disregard the warning. Although I may hear that it's hopeless, the only way I can go on at this point is with hope. Why sit and meditate right now? Why not just go out and play? It seems that everything in this situation is a paradox, but, you know, okay, so I'll be here. Even though I hear it's hopeless, I'll pretend.

TR: That's a hopeful act as well, which is in itself hopeless. It eats itself right up. In other words, you think you are able to deceive the path by being a smart traveler on the path, but you begin to realize that you are the path itself. You can't deceive the path, because you make the path. So you're inevitably going to get a very strong message of hopelessness.

S: The only way to get that, it seems, is to keep playing the game.

TR: That's up to you. You could also give up. You have a very definite choice. You have two very definite alternatives, which I suppose we could call sudden enlightenment or gradual enlightenment. This is entirely dependent upon you, on whether you give up hope on the spot or whether you go on playing the game and improvising all kinds of other entertainments. So the sooner you give up hope, the better.

Student: It seems that you can put up with a hopeless situation only so long. At a certain point, you just can't relate to it anymore and will take advantage of any distraction to turn away from it.

Trungpa Rinpoche: It's up to you.

S: Should you just force yourself again and again, continually, to—

TR: Well, it comes about that way as your life situation goes on.

Student: If the whole situation is hopeless, on what basis do you make decisions like whether to kill one buffalo to feed your family or five hundred buffalo to have their heads on the wall?

Trungpa Rinpoche: Both alternatives are hopeless. Both are ways of trying to survive, which is hope. So both are equally hopeless. We have to learn to work with hopelessness. Nontheistic religion is a hopeless approach of not believing anything. And theistic religion is hopeful, believing in the separateness of me and the nipple I suck on, so to speak. Sorry to be crude, but roughly it works that way.

Student: You said there's no God, there's no self. Is there any so-called true self? Is there anything outside of hopelessness?

Trungpa Rinpoche: I should remind you that this whole thing is the preparation for crazy wisdom, which does not know any kind of truth other than itself. From that point of view, there's no true self, because when you talk about true self or buddha nature, then that in itself is trying to insert some positive attitude, something to the effect that you are okay. That doesn't exist in this hopelessness.

Student: This hopelessness seems to me to be a restatement of the idea of stopping self-protection, stopping a sense of trying to improve the situation. According to our stereotyped understanding of enlightenment, it is in the moment that we stop protecting and improving that real understanding can begin. Is that what you're saying?

Trungpa Rinpoche: As far as this process is concerned, there's no promise of anything at all, none whatsoever. It's giving up everything, including the self.

S: Then that hopelessness puts you in the here and now.

TR: Much more than that. It doesn't put you anywhere. You have no ground to stand on, absolutely none. You are completely desolate. And even desolation is not regarded as home, because you are so desolately, absolutely hopeless that even loneliness is not a refuge anymore. Everything is completely hopeless. Even *itself* [*shouts "itself" and snaps fingers*]. It's totally taken away from you, absolutely completely. Any kind of energy that's happening in order to preserve itself is also hopeless.

Student: The energy that was preserving the self, that forms a kind of shell around the self, if that stops, then it just escapes into no division between itself and what's all around it?

Trungpa Rinpoche: It doesn't give you any reassurance. When we talk about hopelessness, it means literal hopelessness. The sense of hope here is hope as opposed to loss. There's no means by which you could get something in return anymore at all. Absolutely not. Even itself.

S: It's lost its self?

TR: Lost itself, precisely.

S: That kind of groundlessness seems to be more than hopelessness. I mean, in hopelessness there's still some sense of there being *someone* who is without hope.

TR: Even that is suspicious.

S: What happens to the ground? The ground drops away. I don't understand.

TR: The ground is hopelessness as well. There's no solidity in the ground either.

S: I hear what you're saying. You're saying that no matter what direction one looks in—

TR: Yes, you are overwhelmed by hopelessness. All over. Utterly. Completely. Profusely. You are a claustrophobic situation of hopelessness.

We're talking about a sense of hopelessness as an *experience* of no ground. We are talking about experience. We are talking about an experience, which is one little thread in the whole thing. We are talking about the experience of hopelessness. This is an experience that cannot be forgotten or rejected. It might reject itself, but still there is experience. It is just a kind of thread that goes on. I thought we could discuss this further in connection with Padmasambhava's experience of experience. But the fact that this is Padmasambhava's experience of experience doesn't mean anything. It's still hopeless.

Student: You seem to be saying that where there's no hope, it's intelligent. And when you think there's hope, then that's ignorance.

Trungpa Rinpoche: I don't think so, my dear. It's completely hopeless.

Student: When you talk about hopelessness, the whole thing seems totally depressing. And it seems you could very easily be overwhelmed by that depression to the point where you just retreat into a shell or insanity.

Trungpa Rinpoche: It's up to you. It's completely up to you. That's the whole point.

S: Is there anything—

TR: You see, the whole point is that I'm not manufacturing an absolute model of hopelessness with complete and delicately worked-out patterns of all kinds, presenting it to you, and asking you to work on that. Your goodness, your hopelessness, is the only model there is. If I manufactured something, it would be just a trick, unrealistic. Rather, it's your hopelessness, it's your world, your family heirloom, your inheritance. That hopelessness comes in your existence, your psychology. It's a matter of bringing it out as it is. But it's still hopeless. As hopeful as you might try to make it, it's still hopeless. And I can't reshape it, remodel it, or refinish it at all. It's not like a political candidate going on television, where people powder his face and put lipstick on his mouth to make him presentable. One cannot do that. In this case, it's hopeless; it's absolutely hopeless. You have to do it in your own way.

Student: Is it possible for someone to be aware that it's all hopeless but yet be joyous?

Trungpa Rinpoche: Well, I mean we could have all kinds of hopeless situations, but they are all the expression of hopelessness. I suppose what you described could happen, but who are you trying to con?

Student: The situation with Naropa having his visions and having the possibility of choosing to jump over the bitch or deal with the bitch, is that the same situation of "yes" or "no" you described in your talk?

Trungpa Rinpoche: I think so, yes.

S: And Naropa's hopelessness at the end—

TR: Naropa's state of hopelessness before he actually saw his guru was absolute. Understanding Padmasambhava's life without a sense of hopelessness would be completely impossible.

TWO

Hopelessness and the Trikaya

THE SENSE OF HOPELESSNESS is the starting point for relating with crazy wisdom. If the sense of hopelessness is able to cut through unrealistic goals, then the hopelessness becomes something more definite. It becomes definite because we are not trying to manufacture anything other than what there is not. So a sense of hopelessness could provide the basic approach to nonduality.

The sense of hopelessness connects directly with the practical level of our everyday lives. Life on the practical level does not contain any subtle philosophy or subtle mystical experience. It just is. If we are able to see that isness, so to speak, then there is a sense of realization. We experience sudden enlightenment. Without a sense of hopelessness, there is no way to give birth to sudden enlightenment. Only giving up our projects brings about the ultimate, definite, positive state of being, which is the realization that we are already enlightened beings here and now.

In discussing the details of this state, we could say that even in experiencing a sense of buddha nature, we still have to have that experience, which is connected with the samsaric, or confused, part of our being in that it is dependent on the experience of something. Experience involves a sense of duality. You have an experience and you relate with that experience; you relate with it as something separate; there is a separation between you and what you experience. You are dealing with a subject matter, experience.

Though there is still a sense of separateness, of duality, nevertheless it is an experience of being awake, of realizing buddha within us. So we begin to develop some sense of space between the experience and the projection of the experience. There is a forward-moving journey of trying to catch some particular aspect in us that is sane. And making that effort, becoming involved in that particular relationship, brings our sense of space somewhere.

It is like when we are just about to say something. First we have to experience the unsaid things. We feel the space of what we haven't said yet. We feel the space, and then we say whatever we say, which accentuates the space in a certain way, makes it into a definite perspective. In order to express space, we have to draw the boundary of space.

That kind of sense of openness that happens when we are just about to say something or just about to experience something is a kind of sense of emptiness. It is a sense of fertile emptiness, pregnant emptiness. That experience of emptiness is the dharmakaya. In order to give birth, we have to have an accommodation for giving birth. The sense of the absence of that birth before giving birth is the dharmakaya.

Dharmakaya is unconditioned. The leap has already been made. When we definitely decide to leap, we have leapt already. The leaping itself is somewhat repetitious or redundant. Once we have already decided to leap, we have leapt. We are talking about that kind of sense of space in which the leap, the birth, is already given though not yet manifested. It is not yet manifested, but it is as good as already manifested. In that state of mind in which we are about to experience, say, drinking a cup of tea, we have drunk a cup of tea already before we drink it. And we have said things already before we actually say them on a manifest level.

That kind of pregnant, embryonic, fertile ground that happens in our state of mind constantly is also unconditioned [i.e., as well as pregnant with something]. It is unconditioned in relation to my ego, or dualistic mind, my actions, my love and hate, and so on. In relation to all that, it is unconditioned. Thus, we have that kind of unconditioned glimpse happening in our state of mind constantly.

The dharmakaya state is the starting point or ground of Padmasambhava. The embryonic manifestation here is the dharma, the dharma of possibilities that have happened already, existing things that exist in nonexistence. It is the sense of fertility, complete fullness yet intangibility, in our daily experience. Before the emotions arise, there are preparations toward that. Before we put our actions into effect, there are preparations toward that. That sense of occupied space, self-existing space, is dharma. *Kaya* is "form," or "body," the statement that such dharma does exist. The body of dharma is the dharmakaya.

Then we have the second level of manifestation of Padmasambhava, the sambhava, the sambhogakaya, in our state of being. This is the borderline between fullness and emptiness. There is the sense that the fullness of it becomes valid, because it is emptiness. In other words, it is a kind of affirmation of the existence of emptiness. There is the spaciousness where the emotions begin to arise, where anger is just about to burst out or has burst out already, but there still needs to be a journey forward toward giving final birth. This [forward movement] is the sambhogakaya. *Sam* means "complete," *bhoga* means "joy." Joy here is occupation or energy, rather than joy in the sense of pleasure as opposed to pain. It is occupation, action existing for itself, emotions existing for themselves. But though they exist for themselves, they are rootless as far as basic validity is concerned. There is no basic validity, but still emotions occur out of nowhere, and their energy springs forth, sparks out, constantly.

Then we have nirmanakaya. *Nirmana*, in this case, is the emanation, or manifestation—the complete manifestation or final accent. It is like when a child has already been born and the doctor cuts the umbilical cord to make sure that the child is separate from its father and mother. It is now an independent entity. This is parallel to the bursting of the emotions into the fascinated world outside. At this point, the object of passion or the object of aggression, or whatever, comes out very powerfully and very definitely.

This does not particularly refer to applying the emotions, for example, using anger as an influence for killing a person or passion as an influence for magnetizing a person. Still, there is a sense that, before actual words are spoken or actual bodily movements have occurred, the emotions have occurred; there has been a final definition of the emotions and they have become separate from you. You have officially cut the umbilical cord between you and your emotions. They have already occurred outwardly—they have become a satellite already, your satellite already, a separate thing. This is final manifestation.

When we talk here about anger or passion or ignorance/bewilderment, whatever we talk about, we are not speaking in moralistic terms of good and bad. We are speaking of tremendously highly charged emotions that contain the energy of their vividness. We could say that our lives consist of this tremendous vividness all the time: the vividness of being bored, being angry, being in love, being proud, being jealous. Our lives consist of all these kinds of vividness rather than of virtues or sins created by those.

What we are talking about here is the essence of Padmasambhava. There is this vividness of Padmasambhava manifesting in our lives constantly through the process of giving birth: experiencing a sense of space, then manifesting, then finally concluding that manifestation. So there is the threefold process, of the dharmakaya as the embryonic space, the sambhogakaya as the forwarding quality, and the nirmanakaya in which it actually finally manifests itself. All those situations are the vividness of Padmasambhava.

It seems that before discussing the eight aspects of Padmasambhava, it is important to understand the three principles of the trikaya. Unless we realize the subtleties of the energies involved in Padmasambhava's life, we have no chance of understanding it. Without understanding the trikaya, we might think that when Padmasambhava manifests in the different aspects it is like one person wearing different hats: his business hat, his hunting hat, his yogi hat, his scholar hat, and so on. It is not like that. It is not like one person changing costumes; rather it has to do with the vividness of life.

In talking about Padmasambhava, we are not referring purely to a historical person: "once upon a time, there was a person, Padmasambhava, who was born in India." Somehow that does not really make sense. If we were doing that, we would just be having a history lesson. Instead, what we are trying to point to here is that Padmasambhava is our experience. We are trying to relate with the Padmasambhava-*ness* in us, in our state of being. The Padmasambhava-ness consists of those three constituents: the dharmakaya, or open space; the sambhogakaya, or forward energy; and the nirmanakaya, or actual manifestation.

We might say to ourselves at this point, "This is supposed to be crazy wisdom; what's so crazy about those things? Energy happens, space is there. Is there anything about this that is unusual, anything crazy or wise?" Actually, there is nothing—nothing crazy abut it and nothing wise about it. The only thing that makes it extraordinary is that it happens to be true. We are infested with Padmasambhava in ourselves. We are haunted by him. Our whole being is completely made out of Padmasambhava. So when we try to relate with him "out there," as a person who lives on a copper-colored mountain on some remote island off the coast of India, that does not make sense.

It would be very easy to relate with him that way, because then we could have a sense of ambition. We could feel that we would like to go where he is, or find out whether he is a purely mythical being or actually does exist. We could take a plane, we could take a boat; we could find out where those places are where Padmasambhava is still supposed to be living. Trying to invoke Padmasambhava, to bring him about in our being from the outside, is like waiting for Godot. The result never happens.

There was a great Tibetan siddha called the Madman of Tsang. He lived in Tsang, which is in East Tibet, near a mountain called Anye Machen, where my guru, Jamgön Kongtrül, visited him. This was about five years before I met my guru. He used to tell us the story of his meeting with the Madman of Tsang, who was an ordinary farmer who had achieved the essence of crazy wisdom. He had these very precious things stored in his treasury, bags and bags supposedly full of valuable things. But the bags turned out to contain just driftwood and rocks. My guru told us that he asked the Madman of Tsang, "How should we go about uniting ourselves with Padmasambhava?" The madman told him the following.

"When I was a young student and a very devout Buddhist, full of faith, I used to want my body to become one with Padmasambhava's body. I did countless recitations, thousands and millions of mantras and invocations. I used to shout myself half to death reciting mantras. I even felt that I was wasting my time by breathing in during these recitations. I called and called and called to Padmasambhava, trying to make my body one with his. But then suddenly I just realized: I am—my body is—Padmasambhava. I could go on calling on him until my voice breaks down, but it wouldn't make any sense. So I decided not to call on him anymore. Then I found that Padmasambhava was calling on me. I tried to suppress it, but I couldn't control it. Padmasambhava wanted me, and he kept on calling my name."

This is the kind of situation we are discussing, I suppose. Instead of our looking out there for him, he is looking in at us. In order to make these things real and ordinary in our lives, it seems that we need some kind of conviction in us. We have to realize that there is a sense of energy that is always there, and that that energy contains totality. That energy is not dualistic or interdependent; it is a self-existing energy in us. We have our passion, our aggression; we have our own space, our own energy—it's there already. It exists without any dependency on situations. It is absolute and perfect and independent. It is free from any form of relationships.

That seems to be the point about Padmasambhava here. The principle of Padmasambhava consists in freedom from any speculative ideas or theories or activity of watching oneself. It is the living experience of emotions and experiences without a watcher. Because we are buddha already, we are Padmasambhava already. Gaining such confidence, such vajra pride, gives us a further opportunity. It is not hard to imagine that when you know what you are and who you are completely, then you can explore the rest of the world, because you don't have to explore yourself anymore.

Student: Rinpoche, if the dharmakaya is a pregnant state already, or a fertile state already, does that mean that there isn't any completely empty dharmakaya that doesn't apply to anything? Are you saying that the dharmakaya always has some sense of application already?

Trungpa Rinpoche: You see, the dharmakaya in this case is similar to experience. It's quite different from the dharmadhatu, the greater dharmadhatu. When you refer to it as dharma and kaya, it is, in some sense, conditioned. It's conditioned because it's pregnant already.[3]

S: So does that mean that the dharmadhatu is theoretical, purely a matter of theoretical background?

TR: I wouldn't even say it's theoretical. It hardly has a name at all. Talking about dharmadhatu makes us more self-conscious, so then dharmadhatu becomes self-conscious; or rather, inventing words about it makes dharmadhatu more self-conscious from our point of view.

S: Is dharmadhatu experientially different from dharmakaya?

TR: Yes. Dharmadhatu is no experience.

S: And that's the space in which the kayas—

TR: Take place, yes. Dharmakaya is already experience. Dharmakaya is referred to in Tibetan as *tangpo sangye,* which means "the primordial buddha," the buddha who never became a buddha through practice but who is realization on the spot. That is the nondualism of the dharmakaya. Whereas the dharmadhatu is total accommodation of some kind that doesn't have its own entity at all.

You see, the dharmakaya is, so to speak, a kind of credential. Somebody has to have a credential of some kind in order to be dharmakaya. That is why it is pregnant. But this sense of credential should not be regarded in a pejorative or negative way at all. The exciting things happening with the samsaric world are part of that manifestation. The dharma itself, as a teaching, is part of it; the teaching wouldn't exist unless there were somebody to teach. It's that kind of situation.

S: What does Padmasambhava have to do with the dharmadhatu?

TR: Nothing.

S: Well, what is the difference then between the sense of possibility in dharmakaya, the sense of a pregnant situation, and expectation in the negative Buddhist sense of desire, of looking forward to something? In other words, you spoke of dharmakaya as a sense of possibility, as if you had your tea before you even drank it. How does that differ from wanting a cup of tea in the grasping way?

TR: There's no difference at all. If we look at grasping in a matter-of-fact way, it's actually very spacious. But we regard grasping as an insult to ourselves. That's why it becomes an insult. But grasping as it is, is actually very spacious. It's a hollow question. Very spacious. That's the dharmakaya itself.

S: Is there a momentum that brings it beyond the sense of potential or pregnancy of the dharmakaya stage to the point where it is actually moving toward becoming something?

TR: There is momentum already, because there is experience. Momentum begins when you regard experience as something experience-able. The momentum is there already, so dharmakaya is a part of that energy. That's why all three kayas are connected with energy. There is the most transparent energy, the energy of movement, and the energy of manifestation. Those three kayas are all included in that energy. That's why they are called kayas.

S: It seems as though within the pregnant space of the dharmakaya, there is also sambhogakaya and nirmanakaya.

TR: Yes.

S: It seems to me that in the journey from dharmakaya to nirmanakaya, if the manifestation is going to end up to be something samsaric and the dharmakaya is already pregnant with it, then there is a samsaric factor that is already part of the dharmakaya. For instance, if we have the cup of tea before we actually drink it, then there is all the conditioning from past tea-drinking experiences that is part of determining that experience.

TR: You see, the whole point when we talk about Padmasambhava is that Padmasambhava is the trikaya principle, which is made out of a combination of both samsara and nirvana at the same time, so any conditions or conditioning are valid. At this point, as far as that experience is concerned, samsara and nirvana are one within the experience. What we are concerned with here is that it is purely free energy. It's neither conditioned nor unconditioned, but rather its own existence is absolute in its own way. So we don't have to try to make it valid by persuading ourselves that there is nothing samsaric that is part of it. Without that [samsaric element], we would have nothing to be crazy about. This *is* crazy wisdom, you know.

S: What's the nirmanakaya part?

TR: The sense of relating with the tea as an external object, which is like cutting the umbilical cord. Relating with the tea as the teaness out there is the nirmanakaya. But this does not necessarily mean physically doing it, particularly. Rather, it's that there are three types of solidification of experience related with tea, the threefold states of being of the mind.

S: So the nirmanakaya is the sort of "ness."

TR: Yes, it's the cupness and potness and teaness.

S: So what's the sambhogakaya?

TR: The sambhogakaya is the sense of slight separateness, as opposed to the abstract idea of having tea. There's some journey.

S: There's some sense in experiencing the potness and cupness that they might become exiled from the whole process of birth, cut off from the experiencing process that bore them in the first place?

TR: That's happened already. Once you are pregnant, it is already a statement of separation, and it is a further expression of separation when you give birth; then the final statement is when you cut the umbilical cord; that is the final state of separateness.

S: And you accept that separateness fully?

TR: Yes. Otherwise it becomes very confusing in terms of the partnership with nirvana or whatever you would like to call it—sanity, nirvana.

Student: I don't see how this relates with hopelessness. I mean, I don't see how these first two lectures go together.

Trungpa Rinpoche: Well, hopelessness comes from the fact that this process we have been describing does not bring any comfort. We could say that dharmakaya exists, sambhogakaya exists, nirmanakaya exists, and each has its functions. But so what? Still there's no recipe for how to make yourself happy. At this point, it has nothing to do with bringing happiness into our lives, or goodness or comfort or anything else like that. It's still a hopeless situation.

Realistically, even if you know the dharmakaya, sambhogakaya, and nirmanakaya from back to front, what does that mean to you? You will just understand the energy principle and the independency and potency of your energy. But apart from that, there's no medication. It's still hopeless.

Student: Rinpoche, is seeing things as they are still experiential?

Trungpa Rinpoche: Yes, we could say that seeing things as they are is not quite crazy enough.

Student: Rinpoche, you've described the movement from dharmakaya to sambhogakaya to nirmanakaya as a movement of energy outward. Could that process be reversed? Does the energy also go from nirmanakaya to sambhogakaya to dharmakaya?

Trungpa Rinpoche: That also happens constantly. It's sort of recycling itself. That's no big deal.

Student: You've said that we have a choice between gradual and sudden realization.

Trungpa Rinpoche: Yes.

S: Yet hopelessness is there all the time.

TR: Yes.

S: Well, what is it that we could do, then?

TR: There is an old saying that the path is the goal and the goal is the path. You make your journey, you get to your destination, and arriving at that destination brings on another question: how to proceed from there. In that way, each goal itself becomes the path. Particularly from the tantric point of view, you don't achieve anything except path. Discovery of the path is achieving. You see what I mean?

S: Well, what's sudden about it?

TR: It's always sudden.

S: All the time.

TR: All the time, yes. Until you give up the path—and the goal—there's still sudden enlightenment all the time. So the only *final* sudden thing is that you have to give up sudden discovery. That's very shocking. And very sudden.

S: But that sudden flash that goes on all the time, you're saying, is different from the gradual path?

TR: Yes, definitely. The nature of the gradual path from this point of view, if I may say so, is that the gradual path regards the goal as the goal and the path as the doctrine. And the sudden path regards the path as the goal as well as the goal as the path. There's no room for doctrine. It is just a matter of personal experience all the time. If you had to give an Oxford dictionary definition of the difference between gradual and sudden enlightenment, that could be it.

Student: Rinpoche, does this process of solidification from dharmakaya to nirmanakaya and the attitude toward it also apply on the psychological level to the process of projection—to your projections becoming more solid and your attitude toward that?

Trungpa Rinpoche: Naturally. The whole existence of the three kayas is a kind of projection in which you manufacture the projections. So in other words, the very existence of the dharma itself is a projection. Insanity and sanity both are projections. And since everything is done that way, the whole thing becomes a projection and solidity at the same time.

Student: In the story of the man worshiping Padmasambhava with so many mantras and recitations, I wasn't sure of the point. Is that kind of devotional practice purely a waste of time? Or is there some value in it?

Trungpa Rinpoche: Well, both are the same thing in a way. In order to gain valuation of time, to begin with you have to waste time, which is part of gaining valuation of time.

S: So he was wasting time?

TR: But he understood something out of it. He realized, finally, that he was wasting time, by wasting time.

S: Is that all that was happening there?

TR: Yes.

S: It doesn't sound like a waste of time at all.

TR: That's up to you. That's what I'm saying.

Student: When you say the journey need never be made, do you really mean that? We don't have to make the trip?

Trungpa Rinpoche: But then you don't know what the trip is.

S: Why do we need to know that?

TR: To realize you need never make it—it's a seamless web.

Student: Is there a certain determinism involved in the dharmakaya? Is there a kind of inevitability in the progression from dharmakaya to sambhogakaya to nirmanakaya?

Trungpa Rinpoche: I think probably the only determinism on the part of the dharmakaya is the self-consciousness of its own existence, of its own pregnancy. And that's the first expression of dualism.

Student: What's the relation between the three kayas and the charnel ground you mentioned? Is there a relation?

Trungpa Rinpoche: Each time you develop a manifestation, you create your own stuff—right at the beginning. Dharmakaya creates its own existence and its environment as well. The environment is the charnel ground—a place to dissolve, a place to manifest.

Student: I don't see that strong a difference between the sambhogakaya and the nirmanakaya. The dharmakaya seems to have parent status, so to speak, and the sambhogakaya seems to be like giving birth—you know, first expression. And I don't see where the final step from the sambhogakaya to the nirmanakaya comes in. It seems that both of them represent completion of some sort.

Trungpa Rinpoche: Well, the sambhogakaya is acknowledging the energy, you could say, and the nirmanakaya is executing, like the analogy of cutting the umbilical cord. Apart from that, there's no difference.

S: But the sambhogakaya, you said, was analogous to giving birth. That also seems pretty final.

TR: The sambhogakaya is acknowledging the energy in the sense of the receptiveness of reality. It is acknowledging that your projections are separate, definitely separate; and then what you do with the separateness, your projections, is handled by the nirmanakaya. The nirmanakaya could be described as the domestic matter of how to handle your kitchen-sink problem, whereas the sambhogakaya is like getting married to begin with to create the kitchen-sink problem. And the dharmakaya is like courting; it contains those possibilities, is already fraught with all kinds of possibilities.

S: Before, I thought you said that this process of the trikaya, looked at in the context of the self, would be samsaric, whereas in the context of the dharmadhatu, it would be nirvanic?

TR: We never discussed the nirvana aspect of it, because for one thing, it becomes too idealistic. For another thing, it becomes inaccurate, because we never see it. So we are speaking from the samsaric point of view of enlightenment at this point.

S: Why don't we see it?

TR: We still want to have answers and conclusions, which is an experience of separateness, which is samsaric. You want logic, and logic depends on samsaric mind.

S: It seems that this three-kaya process is a different perspective on the same process as the twelve nidanas and the six realms of the world and the different bardo states. Is that so?

TR: Same thing.

THREE

Fearlessness

HAVING ALREADY DISCUSSED the three-kaya principle by way of preparation, we might now consider Padmasambhava as a representative of crazy wisdom as opposed to any other type of manifestation of a vidyadhara. We might say that the unique quality of crazy wisdom in Padmasambhava's case is that of sudden enlightenment. The eight aspects of Padmasambhava are not a lineal process; they are simultaneous. In fact, the traditional expression is "eight names" of Padmasambhava rather than "eight aspects.

What is the name principle? Why is it called a *name* rather than an *aspect*? When we refer to aspects, usually we are referring to differences in basic being. We might speak of a man's father aspect, his teacher aspect, his businessman aspect. In this ordinary usage, there is the idea of a change that goes with the different roles. This usual idea of different aspects—which would imply that Padmasambhava transformed himself, entered into different parts of his being, or manifested different expressions—does not apply to Padmasambhava. Rather, his having different names is connected with the attitudes of his students and of other beings toward him. The different names have to do with the different ways other people see Padmasambhava rather than with his changing. So "name" here has the sense of "title." The Tibetan phrase is *guru tsen gye*, "the eight names of the guru." *Tsen* is the honorific Tibetan word for "name." Some people might see Padmasambhava as fatherly, others as brotherly, and still others might see him as an enemy. The views imposed by the way people see him are the basis for the eight names of

Padmasambhava. Nevertheless, his only manifestation is that of crazy wisdom.

A description for a crazy-wisdom person found in the scriptures is, "He subdues whoever needs to be subdued and destroys whoever needs to be destroyed." The idea here is that whatever your neurosis demands, when you relate with a crazy-wisdom person, you get hit back with that. Crazy wisdom presents you with a mirror reflection. That is why Padmasambhava's crazy wisdom is universal. Crazy wisdom knows no limitation and no logic regarding the form it takes. A mirror will not compromise with you if you are ugly. And there is no point in blaming the mirror or breaking it. The more you break the mirror, the more reflections of your face come about from further pieces of the mirror. So the nature of Padmasambhava's wisdom is that it knows no limitation and no compromise.

The first aspect of Padmasambhava is called Pema Gyalpo or, in Sanskrit, Padma Raja. Padma Raja was born in the Himalayan region between India and Afghanistan, in a place called Uddiyana that has since been called Swat. It was a very beautiful place surrounded by snow-capped mountains. The whole area resembled a man-made park. There were lakes and lotus ponds; the air was fresh, the climate ideal. One of the lakes was called Dhanakosha, or Lake Sindhu. It was covered with the leaves and petals of lotuses. One particular lotus was unusually huge and did not follow the usual pattern of changing with the seasons. It appeared at the beginning of the Year of the Monkey and continued its growth straight through the seasons. Winter came, spring came, autumn came, and summer came, and the lotus never opened. At last, on the tenth day of the tenth month of the Year of the Monkey, the lotus opened. There was a beautiful child inside, sitting on the calyx of the lotus. He had the appearance of a child of eight. He was dignified and inquisitive. The bees and birds congregated about this beautiful child, praising him. The sound of music without a player was heard. The whole place was pervaded with a sense of wholesomeness, health, and mystery.

The child looked like a well-looked-after prince. Could that be possible? He had no fear and seemed to be amused by his surroundings, constantly fascinated by the world outside.

That was the birth of Padmasambhava.

The whole point here is the infant quality of Padmasambhava. He was an aged infant—this is a contradiction, of course—a beautiful grown-up infant; an infant who was wise and powerful; an infant who did not nurse on milk or eat any other food, but who lived on thin air. It is because of this youthfulness that he is known as Padma Raja, "Prince of the Lotus."

We have that element of youthfulness in us as well. We have that beautiful infantlike quality in us. The experience that has taken place in our life situation is like the mud surrounding the roots of a lotus at the bottom of a lake. There is desire, passion, aggression, neuroses of all kinds. Nevertheless, out of these, some quality of freshness comes up always: that infant quality in us, completely young, youthful, inquisitive, comes up.

The inquisitiveness of that infant aspect in us is not neurotically inquisitive, but basically inquisitive. Since we want to explore the depth of pain, since we want to explore the warmth of joy, doing so seems natural. This is the Padmasambhava quality in us. We could call it buddha nature or basic enlightenment. We would like to pick up a toy, hold it in our hands, explore it, drop it, bash it around, see it falling apart, unscrew it, put it together. We always do that, just as an infant does. This infant quality is the quality of enlightenment.

When people talk about enlightenment, they usually have the idea of someone old and wise. An enlightened person, they think, is one who has been aged by experience and has thus become wise—in fact, learned. He has collected hundreds of millions of pieces of information. This makes him old and wise, trustworthy and good—enlightened. But from the point of view of crazy wisdom, enlightenment is entirely different from this. It doesn't particularly have anything to do with being old and wise. It is more like being young and wise, because it has tremendous openness toward exploring the experiences that go on in our lives— toward exploring them psychologically, on the relationship level, on the domestic level, on the practical level, on the philosophical level, and so forth.

There is also a quality of fearlessness in enlightenment, not regarding the world as an enemy, not feeling that the world is going to attack us if we do not take care of ourselves. Instead, there is tremendous delight in exploring the razor's edge, like a child who happens to pick up a razor blade with honey on it. It starts to lick it; it encounters the sweet taste and the blood dripping off its tongue at the same time. Simultaneous pain and pleasure are worth exploring, from the point of view of the sanity of crazy wisdom. This [natural inquisitiveness] is the youthful-prince quality of Padmasambhava. It is the epitome of noncaring but at the same time caring so very much—being eager to learn and eager to explore.

Probably the word *learn* is wrong here. It is not learning in the sense of collecting information; rather, it is absorbing what is happening around us, constantly relating to it. In this kind of learning, we do not at all learn things so that we can use them at some point to defend ourselves. We learn things because they are pleasurable to learn, fantastic to learn. It is like children playing with toys. They discover toys out of nowhere: they are not educational toys, but just things that are around.

Padmasambhava was born from a lotus without parents, because he had no need to be educated. He had no need for parents to bring him up to responsible, sensible adulthood. It is said that he was born from a lotus as though already eight years old. But we could say he was born from a lotus as though already eighty years old. There's no age limit. Whatever his age, he would still be a young baby, or let's say an old baby. Both amount to the same thing.

One of the most important points here is a sense of exploration of our state of being that is independent of education and information collecting. We just explore because we are delighted, like children playing with toys. That childlike quality is always in us, constantly. That is the quality of Padmasambhava.

Once again, this quality also contains fearlessness. The problem we have with fearlessness is that our samsaric way of approaching things prevents us from exploring freely. Although we have a tremendous yearning toward it, we feel that we might get hurt if we explore too much. That is fear. The infant quality of Padmasambhava is fearless, because he is not concerned with being hurt. It is not that he is masochistic or sadistic at all. It is just that he has a sense of appreciation, a sense of complete openness in relating with things—simply, directly. He does not relate with things because they are educational, but just because they are there. The relationship just happens, it develops.

The young prince born from a lotus was discovered by Indrabhuti, the king of Uddiyana. For a long time, King Indrabhuti had been praying to be granted a son, but he had been unable to have one. One day one of his court attendants went to Lake Dhanakosha to collect flowers for the royal household and discovered the mysterious lotus. It had opened, and a young and funny, inquisitive and beautiful child was sitting on it. The attendant reported this to the king, who decided to have the child brought back to the court and to adopt him as his son, as the future king.

Padmasambhava explored the pleasurable situations in the royal palace. After some time, food and wealth and comforts of all kinds began to bore him. Indrabhuti decided to arrange a marriage for Padmasambhava with the daughter of a neighboring king so that Padmasambhava would have a playmate. The marriage took place and Padmasambhava continued to explore things. He explored sexuality, companionship, food, wealth, and so on.

One thing I would like to make completely clear here is that this whole situation was not just a matter of Padmasambhava having to grow up or gain information about life. Padmasambhava's becoming a prince—even the very fact of his being born in a lotus—was not his trip, so to speak, but Indrabhuti's trip. Indrabhuti's version of Padmasambhava had to be given food and clothes and the companionship of women. Padmasambhava then broke through that hospitality by dancing on the palace roof holding a trident and a vajra. He was dancing around up there, and as if by accident, he let go of his two scepters and they fell from the roof. The trident pierced the heart of a minister's wife who was walking below, and the vajra landed on her son's skull. Both mother and child died instantly.

What do you think happened next? Padmasambhava was expelled from the kingdom. His deed was against the law. Murderers were not allowed in the kingdom. Everything in the kingdom was done properly, in accordance with law, so even that mysterious child born from a lotus had to leave—which is what Padmasambhava was asking for. He was going to cut through that situation and continue his explorations of all kinds.

Of course, we as students do not necessarily have to follow Padmasambhava's style exactly. We do not necessarily have to go through all the processes that he went through. In fact, it would be impossible; our situation would not permit it. Nevertheless, his example of exploring passion and aggression is a very, very interesting one—one worth relating to, worth exploring. However, being able to explore depends on fearlessness. Our degree of fearlessness should be, so to speak, the speedometer of our sanity [i.e., the indicator of how far we can go]. The awakened state of mind is shining through [and to the extent that it is, we go ahead]. As the scriptures say, an ordinary person should not act like a yogi, a yogi should not act like a bodhisattva, a bodhisattva should not act like a siddha, and a siddha should not act like a buddha. If we go beyond our limit, if we decide to get wild and freak out, we get hurt. We get feedback; a very strong message comes back to us. If we go beyond our limit, it becomes destructive.

So the idea of crazy wisdom is not just getting wild and freaking out. Rather, it is relating with your fear. How much you explore depends on how much fundamental fear has been related with—I wouldn't say conquered. If you do it in accordance with how much fundamental fear you have related with, then you are not going beyond your limitation.

So, strangely enough, it could be said that crazy wisdom is very timid or cowardly. Cowardice breeds crazy wisdom. Discretion is the better part of valor.

Crazy wisdom is unlike any of the other notions of the path we have discussed elsewhere. For example, in the bodhisattva path, you age or grow up from the first bhumi to the second and so on up to the tenth, and then, finally, the eleventh, the enlightened state. The teaching concerning the bodhisattva path is based on aging, growing old, gaining more and more experience. You collect one paramita after the other. You gain information, understanding, and by building yourself up higher and higher, you become a great scholar as well as a great buddha in some sense. But as far as Padmasambhava's example is concerned, there is no notion of enlightment and realization coming about through collecting stuff, experiences. Padmasambhava's style is one of purely experiencing life situations as a spontaneously existing infant and being willing to be an infant forever. One of the terms developed in the maha ati tradition for this principle is *shönü pum ku,* "youthful prince in a vase."

The vase represents an embryonic situation—embryonic, but at the same time youthful. Breaking the vase is reversing the trikaya principle. You have gained dharmakaya; when the vase is broken, you come back down to sambhogakaya and nirmanakaya; you come back down to earth. A similar process is symbolized by the Zen Ox-Herding Pictures. After the point where there is no more ox and no more ox herd, you return to the world.

So the main focus here is the youthfulness of the enlightened state of being. This youthfulness is the immediacy of experience, the exploratory quality of it.

"But wouldn't exploring age us, make us old?" we might ask. We have to put so much energy into exploring. Do we not become like a traveler who grows old through traveling? From the point of view of crazy wisdom, this is not the case. Exploring is no strain. You might have to do the same thing again and again, but each time, you discover new facets of it, which makes you younger.

Discovery is related with energy that feeds you constantly. It brings your life to a very full, healthy state. So each time you explore, you gain new health. You constantly come back to a sense of being up-to-date in your experience of the world, of your life. So the whole thing becomes constant rejuvenation.

Now that the Padma Raja, the beautiful child, has been kicked out of his kingdom and is wandering somewhere in the suburbs of Indrabhuti's city, experiencing charnel grounds and wastelands with their poisonous snakes, tigers, and so on, let us pause in our story.

Student: The "prince in the vase" already has the dharmakaya quality. When you break the vase, that begins his movement back toward nirmanakaya?

Trungpa Rinpoche: Yes. It is reversing the trikaya.

S: Padmasambhava was born already dharmakaya-like?

TR: Yes. Then he comes down to earth. The gravity pull is compassion. Once you are dharmakaya, you can't just stay there. You return to the world by means of the sambhogakaya and the nirmanakaya.

Student: I encountered the metaphor you used of licking honey from a razor blade in *The Life and Teaching of Naropa*.[4] There it appeared as a simile connected with the four noble truths, that is, portraying suffering that ought to be avoided or that an enlightened person would avoid, knowing it was there. Does your use of it here mean that from Padmasambhava's viewpoint the four noble truths are no longer true?

Trungpa Rinpoche: It's a different way of approaching the truths—or not exactly different, but authentic, we might say. Here, suffering is not regarded as something that you should avoid or abandon; rather, it should be regarded as truth. See what I mean?

S: It's what you taste.

TR: It's what you taste, yes, while exploring the subtleties of everything as an infant would.

S: Does that exploration have to be painful?

TR: Pain is arbitrary at this point. Experiences are not particularly regarded as painful or pleasurable. They just are.

Student: You said that the child was fearless. And then you said that cowardice is the path. Aren't those two contradictory?

Trungpa Rinpoche: They both amount to the same thing at this point. You are fearless because you don't go beyond certain limitations; you are fearless "as it is," and therefore you are a coward at the same time. That may be very difficult to grasp. I don't know whether I am making myself clear.

Student: I have the same question. When you tell us, "It's up to you," it seems that we have a choice about what our limitations are, almost as though we created them ourselves.

Trungpa Rinpoche: I don't see why not, because your limitations are *your* limitations.

S: They don't feel like *my* limitations. They're something that I discover as I go along.

TR: Well, you had to discover them, so you manufactured them as you went along.

S: You mean to say, if I wanted to, I could discover other limitations instead?

TR: Precisely! That's the whole point.

S: What's the point about going beyond them? You seemed to say that crazy wisdom discouraged going beyond them.

TR: Yes.

S: Going beyond them would be like going into some realm of utter fear or something?

TR: Well, this is very simple—kindergarten level. Going beyond your limitations is making things up rather than actually going beyond your limitations. It's manufacturing a dream world.

S: Are you making a distinction between made-up limitations and more real ones?

TR: Sure.

S: And you shouldn't try to go beyond the more real ones?

TR: You can't go beyond them anyway. They're real ones. You can't. you can't relate with them. You'd be going beyond your strength.

S: Then there's no danger of going beyond the natural limitation?

TR: Well, one tends very often to try to explore it.

S: Then what's the difference between exploring it and going beyond it?

TR: The difference is if you go beyond your own limitation, you get hurt. You get some message.

S: So how does fearlessness apply in this situation?

TR: You see, the point is, we do not even trust our own abilities. Usually we don't. That's where fearlessness could play an important part—in exploring the complete realm of your strength. But then going beyond that is frivolous; if you do that, you're subject to destruction. So fearlessness is not a matter of doing something outrageous outside of your realm, but of exploring the complete range of your whole strength.

S: What would keep a fearless person from exploring beyond his own strength?

TR: Some message will come back to that person.

S: Would that really prevent a person who is fearless from going beyond, from exploring everything?

TR: Fearlessness is still a conditional situation; such a person wouldn't be fearless of *everything*.

S: Is this the use of cowardice as intelligence?

TR: Yes.

S: Is that the wisdom part of crazy wisdom?

TR: Somewhat. If you regard crazy wisdom as just being completely outrageous, that's not particularly good or healthy. You are letting yourself in for destruction. That's the usual idea people have, you know: if you're trying to freak out, just push more, push more.

S: It seems that such boundaries presuppose a structure that is independent of oneself—a structure of boundaries out there beyond which a person shouldn't really venture.

TR: Not quite. It is dependent upon one's relationship with the structure.

S: The message that I get out of all this is one should try to be aware of one's limitations so as not to step over them and get hurt.

TR: Not exactly. It's a question of being cautious.

S: How do you know when you're being cautious? This seems to be the point. How do you know when you should pull back or when you should go forward?

TR: You have to relate to what's happening in the whole process. When you begin to notice a deceptive attitude like "Maybe I could try something better than this," then you have begun to develop fear already because you haven't actually ventured into that area before. A warning comes from the sense of self-deception.

S: How do you become aware of that deception?

TR: It's very obvious. Only we know ourselves. We are the closest person to ourselves that we have. We know when we are deceiving ourselves and when we are not. There's no demonstration needed for that. That's something that's understood between you and yourself.

S: Probably a teacher is very helpful to encourage you in certain areas.

TR: You have your areas already. You already have the possibility of rediscovering your strengths and abilities. Teachers can't follow you, live with you, be your bedfellows all the time. Your teacher cannot always be there to guide you, but your self-deception guides you all the time.

Student: Does karma begin to form in the dharmakaya?

Trungpa Rinpoche: We run into different philosophical opinions of different schools on this point. Some people say that no karma develops at that point, and some say that there is karma in the dharmakaya, because the dharmakaya is also a separate entity and has an allegiance toward nirvana. Longchen Rabjam, the great maha ati teacher, would say that karma has developed already; so our school would say that karma has developed already at the dharmakaya level. The dharmakaya brings you a message of sanity because of the insanity that you have already. So that is a relational action; relational action has already happened. In other words, the potter's wheel of the second nidana has already developed.

Student: Why does Padmasambhava choose such a dramatic means of expressing his dissatisfaction with living in a palace? Why does he have to throw a trident and drop his vajra, piercing a heart and cracking a skull? Why doesn't he just walk out?

Trungpa Rinpoche: Walking out sounds like a cop-out. For him just to disappear and just be discovered as missing sounds like the action of a very transparent person who's afraid to communicate with anything and just flees. Padmasambhava is much more heavy-handed than that.

Student: Is fear something other than just projections?

Trungpa Rinpoche: Fear is the message as well as the radar. It is usually a relationship situation. It's not absolute. It's not independent of dualism. I think the crazy-wisdom approach to fear is not regarding it as a hang-up alone, but realizing it is intelligent. It has a message of its own. Fear is worth respecting. If we dismiss fear as an obstacle and ignore it, then we might end up with accidents. In other words, fear is a very wise message.

S: My experience of fear is that it seems to be a really major manifestation of my confusion. One of the daily experiences is that it's a lie and a trap, a tremendous energy trap. I just try to keep from getting caught up in the impulse of it.

TR: Well, you see, the point is, you can't con fear or frighten fear. You have to respect fear. You might try to tell yourself that it's not real, that it's just false. But that kind of approach is very questionable. It is better to develop some kind of respect, realizing that neurosis also is a message, rather than garbage that you should just throw away. That's the whole starting point—the idea of samsara and nirvana being one. Samsara is not regarded as a nuisance alone, but it has its own potent message that is worthy of respect.

S: I'm far from throwing it away, but at the same time, I don't want to centralize it as an issue, to make a mystery out of it. So it's a very fine balance between not throwing it away and trying to let it go.

TR: Well, you have experience already and you don't have to question the experiencer on how to handle it diplomatically.

S: There doesn't seem to be much choice. The fear has such tremendous power.

TR: Well, that's fine. Then you have no chance to think about it or strategize it. Just leap.

S: There's a kind of fear that's a threat to the ego, when it's one of your illusions that feels threatened. Is there a difference between that kind of fear and the fear of going beyond your real limitations?

TR: There seems to be one, yes. There is the fear of not being able to handle what you have, and there's also a sense of needing something more than what you have. Hesitation to deal with what you have can be conquered by a leap, but needing to improvise further entertainment is a deception.

S: The deception of going beyond your limitations.

TR: Yes.

S: Can you take a leap without worrying about your limitations?

TR: Well, if you can, leap. Otherwise, you can't leap either. If you can, take a leap. Then, as you leap, you come back naturally [to the proper relationship to your limitations]. Unless you try to take a sensational leap. In that case, you don't even know what you're doing, but you do it because you want to entertain yourself. It's like taking an overdose.

Student: Is the sense of discovery you talk about the same as keeping your space open, or is it a different idea?

Trungpa Rinpoche: Well, that seems to be it. Discovery doesn't have to be a manifestation of something. It's an attitude of being willing to accommodate whatever comes along. It is somewhat a sense of the duality of something.

S: Quite often in spiritual trips, particularly when they have spectacular practices, there's a tendency to want some practice that you don't know anything about. Would you think of that as a case of helpful inquisitiveness or discovery?

TR: Not if you don't know what you're getting into. There's a difference between exploring what is there and exploring what isn't there. When a child is playing with the razor's edge, the razor is there and the honey is there on the razor's edge. But if the child is exploring something outside, beyond the edge of the balcony, there's nothing beyond the balcony except a sheer drop. That is suicidal.

Student: When one comes to crazy wisdom, why does one man become like the Madman of Tsang and another become a person like your guru?

Trungpa Rinpoche: I think it just depends on our manifestation and our way of viewing things. It's a question of what we are ready for. My guru was the audience for the Madman of Tsang, and I was the audience for my guru. I wasn't all that crazy at the time, so he wasn't very crazy. But the Madman of Tsang was as crazy as he was because my guru was crazy enough to relate it.

FOUR

Death and the Sense of Experience

THE YOUTHFUL PRINCE'S EXPLORATION of life situations is connected with a sense of eternity. Exploring life situations is making friends with the world, and making friends with the world consists of regarding the world as trustworthy. [It becomes trustworthy because] there is something eternal about it. When we talk about eternity, we are not talking about the eternity of one particular entity continuing on and on, as in the philosophical beliefs of the eternalists. In this case, discontinuity is also an expression of eternity. But before discussing eternity, it might be good to discuss death.

Death is the desolate experience in which our habitual patterns cannot continue as we would like them to. Our habitual patterns cease to function. A new force, a new energy, takes us over, which is "deathness," or discontinuity. It is impossible to approach that discontinuity from any angle. That discontinuity is something you cannot communicate with, because you cannot please that particular force. You can't make friends with it, you can't con it, you can't talk it into anything. It is extremely powerful and uncompromising.

This uncompromisingness also blocks expectations for the future. We have our plans—projects of all kinds that we would like to work on. Even if we are bored with life, we would still like to be able to recover that boredom. There is constant hope that something better might come out of the painful situations of life, or that we might discover some further way to expand pleasurable situations. But the sense of death is very powerful, very organic, and very real.

Nyima Öser.

When you are about to die, it may be that your doctors, your relatives, or your closest friends won't tell you you are going to die. They might find it difficult to communicate this to you. But they communicate an unspoken sympathy, and there is something behind it.

In the conventional world, people do not want to relate with a friend who is dying. They do not want to relate to their friend's experience of death as something personal. It is a mutual embarrassment, a mutual tragedy that they don't want to talk about. If we belong to less conventional circles, we might approach a dying person and say, "You are dying," but at the same time, we try to tell him, "After all, this is nothing bad that's happening to you. You are going to be okay. Think of those promises about ongoing eternity you've heard. Think of God, think of salvation." We still don't want to get to the heart of the matter. We don't talk about purgatory or hell or the tormenting experience of the bardo. We are trying to face the situation, but it is embarrassing. Though we are brave enough to say that someone is going to die, we say, "But still, you're going to be okay. Everybody around you feels positive about this, and we love you. Take the love that we feel toward you with you and make something of it as you pass from this world, as you die." That's the attitude [of avoidance] we have toward death.

The actual experience of death, as I have already explained, is a sense of ceasing to exist. The normal routine of your daily life ceases to function and you turn into something else. The basic impact of the experience is the same whether you believe in rebirth or not: it is the discontinuity of what you are doing. You are leaving your present associates behind. You will no longer be able to read that book that you didn't finish. You will not be able to continue the course you were taking. Maybe people who are involved with the doctrine of rebirth might try to tell you, "When you come back, you will finish this book. You'll be back with us. Maybe you'll be one of our children. Think of those possibilities." They tend to say those kinds of things and make promises of all kinds. They make promises about being with God or coming back to the world and continuing with things you have left behind.

In this kind of talk, there is something that is not quite open. There is some kind of fear, mutual fear, even in spite of beliefs about eternity or reincarnation. There is fear or embarrassment about relating to death. There is always a feeling of something undesirable, even if you are reading your friend a chapter from the *Tibetan Book of the Dead*,[5] or whatever.

You might tell your friend, "Though something terrible is happening to you, there is a greater thing. Now you are actually going to have a chance to get into those experiences described in the *Tibetan Book of the Dead*. And we'll help you do it!" But no matter what we try, there is this sense of something that can't be made all right, no matter what kind of positive picture we try to paint.

It seems, quite surprisingly, that for many people, particularly in the West, reading the *Tibetan Book of the Dead* for the first time is very exciting. Pondering on this fact, I have come to the conclusion that the excitement comes from the fact that tremendous promises are being made. Fascination with the promises made in the *Book of the Dead* almost undermines death itself. We have been looking for so long for a way to undermine our irritations, including death itself. Rich people spend a lot of money on coffins, on makeup for the corpse, on good clothes to dress it up in. They pay for expensive funeral systems. They will try any way at all to undermine the embarrassment connected with death. That is why the *Tibetan Book of the Dead* is so popular and is considered to be so fantastic.

People were very excited and celebratory about the idea of reincarnation in the same way. A few decades ago when the idea of reincarnation became current for the first time, everybody was excited about it. That's another way of undermining death. "You're going to continue; you have your karmic debts to work out and your friends to come back to. Maybe you will come back as my child." Nobody stopped to consider that they might come back as a mosquito or a pet dog or cat.

The type of approach to death we have been discussing is very strange, extremely strange.

When we discuss the discovery of eternity by Vajradhara, as the next aspect of Padmasambhava is called, we are not looking at it as a victory over death or as a replacement for the irritations of death or anything of that nature. Eternity in this sense is connected with a true vision of the facts of life. Pain exists and pleasure exists. A negative aspect of the world does exist. Yet you can still relate with it. Fundamentally, developing this kind of sense of eternity is making friends. We might regard a certain person as a good friend in spite of his threatening qualities. In fact, that is the reason we become friends.

Relating with eternity in this sense is becoming a king of life, a lord of life. And if the lord of life is really a lord, his empire extends to death as well. So the lord of life is the lord of life and death. And this lord of life is known as Vajradhara.

The young prince who has just fled from his kingdom suddenly decides to adapt to the savagery of the charnel ground and to the fundamental principle of eternity, which is often known as the mahamudra experience. The mahamudra experience here is the experience that relates with the living quality of phenomena. That is to say, the whole scene in the charnel ground is *real*. There are skeletons, pieces of bodies, wild animals, ravens, jackals, and so forth.

In the charnel ground, the young prince discovers a new approach to life, or rather, a new approach to life discovers him. We could say that at this stage Padmasambhava becomes a solid citizen, because the sense of eternity brings indestructibility, indestructibility in the sense that nothing can be a threat and nothing can produce comfort. That is the kind of eternity we are referring to here. Death is no longer regarded as a threat. Padmasambhava's experience of death is an experience of one of the aspects of life. He is not concerned with perpetuating his personality and existence. We could say that this approach is more than the yogi's or siddha's approach. This approach is more that of a buddha, since these experiences are not regarded as achievements of any kind—they are not discoveries, victories, or forms of revenge. These experiences simple take place, and because they happen, Padmasambhava tunes in to them. So Padmasambhava as Vajradhara becomes the lord of life and death, the holder of the vajra, the holder of indestructible energy—a sambhogakaya buddha.

The next journey that Padmasambhava makes is connected with his wanting to explore all kinds of teaching situations and wanting to relate with the great teachers of the world of that time. He visits one of the leading teachers of the maha ati tradition, Shri Simha, who supposedly came from Thailand (Siam) and was living in a cave in another charnel ground. Vajradhara, the sambhogakaya aspect of Padmasambhava, went and asked him how to destroy the sense of experience. And Shri Simha reduced Padmasambhava to the syllable HUM, which is penetration. You don't try to dissolve experience or try to regard it as a fallacy. You penetrate experience. Experience is like a container with lots of holes in it, which means that it cannot give you proper shelter, proper comfort. Penetrating or puncturing this is like puncturing a comfortable hammock hanging underneath a tree: [once it is punctured,] when you approach it and try to sit in it, you find that you end up on the ground. That's the penetration of the seed syllable HUM. Reducing Padmasambhava to HUM, Shri Simha swallows him through his mouth and shits him out through his anus. This is bringing him to the nirmanakaya experience of being able to penetrate the phenomenal world thoroughly and completely, of being able to transmit a message to the phenomenal world.

Having destroyed his own sense of survival and achieved a sense of eternity, Padmasambhava now develops a sense of penetration. (Of course, he isn't really developing anything, he is just going through these phases. We are telling the story of Padmasambhava in accordance with how we have manufactured him, rather than trying to express that he did all those things.) This is when Padmasambhava became known as the great yogi who could control time, who could control day and night and the four seasons. This yogi aspect of Padmasambhava is called Nyima Öser. Nyima Öser penetrated all the conceptualizations of time, day and night, the four seasons. In his iconography, he is seen holding the sun still, using its rays as a tether.

The idea here is not that some achievement of a subtle experience can bring you to such complete absorption that you cease to experience the distinctions between night and day and the four seasons. Rather, the conceptualized attitudes toward day and night and the four seasons—or toward pain and pleasure or whatever—are penetrated through. Usually, day and night and the four seasons bring us comfort by giving us the feeling we are relating with reality, with the elements: "Now we are relating with summer, now we are relating with autumn, now we are relating with winter, and now we are relating with spring. How good to be alive! How good to be on earth, man's best place, his home! It's getting late; it's time for dinner. We could begin the day with a hearty breakfast." And so forth. Our lifestyle is governed by these concepts. There are lots of things to do as time goes along, and relating with them is like swinging in a hammock, a comfortable bed in the open air. But Nyima Öser punctured this hammock. Now you can't have a good time swinging and having a comfortable snooze in the open air. That's the penetrating quality here.

Student: You are having a comfortable snooze in this hammock. Then you penetrate the comfortable appearance of this hammock. So where does that leave you—standing up?

Trungpa Rinpoche: You find yourself on the ground.

S: But alert somehow?

TR: Yes. One of the qualities seems to be a sense of awake rather than absorption.

Student: If Padmasambhava is the great yogi who controls time, does that mean that time doesn't control him the way it does us?

Trungpa Rinpoche: It's not really a matter of controlling time or not being controlled by it. It's discovering timelessness. If you translate this into a kind of peasant language, then you could say "controlling time."

Student: You have repeatedly emphasized that Padmasambhava doesn't learn anything and in a sense knows everything. I don't understand why we can't look upon him as an ordinary human, like any one of us, who has learned various things at various stages.

Trungpa Rinpoche: We could equally well relate with our own stages in this way. Our process of spiritual development, or whatever you want to call it, is an unlearning process rather than one of collecting new experiences. Padmasambhava's style is unmasking, unlearning—layers and layers of phenomenal covering are gradually removed.

S: The unmasking, or unlearning, process seems to be like a series of deaths. Why does that have to be so painful? Why can't it be like a kind of liberation and have a kind of joyous feeling?

TR: Well, it is joyous, and maybe we are complaining too much. We are more aware of the intensity of the darkness than of the brilliance of the light.

S: It seems that the proper way to relate to death is without any strategy. Do you have to give up your fear before you can be without a strategy? Or can you just relate to your fear?

TR: Fear is a very interesting thing, actually. It has insight as well as the panicky blind quality. So it seems that if you give up hope of attaining anything, then tuning in to fear is tuning in to insight. And skillful means arise spontaneously out of fear itself, because fear seems to be extremely resourceful. It is the opposite of hopelessness, in fact. But fear also has the element of panic and the deaf and dumb quality—you know, doing the best you can. But fear without hope seems to be something very insightful.

S: Is fear insightful in that it points to why you were afraid in the first place?

TR: Not only that. It has its own intuitive aspect going beyond just logical conclusions. It has spontaneously existing resourcefulness.

S: Could you say more about that?

TR: When you connect with your fear, you realize you have already leapt, you are already in midair. You realize that, and then you become resourceful.

S: Isn't that what we are all doing—being resourceful out of no-where?

TR: We don't realize that we're already in midair.

Student: Rinpoche, you say that fear without hope would be intelligent. Could the same be said about the other intense emotions?

Trungpa Rinpoche: Hope and fear largely constitute the rest of the emotions. Hope and fear represent the kind of pushing and pulling quality of duality, and all the emotions consist of that. They are different aspects of that; they all seem to be made out of hope and fear of something—pulling and magnetizing or fending off.

S: Is having fear also desire of the same thing you are afraid of?

TR: Yes, that's the way it is. But when you realize that there is nothing to be desirous *of* (you know, the desire is the hope aspect of the fear), when you realize that, then you and your fear are left nakedly standing alone.

S: So you just connect with the fear without hope. But how do you do that?

TR: It's relating without feedback. Then the situation automatically intensifies or becomes clear.

S: Can you apply the same approach to anger? If I'm angry, instead of either expressing or suppressing it, I just relate to it? I stop the anger and just relate to the thought process?

TR: You don't stop the anger, you just *are* the anger. Anger just hangs out as it is. That is relating with the anger. Then the anger becomes vivid and directionless, and it diffuses into energy. The idea of relating with it has nothing to do with expressing yourself to the other person. The Tibetan expression for that is *rang sar shak*, which means "leave it in its own place." Let anger be in its own place.

Student: I still don't understand what we should try to communicate to a dying person.

Trungpa Rinpoche: You see, death is a very *real* experience. Usually, we do not connect with a sense of reality. If we have an accident—or whatever happens in our lives—we do not regard it as a real experience, even though it may hurt us. It is real to us as far as pain and physical damages are concerned, but still it's not real for us because we immediately look at it in terms of how it could be otherwise. There's always the idea of first aid or some other redeeming aspect of the situation. If you are talking to a dying friend or relative, you should transmit the idea that death is a real experience, rather than that it's just a joke and the person could get better. Often people tell the dying person things like, "Life is really a joke altogether. The great saints say it's not real. Life is unreal. What is death, anyway?" When we try to take this kind of approach, we become jumpy ourselves; and that jumpiness is what we end up communicating to the dying person. We should help them to understand that death is real.

FIVE

The Lion's Roar

W E HAVE LOOKED INTO THE IDEA of timelessness, or eternity. It might be necessary for us now to look a bit further. Conquering or transcending the sense of experience brings us to something completely nondualistic. We might call it sanity. The aspect of Padmasambhava known as Nyima Öser displayed sanity in relating to the concept of time and to ideas or experience connected with spiritual achievement. Having looked briefly into his example, we might now go ahead and discuss another aspect of Padmasambhava: Shakya Senge, Padmasambhava as buddha

The principle connected with this aspect of Padmasambhava is that, once one has already conquered any sense of gaining anything in the relative world, one has to go ahead and make a relationship with complete and total sanity, the awakened state of mind. Shakya Senge, Padmasambhava as buddha, is concerned with this. Shakya Senge is not buddha in the hinayana sense but in the mahayana sense. The mahayana style of Padmasambhava has to do with utterance of the lion's roar, which in the mahayana teaching refers to proclaiming the teaching of shunyata, the ultimate sanity. So, this aspect of Padmasambhava is connected with the expression of the ultimate sanity.

You might ask, "How could this ultimate sanity go further than conquering conceptuality and the sense of experience? Is there something more than that? Isn't that enough?" At this point, there is something more subtle than that. Conquering conceptuality and the sense of experience is a step toward proclamation. First you have to conquer the enemy, then you can proclaim that you have gained victory over him. In making the proclamation referred to as the lion's roar, Padmasambhava as buddha further emphasizes that sanity. The lion's roar is not regarded as a challenge, but as an adornment. It is not a challenge concerning whether the conquering process has been accomplished or not. Rather, when you have already achieved victory, then the victory brings a sense of good news. Proclamation of this good news is the lion's roar.

In connection with Padmasambhava's life, good news is ultimate good news. It is the good news that the spiritual journey need never have been made. The journey has already been completed; therefore, there's no point in searching or trying to gain further insights. The needlessness of making the spiritual journey is the good news. That is the lion's roar. This is something much more than what the mahayana sutras talk about. The mahayana sutras talk about attainment of perfect sanity through realizing that form is emptiness and emptiness is form, and so forth. But the lion's roar that we are talking about here is something much more than that. It goes further in that the ultimate good news is independent of any victory. It is ultimate.

What is Padmasambhava's style of manifesting crazy wisdom in this context? He is the universal monarch who looks down over the yanas of the teachings rather than up to them.

According to the story, Padmasambhava studied with Ananda, the attendant and disciple of the Buddha. He was ordained by Ananda as a bhikshu, and he attained understanding of the message of the Buddha. Padmasambhava regarded Ananda, the Buddha's disciple, more as a guru than as a preceptor. That is an important distinction. He regarded him as a guru rather than as a master of discipline, an informant, a professor, or a teacher in the ordinary sense, because Ananda was in the direct lineage of transmission from the Buddha. This meant that working with him involved a living relationship with the teachings.

Padmasambhava's realization here is something we can relate to as well. The sense of dignity that speaks out and expresses that the journey need never have been made is true. The idea that the spiritual journey needs to be made is a deception. From that point of view, even the ten bhumis of the bodhisattva path are a sophistry. Since there are no bhumis at all, how could there be ten of them?

Seeing things in this way is a part of the crazy wisdom of directness, complete directness. It involves directly relating with sanity, or bodhi mind, with the experience of the Buddha when he attained vajra-like samadhi sitting in the shade of the bodhi tree. It is also a further step toward trusting in buddha nature. At this point, we cannot even call it buddha *nature,* because "nature" automatically implies something embryonic. But in this case, we are not talking about something embryonic but about the living Buddha. Padmasambhava associated himself with the Buddha and discovered sanity. He related with Ananda as the messenger who awakened his inspiration.

A guru does not really transmit spiritual entities into us or through us. A guru just reminds us that there is sanity already in us. So Ananda only provided—or for that matter, Padmasambhava only provides—a reminder that things are so in this way.

We might find it difficult to follow what this experience is about or to identify ourselves with it. We might find hearing about this like listening to a story in which such-and-such a thing happened and then after that everybody lived happily ever after. But the story of Padmasambhava should be something more than that. If we actually relate with what happens in the life of Padmasambhava, we will find that it is quite realistic and personal. We acknowledge sanity, and then sanity comes about by itself.

Acknowledging sanity is a discipline or a pretense: you pretend to be the Buddha; you believe you *are* the Buddha. Again, we are not talking about buddha nature as an embryonic state, but of the living situation of buddhahood having already happened. We adopt such a pretense at the beginning, or maybe we should call it a belief. It is a belief in the sense that our buddhahood is seemingly not real, but we take it as a reality. Some element of mind's trickery is necessary. And then we find ourselves having been tricked into enlightenment.

There are all kinds of tricks that exist as part of the teaching process. They are known as skillful means. That seems to be something of a euphemism.

Skillful means are part of the spiritual tradition. The lineage gurus' conduct in relating with students is a traditional discipline. Skillful means are necessary, because there is a tendency to run away from sanity of this nature. Students might find sanity too spacious, too irritating. We would prefer a little claustrophobic insanity, snug and comforting insanity. Getting into that is like crawling back into a marsupial's pouch. That's the usual tendency, because acknowledging precision and sanity is too crispy, too cool, too cold. It's too early to wake up; we'd rather go back to bed. Going back to bed is relating to the mind's deceptions, which in fact we prefer. We like to get a little bit confused and set up our homes in that. We don't prefer sanity or enlightenment in fact. That seems to be the problem rather than that we don't have it or can't get it. If we really prefer basic sanity or enlightenment, it's irritatingly possible to get into it.

That seems to have been the approach of Padmasambhava's Shakya Senge aspect: he preferred to become like the Buddha. He went to see Ananda and talked to him about the Buddha. He studied with Ananda, worked with him, and he became buddha. You might say, "That's too quick," but nevertheless, it happened.

Then we have another aspect of Padmasambhava, called Senge Dradrok, which again is connected with the lion's roar. The name actually means "lion's roar" or, more literally, "making a noise like a lion." In this aspect, Padmasambhava manifests as a defender of the faith, a great magician.

At that time in India, there were major incursions of heretics, or tirthikas, as they are called in Sanskrit. They were Hindus. They are referred to as heretics because of their belief in duality—in the existence of an external divine being and in the existence of atman as the recipient of that divine being.

Of course, you might criticize this approach, saying that we all should have high regard for the sacred writings of Hinduism, especially the mystical teachings of Hinduism such as the Vedanta. And actually, the vedantic writings themselves do not quite express things dualistically; they are not quite in the dualistic style of spirituality. But the heretics that Padmasambhava was dealing with were believers in the literal truth of dualism. They misunderstood the real depth of the mystic teachings and believed in an external god and an internal ego. Strangely enough, believing in this kind of separateness can bring about very powerful psychic powers. Miracles of all kinds can be performed, and some technical and intellectual understanding of the teachings can be developed.

In relation to these heretics, Padmasambhava acted as an organic agent, an agent of the natural action of the elements. If you mistreat the fire in your fireplace, your house will catch fire. If you don't pay enough attention while cutting your carrots, you might cut your finger. It is this mindlessness and mistreatment of the natural situation that is the heretical quality. Rather than regarding existing situations of nonduality as they are, you try to interpret them a bit so that they help to maintain your existence. For example, believing in God is a way of making sure that *you* exist. Singing a song of praise to God makes *you* happier, because *you* are singing the song about him. Since there is a good audience, a good recipient, therefore God exists. That kind of approach is heretical from the Buddhist point of view.

At that time, the great Buddhist monasteries in a certain part of India were being challenged by Hindu pandits. The Hindu pandits were coming to the monasteries and teaching, and the monks were rapidly turning into Hindus. It was a tremendous catastrophe. So Padmasambhava was asked to come. Those who invited him said, "We can't seem to match those Hindu pandits intellectually, so please save us by performing some magic for us. Maybe that is the only solution."

Padmasambhava came to live in one of the monasteries. One day, he produced an earthquake by pointing his trident in the direction of the Hindu pandits. There were landslides, and five hundred Hindu pandits were destroyed.

What do you make of that?

When somebody becomes unreasonable, they create their own destruction. By putting it that way, I am not trying to make sure that you are not put off by Padmasambhava and his activities. I am not acting as his spokesman and saying, "He's good anyway, in spite of those actions of his." It is simply that with him acting as the agent of the elements, of the organic process, the unreasonable and man-made element had to be diminished.

People in Bhutan were recently trying to build a road from India to Bhutan, called the Bhutan National Highway. They were building and building. They had bulldozers and they had Indian road-making experts. They spent millions and millions of rupees, and they built a beautiful road. But when the rainy season came, the whole road was swept away by tremendous landslides. By building a road, you interfere with the mountain, with the structure of the rock. As the only possible reaction of nature to that disturbance, landslides develop. Then once again there is another project requiring millions of rupees, and this process goes on and on.

The last time it happened was when the president of India was paying a state visit to Bhutan. The airplane that was carrying India's gifts to the Bhutanese king and government got lost in the mist and crashed in the Bhutanese mountains. And as the Indian president was preparing to return to India, sudden landslides took place as a farewell gesture to him.

I'm not saying that the president of India is a heretic, but the definition of heresy here is very delicate. If you are not in tune with the nature of reality, you are making yourself into a target, an extra satellite. And there's no one to feed you. There's no fuel for you except your own resources, and you are bound to die because you can't keep regenerating without further resources. That is what happened to the pandits whom Padmasambhava killed. This is very uncompassionate or outrageous, but Padmasambhava in this case is representing the nature of reality rather than acting as a black magician or white magician.

It seems that we cannot be instructed how to perform acts such as the destruction of the pandits. Although the teachings have been handed down through generations and generations without interruption or perversion, so that even now we possess the complete teachings of Padmasambhava, none of those teachings talk about how to kill heretics. There are no such teachings. But the teachings do talk about how to work with practice and your attitude toward it organically. You do that, and the perverters of the teachings destroy themselves. That seems to be the basic message here. That seems to be the aspect of Padmasambhava called "Lion's Roar," or Senge Dradrok.

Student: Will the elements also organically protect those who don't pervert the teachings?
Trungpa Rinpoche: Maybe.

Student: Is Padmasambhava's organic action in connection with the elements the same as the action of the dharmapalas, the protectors of the teachings?
Trungpa Rinpoche: Somewhat, yes. But it is also more than the action of the dharmapalas. The dharmapalas are just sort of reminders. But in this case, there is a complete message.
S: Isn't what you are calling the "action of the elements" or "a complete message" in a sense just karmic action?
TR: It is karmic action in the sense that there is an organic thing happening, but there's also something specially organic, which has the

quality of being deliberate. There seem to be two patterns. There is a difference between a landslide occurring in the area of a coal mine and the landslide that happened in the heretics' home.

Student: This business of tricking yourself into being buddha is not at all clear to me. It sounds so un-Buddhist to use your mind to trick yourself. Is that different from what you talk about as deception, as conning yourself, conning experience?

Trungpa Rinpoche: It's quite different. The deception of conning yourself has to be based on elaborate strategies. Tricking yourself into becoming buddha is immediate. It happens on the spot.

S: But if I say to myself, "I am buddha," when I don't really know what buddha is—

TR: It doesn't really matter. That's the whole point—we don't know what buddha is. And maybe not knowing what buddha is, is buddha.

S: Well, it doesn't seem like you actually do anything then. Do you do something?

TR: It's up to you. You have to develop your own system.

S: Does it differ from just confidence?

TR: Yes. It's a quick switch, as if the carpet were being pulled out from under your feet. Or your feet were being pulled over the carpet. It's true. It can be done.

S: It's like tripping out then?

TR: Tripping out takes a lot of preparation. But if you are tricked, it takes you by surprise, as though nothing had happened.

S: Is that connected with visualizations and mantra practice?

TR: It's something much more immediate than that. It's just a change of attitude. Instead of trying to become buddha, you suddenly realize that buddha is trying to become you.

S: Does this have anything to do with an abhisheka, an empowerment?

TR: I think so, yes. That's what's called the fourth abhisheka, the sudden introduction of nowness.

S: It seems that there's a whole process of preparation that's necessary for this shift in perspective to take place.

TR: You have to be willing to do that. That's liberation. Apart from that, there is nothing more. It's a question of your being willing to do it; that's the important point. You have to be willing to commit yourself to going through the discomforts that might occur after you are buddha.

Student: Earlier you talked about eternity and Padmasambhava being turned into a HUM. Would being turned into a HUM be like a death experience? Would you have to dissolve in order to penetrate experience? Would you have to die?

Trungpa Rinpoche: Penetration is not particularly connected with death. Being turned into a HUM is becoming an intense person. You become a capsulized being. You are reduced to a capsule, a very concentrated sense of being yourself. You are just a grain of sand. It is not dissolving but being intensified into one dot.

S: When Shri Simha swallowed Padmasambhava and shat him out, was that still him?

TR: Naturally. The analogy is swallowing a diamond. When you shit it out, it's still a genuine diamond.

Student: Penetration seems to involve a sense of sharpness. You're in the midst of an egoistic manipulation, and then something wakes you up with a kind of sharpness.

Trungpa Rinpoche: The sharpness that cuts through neurotic mind seems to be like a two-edged razor that cuts in both directions simultaneously, so the only thing that exists is the sharpness itself. It's not like a needle, not like an ax. It cuts both the projection and the projector at the same time. That is why there is a craziness aspect: the user gets cut by that razor as does what he is using it on. That makes it humorous, too. Nobody wins the battle. The enemy gets destroyed and the defender gets destroyed as well—simultaneously—so it's very crazy. Usually, if you're fighting against something, you're supposed to win, but in this case you don't. Both sides get destroyed. Nobody wins. In other words, both win.

Student: This seems to be connected with shunyata. There could be a gap at any instant, and then there seems to be another kind of sharpness—

Trungpa Rinpoche: That's quite different. When there's a sense of gap, there's no blade to cut anything. It's self-perpetuating in the sense of HUM. From that point of view, the shunyata experience and crazy wisdom are different. Compared to crazy wisdom, shunyata provides a home, a mutual home, a comfortable home, whereas crazy wisdom provides a constant cutting process. The tantric approach is related with energy; the shunyata experience is just wisdom alone, wisdom without energy. It's a discovery, an experience, a nest of some kind.

Student: What was Padmasambhava's motivation in wanting to become buddha? I'm thinking of what you said earlier: we don't want that uncomfortable state; we want the comfort of claustrophobia and insanity.

Trungpa Rinpoche: Yes. I suppose as far as samsaric mind is concerned, it's a perverted motivation. It is going against that tendency of wanting a home. It goes against the grain of what our parents always say to us: "Don't you want to get married and have a job and a comfortable home instead of just sitting and meditating?"

S: But is there some motivation that is not from the samsaric point of view but that exists in its own right?

TR: Outlandishness. Being uncivilized.

S: Is that a part of ourselves that we could discover or cultivate in some way?

TR: That's what we have to see. That's what we have to find out. There's no prescription.

S: Is this outlandishness something that we already experience occasionally as part of our lives or something we haven't experienced yet?

TR: I don't know. Let's find out.

Student: Is what you said before about buddha trying to become you—is that the motivating factor?

Trungpa Rinpoche: Well, there is something very strange going on. You are absolutely comfortable and happy the way you are, yet at the same time, you find it excruciatingly painful. You are not certain whether you want to stay the way you are, which is very pleasurable, or not stay the way you are, because it is very painful at the same time. That kind of pushing and pulling happens all the time. That seems to be the motivation. You want to keep your habitual patterns, but at the same time, you find them too monotonous—that's the kind of motivation. I mean, we cannot define that as being something special. We cannot say you are making a journey in some particular direction. The directions are confused. You are *not* confused about whether you are coming or going, but you *still* want to do something about the situation. That is the contagious quality of buddha nature, which is trying to shine through all the time, seemingly.

SIX

Intellect and Working with Negativity

THE NEXT ASPECT of Padmasambhava is actually called Padmasambhava. For some strange reason, "Padmasambhava" became popular as the general name for all the iconographical aspects of this figure. Maybe a certain Gelukpa influence crept into the naming process. Followers of Padmasambhava in Tibet usually refer to him as Guru Rinpoche or Pema Jungne, "the Lotus-Born," which is Padmakara in Sanskrit. Padmasambhava is then the name of only one of the aspects. It seems this has something to do with a sectarian squabble in which one party holds that Padmasambhava is not a cosmic principle, but just a pandit named Padmasambhava.

In any case, the particular aspect known as Padmasambhava was a pandit, a scholar. He entered Nalanda University and studied what is known as the threefold discipline: meditation; morality; and knowledge, or learning. Those three disciplines correspond to the three sections of the Buddhist scripture called the Tripitaka. One section of the Tripitaka discusses monastic discipline, another the basic teachings of the sutras, and the third the psychological structure of beings.

People frequently ask, "Wouldn't it be possible on the spiritual path not to do any studying at all? Can't we just meditate a lot and learn everything from our experiences?" Many people believe that if you sit and meditate a lot, you don't have to read scriptures or study anything at all. They say that just by meditating everything will come to you. That approach seems to be one-sided. It leaves no room for sharpening

123

Loden Choksi.

the intellect or for disciplining the mind. It also does not take into account the knowledge that protects us from indulging in states of absorption, knowledge that tells us that it is necessary to let go of particular states and bring ourselves into another frame of mind. Study and scholastic learning play an extremely important part for us. This is what is demonstrated by Padmasambhava in his pandit aspect.

One of the problems connected with intellect and intellectual understanding is that if we look for and come up with answers, conclusions, logical deductions, we tend to end up with a high opinion of our understanding. If we develop that, then we may no longer be able to experience things properly or learn anything more from the teachings at all. We become hardened scholars and bookworms. We might begin to feel that practices are unsafe if we do not know what they are, so we have to study them scholastically first. This attitude might go as far as saying that if you really want to study the Buddhist teachings, first you have to learn Sanskrit as well as Japanese or Tibetan. You can't even begin to practice meditation until you have learned those languages and studied the appropriate texts.

This attitude suggests that the student should become a superscholar. When the student has become an extremely perfect scholar, he has attained buddhahood. He has all the answers; he knows everything inside out. This kind of omniscience, according to this view, makes one a buddha.

This view that the enlightened being is a learned person, a great scholar, is a misunderstanding, another extreme. Enlightenment is not purely a matter of collecting information. If a buddha didn't know how to change his snow tires, for example, a person with this view might begin to have doubts about him. After all, he is supposed to be the omniscient one; how could he be a buddha if he doesn't know how to do that? The perfect buddha would be able to surprise you with his knowledge in every area. He would be a good cook, a good mechanic, a good scientist, a good poet, a good musician—he would be good at everything. That is a diluted and diffused idea of buddha, to say the least. He is not that kind of universal expert nor a superprofessor.

But if the proper idea of intellectual understanding and sharpening the intellect is not feeding oneself millions of bits of information and making oneself into a walking library, then what is it? It is connected with developing sharpness and precision in relating with the nature of reality. This has nothing to do with dwelling on logical conclusions or concepts. One has to have a neutral attitude in one's intellectual study of the teaching, one that is neither purely critical nor purely devotional. One doesn't try to come to conclusions. The purpose of study, rather than to come to conclusions, is to experience things logically and sensibly. This seems to be the middle way [between the two extremes of rejecting the intellect and emphasizing it exclusively].

Becoming accomplished in intellectual study usually means forming strong opinions. If you are a scholar, your name becomes worth mentioning if you have made some intellectual discovery. But what we are talking about here is not exactly discovery in the professorial sense, but rather discovery on the level of examining and dealing with personal experience. Through such a process, your personal experience is worked through—it is beaten, burned, and hammered as in working with gold, to use a scriptural analogy. In dealing with your experience, you eat, you chew, and you finally swallow and digest. In this way, the *whole thing* becomes workable; your focus is not purely on highlights, such as developing your personality into that of a great learned person—a Buddhologist or a Tibetologist or something like that.

In other words, intellect here means absence of a watcher. If we watch ourselves learning—watch ourselves growing, developing, becoming more and more scholastic people—then we are comparing ourselves with "other." We are constantly gaining weight in our egos, because we are comparing ourselves with "other." Whereas if there is experience of intellectual study going on without a watcher, it becomes very simple and direct. This kind of intellect without a watcher has qualities similar to what we were describing earlier in connection with the experience of the young prince. It is open, willing to explore. It is without a particular attitude. It is without a sense that you want what is happening to be replaced by information. It is a constant discovery of new situations in life and what the teachings and scriptures have to say about them. It means discovering the subtleties and feelings related with different aspects of Buddhism. It means understanding the whole geography of the teachings, so that you are not bewildered by some new approach, some new wisdom. You are not bewildered, because you know what area of human psychology a particular approach is connected with. In this way, whatever comes up in relation to the teaching becomes very simple, very easy and workable. This was the practice exemplified by Padmasambhava as Padmasambhava. He became a great pandit because he worked with his intellect without a watcher. On the basis of his example, we can also work with intellect without a watcher.

You might ask, "If there is no watcher, how do we know that we have understood what we have learned?" But it is possible to approach learning and understanding other than by collecting information for the sake of gaining a new personality or developing a new ego. That is not the only way. There are other ways for one to be highly scholastic, highly intellectual. It is possible to do that without a watcher.

Another aspect of Padmasambhava is known as Loden Choksi, who was a rajguru, as they called the spiritual teacher of a royal family in India. The way Loden Choksi came to be a rajguru is an interesting story. He was wandering from place to place when he came to a nunnery. He began instructing the head nun there, who was the princess of the kingdom of Sahor. Sahor was somewhere in the area of Himachal Pradesh in present-day northern India. The princess was very precious for this kingdom, because she had been invited to become the queen of a number of neighboring kingdoms, as well as of important kingdoms like China, Persia, and (according to the story) the Roman Empire. Despite these invitations, the princess refused to have anything to do with worldly power and pleasures. She wanted to become a Buddhist nun, and she did. The king of Sahor was extremely fearful that if the princess was not successful in maintaining her nunhood [this would be regarded as a deception and a political affront by those kingdoms whose invitations she had rejected and] that they might attack his kingdom. [Therefore, the king surrounded her with five hundred nuns to guard her in her discipline.]

So Padmasambhava was there giving teachings to the princess and the five hundred nuns when a local cowherd passed by and heard a man's voice coming out of the nunnery. Word of this spread throughout the kingdom and created a huge scandal. At some point, the king and queen and their ministers heard the story. They hoped to be able to expose the scandal as based on a false rumor, but were unable to track down the cowherd who was the original witness. They had a collection of lots of gifts placed at the entrance to the royal courtyard and let it be known that if the original witness would come forward and tell his story, he would receive all these gifts. There was gold, silver, jewelry, silks, and so on. Finally, the herdsman appeared and told his story, which actually seemed to be true. He had no ulterior motive for spreading a scandal in the kingdom.

The king sent one of his ministers to find out what was happening at the nunnery. The minister found the doors completely locked, and the nuns would not let anyone inside, even if it was a messenger from the king who just wanted to inspect. The king suspected that something funny was going on at the nunnery and sent his soldiers to break in. They did so and found Padmasambhava sitting on the throne in the assembly hall, instructing the nuns.

The soldiers tried to seize Padmasambhava but found it very difficult, bewilderingly difficult, to get hold of him. They couldn't catch him at all. At this point, the king became extremely upset and angry and sent a huge number of troops to the nunnery. The troops finally captured Padmasambhava and all the nuns.

The traditional means of execution of this country was burning the prisoner alive in a sandalwood fire. So they put Padmasambhava in a sandalwood fire, and the princess was put into a dungeon filled with thorns. The sandalwood fire, which usually died after twenty-four hours, continued to burn for a long time. With other criminals, there was usually no difficulty, but in this case, the fire continued to burn and smoke for about three weeks. The king and the people began to wonder what the problem was. Could it be possible that there was something unusual about this wanderer they had burned? The king decided he wanted to collect some pieces of this wanderer's bones in case they might have interesting magical properties. He sent a messenger to the place where the fire was, an the messenger found that a huge lake had appeared on the spot, with logs still aflame around the edges of it. In the middle of this lake was a lotus flower with Padmasambhava sitting on it.

The king realized he had made a big mistake and began speaking to Padmasambhava. Padmasambhava sang a song, saying, "Welcome to the great sinner, welcome to the king trapped in confusion," and so forth. The king invited Padmasambhava to come to his palace. Padmasambhava finally accepted his invitation. At this point, according to the story, Padmasambhava conducted sadhana practices of the vajradhatu mandala at the king's palace. The result, according to the story, is that the kingdom was completely emptied out in seven years' time. The whole civilization dissolved as people became great yogis and found there was no point in sticking to ordinary domestic work. They all became crazy.

In this story, Loden Choksi, the rajguru aspect of Padmasambhava, performed a miracle. His miracle was not merely converting the king; the miracle was his manner of dealing with whatever threats or accusations arose. Loden Choksi manifested the invincibility of Padmasambhava. Any challenge to him, rather than being viewed as a threat, turned into a further adornment of his action. Using obstacles as a way of working with life situations plays a very important part in crazy wisdom.

This may be a familiar idea for people already exposed to the teachings of crazy wisdom, but for most people, who think of spirituality as based purely on goodness, any kind of opposition or obstacle is considered a manifestation of evil. Regarding obstacles as adornments is quite an unusual idea. If there is a threat to the teacher or the teaching, it tends to be categorized immediately as the "work of the devil." In this view, the idea is to try not to relate to the obstacles or threats, but to cast them out as something bad, something antagonistic to the teaching. You should just purify yourself of this work of the devil. You should abandon it, rather than exploring it as part of the organic and integral development of the situation you are working with. You regard it purely as a problem.

I suppose if those of us already familiar with these teachings would look into ourselves on a very subtle level, we might still find some element of this approach. Although we know the philosophy and the ideas—we know we are supposed to work with negativity and use it as an adornment—nevertheless, there is still some sense of trying to find alternatives, of trying to find some kind of underlying promise.

Actually, this happens quite a lot with our students. People talk about relating to negativity as part of the development of the situation, but then they regard this approach in itself as an alternative way of solving the problem of negativity. Even older students are constantly asking questions, publicly and in private, based on this alternative-solution approach. They still believe that there is a "best way"; they still believe there is a way to some kind of happiness. Although we know we are supposed to relate to pain and misery as part of the path, we still try to regard *that* as a way to happiness, as a way of solving the problem, as a better alternative. If we had been Padmasambhava as the rajguru, we would have tried to talk to the guards who arrested us before they put us in the fire. We would have said, "This is a great mistake; you mustn't do this. You don't understand what you're doing." We would try this, rather than letting the event happen, rather than letting action speak louder than words.

There still seems to be some kind of timidity in our general approach. We are timid in the sense that, no matter how subtle or obvious the teachings may be, we are still not reconciled to the notion that "pain and pleasure alike are ornaments which it is pleasant to wear."⁶ We might read it, we might say it, but still we find it magnificent to twist the twist and feel that misery or negativity is good: "We have to work with it. Okay, I've been doing that. Lately I've been finding all kinds of rough and rugged things going on in my mind and in my life. It's not particularly pleasant, but all in all it's *interesting* for me." There is some tinge of hope. The idea of finding the negativity "interesting" is that somehow as we go along we will be saved. The unspoken implication is that finally the whole thing is going to be good and pleasurable. It's very subtle. It is almost as though there's an unspoken agreement that in the end all roads are going to lead to Rome.

We are still struggling along with the hinayana mentality, even though we are talking about the most profound teachings of crazy wisdom. We are still thinking this crazy wisdom might lead us to happiness, that the crutches of the vajrayana might help us to walk on a good hinayana path. This shows that we have not related to the whole thing as hopeless—absolutely hopeless—at all. Even hopelessness has been regarded as a solution. That cop-out is still happening. We are still going on as though there were this silent agreement that, no matter what we say, we are working toward some kind of happiness. But Padmasambhava, in his aspect of rajguru, was not concerned about that at all. His approach was, "Let happiness present *itself* if it happens, but in the meantime, let me be executed if necessary."

Acknowledge yourself as the criminal—go ahead and do it! He did it. He was executed as a criminal. But then something changed.

Acknowledging other people's mistakes as yours seems to be very difficult to do; however, pain is the path. We don't want to get blamed for somebody else's action. We will immediately say that we didn't do it. "It wasn't my fault." We can't bear to be blamed unjustly. Well, that is quite sensible, I suppose—people don't like to be blamed. But suppose we decide to take the whole thing on ourselves and let ourselves be blamed, then what would happen? It would be very interesting to find out—purely by following the example of Padmasambhava (if that makes you feel any better).

That is a very interesting kind of approach. It is not particularly subtle; it is obvious. It becomes subtle only with the twist of the twist of the twist of deception, which is a twist toward a goal.

Student: I'd like to know a little bit more about this twist of deception.

Trungpa Rinpoche: Well, we could speak about it a lot, but the main point seems to be to cut the self-justification of "It's going to be okay, there's some kind of promise of a reward *anyway*." Even believing in no promise is a promise of some kind. That kind of twist is always there. And unless we are willing to get blamed unjustly, we can't cut our deception at all. Which is very difficult to do. We are willing to lie for ourselves, but we are not willing to lie for the sake of others. We are not at all willing to take somebody else's pain. Unless maybe we talk to the people whose pain we are taking and say, "Look, I'm doing a good job for you; this is all for you." You feel you would like to have a word with that person before you give in.

Student: Padmasambhava is the lion of the dharma. Somebody wants to blame him for his own bad action. Padmasambhava says, "Sure, go ahead, blacken my name." I don't understand that exactly. Maybe if that was the only thing he could do, it would make sense, but it seems there are other modes of action available. He could pacify, enrich, magnetize, and so on. But just going along with the misplaced blame seems almost like avoiding the situation. I don't see the intelligent quality of his behaving as he did in that situation.

Trungpa Rinpoche: In this case, because he didn't try to magnetize, the whole thing became more powerful. Instead, he gave in, but he gave in in such a powerful way that the others automatically got rebounds from the situation. The result was that in fact Padmasambhava didn't have to talk himself out of his situation, but the others had to do it for him.

The message to us as followers of his is that, since we don't use such techniques too often (to say the least), it is worth trying to practice this approach. We don't have to conceptualize and say that giving in to the situation is the *only* way. That is not the point. We have all the riches and wealth of all kinds of techniques, and this one is also one of the interesting ones. It is worth looking at. I mean, you have eight styles for dealing with your life—Padmasambhava's eight aspects each have different messages—and this is one of them.

Student: Was giving in in this way what Christ did? Just permitting his situation to happen?
Trungpa Rinpoche: That seems to be very obvious, yes. He just took the blame.

Student: I don't understand the idea of not avoiding pain. If we are not trying to avoid pain, then what is the meaning of the noble truth about the cessation of pain?
Trungpa Rinpoche: Here the cessation of pain is the sense of seeing the pain from a reverse angle—from behind—rather than eliminating it.
S: You mean you just end up on the other side of the pain?
TR: Yes, [on the other side of] the creator of the pain, which is confusion.

Student: It seems that both Christ and Padmasambhava had to use magic in order to achieve their final victory.
Trungpa Rinpoche: Not necessarily. It might have become magic by itself.
S: I mean the lake and sitting in the lotus flower and—
TR: That was not magic particularly. That was just what happened. And for that matter, the resurrection could be said not to have been magic at all. It's just what happened in the case of Christ.
S: It's magical in the sense that it's very unusual. I mean, if that isn't magic, what is?
TR: Well, in that case, what we're doing here is magic. We are doing something extremely unusual for America. It happens to have developed by itself. We couldn't have created the whole situation. Our getting together and discussing this subject just happened by itself.

Student: Rinpoche, what you were saying about using pain as an adornment seemed to me like the difference between collecting information and really experiencing the implications of it. But I don't see how you can be sure that you are really making contact with your experience.
Trungpa Rinpoche: One shouldn't regard the whole thing as a way of

getting ahead of ego. Just relate to it as an ongoing process. Don't do anything with it, just go on. It's a very casual matter.

Student: What does Loden Choksi mean?

Trungpa Rinpoche: Loden means "possessing intelligence"; *choksi* means "supreme world" or "supreme existence." In this case, the name does not seem to be as significant as with some of the other aspects. It is not nearly as vivid as, for example, Senge Dradrok or Dorje Trolö. Loden Choksi has something to do with being skillful.

Student: What is the difference between the kind of direct intellectual perception you were talking about here and other kinds of perception?

Trungpa Rinpoche: It seems that if you are purely looking for answers, then you don't perceive anything. In the proper use of intellect, you don't look for answers, you just see; you just take notes in your mind. And even then, you don't have the goal of collecting information; you just relate to what is there as an expression of intelligence. That way, your intelligence can't be conned by extraneous suggestions. Rather, you have sharpened your intellect and you can relate directly to what is happening.

S: But how would you differentiate that from other kinds of perception?

TR: In general, we have perceptions with all kinds of things mixed in; that is, we have conditioned perceptions which contain a purpose of magnetizing or destroying. Such perceptions contain passion and aggression and all the rest of it. There are ulterior motives of all kinds, as opposed to just seeing clearly, just looking at things very precisely, sharply.

Dorje Trolö.

Dorje Trolö and the Three Styles of Transmission

T HE EIGHTH ASPECT of Padmasambhava is Dorje Trolö, the final and absolute aspect of crazy wisdom. To discuss this eighth aspect of Padmasambhava, we have to have some background knowledge about [traditional] ways of communicating the teachings. The idea of lineage is associated with the transmission of the message of *adhishthana*, which means "energy" or, if you like, "grace." This is transmitted like an electric current from the trikaya guru to sentient beings. In other words, crazy wisdom is a continual energy that flows and that, as it flows, regenerates itself. The only way to regenerate this energy is by radiating or communicating it, by putting it into practice or acting it out. It is unlike other energies, which, when you use them, move toward cessation or extinction. The energy of crazy wisdom regenerates itself through the process of our living it. As you live this energy, it regenerates itself; you don't live for death, but you live for birth. Living is a constant birth process rather than a wearing-out process.

The lineage has three styles of transmitting this energy. The first is called the *kangsaknyen gyü*. Here, the energy of the lineage is transmitted by word of mouth using ideas and concepts. In some sense, this is a crude or primitive method, a somewhat dualistic approach. However, in this case, the dualistic approach is functional and worthwhile.

If you sit cross-legged as if you were meditating, the chances are you might actually find yourself meditating after a while. This is like achieving sanity by pushing yourself to imitate it, by behaving as though you were sane already. In the same way, it is possible to use words, terms, images, and ideas—teaching orally or in writing—as though they were an absolutely perfect means of transmission. The procedure is to present an idea, then the refutation of [the opposite of] that idea, and then to associate the idea with an authentic scripture or teaching that has been given in the past.

Believing in the sacredness of certain things on a primitive level is the first step in transmission. Traditionally, scriptures or holy books are not to be trodden upon, sat upon, or otherwise mistreated, because very powerful things are said in them. The idea is that by mistreating the books, you mistreat the messages they contain. This is a way of believing in some kind of entity, or energy, or force—in the living quality of something.

The second style of communicating, or teaching, is the *rigdzin da gyü*. This is the method of crazy wisdom, but on the relative level, not the absolute level. Here you communicate by creating incidents that seem to happen by themselves. Such incidents are seemingly blameless, but they do have an instigator somewhere. In other words, the guru tunes himself in to the cosmic energy, or whatever you would like to call it. Then if there is a need to create chaos, he directs his attention toward chaos. And quite appropriately, chaos presents itself, as if it happened by accident or mistake. *Da* in Tibetan means "symbol" or "sign." The sense of this is that the crazy-wisdom guru does not speak or teach on the ordinary level, but rather, he or she creates a symbol, or means. A symbol in this case is not like something that stands for something else, but it is something that presents the living quality of life and creates a message out of it.

The third one is called *gyalwa gong gyü*. *Gong gyü* means "thought lineage" or "mind lineage." From the point of view of the thought lineage, even the method of creating situations is crude or primitive. Here, a mutual understanding takes place that creates a general atmosphere—and the message is understood. If the guru of crazy wisdom is an authentic being, then the authentic communication happens, and the means of communication is neither words nor symbols. Rather, just by being, a sense of precision is communicated. Maybe it takes the form of waiting—for nothing. Maybe it takes pretending to meditate together but not doing anything. For that matter, it might involve having a very casual relationship; discussing the weather and the flavor of tea; how to make curry, chop suey, or macrobiotic cuisine; or talking about history or the history of the neighbors—whatever.

The crazy wisdom of the thought lineage takes a form that is some-what disappointing to the eager recipient of the teachings. You might go and pay a visit to the guru, which you have especially prepared for, and he isn't even interested in talking to you. He's busy reading the newspaper. Or for that matter, he might create "black air," a certain intensity that makes the whole environment threatening. And there's nothing happening—nothing happening to such an extent that you walk out with a sense of relief, glad you didn't have to be there any longer. But then something happens to you as if everything did happen during those periods of silence or intensity.

The thought lineage is more of a presence than something happening. Also, it has an extraordinarily ordinary quality.

In traditional abhishekas, or initiation ceremonies, the energy of the thought lineage is transmitted into your system at the level of the fourth abhisheka. At that point, the guru will ask you suddenly, "What is your name?" or "Where is your mind?" This abrupt question momentarily cuts through your subconscious gossip, creating a bewilderment of a different type [from the type already going on in you mind]. You search for an answer and realize you do have a name and he wants to know it. It is as if you were nameless before but have now discovered that you have a name. It is that kind of an abrupt moment.

Of course, such ceremonies are subject to corruption. If the teacher is purely following the scriptures and commentaries, and the student is eagerly expecting something powerful, then both the teacher and the student miss the boat simultaneously.

Thought-lineage communication is the teaching of the dharmakaya; the communication by signs and symbols—creating situations—is the sambhogakaya level of teaching; and the communication by words is the nirmanakaya level of teaching. Those are the three styles in which the crazy-wisdom guru communicates to the potential crazy-wisdom student.

The whole thing is not as outrageous as it may seem. Nevertheless, there is an undercurrent of taking advantage of the mischievousness of reality, and this creates a sense of craziness or a sense that something or other is not too solid. Your sense of security is under attack. So the recipient of crazy wisdom—the ideal crazy-wisdom student—should feel extremely insecure, threatened. That way, you manufacture half of the crazy wisdom and the guru manufacturers the other half. Both the guru and the student are alarmed by the situation. Your mind has nothing to work on. A sudden gap has been created—bewilderment.

This kind of bewilderment is quite different from the bewilderment of ignorance. This is the bewilderment that happens between the question and the answer. It is the boundary between the question and the answer. There is a question, and you are just about to answer that question: there is a gap. You have oozed out your question, and the answer hasn't come through yet. There is already a feeling of a sense of the answer, a sense that something positive is happening—but nothing has happened yet. There is that point where the answer is just about to be born and the question has just died.

There is very strange chemistry there; the combination of the death of the question and the birth of the answer creates uncertainty. It is intelligent uncertainty—sharp, inquisitive. This is unlike ego's bewilderment of ignorance, which has totally and completely lost touch with reality because you have given birth to duality and are uncertain about how to handle the next step. You are bewildered because of ego's approach of duality. But, in this case, it is not bewilderment in the sense of not knowing what to do, but bewilderment because something is just about to happen and hasn't happened yet.

The crazy wisdom of Dorje Trolö is not reasonable but somewhat heavy-handed, because wisdom does not permit compromise. If you compromise between black and white, you come out with a gray color—not quite white and not quite black. It is a sad medium rather than a happy medium—disappointing. You feel sorry that you've let it be compromised. You feel totally wretched that you have compromised. That is why crazy wisdom does not know any compromise. The style of crazy wisdom is to build you up: build up your ego to the level of absurdity, to the point of comedy, to a point that is bizarre—and then suddenly let you go. So you have a big fall, like Humpty Dumpty: "All the king's horses and all the king's men / Couldn't put Humpty Dumpty together again."

To get back to the story of Padmasambhava as Dorje Trolö, he was asked by a local deity in Tibet, "What frightens you the most?" Padmasambhava said, "I'm frightened of neurotic sin." It so happens that the Tibetan word for "sin"—*dikpa*—is also the word for "scorpion," so the local deity thought he could frighten Padmasambhava by manifesting himself as a giant scorpion. The local deity was reduced to dust—as a scorpion.

Tibet is supposedly ringed by snow-capped mountains, and there are twelve goddesses associated with those mountains who are guardians of the country. When Dorje Trolö came to Tibet, one of those goddesses refused to surrender to him. She ran away from him—she ran all over the place. She ran up a mountain thinking she was running away from Padmasambhava and found him already there ahead of her, dancing on the mountaintop. She ran away down a valley and found Padmasambhava already at the bottom, sitting at the confluence of that valley and the neighboring one. No matter where she ran, she couldn't get away. Finally, she decided to jump into a lake and hide there. Padmasambhava turned the lake into boiling iron, and she emerged as a kind of skeleton being. Finally, she had to surrender because Padmasambhava was everywhere. It was extremely claustrophobic in some way.

One of the expressions of crazy wisdom is that you can't get away from it. It's everywhere (whatever "it" is).

At Taktsang in Bhutan, Padmasambhava manifested as Dorje Trolö. He transformed his consort, Yeshe Tsogyal, into a pregnant tigress, and he roamed about the Taktsang hills riding on this pregnant tigress. His manifesting this way had to do with subduing the psychic energies of the country, a country that was infested with primitive beliefs concerning ego and God.

Another expression of crazy wisdom is controlling psychic energies. The way to control psychic energies is not to create a greater psychic energy and try to dominate them. That just escalates the war, and it becomes too expensive—like the Vietnam War. You come up with a counterstrategy and then there is a counter-counterstrategy and then a counter-counter-counterstrategy. So the idea is not to create a super-power. The way to control the psychic energy of primitive beliefs is to instigate chaos. Introduce confusion among those energies, confuse people's logic. Confuse them so that they have to think twice. That is like the moment of the changing of the guards. At that moment when they begin to think twice, the energy of crazy wisdom zaps out.

Dorje Trolö controlled the psychic energies of primitive beliefs by creating confusion. He was half-Indian and half-Tibetan, an Indian-looking person dressed up as a Tibetan madman. He held a vajra and a dagger, flames shot from his body, and he rode a pregnant tigress. It was quite strange. He was not quite a local deity and not quite a conventional guru. He was neither warrior nor king. He was certainly not an ordinary person. Riding on a tiger is regarded as a mistake, but somehow he managed to accomplish it. Was he trying to disguise himself as a Tibetan, or what was he trying to do? He was not particularly teaching anything. You couldn't deal with him as a Bön priest or a missionary. He wasn't converting anybody; that didn't seem to be his style either. He was just instigating chaos all over the place as he went along. Even the local deities were confused—absolutely upset.

When Padmasambhava went to Tibet, the Indians got very alarmed. They felt they were losing something very precious, since it seemed he had decided to give his teachings of crazy wisdom only to the Tibetans. This was a terrible insult for the Indians. They prided themselves on being the supreme Aryans, the most intelligent race, the ones most receptive to high teachings. And now instead of teaching them, Padmasambhava was going to the savage country of Tibet, beyond the border areas; he had decided to teach the Tibetans instead of them. King Surya Simha of Uttar Pradesh, the central province of India, sent three acharyas, or spiritual masters, to the king of Tibet with a polite message saying that this so-called Padmasambhava was a charlatan, a black magician in fact. The Indian king advised that Padmasambhava was too dangerous for the Tibetans to have in their country and that they should send him back.

The interesting point here is that the teachings of crazy wisdom can only be taught in savage countries, where there is more opportunity to take advantage of chaos or speed—or whatever you would like to call that factor.

The crazy-wisdom character of Padmasambhava as Dorje Trolö is that of a guru who is unwilling to compromise with anything. If you stand in his way, you are asking for destruction. If you have doubts about him, he takes advantage of your doubts. If you are too devotional or too dependent on blind faith, he will shock you. He takes the ironic aspect of the world very seriously. He plays practical jokes on a larger scale—devastating ones.

The symbolism of the tiger is also interesting. It is connected with the idea of flame, with fire and smoke. And a pregnant tigress is supposed to be the most vicious of all tigers. She is hungry, slightly crazy, completely illogical. You cannot read her psychology and work with it reasonably. She is quite likely to eat you up at any time. That is the nature of Dorje Trolö's transport, his vehicle. The crazy-wisdom guru rides on dangerous energy, impregnated with all kinds of possibilities. This tiger could be said to represent skillful means, crazy skillful means. And Dorje Trolö, who is crazy wisdom, rides on it. They make an excellent couple.

There is another side to Padmasambhava in Tibet, one that is not part of the eight aspects. For Tibetans, Padmasambhava is a father figure. As such, he is usually referred to as Guru Rinpoche, "*the* guru." He fell in love with the Tibetans and lavished tremendous care on them (not exactly the same way the missionaries fell in love with the Africans). The Tibetans were thought of as stupid. They were too faithful and too practical. Therefore, there was a tremendous opening for introducing the craziness of impracticality: abandon your farm, abandon your livelihood, roam about in the mountains dressed in those funny yogic costumes.

Once the Tibetans began to accept those things as acts of sanity, they made excellent yogis, because their approach to yogic practice was also very practical. As they had farmed faithfully and taken care of their herds faithfully, they followed the yogic calling faithfully as well.

The Tibetans were not artistic like the Japanese. Rather, they were excellent farmers, excellent merchants, excellent magicians. The Bön tradition of Tibet was very earthy. It was purely concerned with the realities of life. Bön ceremonies are also sometimes very practical ones. One of the sacred ceremonies involves making a campfire up in the mountains—which keeps you warm. It seems that the deviousness Tibetans have shown in the course of the political intrigues of the twentieth century is entirely out of character. This kind of corruption and political intrigue came to Tibet from the outside—from the Aryan philosophers of India and from the imperial politicians of China.

Padmasambhava's approach was a very beautiful one, and his prophecies actually foretell everything that happened in Tibet, including the corruption. For example, the prophecies tell us that in the end Tibet would be conquered by China, that the Chinese would enter the country in the Year of the Horse, and that they would rush in in the manner of a horse. The Chinese Communists did invade in the Year of the Horse, and they built roads from China to Tibet and all over Tibet and introduced motor vehicles. The prophecies also say something to the effect that in the Year of the Pig, the country would be reduced to the level of a pig, which refers to primitive beliefs, the indoctrination of the Tibetans with foreign ideas.

Another prophecy of Padmasambhava says that the end of Tibet would occur when the household objects of Tsang, the upper province, would be found in Kongpo, the lower province. In fact, it happened that there was a huge flood in the upper province of Tsang when the top of a glaciated mountain fell into the lake below. The whole of the Brahmaputra River was flooded, and it swept villages and monasteries along in its course. Many of the household articles from these places were found in Kongpo, where the river had carried them. His prophecies also say that another sign of the end of Tibet would be the building of a yellow temple at the foot of the Potala Palace in Lhasa. In fact, the thirteenth Dalai Lama had a vision that a temple of Kalachakra should be built there, and they painted it yellow. Another of Padmasambhava's prophecies says that at the fourteenth stage, the rainbow of the Potala would disappear. The "fourteenth stage" refers to the time of the present, the fourteenth, Dalai Lama. Of course, the Potala is the winter palace of the Dalai Lama.

When Padmasambhava told these stories, the Tibetan king and his ministers were extremely upset, and they asked Padmasambhava to help them. "What is the best thing we can do to preserve our nation?" they asked him. "There is nothing we can do," he replied, "other than preserve the teachings that are being given now and place them in safekeeping somewhere." Then he introduced the idea of burying treasures, sacred writings.

He had various writings of his put in gold and silver containers like capsules and buried in certain appropriate places in the different parts of Tibet so that people of the future would rediscover them. He also had domestic articles buried: jewelry of his, jewelry belonging to the king and the royal household, and articles from ordinary farming households as well. The idea was that people would become more primitive, human intelligence would regress, and people would no longer be able to work properly with their hands and produce objects on that kind of artistic level.

So there things were buried all over Tibet, making use of scientific knowledge—quite possibly from India—on how best to preserve the parchments and other kinds of objects. The treasures were buried in many protective layers, including layers of charcoal, ground chalk, and other materials with various chemical properties. Also, for security, there was a layer of poison around the outside, so that thieves or other people without the right knowledge would be unable to dig them out. Such treasures have been discovered lately by great teachers who were supposedly tulkus of Padmasambhava's disciples. They had psychic visions (whatever those are) of certain places where they should dig. Then they set up the unburying process as a ceremony. The devotees would be assembled as well as workmen to do the digging. Sometimes the treasure would have to be dug out of a rock.

This process of rediscovering the treasures has been happening all along, and a lot of sacred teachings have been revealed. One example is the *Tibetan Book of the Dead*.

Another approach to preserving treasures of wisdom is the style of the thought lineage. Teachings have been rediscovered by certain appropriate teachers who have had memories of them and written them down from memory. This is another kind of hidden treasure.

An example of Padmasambhava's acting as a father figure for Tibet was the warning that he gave King Trisong Detsen. The New Year's celebration was about to be held, which traditionally included horse racing and archery, among the other events. Padmasambhava said, "There shouldn't be horse racing or archery this time." But the people around the king found a way to get around Padmasambhava's warning, and the king was killed by the arrow of an unknown assassin at the time of the horse racing and archery.

Padmasambhava loved Tibet and its people dearly, and one might have expected him to stay there. But another interesting part of the story is that, at a certain point, he left. It seems that there is just a certain time to care for and look after situations. Once the country had gotten itself together spiritually and domestically and people had developed *some* sense of sanity, Padmasambhava left Tibet.

Padmasambhava still lives, literally. He is not living in South America, but in some remote place—on a continent of vampires, at a place there called Sangdok Pelri, "Glorious Copper-Colored Mountain." He still lives. Since he *is* the state of dharmakaya, the fact of physical bodies dissolving back into nature is not regarded as a big deal. So if we search for him, we might find him. But I'm sure you will be very disappointed when you see him.

Of course, we are no longer talking about his eight aspects alone. I am sure that since then he has developed millions of aspects.

Student: You talked about the thought-lineage transmission. You said that the teacher creates half of it and the student creates the other half. I thought that crazy wisdom was uncreated.

Trungpa Rinpoche: Yes. It is uncreated, but it is spontaneously existing. You have one half and the teacher has the other half. It wasn't manufactured on the spot; it was *there.*

Student: Do you think America is savage enough for crazy wisdom?
Trungpa Rinpoche: Needless to say.

Student: I didn't understand a phrase you used: "living for death." Could you explain that?

Trungpa Rinpoche: The usual approach to living is the notion that each time we breathe in and out we are approaching closer to death. Every hour brings us closer to death. Whereas in the case of the crazy-wisdom principle, energy is rejuvenated continuously.

Student: Rinpoche, you made the statement that Guru Rinpoche is literally alive in some country. Are you serious? You used the word *literally.*

Trungpa Rinpoche: At this point, it is uncertain what is serious—or what is literal, for that matter.

S: So you could say anything?
TR: I suppose so.

Student: You mentioned the "black air" that the teacher creates. Is part of that created by the student as well?

Trungpa Rinpoche: Yes, by the student's timidity.

S: You also said if the student had doubts, the crazy-wisdom guru would take advantage of the doubts.

TR: Yes.

S: In what way might he take advantage of the student's doubts?

TR: I wonder if I should give away the game. . . . The doubt is a moment of uncertainty. For example, if you're physically weak, you can catch flu and colds easily. If you're not prepared and you're not defending yourself, you can be caught in that weak moment. That seems to be it.

Student: I remember you once said that when the abhisheka was about to happen, there was a sort of moment of fear. How does that relate to insecurity and the student losing his ground?

Trungpa Rinpoche: Well, any relationship between the student and the crazy-wisdom guru is regarded as an abhisheka.

Student: In the case of self-existing crazy wisdom, is Padmasambhava the activator principle?

Trungpa Rinpoche: The activator as well as the background. Because he also consists of dharmakaya as well as sambhogakaya and nirmanakaya.

Student: You talked of the crazy-wisdom process as being one of building up and building up ego until there's a tremendous drop. But at one point, you also talked about a process of hopelessness that does not come all at once but develops situationally little by little. I don't see how those two processes can go on simultaneously. They're going in opposite directions.

Trungpa Rinpoche: Building you up until you have a big fall is the strategy of the crazy-wisdom teacher. Meanwhile, you go along gradually developing hopelessness.

S: When the thought-lineage transmission occurs, there's this openness, this gap. Is that in itself the transmission?

TR: Yes, that's it. Yes, that's it. And there is also the environment around that, which is somewhat global, almost creating a landscape. In the midst of that, the gap is the highlight.

S: It seems that we constantly find ourselves in situations of openness and slip out. What is the benefit of going back to it? Is it kind of a practice, seeing that space so you can go back to it?

TR: Well, you see, you can't re-create that. But you can create your own abhisheka every moment. After the first experience. After that, you can develop your own inner guru; and you create your own abhisheka, rather than trying to memorize what happened already in that past. If you keep going back to that moment in the past, it becomes kind of a special treasure, which doesn't help.

S: Doesn't help?

TR: Doesn't help.

S: But it's necessary to have that experience—

TR: That experience is a catalyst. For example, if you have once had an accident, each time after that when you drive with some crazy driver, you have a really living idea of an accident. You have the sense that you might die at any moment, which is true.

Student: We are talking of openness as a very special situation taking place in transmission, and yet, it seems that it's spontaneously there, subliminally and very often here and there and everywhere. It's naturally behind neurosis as it passes through you, kind of passing with it. Can you speak more about the situation of the naturalness of the openness?

Trungpa Rinpoche: It seems that at this point if we try to be more specific in describing the details, it won't particularly help. It would be like creating special tactics and telling you how to reproduce them—like trying to be spontaneous by textbook—which doesn't seem to do any good. Probably we have to go through some kind of a trial period.

Senge Dradrok.

Notes

Seminar I

Chapter 5

1. Bön (often written "Pön") is an indigenous pre-Buddhist religion of Tibet. [Ed.]

Seminar II

Chapter 1

2. "Simultaneous birth" is a reference to the tantric notion of coemergence, or coemergent wisdom (Tib. *ihenchik kyepe yeshe*). Samsara and nirvana arise together, naturally giving birth to wisdom. [Ed.]

Chapter 2

3. This does not contradict Trungpa Rinpoche's description in the main body of this talk, of the dharmakaya as unconditioned. Although conditioned by a sense of pregnancy, the dharmakaya, as he tells us earlier, also remains unaffected by any contents, thus providing the continual possibility of a glimpse of unconditioned mind. Cf. Rinpoche's answer to the question about karma and the dharmakaya, on page 102. [Ed.]

Chapter 3

4. Herbert V. Guenther, trans., *The Life and Teaching of Naropa* (Oxford: Oxford University Press, 1963).

Chapter 4

5. Francesca Fremantle and Chögyam Trungpa, trans., *The Tibetan Book of the Dead: The Great Liberation through Hearing in the Bardo* (Boston and London: Shambhala, 1987).

Chapter 6

6. This is a quotation from the author's *Sadhana of Mahamudra,* a liturgy practiced by his students. [Ed.]

ILLUSION'S GAME

The Life and Teaching of Naropa

EDITED BY
SHERAB CHÖDZIN KOHN

Editor's Foreword

THIS BOOK IS composed of two seminars by the Vidyadhara, the Venerable Chögyam Trungpa Rinpoche, on the life and teachings of Naropa. Naropa, an Indian of the eleventh century, was one of the Vidyadhara's own spiritual forefathers and a seminal figure for the vajrayana Buddhism of Tibet. The Vidyadhara gave a number of seminars on Naropa, each with its own flavor and emphasis. The editor has had to make a more or less arbitrary selection from them for this volume (New York, January 1972, four talks; Tail of the Tiger, Vermont, 1973, six talks). Future volumes, we hope, will complete the availability to the public of the Vidyadhara's teaching on the very profound subject matter surrounding the life of Naropa.

"Great Vajradhara, Telo, Naro, Marpa, Mila; lord of dharma, Gampopa. . . ." So begins the supplication to the lineage of enlightened teachers of the Kagyü, one of the four main orders of Buddhism in Tibet. Vajradhara is the dharmakaya buddha, the ultimate repository of awakened mind. Telo is Tilopa, a great Indian siddha, Naropa's guru, the first human in the lineage. Naro is Naropa, who became the guru of Marpa, the first Tibetan in the lineage. Marpa's disciple was Mila, the renowned Tibetan yogi usually known as Milarepa (Mila the cotton clad). Milarepa's leading disciple, Gampopa, founded the monastic order of the Kagyü, the various branches of which have been headed by Gampopa's successors for the last nine hundred years.

In the vajrayana Buddhism of Tibet, the central event, which remains timelessly new through the generations, is the transmission of the awakened state of mind from guru to disciple through a meeting of minds. As the awakened state itself is independent of word, concept, or thought, the transmission of it is beyond process. Nevertheless it happens in people's lives, and an extraordinarily demanding process of preparation seems to be needed for students to reach the spiritual nakedness that enables them to open directly to the guru's mind. This process, as we see from Naropa's story, is one that requires of the student an extreme level of self-surrender and in which the teacher sometimes resorts to extremely brutal means to break him and strip him down. Doubtless to the workaday world, such a process, with its outrageous suffering, may seem insane. Yet, seen with the greater vision of enlightenment—here spoken of in terms of mahamudra, the "great seal"—this process is the utmost expression of compassion and sanity. The tale of how Naropa came into direct communication with Tilopa and received from him the transmission of awakened mind became a paradigm for the later tradition of vajrayana Buddhism in Tibet, which arose out of their relationship.

Naropa's story makes it possible to delineate in very concrete terms the various levels of spiritual development that lead up to the possibility of meeting the guru's mind. This is the main thrust of the Vidyadhara's presentation to Western students—making them see themselves and their potentialities in Naropa and his journey. In this manner he opens to them the path of devotion and surrender to the guru as the embodiment and spokesman of reality.

The Vidyadhara deals only briefly here with the formal mahamudra teachings and other tantric teachings associated with Naropa's name, notably, the six dharmas of Naropa (Tib. *naro chödruk*), or six Naropa yogas, as they are sometimes called. But in his concise descriptions, particularly in the later part of the book, he catches each one by its experiential essence, conveying in a few simple words an insight that students might well seek in vain elsewhere through hundreds of pages of text or many hours of oral teaching.

The students to whom the Vidyadhara gave these talks were asked to read *The Life and Teaching of Naropa*, the twelfth-century biography translated from Tibetan by the eminent scholar Herbert V. Guenther (Boston: Shambhala Publications, 1986). Reading this book might be a help for readers of the present volume. Nevertheless, the summary of it that follows and the citations and references in the text convey the essentials. Moreover, occasional references and descriptions by the Vidyadhara reveal that he was sometimes referring in his own mind to at least one other version of Naropa's life story.

Naropa lived in northern India in the eleventh century. He was the only son of a royal family. From an early age, he devoted himself single-mindedly to spiritual matters. His mind was filled with compassion for beings, and his primary interest was the study and practice of the bud-dhadharma. In his youth, in view of his parents' strong desire for the continuity of their royal line, Naropa consented to marry. However, after eight years he was once more overcome by his desire to devote himself exclusively to the dharma. His wife, Niguma, agreed to a divorce and became his disciple (and later a great teacher). Naropa entered the great Buddhist monastic university of Nalanda. There he greatly developed his intellectual powers and became extremely learned. So great were his intellectual powers and erudition that he was elevated to the abbacy of Nalanda. He became renowned as the premier teacher of Buddhism of his time.

At this point in his life (at around the age of forty), the event occurred that was to make Naropa of interest to the tantric tradition. One day, as he was reading with his back to the sun (a symbolic description of his spiritual relationship to reality at that time), he had a vision of a very ugly woman, who told him he understood only the words in his book, not their real meaning. She also revealed that the only way to discover the real meaning was to seek a guru, her brother Tilopa (see pages 160–161 for a quotation of this passage). Over the sustained and impassioned objections of the masters and students of Nalanda, who begged Naropa not to leave and deprive them of their guiding light, Naropa departed from the great university and began his lonely journey in search of Tilopa.

This journey turned out to be arduous and daunting in the extreme. Naropa encountered, instead of Tilopa himself, eleven hideous visions (see pages 163–169 for a quotation describing this part of the story). Naropa was about to kill himself when Tilopa finally appeared and accepted him as his student. Tilopa showed Naropa a series of symbols, which Naropa understood. Tilopa then sat motionless for a year. At the end of a year, Tilopa made a slight movement, which provided a pretext for Naropa to prostrate and ask for teaching. Tilopa required him to leap from the roof of a tall temple building. Naropa's body was crushed. He suffered immense pain. Tilopa healed him with a touch of his hand, then gave him instruction.

This pattern was repeated eleven more times. Eleven more times Tilopa remained either motionless or aloof for a year; then Naropa prostrated and asked for teaching. Tilopa caused him to throw himself into a fire where he was thoroughly burned, to be beaten nearly to death, have his blood sucked out by leeches, be pricked with flaming splinters, run till he nearly expired, be thoroughly beaten again, be beaten nearly to death once more, suffer intolerably in a relationship with a woman, give his consort to Tilopa and watch him maltreat her, and cut off his arms and legs and present them to Tilopa in the form of a mandala. After each of these torments, Tilopa restored him with a touch of his hand and bestowed a precious teaching. The teachings gained in this way, including the renowned six dharmas of Naropa, are those that have been passed down for a millennium in the Kagyü and other lineages.

After further tasks and trials and teachings, finally the transmission of mahamudra through the meeting of the minds took place completely. Tilopa then instructed Naropa to bring benefit to beings. Later, as Tilopa foresaw, Marpa crossed the Himalayas from Tibet, found Naropa, and became his disciple. When Naropa had completed his teachings to Marpa, he prophesied to him that he would have a great spiritual son, Milarepa. At that time, Naropa nodded three times in the direction of Tibet. At the same time, all the trees of that region of northern India (Pullahari) bowed three times toward Tibet. They still remain inclined in that direction today.

The Vidyadhara's commentaries on the life of Naropa go far to illuminate the nature of the spiritual path, a subject that is still scarcely understood. In this way they provide a fundamental background for those seeking to fathom his thought. They are especially helpful in explaining why, throughout the nearly twenty years that he taught in the West, he continued to warn against and castigate lukewarm approaches to spirituality that seek to integrate it "reasonably" into conventional life. He decried as spiritual materialism the use of spiritual truths and practices as a means to promote happiness, health, success in society, and other comforts of ego. From the moment Naropa caught a glimpse of the ugly woman, these are precisely the things to which he had to give up his attachment—down to the last trace. Thus, in offering commentary on the life of Naropa, the Vidyadhara can teach us directly of the genuine spirituality—raw and rugged, as he often described it—that he himself abandoned all comforts in order to instill.

SHERAB CHÖDZIN KOHN
Nova Scotia, 1992

Part One

LIFE OF NAROPA SEMINAR I

New York, 1972

ONE

Naropa and Us

WE ARE GOING to discuss the life and teachings of Naropa fully and completely, but not fully and completely in the way you would like. We are going to discuss the outlines of Naropa's life and his relationship with his guru, Tilopa, and the twelve acts of repentance he had to go through. We will also discuss his mahamudra experience. *Mahamudra* means "great symbol"; it is connected with seeing the phenomena of the world as they are. We will close our discussion with the six teachings of Naropa.

I find it necessary to express my negativities about presenting such potent—two hundred percent potent—teachings to the people of the continent of North America, or to the West altogether. Nobody here seems to be ready for this material at all. People are relating with the starting point of practice, and as far as we know, nobody in America has a complete understanding of even the hinayana level of Buddhism. People have hardly any understanding at all. They have a completely schizophrenic attitude: they conceive of a divine, enlightened personality that is opposed to their confused version of themselves. As a result, people regard themselves as abandoned people, completely bad people. Or else they might have some hope, but that again is based on some kind of spiritual pride that does not leave any leeway for confusion at all. So we're hopeless. I'm afraid we're hopeless.

Isn't that a terrible, grim picture? Extremely grim. We are hopeless, absolutely confused. We are so confused we do not even know why we are here listening to this. We wonder why. We are extremely confused, bewildered. What can we do about that? Let alone talking about Naropa? Naropa achieved something. He found his way in the end. Once he became a disciple of Tilopa, he was okay. But before he became a disciple of Tilopa, he was confused, as much as we are.

Spiritual practice is stepping out of the duality of me-ness and my-ness as opposed to otherness, of who is me and who is not me. But in addition to this we have the further confusion of gurus laying their trips on us. Or, as they are called in America, guh-ROOS. That particular species of human beings we call guh-ROOS are mysterious. They save you. They tell you they save you entirely, but on the other hand, they tell you they still have to work on themselves. We are confused. They are broke. It's a hopeless situation.

If we want to write essays about that for our Ph.D., we won't be able to, because we are so confused. Even if we want to become professional gurus, we won't be able to make head or tail of it. Of course a lot of people decide to "make a journey to the East," to live with the natives: study with them, eat with them, and shit with them, whether they use toilet tissue or not. They are serious, obviously, and faithful in playing Burmese games, Japanese games, and so on. They get right into it—sit with the Orientals, eat with them, shit with them. We are getting back a lot of anthropological messages about these "primitive" societies. It seems that though they are primitive, their spiritual understanding is much higher than ours. In any case, these are the trips we have going on.

I would like to call your attention to the following passage from *The Life and Teaching of Naropa*:

Once when 'Jig-med grags-pa (Abhayakirti) [Naropa],[1] with his back to the sun, was studying the books on grammar, epistemology, spiritual precepts, and logic, a terrifying shadow fell on them. Looking round he saw behind him an old woman with thirty-seven ugly features: her eyes were red and deep-hollowed; her hair was fox-coloured and dishevelled; her forehead large and protruding; her face had many wrinkles and was shrivelled up; her ears were long and lumpy; her nose was twisted and inflamed; she had a yellow beard streaked with white; her mouth was distorted and gaping; her teeth were turned in and decayed; her tongue made chewing movements and moistened her lips; she whistled when she yawned; she was

weeping and tears ran down her cheeks; she was shivering and pant-
ing for breath; her complexion was darkish blue; her skin rough and
thick; her body bent and askew; her neck curved; she was hump-
backed; and, being lame, she supported herself on a stick. She said to
Naropa: "What are you looking into?"

"I study the books on grammar, epistemology, spiritual precepts,
and logic," he replied.

"Do you understand them?"

"Yes."

"Do you understand the words or the sense?"

"The words."

The old woman was delighted, rocked with laughter, and began
to dance, waving her stick in the air. Thinking that she might feel still
happier, Naropa added: "I also understand the sense." But then the
woman began to weep and tremble and she threw her stick down.

"How is it that you were happy when I said that I understood the
words, but became miserable when I added that I also understood
the sense?"

"I felt happy because you, a great scholar, did not lie and frankly
admitted that you only understood the words. But I felt sad when
you told a lie by stating that you understood the sense, which you
do not."

"Who, then, understands the sense?"

"My brother."

"Introduce me to him wherever he may be."

"Go yourself, pay your respects to him, and beg him that you
may come to grasp the sense."

With these words, the old woman disappeared like a rainbow in
the sky.

[*The Life and Teaching of Naropa*, trans.
Herbert V. Guenther (Boston & London:
Shambhala Publications, 1986), pp. 24–25]

Naropa was studying epistemology, logic, philosophy, and grammar.
That's where we are at. Of course, everybody is also extremely involved
with art now. Everybody is trying to work out their artistic self-expres-
sion. They might hear the teachings of Naropa in connection with art;
they might see it in terms of "the art of the Tibetan teachings." Then

there is also logic, the question of how the teachings relate with each other, how not and how so. We are involved with logic as well. It could be said that everybody here is in the first stage of Naropa's experience, involved in philosophy and art, as well as epistemology. We are on the same level that Naropa was experiencing before he attained enlightenment. We want an answer; we want definitions. We want a fixed situation rather than something fluid. We feel that concepts are very badly needed.

In this seminar, you are not going to be able to relate with concepts. You're not going to get something out of studying logic, epistemology, grammar, and philosophy—which were a failure for Naropa as well. That is why he had to go through twelve stages of punishment, because of his concepts. We are going to go through the same journey that Naropa went through; we are going to take a tour of Naropa's agony. In some ways, it is going to be like Disneyland. You go through some tunnel and you come out; you're delivered to somewhere else. You see exciting things and you come out on the other end. But in this case, it is related with psychological problems. It is going to be more deathening, more hellish or heavenish. We start at Naropa's starting point of searching for goodness and trying to achieve divinity.

Genuine Madness and Pop Art

And he proceeded onwards in an Eastern direction.

These were the visions he had:

When he had come to a narrow footpath that wound between rocks and a river, he found a leper woman without hands and feet blocking the path.

"Do not block the way, step aside."

"I cannot move. Go round if you are not in a hurry, but if you are, jump over me."

Although he was full of compassion, he closed his nose in disgust and leaped over her. The leper woman rose in the air in a rainbow halo and said:

Listen, Abhayakirti:
The Ultimate in which all become the same
Is free of habit-forming thought and limitations.
How, if still fettered by them,
Can you hope to find the Guru?

At this the woman, the rocks, and the path all vanished and Naropa fell into a swoon on a sandy plateau. When he recovered consciousness he thought: "I did not recognize this to be the Guru, now I shall ask anyone I meet for instruction." Then he got up and went on his way praying.

On a narrow road he met a stinking bitch crawling with vermin.

He closed his nose and jumped over the animal, which then appeared in the sky in a rainbow halo and said:

> All living beings by nature are one's parents.
> How will you find the Guru, if
> Without developing compassion
> On the Mahayana path
> You seek in the wrong direction?
> How will you find the guru to accept you
> When you look down on others?

After these words the bitch and the rocks disappeared and Naropa again swooned on a sandy plateau.

When he came to, he resumed his prayers and his journey, and met a man carrying a load.

"Have you seen the venerable Tilopa?"

"I have not seen him. However, you will find behind this mountain a man playing tricks on his parents. Ask him."

When he had crossed the mountain, he found the man, who said:

"I have seen him, but before I tell you, help me to turn my parents' head."

But Abhayakirti thought: "Even if I should not find the venerable Tilopa, I cannot associate with a scoundrel, because I am a prince, a Bhikshu, and a scholar. If I seek the Guru I will do so in a respectable way according to the dharma."

Everything happened as before, the man receded into the centre of a rainbow halo and said:

> How will you find the Guru, if
> In this doctrine of Great Compassion
> You do not crack the skull of egotism
> With the mallet of non-Pure-Egoness and nothingness?

The man disappeared like a rainbow and Naropa fell senseless to the ground. When he woke up there was nothing and he walked on praying as he went.

Beyond another mountain he found a man who was tearing the intestines out of a human corpse and cutting them up. Asked whether he had seen Tilopa, he answered:

"Yes, but before I show him to you, help me to cut up the intestines of this decayed corpse."

Since Naropa did not do so, the man moved away into the centre of a rainbow-coloured light and said:

How will you find the Guru, if
You cut not Samsara's ties
With the unoriginatedness of the Ultimate
In its realm of non-reference?

And the man disappeared like a rainbow.

When Naropa had recovered from his swoon and gone on his way praying, he found on the bank of a river a rascal who had opened the stomach of a live man and was washing it with warm water. When he asked him whether he had seen the venerable Tilopa, he replied:

"Yes, but before I show him, help me."

Again Naropa refused, and the man appearing in a centre of light in the sky said:

How will you find the Guru, if
With the water of profound instruction
You cleanse not Samsara, which by nature [is] free
Yet represents the dirt of habit-forming thoughts?

And the man disappeared in the sky.

After having woken from his swoon Naropa prayed and journeyed on until he came to the city of a great king, whom he asked whether he had seen Tilopa. The king replied:

"I have seen him, but marry my daughter before I show him to you."

Having taken her, he seemed to spend a long time. Then the king, not wishing to let him go, took back the girl and the dowry and left the room. Not recognizing this as a magic spell, but thinking that he would have to employ force with the aid of the *bDe-mchog rtsa-rgyud*, *Abhidhana-uttaratantra*, he heard a voice say:

Are you not deceived by a magic show?
How then will you find the Guru

If through desire and dislike you fall
Into the three forms of evil life?

And the whole kingdom disappeared.

When Naropa came to, he travelled in prayer until he met a dark man with a pack of hounds, a bow and arrows.

"Have you seen Tilopa?"

"Yes."

"Show him to me."

"Take this bow and arrow and kill that deer."

When Naropa refused, the man said:

A hunter, I have drawn the arrow
Of the phantom body which from desires is free
In the bow, of radiant light the essence:
I shall kill the fleeing deer of this and that,
On the mountain of the body believing in an I.
Tomorrow I go fishing in the lake.

So saying, he disappeared.

When Naropa had recovered he continued prayerfully in search of the Guru and came to the shore of a lake full of fish. Nearby two old people were ploughing a field, killing and eating the insects they found in the furrows.

"Have you seen Tilopa?"

"He stayed with us, but before I show him to you—hallo, wife, come and get this Bhikshu something to eat."

The old woman took some fish and frogs from her net and cooked them alive. When she invited Naropa to eat, he said: "Since I am a Bhikshu I no longer have an evening meal, and besides that I do not eat meat." Thinking, "I must have violated the doctrine of the Buddha to be asked to dine by an old woman who cooks fish and frogs alive," he sat there miserably. Then the old man came up with an ox on his shoulders and asked his wife: "Have you prepared some food for the Bhikshu?" She replied: "He seems to be stupid; I cooked some food, but he said that he did not want to eat."

Then the old man threw the pan into the fire while fish and frogs flew up into the sky. He said:

Fettered by habit-forming thoughts, 'tis hard to find the
   Guru.
How will you find the Guru if you eat not
This fish of habit-forming thoughts, but hanker
After pleasures (which enhance the sense of ego)?
Tomorrow I will kill my parents.

He then disappeared.

After his recovery Naropa came upon a man who had impaled his
father on a stake, put his mother into a dungeon, and was about to
kill them. They cried loudly: "Oh son, do not be so cruel." Although
Naropa was revolted at the sight, he asked the man whether he had
seen Tilopa, and was answered: "Help me to kill the parents who
have brought me misfortune and I will then show you Tilopa."

But since Naropa felt compassion for the man's parents, he did
not make friends with this murderer. Then with the words:

You will find it hard to find the Guru
If you kill not the three poisons that derive
From your parents, the dichotomy of this and that.
Tomorrow I will go and beg,

the man disappeared.

When Naropa had recovered from his swoon and gone on in
prayer, he came to a hermitage. One of the inmates recognized him
as Abhayakirti and asked: "Why have you come? Is it to meet us?"

"I am merely a Ku-su-li-pa,[1] there is no need for a reception."

The hermit, however, did not heed his words and received him
with due honours. Asked for the reason for his coming, Naropa said:
"I seek Tilopa. Have you seen him?"

"You will find that your search has come to an end. Inside is a
beggar who claims to be Tilopa."

Naropa found him within sitting by the fire and frying live fish.
When the hermits saw this, they began angrily to beat the beggar,
who asked: "Don't you like what I do?"

"How can we when evil is done in a hermitage?"

The beggar snapped his fingers, said "Lohivagaja,"[2] and the fish
returned to the lake. Naropa, realizing that this man must be Tilopa,

folded his hands and begged for instruction. The Guru passed him a handful of lice, saying:

> If you would kill the misery of habit-forming thoughts
> And ingrained tendencies on the endless path
> To the ultimate nature of all beings,
> First you must kill (these lice).

But when Naropa was unable to do so, the man disappeared with the words:

> You will find it hard to find the Guru
> If you kill not the louse of habit-forming thoughts,
> Self-originated and self-destructive.
> Tomorrow I will visit a freak show.

Dejectedly Naropa got up and continued his search. Coming to a wide plain, he found many one-eyed people, a blind man with sight, an earless one who could hear, a man without a tongue speaking, a lame man running about, and a corpse gently fanning itself. When Naropa asked them if they had seen Tilopa, they declared:

"We haven't seen him or anyone else. If you really want to find him, do as follows":

> Out of confidence, devotion, and certainty, become
> A worthy vessel, a disciple with the courage of conviction.
> Cling to the spirituality of a Teacher in the spiritual fold,
> Wield the razor of intuitive understanding as the viewpoint,
> Ride the horse of bliss and radiance as the method of
> attention,
> Free yourself from the bonds of this and that as the way of
> conduct.
> Then shines the sun of self-lustre which understands
> One-eyedness as the quality of many,
> Blindness as seeing without seeing a thing,
> Deafness as hearing without hearing a thing,
> Muteness as speaking without saying something,
> Lameness as moving without being hurried,

Death's immobility as the breeze of the Unoriginated (like
air moved by a fan).

In this way the symbols of Mahamudra were pointed out, where-
after everything disappeared.

[Pp. 30–36]

In the teachings proclaimed by the Kagyü lineage, we find a lot of
processes that have to be gone through and understandings that have to
be developed. This is by no means easy. It is extremely difficult to understand that there is some basic confusion we have created, and that within
that confusion there is also some kind of madness. Strangely enough, the
madness is not confused. There is sanity in the confusion and the madness. Confusion in dealing with the situation of life as a fixed thing seems
to be a sane approach. So what seems to be insane is enlightenment.

Naropa's approach to his successive discoveries in his visions—or
whatever they are, phantoms that he sees—is connected with his seeming sanity. Because Naropa was born a prince and was educated and became a professor at Nalanda University, he regards himself as a sensible
person, an educated, sensible person, someone highly respected. But this
sensible quality, this sanity of his, turns out to be a very clumsy way of
relating with the teachings of Tilopa—the teachings of the Kagyü lineage. Because he was not enough of a freak, because he was not insane
enough, he couldn't relate with them at all.

Insanity in this case is giving up logical arguments, giving up concept.
Things as they are conceptualized are not things as they are. We have to
try to see within the conceptualized situation, according to which fire is
hot and the sky is blue. Maybe the sky is green; maybe fire is cold.
There's that possibility, always.

When we hear someone say such a thing, we become extremely per-
plexed and annoyed. We think, "Of course, fire is hot; fire is not cold. Of
course, the sky is blue, not green. That's nonsense! I'm not going to have
anything to do with that kind of nonsense. I'm going to stick to my sensible outlook. The sky is blue and fire is hot; that gives me a sense of
security, satisfaction, and sanity. If fire is hot, I'm quite happy with it. if
the sky is blue, I'm also happy with that. I don't want any interference
with my regular line of thought."

On the other hand, the idea of insanity we are looking into here does not mean that you should drop your ordinary sanity and be swinging and hip, to use current conventional terms. I am not saying you should change your entire perspective around, that instead of being clean, you should be dirty because that's a more hip way to behave, or that you should adopt any of the rest of that kind of approach. That is not quite the point. People might think that Naropa's hang-up was that he was not hip enough to experience Tilopa's doctrine or teaching. That is not quite so. There is a problem in communicating this situation to late-twentieth-century Americans. We have an enormous problem there.

One of the biggest problems we face is the popularity of Tibetan Buddhism and Tibetan Buddhist works of art. Everything is regarded as fabulous, a fantastic display. "It is so fantastic! It matches what I saw in my acid trip! It's fabulous!" Looking at it with this attitude, the style of Naropa and his hang-ups and the style of Tilopa and his teachings might be seen as pop art, with people just thinking, "It's a far-out thing." Tibetan wrathful deities in paintings and thangkas demonstrate a crazy-wisdom quality, which is pop art from the point of view of those who regard connecting with the teachings as a hip thing to do.

There are problems with that. Take the example of going into retreat in a cabin in the woods under severe conditions. That should not be regarded as an alternative form of luxury. The retreat cabin you meditate in has nothing to do with your reaction against your central-heated home or your penthouse. It has nothing to do with that at all. It just provides another life situation, and that's all. Meditating in retreat in a cabin in the remote countryside is not pop art. The same is true for visualizing all kinds of deities and mandalas as some American students have been instructed to do. The first impact on them seems to be, "At last I am able to relate with those beautiful, colorful, groovy things that are in the Tibetan thangkas. At last I have managed to get to relate with that. At last the dream comes true, and I am able to live real pop art. I'm not only thinking of them or painting them; by visualizing, I'm becoming part of them. It's an exciting, outlandish thing to do." It's a kind of pop art.

To come back to Naropa, this seems to be precisely Naropa's hang-up. He had so much fascination about Tilopa and receiving the tantric teachings from him that he also looked at it as the next groovy thing to do. And he walked and walked and walked and went on and on. But at each point he got hit because he regarded the whole thing as pop art, according to the conception of that particular age. And it is possible that we ourselves might experience the same kind of situation as well, if we impulsively regard the whole thing as pop art—as colorful, inspiring, and, at the same time, artistic. As long as we regard it as something we might tune in to at any time, whenever we like, thinking that as soon as we do, it will relieve us from all our pressures and tensions—as long as we regard it as another escape, another sidetrack—being hit like Naropa could happen to us too.

All the successive situations that Naropa went through in experiencing Tilopa's different qualities—the leper woman, the decaying dog, the criminal, and so on—involve a psychological expectation that is an extremely confused one. And we try to make pictures out of that psychological confusion. And the only kind of picture we can come up with is a beautiful, colorful, artistic kind of picture with a dreamy quality connected with possibly achieving a goal, an aim, an object. In other words, our picture is connected with the idea of reaching heaven. That seems to be the problem—because such an idea has nothing to do with truth or reality as the Kagyü lineage speaks of it, nothing to do with the mahamudra experience. Such ideas are not real truth. Bliss is not the real truth. Meditative absorption is not the real truth. It seems the real truth is naked and direct, uncolored, unshaded, and not manufactured—the simple existence of a solitary rock—which seems to be extremely boring to experience. We might think, "If I'm not going to get any excitement or understanding out of experiencing such a truth, what the hell am I getting into this trip for?"

And that seems to be our problem. When we try to get into something, we expect a lot—entertainment, precision, an answer, reassurance, clarity. We expect all kinds of things. By expecting clarity, we are confusing the whole issue; we are producing confusion. By expecting reassurance, by expecting to be reassured that the trip we are getting into is right, we are creating more paranoia. Paranoia and reassurance speak the same language; they're on the same level; they're always interdependent. By looking for precise understanding, we are arousing fear of confusion; we are making more confusion constantly. When we think of bliss, we are making a reference point out of this blissful state, therefore we are arousing fear of pain; we are creating further pain under the pretense of trying to create bliss. These are the things that Naropa experienced in his search for Tilopa. And that is also what we are experiencing. That is what generally happens. We try to grasp every situation of confusion as fast as possible; we grasp it, dwell on it, make it into a mother, suck as much milk as possible out of it, dwell further on it, bounce on it.

In a sense, it is beautiful that we can relate to Naropa's confusion as our confusion. It is extremely beautiful that we can relate with him. We can also relate with his understanding. We ourselves could become like Naropa, the father of the Kagyü lineage. This whole room we are in together is filled with potential Naropas, because the whole room is filled with the potentiality of Naropa's confusion. It is quite beautiful.

It seems that in relation to the whole thing we are talking about, Naropa's attainment of enlightenment is not that important. It is Naropa's confusion that is important for us as ordinary people. Connecting with that provides a basis for progress, for a step toward understanding. So let us relate with his story that way. All the hang-ups that Naropa experienced, all his imaginations—his visual mind, his auditory mind as he experienced them—are part of our makeup as well. And there are possibilities of stepping out of that confusion.

Student: I am confused by some of the things Naropa was asked to do. Seemingly there shouldn't be any contradiction between a guru's teaching and the Buddha's teaching. And yet in the visions there seem to be a lot of them. For example, asking him to kill lice seems to be a direct contradiction. On the one hand, his "sane," sensible mind is saying, "Don't do this"; on the other, it is saying, "Do this." It seems either way the poor guy turns, he gets cut down. What would have happened if he had killed the lice? He still would have been in violation, so to speak.

Trungpa Rinpoche: Probably at that moment there was no such thing as lice to be killed. Physically there may have been no lice at all.

S: Still, you're killing, whether it's only a projection or not. If you kill somebody in a dream, isn't that the same as actually carrying out the action?

TR: It's quite different. You're dealing with your own projections in a dream. If you dreamed that you became a millionaire, you wouldn't actually become a millionaire.

S: It still sounds suicidal. Even if the lice aren't there, something exists.

TR: Yes, something exists, which is your projections, your dogma, your resistance, which has to be killed. Of course there is something there; not only something, but *the* thing is there.

S: If it's killed, you're still left a killer aren't you?

TR: Attaining enlightenment could be described as killing ego.

S: It sounds suicidal and hence not complete.

TR: It is complete. When you attain enlightenment, the killer of ego is so efficient and precise that ego cannot arise again at all, not even a memory of it. It does a very fine job. When we kill somebody in the literal sense, we cannot kill them completely. We can't kill their name, we can't kill their relatives—something is left. But in killing ego in connection with the attainment of enlightenment, we do a complete job—the name and the concept are killed as well.

S: Sometimes you talk about meditation in terms of making friends with yourself. Is this what you call making friends with yourself?

TR: What self?

S: It just doesn't seem very friendly.

TR: It is the act of a friend, an act of compassion. Ego is murdered out of compassion, out of love. Usually murder takes place out of hate. It is because the murder of ego is done out of compassion that, quite surprisingly, it is complete. The murder of ego is a complete murder, in contrast to the other kind.

S: Putting it out of its misery.

TR: Not quite. Respecting the misery.

Student: Rinpoche, it sounds as though you're saying we have to go beyond, transcend ego, before we even have the right to get into tantra.

Trungpa Rinpoche: Go beyond? I think we have to, yes. It seems that in the current situation in America, we are in the stage of being haunted by the lady with the thirty-seven ugly marks as Naropa was. We haven't developed to the next stages of Naropa's search for Tilopa at all yet. We have just stayed at the beginning. At the moment we seem to be just discovering the difference between the words and the sense. The discovery of the word seems to be the sense, but that is not quite the case. Discovering the words was what Naropa was doing reading that particular book with his back to the sun. Reading a book on logic. We seem to be at that level. So we have a long way to go.

Student: Is each one of these situations that Naropa goes through a step in developing out of his confusion?

Trungpa Rinpoche: Each situation has a different symbolism related with that, yes.

Student: Who is arranging all these visions?
Trungpa Rinpoche: Nobody. It just seems to happen that way.

Student: Rinpoche, could you say more about the madness or insanity you were talking about?
Trungpa Rinpoche: It is madness beyond the conceptualized point of view of ego. For example, if you are in an outrageous state of hatred and trying to relate with somebody as an object of that hatred, if that person doesn't communicate back to you in terms of hate, you might think he is a mad person. You think he is mad because he doesn't fight you back. As far as you are concerned, that person is mad, because he has lost his perspective of aggression and passion as it should be from the point of view . . .
S: From the point of view of samsara?
TR: Yes. From the point of view of samsara, Buddha is mad. There's a story in the Indian scriptures that in a particular country, a soothsayer predicted to the king that there would be seven days of rain containing a substance that would make people mad. Whoever drank the water would go mad. So his whole kingdom was going to go mad. Hearing this prediction, the king collected gallons and gallons of water for his private use to keep himself from going mad. Then the rain fell and everyone else went mad. Then they all began accusing the king of being mad. Finally he gave in and decided to drink the water of madness in order to fit in with the rest of the kingdom. He couldn't be bothered keeping himself "insane."

Student: In the different visions that Naropa has, he doesn't want to do the things he's asked to do, presumably because he thinks they're immoral. So are we to conclude from this that morality and the moral law are purely something that operates in the ego realm, and that an enlightened person in the position of Tilopa follows no moral law?
Trungpa Rinpoche: Tilopa does follow the moral law in its absolute perfection.
S: What does that mean?
TR: The conventional moral law purely has to do with relating with

your conscience rather than dealing with situations. Dealing with situations, with what is right and what is wrong in situations, is Tilopa's fashion. If you relate with a situation in terms of your conscience or your perceptions, it means you don't actually relate with the situation at all; you don't even have any idea of understanding the situation. This seems to be what happens in general in life. You have to try to understand situations as precisely as possible, but there are situations that you regard as bad to understand. For example, if you had to investigate a murder case, you might want to dissociate yourself from the case altogether, thinking, "I don't want to be involved with murder at all." Then you have no way at all of understanding how and why one person murdered the other. You could let yourself become involved with that murder case and try to understand the rightness and wrongness of what was done as scientifically as possible. You could look into the situation in terms of cause and effect and gain some understanding of it. But on the other hand, if you think, "Becoming involved with murder will just get me in contact with bad vibrations, so I'll have nothing to do with that," then you seal yourself off completely.

That is exactly the same thing that seems to be happening in present-day society. Particularly the young generation doesn't want to have anything to do with society—let alone understand it—because it's something ugly, something terrible. This creates tremendous confusion and conflict. Whereas if people were to get into society and try to understand what is wrong, there might be some intelligence coming out of that. Complete rejection without discrimination seems to be the problem.

Student: So should we register to vote?
Trungpa Rinpoche: Why not? Add your energies to the country's.

Student: Don't you think there have been some things we've all learned from that rejection you were just talking about?
Trungpa Rinpoche: Yes and no—both. A lot of people have rejected Christianity and gone to Hinduism or Buddhism. They feel that they no longer have any associations with Christianity at all. Then later—from the point of view of aliens—they begin to realize that Christianity speaks some kind of profound truth. They only see that from the point of view of aliens, having gone away. They begin to appreciate the culture they

were brought up in. Finally they become the best Christians, people with much more understanding of Christianity than ordinary Christians.

You can't reject your history. You can't say that your hair is black if it is blond. You have to accept your history. Those wanting to imitate Oriental culture might go so far as to become 100 percent Hindu or 100 percent Japanese, even to the point of undergoing plastic surgery. But somehow denying your existence—your body, your makeup, your psychological approach—does not help. In fact, it brings more problems. You have to be what you are. You have to relate with your country, the state of your country, its politics, its culture. That is extremely important, since you cannot become someone else. And it is such a blessing.

If we could become someone else, or halfway someone else, that would provide us with a tremendous number of sidetracks and possibilities for escape. We should be thankful that we have a body, a culture, a race, and a country that is honestly ours, and we should relate with those. We can't reject all that. That represents our relationship to the earth as a whole, our national karma, and all the rest of it. That seems to be the starting point for attaining enlightenment, becoming a buddha, an American buddha.

Student: Rinpoche, Naropa's experiences seem to be all symbols. Can't we go too far in taking everything as a symbol? How do we prevent ourselves from going too far in that sense?

Trungpa Rinpoche: Naropa, in a sense, failed in this way because he didn't have the chance of relating with Tilopa immediately. For that very reason, he got too much involved in symbolism. The same could apply to us as well. It's not so much a matter of too much symbolism as of too much fascination with the context. For example, you could be completely fooled by a salesman if you're in a shop. The salesman might say, "This is such beautiful material. This is such a functional item. It's of good quality, yet cheap. It's so beautiful; you'll be getting your money's worth." At that point, you can't deny that what the salesman is telling you is the truth. He's absolutely telling the truth. The thing he's trying to sell you does have those good qualities. But if you ended up buying it on the basis of fascination, you might be disappointed afterward, because somehow afterward you're not relating with it on the same level of fascination anymore. You might find at that point that your fascination is rejected by the experience you had in your first glimpse before the salesman began to fascinate you. The whole thing is based on fascination.

S: What I was asking about was if there was a point where one had gone too far in taking experiences as symbolic, a point where the whole thing's a projection.

TR: Yes, that is related with fascination, not being able to relate with yourself. One has to relate to one's whole being rather than just purely dealing with accuracy and beautiful display.

Student: In the Buddhist tradition, after the death of ego, is there any self left? Does self exist?

Trungpa Rinpoche: That's a very old question. You see, in order to have the continuity of something, you have to have somebody constantly watching this continuity happening. If you have ego continuing, you also have to have the observer observing that ego is continuing. This is because the whole thing is based on a mirage. If there's no watcher, there's no mirage. If there's a watcher to acknowledge that the mirage exists, there will be a mirage. After enlightenment, there's no watcher anymore; therefore the watcher's object does not exist anymore.

S: Does the being exist after that?

TR: The being is self-consciousness, making sure you are there. And you don't watch yourself being there anymore. It's not a question of whether being exists or does not exist. If you see being as not existing, then you have to watch that, make sure that being does not exist anymore, which is continuing the being anyhow.

S: So in other words, there is a death or an identity after ego death, and the death or ego is the death of confusion about it?

TR: Well, the watcher dissolves, so we cannot say yes or no either. It's beyond remark.

Student: Regarding relating with our culture, Alan Watts says that one thing that has given our culture a great neurosis is seeing things in terms of the conflict between good and evil rather than just seeing them as they are. This makes me want to ask you about the Buddhist view of what the devil is or the black magician. A lot of our cultural history that is still going on has to do with black magic.

Trungpa Rinpoche: Defining good and evil or the devil and black magic is very much related to our topic of sanity and insanity, and the whole subject of meditation is related with that as well. The result of any situation that is connected with self-enrichment, or an attempt at self-perpetuation, either in an ego-centered way or a very innocent and kind way—the result of anything aimed at enriching the ego—is destruction, complete confusion, perpetual confusion. There is no killing of ego here. From a black magician's point of view, you don't kill somebody's ego, you kill somebody's non-ego.

S: How can you do that?

TR: You just do it out of conviction, belief. In other words, you can't destroy it completely, but you put a smear of ink over it, and you don't look again; you just hope for the best—that you killed it. The whole thing is connected with spiritual materialism, which I talk so much about. Spiritual materialism means enriching the ego. Anything related with spiritual materialism is a step toward the black magician, if I may say so. It could be a step toward the black magician or the white magician actually, but in any case toward the magician, toward gaining power. If you want to help your friend, you just do it. If you want to destroy your enemy, you just do it. In that way, you have the potential of the black magician, even if you are regarded as a kind person who is at the same time a powerful person.

The whole question is how much the relationship with ego becomes a central theme in spiritual practice. When it does, you get good and bad, what is and what is not, which is called duality in Buddhist terminology. The whole thing of who you are is purely related with the watcher. You can't measure anything without a starting point. And you can't count unless you can start from zero. So zero is you, ego. You start from there and you build your number series, you build your measurement system, you build your relationships. Once you do that, you get an overwhelming sense of good and kind or bad and destructive. You build all kinds of things based on that basic reference point. It seems that the whole thing is based on how much you are involved with ego. That seems to be the basis for defining goodness or wickedness.

Student: What are the methods in your way for killing the ego? What methods would you use in our society?

Trungpa Rinpoche: It has nothing to do with society at all. It is purely a matter of dealing with one's psychological state of being. Sociological styles don't make any difference in this regard. Sociological approaches or styles are just a photograph. The direct way of dealing with ourselves here is getting into the nitty-gritty of our whole existence and dealing with excruciating pain and excruciating pleasure as directly as possible. That way we begin to realize that pain and pleasure do not exist in a centralized way, but pain and pleasure exist in an expansive, joyful way. So we don't have to nurse anything.

Student: Rinpoche, you spoke of compassion as being bad medicine for ego. Yet Naropa violates our definition of compassion in a number of ways.

Trungpa Rinpoche: There are two different types of compassion. There is actual compassion, direct compassion, absolute compassion. Then there is the other kind of compassion that Mr. Gurdjieff[3] calls "idiot compassion," which is compassion with neurosis, a slimy way of trying to fulfill your desire secretly. This is your aim, but you give the appearance of being generous and impersonal.

S: What is absolute compassion?

TR: Absolute compassion is seeing the situation as it is, directly and thoroughly. If you have to be tough, you just do it. In other words, idiot compassion contains a sort of opium—constantly trying to be good and kind—and absolute compassion is more literal, more discriminating, and more definite. You are willing to hurt somebody, even though you do not want to hurt that person; but in order to wake that person up, you might have to hurt him or her, you might have to inflict pain.

That is precisely why, in the Buddhist tradition, we don't start with the teaching of compassion, the mahayana, but we start with teaching of the lesser vehicle, the hinayana. In the hinayana, you try to get yourself together. Then you start applying your compassion after that, having gotten yourself together, having built the foundation. You can't just work on the level of absolute compassion right from the beginning. You have to develop toward it.

Student: I think you said earlier that one of the obstacles to developing in this way is the need for reassurance. How does one get away from the need for reassurance?

Trungpa Rinpoche: Acknowledge needing reassurance, acknowledge it as an effigy that looks in only one direction and does not look around. An effigy with one face, possibly only one eye. Doesn't see around, doesn't see the whole situation. Do you see what I mean?

S: The effigy only looks one way. Is this the person who needs reassurance?

TR: Yes, because that reassurance has to be attached to that one situation. Whenever you need reassurance, that means you have a fixed idea of what ought to be. And because of that you fix your vision on one situation, one particular thing. And those situations that are not being observed because of the point of view of needing reassurance, that we are not looking at, are a source of paranoia. We wish we could cover the whole ground, but since we can't do that physiologically, we have to try to stick to that one thing as much as we can. So the need for reassurance has only one eye.

S: And the way to get beyond that one-eyed vision?

TR: Develop more eyes, rather than just a unidirectional radar system. You don't have to fix your eye on one thing. You can have panoramic vision, vision all around at once.

Student: Something like a fish-eye lens.

Trungpa Rinpoche: Something like that, but even that has a camera behind it.

THREE

An Operation without Anesthetics

NAROPA'S EXPERIENCE of discovering Tilopa is connected with finally giving up hope, giving up hope of getting what we wanted to get. For Naropa, that search for an ultimate answer finally had to be given up. But this is not easy to give up, because each time we try to give up having the ultimate answer—our final answer, the truth—giving up the truth is discovered as another truth. So we could go on and on and on giving up truths. Giving up hope becomes another hope of getting something out of giving up hope.

We seem to love ourselves enormously. We love ourselves so much that we reach the point where we might kill ourselves. A kind of love-hate relationship goes on in which our extreme desire, our extreme love of ourselves, becomes hatred in practice. This is precisely why samsaric mind, the samsaric point of view of gaining happiness, is regarded by the Buddhist teaching as holding the wrong end of the stick. That is precisely why confusion is regarded as off.

Looking at Naropa's situation, we see that to have found a teacher like Tilopa, we have to give up our conceptualized way of thinking and our conceptualized attitudes. We have to learn that lesson: to become tired of the dreams, sick of them. The dreams have no root. They are purely fantasies. But then, after that, when the dreams cease to function, there is something else to relate with. That is the shell of the dreams. The shell, or the shadow, of the dreams becomes tough and strong. Having woken up, we face reality.

Having given up hope of meeting Tilopa, Naropa finally meets

Tilopa. But that turns out to be another problem. That is another uneasy situation. Having gone through the fantasies and used them up, we are faced with the reality or ultimate truth, or whatever you would like to call it. What do we do with the reality? How shall we handle this reality? Having woken up, what shall we do?

A lot of the great Tibetan teachers talk about transcending the phantom of mind and facing reality. Once one faces it, reality is like pure gold. One has to examine that gold, process it—hammer it and mold out of it whatever shapes one wants. Or we could also say that when one faces reality, it is like dough, and processing it is like kneading dough. If you want good bread, you have to knead the dough with complete strength. And it is said that the important point in this is not kneading the dough but cleaning the bowl. If you are good at kneading, you clean the bowl with the dough. The result might be good bread, but this is still uncertain.

Dealing with reality is an extremely big problem, a much bigger one than dealing with the phantoms of our imagination. In our meditation practice, dealing with thought processes is relatively simple. You just relate with thoughts as thoughts, and the thought process becomes transparent. But dealing with the technique of meditation is another matter; dealing with your body is another matter. That is the most difficult problem of all.

Dealing with reality is difficult because we are still approaching it in an unrealistic way. There is reality in its full glory. Should we look at it as a spectrum? Should we regard it as something that belongs to us? Should we regard it as a show? If we don't regard it in any way at all, how are we going to deal with that reality in its full splendor? In fact, we do not know what to do with reality. Having been presented with it, we are completely bewildered.

It's like meeting your favorite film star on the street. If you suddenly bumped into him or her on the street, you would have to make up your mind what to say, what to do. Somehow it's a dream coming true; it's real. There is something real about meeting that particular person, but at the same time, there is something unreal because you are not prepared for that reality. It happened by accident.

Meeting reality usually takes the form of an accident. We are bewildered by this accident, by this accidental discovery of reality, and then we are uncertain what to do. Should we pull it, push it, possess it, play with it, or what? But actually we don't have to do anything with it. Just let that reality be there. And that seems to be the problem that Naropa encountered in his meeting with Tilopa. He regarded himself as a student and thought he had to do something—ask for Tilopa's teaching. Thus he was still seeing Tilopa as an external person rather than as a part of his own psychological makeup presenting itself as Tilopa.

Dealing with spiritual masters is very tricky. They may be individual persons with a name and age and so on, born in such-and-such a place, with a particular lifestyle. Yet such a master is part of your ghost, part of your shadow; he's your phantom, coming back because you would like to deal with him on the level of spirituality rather than in terms of ego's language.

If you try to deal with him directly in terms of ego's language, it is very, very complicated. Dealing with a lawyer or a salesman is quite simple. If it's a salesman, you just examine the merchandise and pay him money, take your merchandise, and go home. That's a very realistic relationship. But with a spiritual friend, it is quite different. You can't pay him with material objects. You can't pay him by being ingratiating or by being aggressive and insisting on getting something out of him: "If you don't teach me, I'll kill you." That doesn't work either. Somehow there is always a very subtle relationship involved. Although there is some kind of exchange, that exchange is very subtle, almost bewildering. And most of us do not know how to relate with it.

Even Naropa, for instance, didn't know how to relate with it. Naropa was one of the world's most educated men, one of the world's most intelligent scholars. As a professor, Naropa was often referred to as "the only eye of the world." Still, something did not work in the way he dealt with Tilopa. In spite of his scholastic, philosophical, and metaphysical understanding of the dharma, somehow something didn't click at all. In fact, things went the opposite way altogether.

It seems that the relationship between the student and the teacher is a very subtle relationship, and if that subtle relationship does not work, then it works its way into a very painful process. We cannot present ourselves in that subtle relationship as a friend. We have to reduce ourselves to a patient, a sick person. We could be a friend at the same time, but still our main style of presenting ourselves to our spiritual friend is as a physically or mentally fucked-up person—rather than just a friend who is gracious, intelligent, friendly, and loving. Someone might try to present himself that way, but somehow his whole way of carrying his being makes it very difficult for the spiritual friend to accept him in this role of friend.

As a spiritual friend, you see this person inviting himself onto your doorstep. He is frantically shivering, shaking, freaking. Obviously, you invite him in, give him a seat, calm him down. And then you find out what is wrong with this person. Does this person need an operation, or would just some instant medicine help? Usually the person needs an operation more than hospitality.

This operation has different stages. To begin with, one has to deal with the body and the environment. (When I say "body," I am referring to mind-body). The whole problem of this person who has come to you, the kind of sickness he has, is a conflict between "that" and "this." *That,* in this case, refers to the projections we put out. When we put out projections, they bounce back on us, manifesting as seductive or threatening, or whatever. *This* is the perceiver of those projections.

So there is a conflict between "that" and "this" constantly, all the time. That is the cause of the symptoms of the sicknesses of all kinds that the person who has come to us is going through—all kinds of suffering. It is a sickness of cosmic chaos, a sickness of cosmic misunderstanding, a sickness of losing ground either here or there, losing the ground of "that" or losing the ground of "this." Therefore, the operation is not so much one of cutting out pieces of sickness and sewing the person back up. That doesn't cure. Cutting out the areas of sickness and sewing him back up doesn't mean anything. He still has the sickness; he still has the body.

The only operation that the spiritual friend can perform is a mutual operation. The student should not be under anesthetics of any kind. No anesthetics. It is the experience of the operation that is important rather than the operation itself. A mother might want to have natural childbirth because she wants to see her child being born, brought out of her. She doesn't want to be put under anesthetics. She wants to take part in the whole process of the birth. Here, it is exactly the same: we have to have a natural operation rather than one with anesthetics.

And of course, every penetration of the knife that cuts the tense skin, full of muscular tension that has developed from the chaos, from the conflict between "this" and "that," is enormously powerful. This tension is just about to explode; that is why the operation is needed. No matter how gentle the physician is, there will be pain. In fact, the gentler the physician, the more acute the pain will be, because the physician does not take any chances. He does not just chop something off, but he is deliberate, very slow and very careful. The stroke of his knife is a very slow movement, extremely slow and kind.

This is exactly the kind of operation that Tilopa performs on Naropa. His operating knife is extremely sharp. At the beginning you hardly notice it's cut, but sometime later it becomes overwhelming. That kind gesture, which we talked about earlier as the absence of idiot compassion, is part of dealing with reality, the absolute quality of the world.

It seems that we do not have the time and space here to go into the symbolism of the twelve successive situations that Naropa faced. Each one contains a different symbolism. But we can describe the whole process that those twelve experiences make up. To begin with, it is a process of cutting and opening up, releasing the tension in the skin. The skin is extremely tense because there is pressure from inside and pressure from outside. The inside pressure is confusion and uncertainty about how to relate with things. The external pressure comes from the fact that things we have put out have begun to bounce back on us. There is this extraordinary pressure that builds up, so we cut open the patient's skin and remove a certain part of his organism that is producing this neurological pressure.

This seems to describe the subtle level of the twelve experiences Naropa went through. In this process, the first thing is dealing with the facade, then dealing with the inner phenomena, and then dealing with the innermost ones, going deeper, deeper, deeper into social situations, emotions, and so on. To begin with, there are social hesitations of all kinds that are based on conventional rules. Naropa has been brought up as a prince, and he has an upper-class snobbishness. In accordance with this, his life is based on the expectation that everything will be conducted properly and precisely. That kind of gentility in him is connected with the social setup.

Then there are the inner phenomena, which you get into at the level of being just about to give up social jargon. There is conflict, because it is hard to tune in to that inward way of thinking and that inward emotion. This also involves giving up the philosophical and metaphysical beliefs of all kinds that Naropa had acquired.

Then beyond that is naked emotion, direct emotional states.

In other words, these twelve experiences that Naropa went through were a continuous unlearning process. To begin with, he had to unlearn, to undo the cultural facade. Then he had to undo the philosophical and emotional facade. Then he had to step out and become free altogether. This whole process was a very painful and very deliberate operation.

This does not apply to Naropa and his time alone. This could also be something very up-to-date. This operation is applicable as long as we have conflicting emotions and erroneous beliefs about reality. Conflicting emotions and wrong beliefs about reality are known as the two veils. As long as they remain universal, the treatment, the operation without anesthetics, remains very up-to-date. And that is merely the beginning.

Student: Are there several layers of emotional veils, different kinds of emotions constituting more than one layer of the veil of conflicting emotions?

Trungpa Rinpoche: According to Nagarjuna's analysis of human psychology, there is the actual emotion, the direct one that we usually call emotion; then there is the intention of that emotion, of that confusion of emotion; and then there is the activator of the emotion. You see, the whole thing goes back to ego's basic formula of maintaining itself. The ego cannot maintain itself unless there is a subtle way of setting its wheels in motion. Those wheels are set into motion by a slight move; then they roll faster, then finally extremely fast. It's like setting anything in motion: first it's slow, then it's faster, then it's extremely fast.

The layers of emotion begin with fascination. There is the fascination with a feeling that there might be something there, but on the other hand, there might not—that kind of uncertainty about something's being there. Then one begins to get much more adventurous: "Supposing there is something there, let's look for it, or let's get into it." The whole thing moves more rhythmically. And since there is now something you can move, that you have put forward, then finally you are not only just concerned with that movement or that speed, not just concerned with discovery alone, but you begin to be concerned about what comes after the discovery and begin hoping there will be another discovery. And so on and so on.

So the final emotional state is not so much just wanting to have experience of one thing, but wanting to experience the next thing. So the whole process becomes very fast, very speedy.

Student: You were talking about projecting something out and getting it back and the whole thing reflecting some kind of cosmic chaos. I didn't follow that.

Trungpa Rinpoche: When you project something out, that projection also becomes a message for the next thing. If you shout, your echo comes back to you. If you talk to somebody, that person reacts to your communication. If you put out any vibrations, they automatically re-bound back on you. This is a natural thing, which is always there. Scientifically, things happen that way. Because of that, there is the natural situation that it is hard to strategize the whole process. How to deal with the rebounds is the inner level. For that you have to develop another tactic, another policy. Having put something out in the first place was impulse, an impulsive move. But getting what you put out back is an unexpected thing. You will have to work out how to deal with that thing. There's that kind of red tape. Somebody has to be manufacturing foreign policy, so to speak, which makes everything very centralized and self-conscious.

Student: How do you relate to your spiritual friend while you are slowly being cut up by him? You said aggression doesn't work. That seems to be obvious. Various social games don't work. Yet there is this exquisite torture. I suppose that should produce feelings of gratitude, but somehow . . .

Trungpa Rinpoche: Well, you see, he is not dealing with your problems other than through your reactions. Do you see what I mean?

S: No.

TR: The operation is performed on your reactions, not on anything else. Your reactions are the very juicy substance that is cut up and sewn and pieced together. That way you have no room at all to play with, even in the most vague situations like those in the first portion of Naropa's search, before he meets Tilopa. Each time he first meets a situation, he has a reaction against it, which triggers off the next situation automatically. And later on, there is always a message coming through to him, saying things like, "Tomorrow I will visit a freak show." There is a hint. He blindly keeps failing to guess the message, but he reacts to it.

S: If you could control your reactions, would that help? If your reactions weren't so much in conflict with the situation around you or weren't so aggressive toward it, there wouldn't be that friction. . . .

TR: It's not a question of what you should be or what you should be doing. It's a question of what you are. The operation can always be performed on what your potential for reactions is. I mean, you can't escape.

Student: Is it right, then, to say that there must be a fundamental trust in your spiritual friend so that you can allow yourself to react however you're going to, knowing that there is a communication that goes beyond your immediate reactions?

Trungpa Rinpoche: I suppose that's the situation. But at the same time that you have a feeling of fundamental, absolute trust, you also have the feeling that you don't want to walk out of the situation while it's still such a mess. You have started already, so your fate is inevitable. It's an unfinished karmic situation.

Student: I didn't quite follow that part about having to relate with your body. Is it that when you see something new, you don't know what to do with it, so you move into a state where you have to relate more with your body than your thoughts? I didn't understand that point.

Trungpa Rinpoche: Well, the starting point is the physical situation. Usually physical problems bring about the fundamental situations leading to meeting the spiritual friend. For example, Naropa's attempt to commit suicide brings Tilopa there. Because finally Naropa is actually relating with his body; finally he has come to the point where the only solution is relating with the earth. Of course, his particular solution was rather a questionable one.

S: I took that symbolically as the suicide of ego.

TR: Yes, but then you are holding the wrong end of the stick by taking the ego to be body rather than mind. There is a confusion as to what really is ego and what is not. You just think, "If I eliminate this tiresome object that gets in the way all the time . . ." But if you eliminate that, you may have no further opportunity of receiving teaching.

In fact, what hangs around and gets in the way is ego rather than the body. But still, relatively speaking, that was an intelligent move on the part of confused Naropa. He was beginning to get some sense of the symbolism of ego. But he related to that symbolism by seeing the body as ego. That was the only thing available at the time, which is understandable. For example, if people begin feeling claustrophobic sitting in their offices, they might try to open the window or remove a picture from the wall or something else of that nature. At least that's an intelligent gesture symbolically. But it doesn't really help.

Student: You were talking about the emotion, the intention of the emotion, and then a third thing that I didn't understand.

Trungpa Rinpoche: Those are the stages of the development of the emotion. There's the emotion, the intention, and then the possibility of discovering something, which is inquisitive mind. You start with inquisitive mind and then set things in motion, and then that motion becomes more adventurous. Then finally you not only care about discovering, but you care more about the next thing. Getting something is no longer the answer, but getting something more is the answer, which is based again on the inquisitive mind that was there at the beginning. The Tibetan word for the development of inquisitive mind is *gyuwa,* which means a sort of a flicker. It's like a very bright flashlight. While looking with the flashlight, you don't know what is happening. You close your eyes because of this glaring light, but then you move all the faster with your delayed reaction after the light is off. The occurrence is gyuwa, the impulsive moment of fascination, which is much faster than your reaction. It sees the flashlight beam on this brilliant moment and then tries to catch the next one, the next moment.

Student: Don't you outpace yourself that way?

Trungpa Rinpoche: Somehow you don't, actually. You make up for the loss of time. A very efficient administrator is running the whole show there.

All the emotions have that kind of starting point of a sudden manipulative, impulsive move. In other words, you can't have emotions at all without an object for putting your greed or hate or other emotion onto. Then, when you put that emotion out, automatically you get something back. Then you use what you get back as source material for putting out something further. It acts as a kind of fuel. You go on and on like that. When you put out something, you get your fuel back, then you use that fuel for the next one. You build up this whole context.

Student: Could you explain the meaning of Tilopa's repeated formula about how "this body believing in an I" deserves to be gotten rid of, and how Naropa should "look into the mirror of his mind"?

Trungpa Rinpoche: In other words, the ego is the ideal fuel, the fuel that is exciting to burn. Consuming the ego as fuel, that would make a nice fire. If you want to make a good fire, one that is dry and puts out a lot of heat and doesn't leave a lot of cinders, from the point of view of non-ego, ego is *the* best fuel that could be found in the whole universe. Discovering this delightful fuel, this highly efficient fuel, is based on looking into the mirror of your mind. That is what watches the ego burning. The mirror of your mind, you could say, is one's innate nature or buddha mind, or whatever you would like to call it. It has a very intelligent and extremely practical and scientific quality behind it. So if you look into the mirror of the mind, which sees a panoramic vision of everything, you know how to choose your next fuel of ego.

That is the whole idea of using samsaric situations as stepping-stones to enlightenment. And it's also the same idea that if there is no samsara, there is no enlightenment. The two are interdependent.

Student: You're saying that the operation is only a success if the patient dies.

Trungpa Rinpoche: Yes, yes.

Student: In that case, what good does the operation do?

Trungpa Rinpoche: It's a feast, a celebration.

Student: You talked about how the process of projection tends to escalate. It seems there could be two approaches to doing something about it. Either you could de-escalate slowly or attempt to stop cold. Which is the better approach, the one that will work?

Trungpa Rinpoche: To begin with, you don't have to regard the projections as something wrong, something bad you should get rid of. This is precisely the point about ego being the only fuel for wisdom. So projections are welcomed; one is delighted to find projections to work on. One doesn't have to try to shut them off or shut them out, but should take advantage of their presence.

S: How?

TR: By understanding or realizing or appreciating their presence. That appreciation is necessary, of course. If there's appreciation, then obviously the projections won't become demonic or irritating or destructive at all.

Student: How do we arrange to appreciate them?

Trungpa Rinpoche: That probably needs more practice. You don't deliberately try to appreciate them. That doesn't seem to be a particularly accurate way of enjoying oneself. If you feel you have to enjoy something—suppose you felt you had to enjoy a party given by your rich uncle—that doesn't mean you will actually enjoy it. Instead you must just see the factual situations of projections as they are. You don't have to do anything with them. If you don't try to do anything with them, the discoveries come naturally; you have a natural situation there.

Student: Is not trying correlated with a bodily state of relaxation?

Trungpa Rinpoche: Not necessarily. It's actually not trying to do anything at all [even relax]. That's the whole point.

Student: Rinpoche, concerning these twelve tortures, I guess you could call them, that Naropa was put through, I can see that the first one took an incredible amount of courage—or trust or faith. But then he was healed. And each time after that, he was healed. Wouldn't that give the whole thing more of a game quality? Like jumping off a cliff isn't really jumping off a cliff if you know your guru's going to put you back together afterward. So that seems to be cheating a bit.

Trungpa Rinpoche: You have to take into account the extreme and constant sincerity of Naropa. He was a very sincere person. Each time he saw one of those visions, for instance; I mean, by the end of the visions one would expect he would begin to presume there was some message involved. But he was too sincere with himself. He took everything seriously.

S: But he was killed at one time and then revived. I mean, a person has got to notice that!

TR: But still his mind doesn't work that way. The reality is too real for him.

Student: You talked about our dreams and fantasies and said that when those are gone, there is still the shadow of the dreams. What are the shadows?

Trungpa Rinpoche: The shadows are the reality. The shadows of dreams are reality. Dreams are such an insubstantial thing. But that insubstantial thing presents such solid things as its shadow—like a shell.

An experience of the shadow of the outer dream experience is meeting Tilopa, the shadow of the dream. Dreams produce reality; reality produces dreams.

S: But when we dream, that's fantasy, not reality.

TR: But the impact of the dream is reality. Our thought process could be called a dream; what happens in our daily life situations is a fantasy as well.

S: So fantasies are useful?

TR: They could be a hang-up at the same time.

S: How do you distinguish whether they're useful or destructive?

TR: You don't have to particularly. That's the whole problem. When we begin to do that, the whole thing becomes very methodical, too definite, too predictable to be true.

S: So what do you do?

TR: You just float along.

Student: From that point of view, how do you regard the difference between reality and unreality? Or is there any difference?

Trungpa Rinpoche: Well, there seems to be something. I suppose reality is that which is connected with body when you are awake. And unreality is that which is purely connected with your fantasies when you are asleep or when you are in a discursive thought process.

S: Can your fantasies make some impact on your realities? Can some fantasy make you do something real?

TR: That's exactly what I'm saying. The fantasy produces a shell, which is reality. The shadow of the fantasy is reality.

Student: What's the difference between appreciation and fascination?

Trungpa Rinpoche: Fascination works purely in terms of highlights. In other words, appreciation deals with qualities, and fascination deals with the colors of the qualities. One is fascinated by the deep gold quality of gold rather than appreciating gold as something rich and valuable. Fascination is purely involved with the color of gold; appreciation appreciates its value.

S: Fascination is more on the surface.

TR: More on the surface, yes. It's an impulsive thing.

S: You're kind of caught . . .

TR: Caught by the highlights, yes.

Student: You seemed to say that it wasn't necessary to discriminate between useful and destructive fantasies. Is it not necessary to be cautious about the kind of experiences we want to enter into? Don't I have to be concerned about the price I'm paying for an experience? Is there karma?

Trungpa Rinpoche: There's karma always, whatever you do.

S: Then if certain things make more karma, should we avoid entering into those things?

TR: That just creates another karma. Boycotting something also creates karma, as much as taking part in it does.

S: Not less or more?

TR: It's more or less the same, you see, unless the whole process is regarded in terms of the fundamental principle of the creator of the karmic situation. It seems that the practice of meditation is the only way one can step out of planting further karma. Meditation practice has this particular quality of providing a pure gap and not feeding on concepts of any kind. You just deal with the technique. Meditation practice is the only way of providing a gap, of not sowing a further seed. If you're trying to be careful, that also sows a seed. It's almost the same. We could speak in terms of black karma or white karma, but both are a color.

S: Don't certain experiences make it more difficult for us to meditate?

TR: That depends on the context you provide for them, on the way you treat that situation. Some people find complicated or rich surroundings more conducive to meditation. Some people find simple surroundings more conducive.

S: Don't the activities I engage in during the day color my experience when I sit down to meditate?

TR: That depends on how you view them.

S: In a very screwed-up way.

TR: If you view them as something . . .

S: Bad.

TR: . . . bad, that begins to haunt you. If you view something as being extremely good, that also begins to haunt you. The conceptual mind is extremely powerful. It runs the whole show of samsara.

Student: Meditation, then, is the only thing that in and of itself has no color, and therefore . . .

Trungpa Rinpoche: It's at least a primordial gesture. Meditation is a primordial gesture.

FOUR

Something Very Tickling

WHEN NAROPA FINALLY discovered Tilopa, there was no particular gracious occasion. There was no ceremonial initiation of any kind. The initiation consisted in Tilopa's taking off his slipper and slapping Naropa on the cheek, which sent Naropa into a coma, weakened as he was. Then Tilopa sang a song to the effect of "Whatever I have experienced in the mahamudra, Naropa has also experienced, so in the future, whoever is open to the teaching of mahamudra should get it from Naropa."

That was quite interesting and shocking. Naropa achieved realization in a sudden glimpse. But we shouldn't be too optimistic, thinking that we too will experience a sudden transmission like that. Probably we won't. The whole thing is very haphazard, very much a matter of taking a chance.

The teachings of Naropa are known as the six dharmas or six doctrines. The first doctrine connected with his sudden discovery of the mahamudra experience is called illusory body. He discovered that every situation or experience is illusory, is to be regarded as body and nonbody, substance and nonsubstance. He experienced life as like a mirage.

The second doctrine has to do with dream. Our fantasies are involved with trying to pin down experience as something fixed, which actually doesn't exist at all.

Then there is the doctrine related with the bardo experience, which is the intermediate situation between death and birth.

Then we have inner heat, or *tumo* (which in Sanskrit is *chandali*), an inner burning that arouses the universal flame that burns away all conceptualized notions of whatever kind, totally consuming them.

Then there is transference of consciousness. Since you do not believe in physical existence as a solid thing that you can take refuge in, you can switch out of such a belief into nonbelief, transfer your consciousness into open space, a space which has nothing to do with the fixed notion of "me and mine" and "that and this" at all.

The last, the sixth doctrine, is luminosity (*ösel* in Tibetan), all-pervading luminosity. There is nothing at all that is regarded as a dark corner, an area of mystery anymore. The whole thing is seen as open, brilliant, things as they really are. There are no mysterious corners left.

Very crudely, those are the six doctrines of Naropa. I look forward to a situation in which we have time to go into them in a more subtle and fundamental way. That would be extremely good. At this point, I hope we have at least started something in terms of arousing inquisitive mind. There may be something happening somewhere underneath human confusion, which is very tickling.

Let's leave it at that for now and dedicate our actions here, our working together, to American karma. Something is trying to come out of American karma. It's dying to burst, dying to blast. Let's make a homemade bomb out of this seminar.

Part Two

LIFE OF NAROPA SEMINAR II

Karmê Chöling, 1973

ONE

Pain and Hopelessness

W E ARE GOING to discuss the life and teaching of Naropa, which is basically a tantric subject. It will be necessary to know something about tantra in order to understand Naropa. This might be hard, but we can certainly try.

Tantra, or vajrayana, is the most fundamental and final stage of the development of wisdom in Buddhism. It is the final development of the enlightenment experience. The enlightenment experience has three levels. There is the nirmanakaya level, the level of manifestation. On this level, enlightened mind can communicate with ordinary living beings. Then there is the sambhogakaya level, the level that communicates with the emotions and energy of ordinary beings. And then there is the *dharmakaya* level, the wisdom that communicates with the greater depths of ignorance in ordinary sentient beings.

Those three types of buddhas are fully dealt with in tantra. It could be said that they are dealt with in the mahayana too, but the final development of the mahayana state is the tantric state. In other words, there is really no such thing as a mahayana buddha. All the buddhas are fully realized, fully awakened in the tantric fashion. That is to say, advanced mahayana becomes tantra.

In the hinayana, enlightened beings are called arhats. An arhat is a relatively realized person, who can relate to himself but cannot fully relate with other beings. He understands himself, and consequently he is able to demonstrate the teachings and give the teachings to others. People manage to relate to his understanding of himself, and they in turn develop understanding. This is the learning situation relating with arhats.

However, at this point we are going to discuss the vajrayana, tantra, the ultimate experience of realization. We have to understand the basics of tantra. The way to approach tantra is by developing intellect and intuition, mind and body, so that they work together. Mind and body consciousness working together at the beginner's level means the realization of pain and suffering—having hang-ups and realizing them, having pain and noticing it. This is a very basic level. Still, it requires a certain amount of intelligence.

You might say that it is very easy to understand or experience pain. Oh no. It takes a lot of understanding to realize pain. This level of understanding is what is necessary to prepare the ground for tantra. The tantric type of intelligence exists right at the beginning at the ordinary level, the level of pain. So we shouldn't jump the gun and try to be too advanced, to bypass the ground floor and go right to the top floor. At this point, tantric intelligence is understanding, realizing, experiencing pain.

The term *tantra* means "continuity." It refers to a continuity of intelligence that goes on constantly. This kind of intelligence cannot be inhibited or prevented, and it cannot be interrupted. From the Buddhist point of view, our basic being is fundamental intelligence and wakefulness that has been clouded over by all kinds of veils and obscurations. What prevents us from seeing pain is that we fail to see these veils. The method used in tantra to enable us to realize pain is called mantra.

In this case, mantra has nothing to do with some verbal gibberish that you repeat over and over. Mantra here is an upaya, a skillful means. The derivation of the word *mantra* is the Sanskrit *mantraya,* which is a combination of two words. *Manas* means "mind," and *traya* means "protection." So mantra protects the mind, the fundamental intelligence or wakefulness. It does not protect it by using guards or putting it under a glass dome. Protection here is clearing away obstacles, clearing away threats. All threats to that intelligence are cleared away. This is the style of protection here. Not allowing the intelligence to become obscured improves it. This is a different style of protection from the paranoid one of guarding against something, fending something off. The obscurations are removed, and that is the protection.

So mantra is the means or method. We have to have this skillful means in order to realize pain at the beginning. This is the hinayana approach to tantra, which is developing fundamental openness.

Pain is often very serious. Pain is often unspeakable. Not that it is difficult to describe, but we don't want to describe it. From that point of view, pain is synonymous with ego. Ego *is* pain, and pain *is* ego. Pain is neurosis.

Pain, or ego, is unspeakable. It's an enormous secret. It's such a big secret, we don't even have to name it. We can just barely make a reference to it and our colleague or friend will know what we're talking about. You might say, "Today's been a very heavy day." Your friend will never ask, "A heavy day of what?" It's understood. It's mystical communication.

Whenever the possibility of that kind of communication presents itself, we shy away from it. We go just so far and then we turn around. We don't go too far. Maybe we assume that if we went too far, it would be embarrassing for our colleague or friend. But actually it would be embarrassing to us (maybe to our friend or colleagues as well). Pain is the unnameable private parts we don't want to mention. It's a sacred name. It's a samsaric version of God. Its style of protection is the hesitation of not going into it as far as you can because you are threatened by the sense of going into it too far.

There is actually no danger in going too far. The danger, from ego's point of view, is that if we go too far, we may not know how to reassemble ourselves afterward. It's like the nursery rhyme about Humpty Dumpty: "All the king's horses and all the king's men couldn't put Humpty together again." There's no hope. Whatever power we can call on, the greatest of the greatest powers we can put together cannot put our ego together again once it has been exposed. It is impossible, and we *know* that. We are so intelligent. There is a hint of tantra there already: we actually know how to protect ourselves from the protection of ego, that sense of an enormous scheme being there, even though it's a very simple little thing that is taking place. All that is the pain.

It is not so much the actual agony of having something like rheumatism or having been hurt psychologically by somebody and feeling bad about it. That is not quite the pain that is going on here. It is the fundamental mystical experience of "thisness," beingness, and unspeakableness—that thing we don't talk about to ourselves, let alone to others.

We never even *think* of it. That is the pain. And there is a kind of intelligence there.

In Naropa's case, he wanted to overcome this pain, and he decided to leave his home and join a monastic establishment so he could expose himself to the mercies of the teachers and gurus—so he could give up, take refuge, give up arrogance, confusion, and so forth. But according to the example of Naropa's life, only exposing "this" is not quite enough.

Obviously in the West, with encounter groups, confession, psychiatrists, and so on, people have developed the idea of exposing the secret as far as you can, speaking your mind on religious, social, and philosophical subjects of all kinds. The methods range from taking part in orgies to becoming Catholic and confessing oneself. There are so many ways of seemingly exposing oneself. We seem to have some understanding about self-exposure, and we do our best. But that doesn't seem to be quite the same thing we are doing here.

Not that I am criticizing every method that has been developed so far in the West as a failure. Not at all. There is an element of truth in all of them. We seem to be hitting the right nail, but that doesn't mean that we are hitting it on the head. We are hitting the general area of the nail anyway. Generally, things are following the right pattern. Particularly, spiritual, psychological, and philosophical developments that have taken place in this country recently have been remarkably intelligent. But the thing is: what happens then? Should we keep repeating the same ceremonies of exposure of our ego constantly, every day, every hour, every week? There is a limit to how many times we can go to an orgy. There's a limit to how many times we can go to confession. Repeating the same thing over and over again at some point becomes a drug, which gives a sense of relief, of openness or far-outness.

The problem here has nothing to do with the technique being wrong. It is the attitude that seems to be wrong. Through methods of exposing ourselves, we want to get rid of the burden of this secret in us, because somebody might recognize it and use it against us. That is usually the logic. We want to get completely clear and clean so nobody can attack us anymore.

That's a very smart scheme. But interestingly, sometimes during the process of scheming, we discover a new scheme. In the process of going through the techniques and methods of the first scheme, we find another method, another scheme. We end up bombarded by all kinds of alternatives, and we are never able to relate with any of them properly. We get completely lost.

Or else we are very earnest and honest and follow one method in a very methodical, businesslike fashion. We become professional orgy-goers or professional encounter-groupies. In that way, we create another shell. The original trick doesn't work anymore. The trick of repeating the ceremony of uncovering ourselves creates another mask, a very thick mask, and once more we are embedded in the rock. Again and again it happens, and we can't get out of it. The methods themselves become obstacles. There is nothing we can do about it.

The problem seems to be the attitude that the pain should go, then we will be happy. That is our mistaken belief. The pain never goes, and we will never be happy. That is the truth of suffering, duhkha satya. Pain never goes; we will never be happy. There's a mantra for you. It's worth repeating. You've got the first initiation now: you've got a mantra.

It is not so much that pain is an obstacle. Rather, as we go on, pain becomes an obstacle because we want to get rid of it. Of course, at the beginning we may not regard the pain as an obstacle. The first thing is stupidity: not realizing the pain. Then we realize the pain and we become familiar with the hang-ups connected with the pain. Then we want to get rid of that. That's the second veil, regarding the pain as an obstacle.

The idea is to learn to live with the pain in accordance with the Buddhist tradition of taking refuge. This is one of the very prominent, very important methods. Taking refuge here means surrendering hope rather than surrendering fear. When we give up promises, potentials, possibilities, then we begin to realize that there is no burden of further imprisonment. We have been completely freed, even from hope, which is a really refreshing experience. In other words, if we accept the burden as truly burdensome, completely burdensome, then its heaviness does not exist anymore. Because it is truly a burden, truly heavy. It is like identifying with a heavy rock that is pressing you into the ground. If you identify with the rock, you don't exist. You become the rock.

But that, too, becomes very tricky. Once you start looking at it that way, you can turn that into another trick. You create trick after trick that imprisons you with hope, until you finally realize there is no hope.

We are going to go through Naropa's life stage by stage and try to see how it applies to ourselves, rather than looking at it as the myth of Naropa, of a great teacher who got enlightened and lived happily ever after. There must be realities that connect his life with ours. This first step of hopelessness, for example, plays an extremely important part in realizing the foundations for tantra at the hinayana level of the Buddhist path. We can quite safely say that hope, or a sense of promise, is a hindrance on the spiritual path.

Creating this kind of hope is one of the most prominent features of spiritual materialism. There are all kinds of promises, all kinds of proofs. We find the same approach as that of a car salesman. Or it's like someone demonstrating a vacuum cleaner and telling you how well you could clean your house if you would just buy it. If you would just buy that vacuum cleaner, how beautiful your room would be, completely free of dirt and dust, down to the last speck! Whether it is a vacuum-cleaner salesman or a guru, we find the same level of salesmanship. That is why both are included in the same bag of materialists. There are so many promises involved. So much hope is planted in your heart. This is playing on your weakness. It creates further confusion with regard to pain. You forget about the pain altogether and get involved in looking for something other than the pain. And that itself *is* pain. Trying to suppress disbelief, focusing on belief, trying to convince yourself this approach will work (thinking that convincing yourself is what will make it work)— all that *is* pain.

That is what we will go through unless we understand that the basic requirement for treading the spiritual path is hopelessness. Hopelessness is not quite the same as despairing. There is a difference. Despair is laziness, lack of intellect. One is not even willing to look for the reason for the despair. It is a total flop. But hopelessness is very intelligent. You keep looking. You flip page after page, saying, "That's hopeless, that's hopeless." You are still very vigorous, hopelessly vigorous. You're still looking for hope, but each time you have to say, "Oh, no. Yuck!" Hopelessness keeps going; it is very vigorous, very inspiring. It tickles your mind as though there were something you are about to discover. When you discover it, you say, "Ah, now I've found the thing! . . . Oh, no. It's the same old thing again."

There is enormous challenge and excitement in hopelessness. When you give up, when you enter into complete despair with hopelessness after hopelessness, just before despair and laziness take you over, you begin to develop a sense of humor. You develop a sense of humor, and you don't become completely lazy and stupid.

Student: In order for me to begin to attain hopelessness, I have to have some hope. It seems that I have to go back and forth between those two. It seems there has to be that pull from both sides.

Trungpa Rinpoche: The first thing is not hope or a sense of promise as such; it's more like inquisitiveness, inquisitive mind, which explores constantly, including exploring yourself, your embarrassment about yourself, your insanity, your own confusion. That kind of inquisitiveness is not quite on the level of hope. But it is a definite step. Then, once you have found your hang-ups, your hesitation, then you begin to develop the project of getting rid of that pain and confusion. That's what we always do anyway. There's no need for a program for that; that's just what we always do.

The minute you discover your hesitations, confusions, insanity, and so on, you want to get rid of them. You look for all kinds of remedies. You shop around and you find that fundamentally none of them work. They may work great temporarily, but fundamentally, they don't work. Then you start questioning. You question the products you bought at the supermarket. You look into each brand, the instructions on the label, and so on. The salespeople are very kind, making suggestions about the products. You go through all that, and you're still struggling. Then, at a certain point, it becomes necessary to let you have it: to tell you that the only and best remedy is hopelessness—which is your own product. It doesn't cost any money or energy. You don't have to go to the supermarket, and it's cheap and good. It's organic.

Many of you have already gone through this process. You have looked in the supermarket and seen the ads. You've seen it all. Now it's time to give up hope, even give up hope of attaining enlightenment.

Student: Does despair come out of a relationship between energy and pain? If you were to fixate on pain, I think that would dissipate energy and bring despair.

Trungpa Rinpoche: You see, energy is pain in some sense. But it is not one hundred percent. Maybe fifty-fifty. Energy and intelligence create pain. Intelligence in this case means ambition. You feel you have something to achieve that you're unable to achieve. You feel you might be unable to achieve your goal.

Student: Sometimes I think I go looking for pain, that I cultivate it, and this seems masochistic. Also, I think I see other people doing the same thing. What do you think of that?

Trungpa Rinpoche: I think that sounds like a fascination or an occupation—trying to kill boredom. You don't want to look at the greater pain we're discussing—the unnameable. In order to avoid seeing that, you do anything to create a petty pain in order to avoid seeing the greater pain of "thisness," this "thing."

Student: You said that the word *tantra* means "continuity," and that confuses me because my understanding is that one of the basic qualities of an enlightened person is the fact that he is not continuous, he is not solid at all. I thought that solidness was ego, and when he discovers that that's not real, then he's free to be not continuous.

Trungpa Rinpoche: Tantra does mean "continuity." This kind of continuity cannot be challenged, because this kind of continuity never depends on superficial continuity or discontinuity. It is unconditional continuity. Obviously, the enlightenment experience involves the discontinuity of ego with its fixation, but there is also the element of all-pervasiveness—enlightenment is right now but later as well; we are enlightened now, but we will be more enlightened later. There is a thread of enlightenment that goes on all the time. The sense of the nonexistence of ego is the greatest continuity. So continuity here does not mean continuously relating to a single reference point. There is a state without reference point that is basic the way completely outer space, without stars and galaxies and planets, is basic. The stars, galaxies, and planets may be there or not, but still the space will be there.

S: And it contains everything.

TR: It contains nothing in this case, but still it contains itself. It does not need any feedback or maintenance—it does not need anything at all. That is the great umbrella above the little umbrellas.

Student: Does the discovery of hopelessness take care of itself as you go through your life day by day, or is it something you have to work on? Do you have to go out of your way somehow?

Trungpa Rinpoche: It's not easy. It wouldn't just dawn on you. You have to make a definite jump, which is a very painful one. Quite possibly, you need another person to tell you you are hopeless. That is the role of a guru. You need a spiritual friend who says, "Now you're hopeless, and you will never be able to do anything. The outlook is full of nothingness." It seems to be the role of the guru to tell you that you are hopeless or that you will never solve your problem. It has to be a shock of some kind, otherwise it doesn't work. You would just continue on with your mild complaining of all kinds.

Student: Rinpoche, would that shock of hopelessness create a sense of depression at that particular moment?

Trungpa Rinpoche: Yes, I hope so.

Student: I'm having a lot of trouble with your concept of pain. Pain to me is like feeling that I'm bleeding. And when I don't have that sense of pain, when I'm relieved of it, I say, "Well, I'm not in pain." My concept of pain is very visceral, and I feel it quite sharply. You're talking about a kind of pain that is still there when I'm relieved from my visceral pain and feeling good.

Trungpa Rinpoche: I think you have a good understanding of what I mean. That's it. It's the larger notion, the whole thing: you're relieved of pain, and then what? There are a lot of loose ends. You try to look at everything officially as extending from one particular point to another particular point. You have certain boundaries that you don't go beyond. You can't be bothered. And beyond those boundaries are still greater loose ends. And those loose ends begin to lead back to you. Then you try to tidy them up again. This is the greater thing that we don't talk about that everybody knows about.

Student: So these little pains are little things like having to find a job that can be tidied up temporarily.

Trungpa Rinpoche: And that relates with the greater thing. But, you know, if you have an actual practical task to perform, you perform it.

S: But isn't being involved in performing that task some kind of hope? Do you have to give up performing the task?

TR: No, it's not as simple as that. You can go ahead and perform your task. But that doesn't solve your greater problem. Your problem is still there.

S: But you wouldn't even have to go through that to realize the larger situation.

TR: It depends on your intelligence. Some people dream too much, so they have to go through that. And some people already have a realistic vision of the prospects of their life, so they may not have to go through it.

Student: You talked about the fact that we set up tricks for ourselves, getting involved with encounter groups and so on. We're tricking ourselves in some way in thinking that we're being more open and unmasking pain. What happens in hopelessness to those tricks? Does someone who's hopeless realize the tricks will never stop? That they will never end?

Trungpa Rinpoche: I think so. That's good, yes.

Student: Rinpoche, at the same time, I can't help but feel that there's a certain amount of joy attached to realizing the hopelessness of the situation. It seems that there's a sense of opposites coming together there.

Trungpa Rinpoche: Yes, so what?

S: Well, it seems kind of incredible, this coming together of joy and pain.

TR: Well, that's the point. Hopelessness doesn't mean that you are miserable particularly. There's lots of room for energy, more energy and more joy. But *joy* is probably the wrong word—a sense of wholesomeness, healthiness, a sense of well-being because of hopelessness.

S: But somehow without ego.

TR: The sense of well-being does not have to have ego particularly.

S: Are we, evolutionarily speaking, on the verge of hopelessness? If you read the story of Naropa, it seems like Naropa went through so much.

TR: The level of hopelessness we are talking about came at the beginning of Naropa's life, before he became a pandit. We haven't had the level of his hopelessness in dealing with Tilopa yet. That's a tantric one. This is just the beginning level, which Naropa experienced when he took monk's vows and joined the monastery.

S: That sense of hopelessness that made him enter the monastery doesn't seem particularly hopeless. It sounds more like disillusionment. I mean, if you were talking to your parents about joining a dharma group and so on, you'd talk more about disillusionment with the mundane. . . .

TR: Yes, but once he entered the monastery, he began to feel that he was inadequate, and he started pushing too hard, speeding, and so forth. Hopelessness begins there.

S: Then he just wound up going out and looking for a guru.

TR: No. Then he found his intellect. He put himself together. He became a great pandit. Which probably we will talk about tomorrow.

S: So the hopelessness you're talking about is analogous to his hopelessness in the monastic situation.

TR: Yes. You see, things worked alternatingly. First intuition, then intellect, then intuition, and then the final level of intellect. So this was the first intuition—the desire to enter a monastery. Then he entered the monastery and found hopelessness. Then he found some way that clicked in which he could work with his intellect, some way in which his hopelessness became workable. This involved a big chunk of intellect—studying the Tripitaka to the point of knowing it inside out, and so on. Then he came back to the level of intuition again when he began to look for Tilopa. And finally, when he was completely absorbed in Tilopa's teaching and had become enlightened, then he went back to intellect again. At that point, instead of being *prajna,* intellect became *jnana,* wisdom.

Student: Between intellect and intuition, is one more valid than the other?

Trungpa Rinpoche: Both of them are valid, just like your head and arms.

S: What's the difference between them?

TR: Intellect has nothing to do with book learning, becoming a scholar, particularly. It is analytical mind, which is able to see things clearly and precisely. And intuition feels things on the level of pain and pleasure.

TWO

Giving Birth to Intellect

WE HAVE DISCUSSED Naropa's first discovery of pain, or our own discovery of the meaning of Naropa's example, our own discovery of pain. This is a kind of adolescent level, involved with the discovery of the world and its meanings. Naropa joins a monastery—or you join a meditation center. He becomes part of a vihara, which is parallel with becoming part of our meditation center here.

Then, very interestingly, in the midst of practice, suddenly aggression arises—enormous anger and resentment. One does not recognize where this aggression comes from. One does not even want to trace it back. But this aggression arises. There is the aggression of having been tricked into becoming part of an established, disciplined setup, the aggression that says things should happen properly but they are not functioning the way you expected. The sense of aggression becomes everything. In fact, there is enormous awareness; an almost meditative level of absorption in aggression and resentment takes place. You are resentful that your instructor has been unreasonable to you, has disciplined you unreasonably, blamed something on you that you didn't do. There is a certain sense of disgust. In the middle of practice, there are occasional thoughts of quitting and leaving the place, and you daydream about how to work out the project of leaving in detail. But there is also some hesitation; or the project becomes so big that you are afraid to embark on it.

All this kind of aggression takes place after you begin to realize pain, the truth of pain, as a definite thing that you cannot ignore, that you cannot forget. This pain is real pain. You experience this not because you trust and believe doctrines you have been told. Rather your real pain has become obvious. It is not somebody's doctrine. You have discovered your own truth of pain.

This creates a sense of imprisonment, because what you've discovered coincides with what is taught in the books. Being imprisoned in this way by your own realization of pain is by no means pleasant. At the same time, it is exciting that in fact you are in immediate and direct communication with the truth. There is some sense of promise, but not a sense of a happy ending.

The more you look into this situation, the more horrific it becomes. That is the course that the aggression takes. You are resentful about something—about the world, the books, the people, the environment, the lifestyle—and at the same time, you resent your own existence, because you are the creator of the pain and you can't escape from yourself. The more you think about it, the more the whole thing becomes grimmer and grimmer and grimmer. Trying to reach out and kick the nearest piece of furniture doesn't help. Being rude to your colleagues doesn't help. Somehow, complaining about the food doesn't help either. An inevitable depression, a mystical depression, a very powerful one, comes with anger and resentment.

You might ask if this is good or bad. We can't say that it's good or that it's bad. But it *is*. It certainly does exist.

All that anger and resentment and pain, depression, sexual frustration, financial frustration—the things of all kinds that go on in one's head—have one good thing about them. There is one good message here, a really good one, a gem that we are about to discover in ourselves. It is not good in the sense of relieving pain and bringing happiness. It's another subtle form of pain, but it contains an enormous jewel, enormous richness, enormous beauty. It is called intellect. This pain that is happening in you and around you, that is trying to give birth and is not able to, is a message that intellect is just about to be born.

In Naropa's case, he was locked up in a monastic cell. Traditionally, you have an eight-by-eight room. You have to rise at four in the morning and go to sleep about midnight. In the courtyard of the monastery at night, a monk who keeps discipline with his big stick keeps walking around checking to make sure that everybody is up and studying, memorizing scriptures. You read by the dim light of an oil lamp. You read the scriptures, memorize them, and meditate on them.

In the monastery, the only relief comes when you change subjects of study or switch meditative techniques. You meditate and the gong goes; the only break you have is going to study. Then you study and the gong goes, and your only relief is to go back to meditation. Eating in the assembly hall is not particularly festive either. It's as though you are on trial. The monk in charge of discipline might come and reprimand you for your lack of mindfulness at any time. You're not allowed to jump or run. You walk mindfully and you speak softly. You're not allowed to shout. You're not even allowed to draw doodles.

Life at Nalanda University was very dignified, fundamentally very sane, but at the same time very severe. According to historical records, the architecture there was good, wonderful, but it was designed to suit monks. It was not at all lavish or luxurious. The basic minimum was provided. The monks had the encouragement of simplicity and awareness. The walls were designed to bounce back one's own neurotic thoughts. Every inch of one's life was planned, and particular behavior was prescribed for all situations.

The resentment that one can develop in such situations brings prajna. Great teachers like Naropa and Atisha Dipankara and Saraha—a lot of great teachers of that age—came out of such establishments. The resentment turns into prajna. *Prajna* is a Sanskrit word. *Jna* means "knowledge," and *pra* means "supreme." So prajna is supreme knowledge or greater knowledge.

We mustn't confuse that with wisdom. In the nontheistic tradition of Buddhism, knowledge comes first and wisdom comes later. Wisdom is connected with looking, and knowledge is connected with seeing. Knowledge is seeing, being aware. We have to learn how to see first. Having learned how to see, then we begin to look, which is on the wisdom level, the ultimate level.

Prajna is seeing things as they are. At the beginning, if you look without the training of seeing, you don't look at things as they are, because you don't see them. Seeing here is a matter of both awareness and discipline. You're aware of this room. You're aware of the temperature in this room, and you're aware of sitting on chairs. You have a general kind of awareness of how and where you are. The way intellect goes with that is within a state of being, such as being here and sitting on chairs, you can function. You can sit there, and at the same time, you can think and write and look. This manifestation of one's state of being is intellect.

So the intellect we are talking about is not the bookworm type. It doesn't necessarily mean being a scholar or doing research work or anything like that. Intellect in the sense of prajna is a state of being logical and open, open to any information and willing to collect it, chew it, swallow it, digest it, work with it. This is not the ordinary idea of intellect connected with intellectuals in intellectual circles. There, you are given a certain reference point. You are already programmed before you know who and what you are. You are given certain raw material, and you have to fit that raw material into certain pigeonholes that are already prepared for you.

In the case of prajna, you have the raw material with you, but you don't have the pigeonholes. If you like, you can build a pigeonhole for yourself. In that sense, with prajna, everything is homemade; that is why it is greater intellect. The only system you have is that of sharpening your intellect working within the relative frame of reference of logic. Let's take the example of saying, "I feel sick." The reason why I feel sick is that I have the memory "I used to be well; I used to feel fine." I know that I am sick because, compared with that memory, I don't feel good. It's very simple, ordinary logic like that.

Prajna is also the seed of discriminating awareness. In discriminating awareness, you take things in openly, accept everything, but at the same time, everything is examined critically. Being critical in this sense is not rejecting and accepting things in a petty way. It is seeing the values of each thing in its own place, rather than seeing its values from the point of view of whether it is threatening to your ego or helpful to it. You see things as they are with dispassionate judgment. This is again the quality of prajna, greater knowledge or transcendent knowledge—seeing dispassionately but still discriminating.

This is very painful in a way. When you begin to see things without any value judgment in the ordinary sense, without any bias regarding yourself and others, your vision and your logic and your sharpness become very painful. You don't have any filters between you and "that"; you are touching a cold stone. Reality becomes a pain in the ass. An analogy that has been used for that kind of seeing is, on a winter morning, licking a rock with frost on it; your tongue sticks to the rock because your tongue is very naked and warm and the stone is so cold. You think you are licking it, but actually your tongue is stuck. That is reality as seen with prajna. It is so immediate, and it sticks there. That's the kind of pain we are talking about.

The prajna level of pain is so immediate and so, so powerful. The level of pain we were discussing before is relatively mild—in fact, in many ways luxurious. Pain on the prajna level is much more painful than that earlier pain, because before we didn't have a chance to apply our intellect to it. We just felt painful, were imprisoned in the pain. Of course, there was some kind of intellect functioning, but not 100 percent, the way it is on the prajna level. Now we are relating with naked reality without any dualistic padding.

The notion of duality here is not that there are separate things existing and therefore we can speak of duality. The notion of duality here is that things are one, and a big barrier has been put in the middle, which divides it. The oneness on the other side is called "that," and the oneness on this side is called "this." Because of the Suez Canal we built, because of the wall we built, the one is slashed in two. And nonduality is not a matter of the two things melting back into each other, but of taking that barrier completely out. When that happens and the two aspects of the one meet, we find it is quite painful, because we are so used to having separate entities there. Now when we realize that nonduality is being imposed on us, we find it very claustrophobic, very sharp. It is much too sharp and much too powerful to meet this oneness. The "that" does not adjust to the "this," and the "this" does not adjust to the "that." Once the barrier is removed, they become one, with no chance for adjustment at all. That's why the prajna experience is so sharp and immediate and powerful—highly powerful, extraordinarily powerful.

At this prajna level, pain is seen as a hundred times bigger than we saw it at the beginning. You have acquired a brand-new, very powerful microscope, and your little pain is put under that microscope, and you look at it. You see a gigantic monster. And that's not even at the level of tantra yet. We are just barely beginning. But you cannot say that seeing the pain in this magnified way is an exaggeration at all. It is seeing things as they are in their own right perspective, seeing clearly by putting a small object under the microscope.

Naropa began to enjoy being in his monastic cell, being watched and being worked hard, because he was learning how to use language, how to communicate, how to think logically, how to work logically. He engaged in debates; he practiced and he studied, memorized texts. And he felt very comfortable. But at the same time, he felt tortured by his rediscovery of reality from the mahayana point of view. As far as we are concerned, we have a lot to learn from the example of his life. We could learn to trust in our intellect.

I suppose we should make a distinction between analytical mind and intellectual mind. In the case of analytical mind, you already have formulas that have been given to you, and you try to use those formulas to analyze things you come across. You interpret in accordance with certain given methods. With intellectual mind free from analytical mind, the only formula you have is basic logic—you are without set ideas and patterns; you are not bound by any social, philosophical, or religious standards. You are free from that indoctrination; therefore, you are able to see your pain more magnified, as though under a microscope. That is the main difference between analytical mind and intellectual mind, intellectual mind being synonymous with prajna.

Another thing about analytical mind is that there is a certain amount of aggression involved in it. You are defending your faith. You are analyzing in such a way as to fit something into an already worked-out reference point, and there is a spare part missing. Therefore, you are studying matters concerning that spare part. Then, having discovered the spare part, you have to make it fit into the original body—which is very aggressive and very demanding, and it makes you totally blind. You fail to see the rest of the whole. Whereas intellect in the sense of prajna is very open and has never been given a particular project. The only project there is for prajna is to see totality and clarity. In order to understand the parts, you have to relate with the whole body rather than concentrating on the parts. That seems to be prajna's style.

Student: Where does the emotional element come in with prajna? If pain is magnified a hundred times, a lot of emotions must come along with that. Does prajna have the ability to handle those emotions?

Trungpa Rinpoche: We don't have that ability at this point. We don't have the equipment to deal with emotions yet—that is, Naropa doesn't yet have it. That was why he was led on to tantra. He realized that, instead of everything being so clear-cut, he had another problem. The level of prajna we've talked about so far has nothing to do with emotions as such. It's just intellect. It's like the level of a teenager in the puberty stage who is still fascinated by gadgets, who is never concerned with affects and emotions—anger or aggression or anything like that. He is just rediscovering the universe constantly.

S: With logic leading.

TR: Yes, that's precisely how Naropa was.

Student: I thought it was one of the failings of analytical mind that it doesn't take into account the rawer aspects of experiences but rather deals in abstractions. I don't see how prajna or what you call intellectual mind can operate without relating to the emotions.

Trungpa Rinpoche: Analytical mind can analyze the emotions, but there are still certain dogmas and philosophical ideas involved. Prajna, or the intellect, sees emotions as loose ends; it sees them very technically—as part of the five skandhas, for example. From the point of view of prajna, you don't have to get into them particularly. You see them clearly and in fact could describe them to other people and help them. But still this doesn't really work when compared to the tantric level. It doesn't become as fully emotional as it should be, could be. In prajna, you can relate to the raw material by having confidence. You don't really have to get into it exactly. You have to relate to it personally, but not on the emotional level as such.

Student: Is the intellectual approach what the arhats overstressed?

Trungpa Rinpoche: The arhats didn't seem to do that very much. It seems to have been the young ambitious pandits like Naropa, people newly converted to prajna with its dispassionate kind of clarity. Those are the bodhisattvas up to the seventh bhumi.

Student: How is it possible to work through the confusions of the lower bhumis and still maintain that kind of distance?

Trungpa Rinpoche: You can, because your mind is so sharp. Your mind is extraordinarily sharp, and there are no obstacles to it at all. It can see through anything right away. But that is not the same as involving yourself in the confusion or emotion fully, being completely in it, which could happen.

I think the problem on the prajna level is that relationships are taken as a basic reference point with regard to each other, and emotions are taken as a basic reference point with regard to each other. The only thing lacking here is the highest form of fundamental rawness and ruggedness found on the tantric level. Although there is only a superficial understanding of the raw material, there is a certain amount of fearlessness at the same time. You do not hesitate to deal with things as they are, but you are still at the level of seeing. That fearlessness is possible if your mind is really tuned in to prajna, the sword of Manjushri. The sword of Manjushri cuts constantly; it never stays in its sheath.

Student: Is it prajna the way we see and hear everything happening without having any power to stop it or pick and choose? Then subsequently we sort it all out; a split second later we pick and choose. Is prajna the primary receptivity before we say things like, "I like tall more than short?"

Trungpa Rinpoche: Yes, I think so.

S: If you could live totally in that, without the second judgment, without the subsequent activity of the mind, would there be a familiarity from when you knew both things?

TR: Both things?

S: Yes. First you see something clearly, without the overlay quality of judgment. But then, as you go on judging what you saw, you familiarize yourself with it more or less. But before that familiarization, before your bias becomes involved, is there still a sense of familiarity with what you see, or does it become something strange?

TR: I think there's still familiarity, because there's trust in one's own intellect. You may be dealing with completely alien raw material, but at the same time, there's trust in your own intelligence, which creates another level of familiarity with things. It's like a confident general conducting warfare on the battlefield. He probably doesn't know the nature of his enemy, but he's confident he can wipe him out.

Student: Rinpoche, what is aware of prajna? Prajna being awareness of various things, is there something that is aware of prajna? Or is prajna aware of prajna?

Trungpa Rinpoche: There are two levels to that. The first level is prajna being aware of itself in such a way that it cuts its own blade. It's so fast and so precise that it cuts itself. This doesn't blunt its blade; that blade sharpens itself by cutting itself. Then there is another level, which is the awareness of skillful means. It is aware of how and when to use the sword. The use of the sword creates feedback to the swordsman.

But prajna is by no means regarded as absolute. It is still a relative experience, because striking with a sword is going from here to there.

Even though the sword may have two edges, while you're cutting "that," you can't cut "this." You have to cut "this" after "that" has been cut. So there is still a process and a journey involved, which brings a sense of skill, a sense of confidence. The blade of the sword is accuracy and wakefulness, and the body of the sword is confidence and delight in itself.

S: Is prajna cutting itself similar to disowning your own insight?

TR: Definitely, yes. Prajna is an ongoing process—constantly cutting, all the time. So all the time it is cutting, it has to sharpen its own blade. Otherwise you would have to stop cutting to sharpen the blade. So it's a built-in mechanism, so to speak. Cutting through sharpens itself, because it cuts itself as soon as it cuts the other.

Student: Is this sense of confidence the reason that prajna can't handle emotions?

Trungpa Rinpoche: Well, we can't really say that prajna can't handle emotions; rather, emotions never occur on the prajna level; emotions are no longer a part of that particular level. They are just irrelevant from that point of view. Emotions are not particularly dealt with, and the problem of emotions never occurred.

S: Because prajna is just seeing?

TR: Yes.

Student: I was wondering a bit more about the relationship between resentment and prajna. Did you mean to say that resentment caused prajna? Or when that kind of resentment comes on, it's already prajna, understanding?

Trungpa Rinpoche: The resentment gives birth to prajna. You give birth to a sword. It begins to cut through your insides, and there is all kinds of pain and resentment, and you don't know who to blame. Then suddenly, unexpectedly, you give birth to a sword.

S: You described the situation at Nalanda as a typical highly disciplined monastic situation and gave the impression that just the very irritation of the situation contributes toward the development of prajna.

TR: Yes.

S: How does that work? Can irritation cause intellect?

TR: Irritations are intellect, you could quite safely say. Irritations come from logical mind of some kind or other. Without that, we couldn't be irritated.

S: Then I could give a person a little gift of prajna by putting a pebble in his shoe?

TR: Sure. That sharpens prajna.

S: Is that one of the reasons behind a very tight and claustrophobic meditation schedule?

TR: Anything. Anything. Yes, anything.

S: You mean yes and more?

TR: Yes and more, yes. Since we can't have eight-by-eight meditation cells for everybody, we can create time cells.

Student: You said that at the prajna level, emotions are not seen as a problem, and apparently it can go on like that. I still don't understand that.

Trungpa Rinpoche: At the level of prajna, emotions don't apply as a problem, because prajna is very much speeding along, constantly speeding. In order for emotions to ferment, you have to wait for a little while. That explains the analogy of Naropa sitting reading a book. He is obviously constantly cutting through, but here he has relatively slowed down, slowed down a little bit. He has decided to relax a little bit and, for lack of something better to do, to read a book. And then the message came to him that we will be discussing soon.

Student: It seems that a little while ago you were implying that the way to give birth to prajna is by increasing the level of irritation as much as possible. It seems that it really couldn't be that simple, or we could really go wild irritating each other and help each other give birth to prajna.

Trungpa Rinpoche: It's not as simple as that, that's true. I wasn't really recommending putting things in people's shoes as a practical approach. In fact, that level of irritation can be created just by giving a little space to people. In that way, the equivalent of Naropa's setup can be created in a Vermont farmhouse. We are not as learned as Naropa and his colleagues. We don't have such a lavish property. We don't have the patronage of the kings. But still we can do a pretty good job.

Student: Does prajna have a sense of compassion?

Trungpa Rinpoche: It has a sense of trust in oneself, which is basic compassion, warmth, toward oneself. That automatically happens. Without that, you wouldn't be holding a sword. You wouldn't strike because you'd mistrust yourself. The reason the sword of prajna can be handled by a person is that he has a certain amount of trust in himself.

Student: Is prajna related to what Don Juan calls clarity?[1]

Trungpa Rinpoche: We can't discuss the Don Juan issue at the level of prajna. Basically, it is at the level of tantra. There is that element of clarity, which is a hint of prajna at a higher, more mystical level, higher than the mahayana level we are discussing. Obviously, tantra does have prajna.

S: Don Juan says that when clarity develops, it becomes your enemy.

TR: That has something to do with energy. You see, on the prajna level, there is not very much relating to energy as such. Sharpness is the only energy. The other energy I am referring to is a kind of fertility, energy that gives birth to itself. That doesn't happen on the mahayana level; it only happens in tantra.

Student: Do you have to cut everything down before the fertility begins to happen?

Trungpa Rinpoche: I think so, yes. It's more of a plowing process, actually. You have to plow twice. Once to tame the ground and then again to sow the seed.

Student: Does the difference between prajna and jnana, knowledge and wisdom, seeing and looking, have to do with the birth of some kind of aim in a person? Your sword just functions, cuts anything that comes into view. But wisdom would be not having to do that—knowing what you're after and therefore knowing when to cut and when not to.

Trungpa Rinpoche: Prajna is discovering the weapon and the technique for using it. But there is no master there to conduct the whole scheme. Jnana is discovering the wise schemer. At that level, you have the plan that is not planned deliberately, and you also have the weapon and the swordsman. At that point, it becomes a complete kingdom. That's why the buddhas are sometimes referred to in the scriptures as kings or victorious ones. Bodhisattvas are called princes—they're still on the adolescent level.

This contrasts with the look-and-see approach, which is connected with an external deity or God. You have to put an effort into perceiving an external being who is greater. But in the case of the nontheistic tradition, there is no reference to an outsider. There is rediscovering within. That results in the difference between looking in order to see and seeing in order to look.

Student: You were talking about trust in oneself. It seems to me that could only be real after prajna is born. Up until that point, how can you distinguish between ego-based self-confidence and trust in oneself?

Trungpa Rinpoche: Ego doesn't cut its own ground. Ego nurses its ground. An egoless experience like prajna cuts its own ground. That's where the irritations and resentment we have been talking about come from. And within the realm of resentment, a soft heart begins to develop, softness toward oneself. The softer you become toward yourself, the more you want to cut your ground. Somehow the question of ego doesn't apply at that point. Ego is already dissipating and has given up its hold on you. This is an organic thing that happens slowly. Somebody might ask you later, "What happened to your ego?" And you might say, "Oh, I never thought about that."

Student: Resentment gives way to being soft to yourself, and the more soft toward yourself you are, the more you have a need to cut away your own ground? I don't quite follow.

Trungpa Rinpoche: Softness here is a sense of being kind to yourself.

S: How does that grow from resentment?

TR: It grows from resentment because resentment is very intelligent; anger is very intelligent; depression is very intelligent. And usually you are angry at yourself because subconsciously you wanted to be kind to yourself. Otherwise you wouldn't get angry. If you weren't wanting to be kind to yourself, you might just as well give in, let yourself be destroyed. The resentment is an outward-directed defense mechanism for protecting yourself, which automatically suggests a sense of softness, a soft spot in oneself.

S: So where does the cutting come in, the desire to cut more the more one feels the soft spot?

TR: Well, one doesn't cut oneself; one cuts one's ground, which is the same thing resentment does, actually. This is completely the opposite of ego. The ordinary ego approach is that you hate yourself and you love your ground. You are constantly building up your ground, your territory. Still, you regard yourself with distaste. It is suicidal. It's the reverse psychology of what develops when people are put into a monastic situation and disciplined in the way we talked about. They begin to change their logic. They begin to resent the environment rather than themselves. They reject the ground and want to preserve themselves—which is compassion.

Student: Does the resentment come from seeing through the veil that covers the pain?

Trungpa Rinpoche: Yes.

S: And does that high degree of irritation bring a high degree of awareness at the same time, because you're right there?

TR: Yes, yes.

S: So the resentment is actually intelligence itself.

TR: You can't have resentment without being intelligent.

Student: Is resentment an emotion?

Trungpa Rinpoche: There is a definite technical problem with that. Emotion is supposed to be a fundamental, organic process. Resentment may be the vanguard of the emotions, but it is not a real emotion, because it relates with the fringe, the edge of things. Resentment is edgy and not quite hearty.

S: What are real emotions?

TR: Different expressions of being and different ways of relating with being. For example, if you feel your being is lacking something, you create passion. If you feel your being is threatened, you create aggression—and so on. It's connected with a total sense of being. The total sense of being feels not quite complete enough, and you try to balance that. Real emotions are much more dignified than things like resentment, which are at the level of the outskirts. The emotions are the real capital rather than the profit.

Student: Rinpoche, can resentment give way to real emotion if you are willing to get into it?

Trungpa Rinpoche: It could. You see, the resentment we are talking about here is a very special kind of resentment—spiritual-journey resentment. Ordinary resentment doesn't develop; it just goes back and forth, because there's no journey. There's no heart. There's no particular pattern. It's just random.

Student: Would you say an emotion like anger is an expression of your pain, or isn't it rather ego's attempt to cover up the pain—in a sense, to escape itself?

Trungpa Rinpoche: Sure, I think so. Basically the shyness of ego doesn't want to face itself, so it tends to bring up all kinds of things.

Student: If you feel very angry, then there seems to be a need to get beyond your anger.

Trungpa Rinpoche: That depends on the student's level. At the beginner's level, anger has never been understood or experienced properly. Anger has to be acknowledged. At the more advanced level, I suppose we could say that anger can be transmuted into a working basis.

Student: Does that require trust in your anger? Or trust in yourself?

Trungpa Rinpoche: Those two amount to the same thing. Yes, something like that. There is an all-pervasive trust happening in that area. Usually the problem comes when you and your anger are in conflict. The problem is being in conflict with your emotions, which makes things very uncomfortable. If you had no conflict with your emotions, things would be very natural. If there is no conflict, that solves seventy-five percent of the problem.

S: What's the other twenty-five percent?

TR: Self-consciousness about having solved your problem.

S: What do you do about that?

TR: You don't do anything about that. It just falls apart.

THREE

Choiceless Awareness

PRAJNA SEEMS TO BE a way of opening many gates. Through prajna one discovers the real meaning of shunyata. Discovering shunyata is very powerful, and it is also frightening. Prajna could be described as a way of opening up the shunyata experience—that is, a way of being cornered. You get cornered into "this" to the extent that finally you have to escape through the walls. That is, you have to see the walls as empty; otherwise, you cannot escape.

Shunyata is more of a meditative experience than intellect is. It is often referred to as choiceless awareness—you do not develop an understanding of shunyata, but rather it comes to you. When a person has developed his intellect—clarity and sharpness—to a certain level, that provides a kind of ground that makes it possible for him to see the nonexistence of shunyata—and the fullness of shunyata at the same time.

You might say, "But what's left after prajna has done its cutting through?" There is lots left. The process of cutting through also has to be exposed, to the point where the journey no longer exists, the process doesn't exist anymore, the effort doesn't exist anymore. Shunyata is truly choiceless and does not compromise. Once you realize that you have no ground at all, none whatsoever, you are suspended in midair. When you cry for help, nobody is around you, and your voice itself becomes shunyata, so you can't even shout. Your actions to save yourself become nonexistent, which is the result of cutting through. Because you have cut through so much, finally your own ground has been cut through completely. Then the process of cutting through no longer exists. There is no occupation of any kind at all.

We should understand as a general principle the logic of subject and object and their duality, which I mentioned in the previous talk. Duality is not composed of two separate entities. Subject and object are not two different entities. They are one. By creating a wall within the one, we produce duality. Thus, shunyata is simply an expansion of "this." That is why it is called choiceless awareness. "This" pushes the walls out; "this" expands.

You might ask, "If only 'this' exists, does that conflict with the general idea of egolessness?" Absolutely not. Ego and egolessness have nothing to do with "this." Actually ego is based on "that"; failing to realize "this" is what created ego. So the more you realize "this" or "here," the more groundless you become.

You don't have to have ground, but as I mentioned already, at the beginning this is rather frightening. There was an analogous moment in Naropa's life. He had been training for eight years in the monastery and had passed his oral examination, which took the form of logical debates, and he had become the head of Nalanda. At that point, he had a vision of an ugly woman, which was a shock, a sudden shock. According to traditional interpretations, this woman was Vajrayogini, who is a symbol of shunyata. The sudden shock of shunyata was overwhelming. Her shadow fell on the book he was reading—this was the terrifying experience of shunyata. After being through lots and lots of cutting through, so much prajna, you finally realize you have no choice but to seek the guru. This is the result of prajna, intellect. But at the same time, you might say that shunyata itself is also a form of intellect, the highest form. The ugly woman's intellect was much sharper and more powerful than Naropa's was at the time. But at the level of shunyata, intellect is really no longer regarded as prajna. At that level, there is an awareness that is an expression of further compassion. The aspect of softness or nonaggression becomes very intelligent, but not intellectual, not sharp in the style of prajna in action. It is sharp in the manner of prajna as a state of being, so to speak.

Of course, things don't happen as linearly as that. We could have an experience of prajna and a glimpse of shunyata happening simultaneously within ourselves. We could have that. We cut our ground and have a frightening—terrifying—sudden glimpse of groundlessness. Then we try to latch back onto our ground. This sort of thing happens constantly to us if we have any awareness of a journey taking place on the spiritual path. You might make the pretense or actually think that you are freaking out, losing your grip on reality, but it is a mere glimpse of shunyata taking place.

Shunyata is also described in terms of the feminine principle—as the consort of all the buddhas. Prajna is described in terms of the feminine principle, too—as the mother of all the buddhas, she who gives birth to the very idea of enlightenment. This very notion was started by her, by prajna. But she who made the buddhas speak, communicate, is shunyata. Because with shunyata there is a lot of room, openness, groundlessness; therefore, there is no fear of communicating with students as Buddha communicated with his disciples. In the situation of groundlessness, no one is standing on any ground, so communication can take place quite freely.

In Naropa's song after he meets the ugly woman [pp. 25–26 in Guenther's translation], each line is connected with a different attribute of samsara. It shows that somehow his sense of imprisonment has been sharpened. He realizes his inadequacy in being unable to see the reality of shunyata. He has enough prajna, but that doesn't help him anymore. He remains in a state of limbo. Prajna without shunyata is a body without arms, as is traditionally said, like a body without arms trying to climb a rock.

I suppose in order to simplify matters, we could say the real definition of shunyata is awareness without choice, or awareness that contains no experience. That is why shunyata is described as full and empty at the same time. Emptiness here does not mean seeing everything as just energy, so that you could walk through tables and chairs. Rather, you begin to see yourself as tables and chairs or rocks and sky and water. You begin to identify with the phenomenal world completely. Your existence is one of those phenomena, so everything is transparent or fluid. There is a sense of uniformity, sameness. At the same time, there is a sense of difference.

Student: Is shunyata like mindfulness in that you identify with phenomena?

Trungpa Rinpoche: No, I wouldn't say its like mindfulness practice. In the usual approach to mindfulness practice, you project onto "that," onto the tables and chairs. You are the instigator. In the case of shunyata, to a certain extent, the tables and chairs become the instigator. They become the reminder.

S: I thought mindfulness was just seeing things as they are, observing but not reflecting. So, in that sense, I thought mindfulness and shunyata would be the same.

TR: Yes, in that sense, but it's rather tricky. You see, mindfulness contains the idea that you are the original instigator. You thought of the idea of mindfulness rather than having a sense of becoming one of the phenomena. Shunyata is all-pervasive; awareness becomes ubiquitous.

Student: What did you mean when you said that in shunyata there's awareness but no experience?

Trungpa Rinpoche: Experience is a process like eating food. You pick it up, you put it in your mouth, you chew it, and you swallow it. Experience is a process like that if we look at it in slow motion. It may happen very fast, but if we look at it in slow motion, it contains those steps. The content of the experience has to be adapted to one's own being. In this case, no adaptation is needed. It's a one-shot deal, so to speak.

Student: You describe shunyata in terms of nonduality and everything becoming "this," and you talk about pushing out the walls of "this." That all sounds as though there is some maintenance involved, which doesn't really fit.

Trungpa Rinpoche: I suppose it is the opposite of maintenance. Pushing out the walls is a kind of transcendental vandalism.

S: Still, there's the idea of the wall being pushed out. And what's on the other side of the wall?

TR: Nothing. Just the other side.

S: Is that a painful experience?

TR: It's shocking.

Student: Presumably it's not self-conscious enough to be exactly painful.

Trungpa Rinpoche: Yes, it's not exactly painful. Pain is conditional on one's maintaining oneself, and this is just an experience of expanding "this," so there's a certain amount of confidence in the needlessness of maintaining oneself. So it's a surprise. There is a sense of the needlessness of maintaining oneself, but still there is an ongoing process of naiveté. This experience cuts through the naiveté, and suddenly you're seeing something extraordinary arising out of a very ordinary thing.

When one is naive, one expects things to stay as they are; one doesn't expect any surprises. The shunyata experience cuts through that naiveté.

Student: You said that prajna's cutting through to shunyata didn't involve pain. But didn't the visions that Naropa had when he was looking for Tilopa express different aspects of his pain?

Trungpa Rinpoche: We are talking about a different level. We haven't got to that level yet. That's something much more subtle and also much more painful. This is just sort of a rehabilitation process that's taking place now.

S: Well, didn't he find it rather painful when the woman implied he didn't understand the sense of what he was reading?

TR: Not really. If Naropa were to have experienced pain at that point, it would have been because he resented his greatness as a pandit being undermined and insulted. But somehow his state of mind was so sharp that there wasn't any room for that. He took in the message immediately, very clearly, very simply. That's because of the sharpness of prajna. If he had had the slightest involvement with spiritual materialism, he would have been very hurt. But since he didn't, the whole thing was very clear.

Student: If, in the shunyata experience, there's no ground, no subconscious thing going on, does that mean that everything feels extremely fresh and new?

Trungpa Rinpoche: I would say that the first experience would feel new because you haven't had it before. You're still wearing out your hang-ups, so it seems to be new. But once you've become an adult in shunyata, a professional with it, so to speak, instead of seeing things as new, you see them as very ordinary and full of details. Ordinary things full of details. It might feel fresh, not on account of its newness, but rather on account of its ordinariness.

S: Then there's nothing exciting about it.

TR: The details are very exciting, constantly. And there is a potential of mahamudra in seeing the details in their fullness, in their energy aspect. The emptiness is the meditative aspect.

Student: If, in shunyata, there's no process and no experiencer, what's the relationship to the teachings? Ordinarily we would relate to the teachings as a reference point in a process, and it seems that in shunyata that too would dissolve.

Trungpa Rinpoche: You see, this is precisely the point where the teachings become part of you. You are completely identified with the teachings. You yourself become a living teaching; you yourself become living dharma. That's the way it is from this point on up to the highest level of vajrayana. There is constant identification with the teaching. It becomes more and more part of your body, part of your brain, part of your heart. The more you identify with the teachings, the more the reference point takes the form of awareness that constantly reminds you. That's why shunyata is called choiceless awareness. Because you have identified with the teachings, awareness comes to you.

Student: You often speak of aloneness and of the spiritual path as a lonely journey. It sounds like shunyata is the first real experience of aloneness.

Trungpa Rinpoche: Very much so. Yes, there's no ground. But it feels very tough at the same time. We have an expression—"hard fact"—that seems to fit.

Student: Does discipline become more relaxed at this point, more self-initiating?

Trungpa Rinpoche: Very much so. The idea is that when you become more identified with the teachings, discipline becomes a natural habit. On the level of shunyata, discipline becomes very organic, ordinary, spontaneous.

Student: Is the satori experience of Zen an experience of shunyata?

Trungpa Rinpoche: Yes. I think the peak of the shunyata experience is what satori is. The peak of shunyata, a real glimpse of shunyata. Your logic wears out. You have no logic, no reference point of logic, and you become completely exposed to nothingness, or fullness. That is the satori experience of a sudden glimpse of aloneness.

Student: That seems to have a very different taste from Naropa's meeting with the old woman.

Trungpa Rinpoche: Not so different, actually. The only difference is that there are tantric overtones in the images in his life, like meeting the old woman. In the Zen tradition, you don't have a dialogue with Zen. You might have a dialogue with a buddha or somebody else. Nobody has a dialogue with Zen. But here, Naropa is having a dialogue with Zen. That's just a tantric way of looking at the situation.

Student: Is there some reason Naropa doesn't look for a teacher until he's had the experience of shunyata?

Trungpa Rinpoche: He never thought of a teacher from that angle. Obviously he did have a lot of masters, professors, and so forth—teachers but not gurus. The idea of a guru never occurred to him before. He was satisfied that he was being taught, that he was learning, that he was a good student. He never thought in terms of a real teacher who could lead him beyond the technical, theoretical, prajna level.

Student: When the old woman told him he understood the words but not the sense, it seems to me that would be a criticism of analytical mind rather than prajna. Doesn't prajna understand the sense?

Trungpa Rinpoche: Surprisingly not. That's the difference between prajna and jnana. Prajna understands the words completely, to the utmost extent that words can be understood. But to understand the sense, you have to develop jnana, wisdom. That's the whole point. That's why prajna corresponds to the sixth bhumi, or level, of the bodhisattva path, and you have to reach three levels beyond that before you develop jnana, wisdom. Prajna is not quite enough.

Student: What happens to the aggression that characterizes or accompanies prajna when it reaches the level of shunyata?

Trungpa Rinpoche: Aggression is still there in the form of intelligent energy. That still goes on: throughout the journey there will be a sense of energy, the excitement of new discovery. I suppose we could say that aggression becomes energy.

S: Does it level out and become less unbearable?

TR: There's no aggression as such. There's no question of a threshold of pain there. Aggression continues to be present somehow or other in the form of energy. After all, you still have your head. Even when you reach the ati level, you still carry your head with you. You know, you feel you have this thing with you. That kind of awareness is still there. It's very hard to clean up completely.

Student: Where does buddha nature come into this?

Trungpa Rinpoche: That is the essence, the fundamental essence of the wakeful quality, the thing that makes you struggle and proceed along the path. That appears right at the beginning and goes on all the way through. The other day I was talking about tantra as continuity and about the understanding of pain being the starting point of that continuity. That's the expression of buddha nature, which goes on constantly. There's actually a sense of threat connected with it, because you constantly have the potential of sanity.

S: And when you get to shunyata, that energy that is the driving force for the whole thing becomes just as it is, clear of all the other stuff around it?

TR: You don't have to be concerned about clearing away the other things. They just evaporate, so to speak, because you have such conviction, such real experience.

Student: You said that prajna without shunyata was like a man without arms trying to climb a rock. Is the experience of shunyata like acquiring a pair of arms?

Trungpa Rinpoche: Definitely, yes, because shunyata redefines compassion. Often compassion is spoken of in terms of the hook of compassion, like the sucker at the end of the tentacles of an octopus. The more arms you develop, the more powerful is the suction you develop at the same time. Shunyata is very much connected with building up compassion, warmth. So not only do you develop arms, but your arms become very functional.

Student: You said in your first talk that we can never be happy and pain never ends. Is it true that in the shunyata experience, there is still pain, but there is no one to experience it, so it doesn't hurt?

Trungpa Rinpoche: I think we could say that, yes. There will be pain if you are intelligent, but the hurting part or the seeking-for-pleasure part is a neurotic thing. With intelligence comes pain, but without neurosis there is no sorrow.

Student: If the pain is no longer painful, what is there to distinguish between pain and pleasure?

Trungpa Rinpoche: Very simple logic. In ordinary experience you can distinguish between coffee and tea. It's like that.

Student: Shunyata, for me, always seems to have a huge connotation of desolation, but when you talk about it, it also seems to have fullness to it. What is that, or why is that?

Trungpa Rinpoche: I suppose when you feel completely desolate, you begin to help yourself, you make yourself at home. You begin to realize all kinds of beauties around you. It's a question of identifying with the shunyata principle. That's why I said, "Make yourself at home."

Student: Is it possible to confuse the shunyata experience with other levels of experience?

Trungpa Rinpoche: I don't think so. Unless you are completely faking the shunyata experience to yourself, convincing yourself, hypnotizing yourself shunyata-style. Then obviously the whole thing becomes superficial. But at the level of the shunyata experience, you need your teacher much more, so that has a very grounding effect.

Student: Is there a danger in pursuing the shunyata experience?

Trungpa Rinpoche: Yes, very much so. The shunyata experience with ego is Rudrahood.

Student: Is there an equivalent of the shunyata experience on the hinayana level?

Trungpa Rinpoche: The only thing I can think of is the experience of impermanence, which is a glimpse of shunyata in a very literal sense— the all-pervasive feeling of nonexistence and impermanence—and of egolessness, for that matter, as well.

Student: When you talked about expanding "this," it raised the question of Rudrahood for me. Then you said you could have a shunyata experience with ego. This makes me think I don't understand what "this" is.

Trungpa Rinpoche: "This" is this [*puts his hand on his chest*], unmistakably. And "that" is ego, Rudra. "That" has a name, but "this" doesn't have a name.

Student: Does the arhat experience shunyata?

Trungpa Rinpoche: The experience of the arhat is not exactly shunyata as it is described in connection with the bodhisattva path. The arhat experiences a sense of egolessness, transitoriness within him- or herself. It doesn't even extend to objects like tables and chairs. It's just connected with the body and bodily sensations and the breath and emotions and thought patterns. It stops there and it doesn't expand, because there is very little warmth toward oneself at that point. There is very little emphasis on compassion. Since there is very little warmth, the arhat dwells only on his own problem and trying to solve that problem.

Student: Rinpoche, what is the relationship of formal sitting practice to the shunyata experience? Is there any particular technique that would produce that experience?

Trungpa Rinpoche: Vipashyana meditation automatically leads to shunyata. Also, sitting without any technique—just sitting—is shunyata practice. At that level, sitting practice becomes very ordinary and workable. There is quite possibly less struggle involved. Maybe there is just a hint of familiarity that makes it comfortable and easy to sit or to prolong one's sitting practice. But really there is no technique for shunyata. Such a thing would be a contradiction. Shunyata is just a way of being.

S: But would you say that having that experience is dependent upon practicing sitting meditation?

TR: Yes, I think so. There's no way out.

Beyond Shunyata

W<small>E ARE GOING</small> to discuss the basic meaning of going beyond shunyata. The walls of confusion and chaos are eliminated by prajna, and the ground of confusion and chaos is eliminated by the shunyata experience. Now we are suspended in midair. We have to learn how to walk, how to breathe, how to behave. That seems to be the next problem in the situation.

In the case of Naropa, he had decided to leave the monastery and search for Tilopa, but he still didn't know how to behave. Should he still behave like a pandit, a monk, a scholar? Or should he behave like an ordinary person searching for the truth? The answer to these questions is uncertain. Basic confusion is still there, and once again, self-consciousness. He did get the message of the shunyata lady, so to speak, but he did not know how to handle that. She did give him some hint about what to do, but beyond that everything was uncertain. How to go about working with that message was completely and totally uncertain for him.

The reason for this is that shunyata alone does not provide any guidance, even with skillful means. You still need a certain trust toward and respect for magic, the magical aspect of the phenomenal world. Things are very tricky. They are very tricky, and they play tricks on you spontaneously. There's nobody who is the game maker, who conceives of the game. Nobody's playing the tricks on you. But things as they are, are full of trickery.

I suppose in the theistic tradition this might be called something like the mischievousness of God. But in the nontheistic tradition, the whole thing is not based on there being a maker of these tricks. The tricks that happen are tricks in themselves. That magical or miraculous quality of phenomenal display is always there. Particularly, it is always there when we feel we don't want to get into it, when we feel we haven't got time for it. When we are in a hurry to do something, something else happens. A trick is played on us that slows us down. And equally, when we are moved to relax and take our time, a trick is played on us that speeds us up. Such tricks happen constantly in our lives.

This is not hypothetical. This is something very real, extremely real, very definite.

Naropa resigns as abbot of Nalanda and goes to look for Tilopa. The voice of a trick says: "Tilopa is in the east. Go east, toward where the sun rises." Naropa does that, and he finds a leper woman blocking his path. Before encountering the leper woman, he thought he was finally going to meet Tilopa properly, meet the great master, the great guru, the enlightened Tilopa who could tell him the sense beyond the words. And before the leper woman disappears, we have this verse:

> Listen, Abhayakirti
> The Ultimate in which all become the same
> Is free of habit-forming thought and limitations.
> How, if still fettered by them,
> Can you hope to find the Guru?
>
> [p. 30]

There is a pattern in this odyssey, in this journey, which I thought I might relate to you. The eleven experiences [that follow his meeting with the ugly woman] seem to be divided into three sections. The first includes the leper woman, the bitch, the man playing tricks on his parents, and the man opening the body of the corpse. Those four are related to aggression. The next group is opening the stomach of the live man and washing it with hot water, marrying the king's daughter, and the huntsman. Those are connected with passion. The last group is connected with ignorance, a different type of temptation, a different kind of attempt to relate with reality that failed.

So since Naropa is a scholar and a prajna type of person, obviously the first method he would use is that of aggression. The first experience in this category is an interesting one, a real demonstration of aggression.

Seeing through the eyes [of prajna], Naropa has had a real vision, a real look at the experience of shunyata. This has made his mind much more vulnerable, so his aggression is coming out fast. He sees the leper woman with the sense of speed with which he is looking for his teacher. This is quite interesting and noteworthy.

The next thing is that he sees a bitch whose body is infested with worms. He thought he was just about to discover his guru, Tilopa. Instead he sees this further expression of aggression—a bitch with the inside of her body crawling with worms. As the bitch is about to disappear, we have the verse:

> All living beings by nature are one's parents.
> How will you find the Guru, if
> Without developing compassion
> On the Mahayana path
> You seek in the wrong direction?
> How will you find the Guru to accept you
> When you look down on others?
>
> [pp. 30–31]

As we go along, these verses become progressively more tantric. The first section is very ordinary, very basic Buddhism. As we go on, things become deeper in many ways.

The next thing is the man playing tricks on his parents. Again Naropa fails to relate with himself. He still has the notion of being an articulate scholar from Nalanda, an accomplished leader, which makes him approach his search with a very genteel way of doing things. He has not yet gotten into the basic level of life. He hasn't actually related with father, mother, lover, enemy at all. A father and mother are related with the lover and enemy. The mother is the lover and the father is the enemy, the object of aggression. Since Naropa fails to relate with that, he has to journey further. As this particular vision is about to disappear, Tilopa says:

> How will you find the Guru, if
> In this doctrine of Great Compassion
> You do not crack the skull of egotism
> With the mallet of non-Pure-Egoness and nothingness?
>
> [p. 31]

The next one is the man opening the stomach of a corpse. This is a very powerful image, which has the sense that one should abandon the corpse that one is hanging on to. Nalanda University is a corpse for Naropa. He is trying to open that stomach again—trying to reevaluate himself by going through the library, so to speak, again and again. He still carries Nalanda with him as a tortoise carries his shell. He has to reeducate himself to the path of the yogi. As he is seeing this vision, Tilopa says:

> How will you find the Guru, if
> You cut not Samsara's ties
> With the unoriginatedness of the Ultimate
> In its realm of non-reference?
>
> [p. 32]

So that is the first section in which we have a glimpse of the fact that aggression comes from memory of the past. A person might be very proud of his past: "I was brought up in Brooklyn, so nobody can cheat me." Or in this case: "Nalanda is a very powerful place, the center of intelligence of the Indian empire, so no one can touch me." This same applies to the shunyata experience. You have been woken up by the ugly woman, and you still have that memory going on all the time in your state of being.

The next section, the section of passion, begins with the live man, who is a passionate live man who clings to life, which is a symbol of passion. Moreover, his stomach has been opened, which is more of a symbol of passion; there is a sense of the hot-blooded, the fleshy, live, warm. And his stomach is being washed in hot water, a further statement of passion, real passion. The basic message at this point is that Naropa is lacking enormously in compassion. He is treating the world like a shopping center rather than relating with himself. That has been his problem. All this mockery of Naropa comes because he is still shopping. He should look *into* himself and things more rather than looking for Tilopa as an external person. The verse at this point goes:

> How will you find the Guru, if
> With the water of profound instruction
> You cleanse not Samsara, which by nature [is] free
> Yet represents the dirt of habit-forming thoughts?
>
> [p. 32]

The basic theme of passion here has to do with the fact that Naropa still has to communicate with the world outside himself. On the other hand, he has been relating too much to this outsidedness as a shopping center in which Tilopa is the most valuable thing you can buy. He hasn't actually related with *himself* in order to communicate with the world. He hasn't spent a penny at this point. He's just been gazing at the whole universe. He has been fascinated by the world, but nothing has happened with his relationship with it. He is still roaming in the vacuums of shunyata.

This is much more than what we talk about as being "completely spaced out." We feel spaced out because we are spaced out [absent-minded]. Naropa feels completely spaced out because he has no reference point. In that condition, he can't even talk to anyone. He has no one to tell stories to. He has no reference point at all. The whole thing is desolate and deathly in many ways.

In the next vision, he sees the king, who asks him to marry his daughter. That's a very powerful thing. Considering that he is a fully ordained monk, this means he would have to break his vow. Breaking his vow at this point just means relating with the phenomenal world. Up till this point, he has built up an artificial virginity. And now he is breaking that virginity. Before he meets Tilopa, he should become Tilopa properly. He should be reduced to a garbage pile full of worms and flies, then burnt and reduced to dust. Having been reduced to dust, then he might receive instruction. That seems to be the point here. Marrying the king's daughter has nothing at all to do with the tantric teachings concerning the karmamudra or anything like that. It simply has to do with the fact that he is too clean, too slick, and he has to collect more dirt in order to become a really good and seasoned and antique student. In order to antique something, you put wax and dirt on it to make it look antique. So marrying the king's daughter is a process of seasoning. And Tilopa's verse here is:

> Are you not deceived by a magic show?
> How then will you find the Guru
> If through desire and dislike you fall
> Into the three forms of evil life?

[p. 32]

The next one is that Naropa meets a dark-skinned huntsman. The point here is exaggerated passion. Passion is usually interpreted in terms of pleasure. Fulfilling passion is usually related with attaining pleasure. But in this case, it is also connected with love and hate happening at the same time. His journey has to stop at some point. He has to think twice about himself. The verse here is:

> A hunter, I have drawn the arrow
> Of the phantom body which from desires is free
> In the bow, of radiant light the essence:
> I shall kill the fleeing deer of this and that,
> On the mountain of the body believing in an I.
> Tomorrow I go fishing in the lake.

[p. 33]

The next one is the old people plowing the field and eating worms. This is the beginning of the ignorance section. This section is related with the earth quality, earthiness. So it begins with plowing the ground and eating worms, which are also the product of earth. These are very earthy activities, but equally freaky ones as far as Naropa is concerned. He probably regarded ignorance as completely stupid and thought that such ignorant people couldn't even plow or eat worms. But in the case of this kind of intelligent ignorance, people *can* do such things. The woman also cooks fish and frogs alive for Naropa to eat. It is a kind of horrific idea that ignorance is so alive and has managed to improvise all kinds of fantastic things. And discovering this different version of ignorance is like rediscovering himself. The verse here is:

> Fettered by habit-forming thought, 'tis hard to find the
>   Guru.
> How will you find the Guru if you eat not
> This fish of habit-forming thoughts, but hanker
> After pleasures (which enhance the sense of ego)?
> Tomorrow I will kill my parents.

[pp. 33–34]

Killing parents is one of the images of tantra. Now we are getting closer to tantric images. Father is aggression, and mother is passion. In many tantric vows, there are verses that say, "Kill your father; make love to your mother." That's one of the verses defining samaya discipline. It means to relate with your father, aggression, completely, and your mother, passion, completely. Get into them and relate with them. The father is impaled and the mother is put in the dungeon. These are expressions of aggression and passion, but at this point, they are activities of ignorance. You might think that ignorance is just purely lying in the dungeon and being part of the worms and so forth, but you begin to realize that this is not so. There are very powerful things happening, *live* situations. Ignorance has a living quality that is very prominent. Getting into this is part of searching for the guru, actually being like Tilopa. The verse here goes:

> You will find it hard to find the Guru
> If you kill not the three poisons that derive
> From your parents, the dichotomy of this and that.
> Tomorrow I will go and beg . . .

> *[p. 34]*

These hints that begin with the huntsman saying, "Tomorrow I will do this or that," are interesting. Up to the point where those begin, there is no need to sow a further seed of confusion. Naropa is already confused. But after that point, it is necessary to sow a seed of confusion. You don't want to quite leave Naropa to himself so he can work things out completely. So the message about tomorrow sows a seed of expectation, and further confusion comes out of that. The method of teaching at this point is not designed to free Naropa or instruct him at all, but rather to confuse him more and more. That is the essence of the teaching style at this level, which is mahamudra.

The next one on the ignorance level is the beggar frying live fish and bringing dead fish back to life. He also asks Naropa to eat some live lice, which he hands him. Again, this conveys a sense of uncertainty. We could say that eating food is predominantly a mark of uncertainty. It's trying to make sure that we do have our body. We have food and drink when we are uncertain, when the boundaries become fuzzy. When that happens as we drive along on a highway, we decide to pull into a restaurant and eat. It's a way of reassuring ourselves. But eating live food is much more powerful than just stopping at a restaurant. You have to struggle to eat, because your food is struggling to get away from you. It is a very direct message, and at the same time quite horrific. The verses here are:

> If you would kill the misery of habit-forming thoughts
> And ingrained tendencies on the endless path
> To the ultimate nature of all beings,
> First you must kill (these lice).

[p. 35]

But when Naropa was unable to do so, the man disappeared with the words:

> You will find it hard to find the Guru
> If you kill not the louse of habit-forming thoughts,
> Self-originated and self-destructive.
> Tomorrow I will visit a freak show.

We shall do that tomorrow.

Student: Did you say the "tomorrow" messages were designed to confuse Naropa?
Trungpa Rinpoche: Yes.
S: I don't understand.
TR: They don't give any hint. At the beginning, he was still carrying Nalanda University with him and was pretty much together. At that point, he had to be given some means for forgetting that memory. He had to be confused, given another kind of promise about his search for his guru. He had to be lured into it more and at the same time made to forget his past hang-ups about Nalanda. So the way to confuse him was to lure him further in, as with the carrot and the donkey.

Student: It seems that Naropa still has a big ego problem, even after the shunyata experience. You can still have ego, or these "habit-forming thoughts," even while you are experiencing shunyata?
Trungpa Rinpoche: I think so. Much more so, in many ways. They become much more highlighted, I'm afraid. Or rather, I'm pleased to announce.

Student: The effect of Naropa's marrying the king's daughter is to bring out more of his shit. Why doesn't the text say something to the effect "You've got to relate more to your shit," rather than warning him about falling into the traps of samsara?

Trungpa Rinpoche: That's the very clever thing about the whole business.

S: Is it sucking him further in that way?

TR: Of course. It's fantastic that way. The subject matter of all the songs, all the messages, is designed to confuse him. The messages are presented in accordance with certain moral patterns all the way. Even up to the highest mystical level, the messages still have a connection with that moral pattern. That's part of the masterpiece quality of this whole story.

Student: When you say that the whole idea is to confuse him more, do you mean that strictly from ego's point of view? It's confusing ego?

Trungpa Rinpoche: At this point, it's all one. We can't really distinguish points of view. It's the point of view of the thing, the thingness.

S: It's not one person confusing another person?

TR: No, it's just the thing.

S: You mean like the tricks you were talking about?

TR: Yes. It's very tricky.

Student: So the whole thing is just sucking him in all the way down the line. In that case, where does intelligence come in?

Trungpa Rinpoche: At this point, his intelligence is being insulted rather than acknowledged in any way. Naropa has all kinds of intelligence, you know, and has been through all kinds of disciplines, but each time when he tries to pull any one of them out and use it, it is insulted.

Student: By intelligence there, do you mean the—

Trungpa Rinpoche: The prajna type.

Student: No matter what Naropa did, would he be wrong? For example, if the king offered him his daughter and he said, "No, I'm a monk, I can't take her," would the daughter disappear and say, "How can you find Tilopa if you don't accept the king's daughter?"

Trungpa Rinpoche: No. It would be much longer than that. She would probably come out and seduce him. Then at the end she would say the same thing as the present verse does. The whole thing is a fantastic display of the greatest genius that one could ever think of. It's so apt.

Student: It seems Naropa disarms himself with his motivation. He doesn't have any rebuttal for the insults to his intelligence because he's committed to pursuing Tilopa.

Trungpa Rinpoche: He doesn't even think in terms of insults. He doesn't particularly think of discovery either at a certain point. Halfway through the search, before the "tomorrow" messages start coming, he has become dull and dumb and numb. That's the reason for the lines about "Tomorrow you'll see thus-and-such." They're to wake him up more. You don't want just to reduce him into a piece of lead. So the intention that runs through the messages is to keep him up, make him work harder.

Student: Do those messages also tell him that although he's more confused than he was yesterday, he's making progress?

Trungpa Rinpoche: Progress in terms of time and space but not in the amount of his understanding particularly.

S: At least he's getting another message.

TR: Yes, yes.

Student: Is this by way of preparing a kind of a new ground for the meeting of Tilopa? Are all these temptations or confusions setting up a new ground to work with?

Trungpa Rinpoche: Absolutely. Otherwise there's no point. You know, every one of these experiences provides fantastic ground to reflect back on and work on. It's a very ingenious strategy. And it doesn't particularly seem to be Tilopa personally who's doing it. Nobody knows who's doing it. If it had to be done in the ordinary way, the planning of how to handle Naropa would have taken ten years. It would be a million-dollar project in a university laboratory. And all the psychologists in the world would have to get together.

Student: Is shunyata related to form being emptiness, and then is what's happening to Naropa in this later stage going back to the other side of emptiness being form?[1]

Trungpa Rinpoche: I think so, yes.

Student: Does this mean experiencing pain again in relationship with reality?

Trungpa Rinpoche: Very much so. You get blissed out, so to speak, when you first discover shunyata. At that point, Naropa got a message that he had a teacher, he had a guru. Now he's promised to seek his guru, and in that way he loses his ground. He's no longer walking on earth, he's walking on clouds. And those eleven experiences after the ugly woman bring him down and bring more pain, definitely. That's a kind of vajrayana pain that we've just barely discussed. And I think there's further pain just about to come.

Student: You made the point several times that the sequence of situations is extremely apt and has been created by just the situations themselves. In terms of the personal application of this for any individual, is this a certain course that everyone on the path goes through? Is it that at a certain point in your development—after going through prajna and maybe having some first intuition of shunyata—situations will start having this confusing effect on people? Just from the situation, in a way that can't be duplicated, can't be made up? The effect does happen?

Trungpa Rinpoche: I think so, yes. You seem to have got the feeling of the whole thing we have been discussing tonight. Sure.

Student: In that sense, is Naropa sort of like an everyman?

Trungpa Rinpoche: By all means. If there weren't a sense of general application, we might be discussing this in some department of ethnic culture or some place like that. But we have decided to make it part of our study of American karma, which means that it does have some bearing on us, naturally. In fact, since you people decided to take part in this seminar, you have already inherited Naropa's sanity as well as his insanity, without any further choices. Welcome.

Student: Is that a kind of confirmation?

Trungpa Rinpoche: Well, what we're doing is a very minor confirmation.

S: No, I mean isn't the fact that the aptness of the message comes out of the situation itself a confirmation of some kind?

TR: I think so, yes.

Student: Is the meeting with Vajrayogini a kind of archetypal meeting that's universal, that happens to all human beings at the first moment of giving up and letting go? Does that vision happen to most human beings at such a moment?

Trungpa Rinpoche: I think so. It could happen in all kinds of ways. You might have an argument with your landlady or your mother-in-law. Every event like that is meeting the ugly woman. In this case, the ugly woman has nothing to do with male chauvinism. It's a cosmic thing. It's the cosmic principle of womanness. It would have to be a mother who cooks you food, or a girlfriend who bosses you around, or a secretary who minds your business. And every one of them is a cosmic principle and has nothing to do with male chauvinism at all. It's basic womanness in the highest sense.

Student: Could you say something abut Naropa noticing all the woman's marks of ugliness? Is it sort of another mockery of Naropa that he would catalog all that?

Trungpa Rinpoche: I think so, yes. Naropa hasn't reached the tenth bhumi. He's on the level of the sixth bhumi—prajna—and because his vision is not very clear, the woman is ugly. The less clear his vision, the more ugly the woman. Further on, his vision becomes more refined. He has potential when he decides to seek Tilopa, but still his vision is very dull, so the ugly woman sharpens herself into further grotesque images like that of the leper woman and so forth.

S: What's the significance of her having all the ugly characteristics at that point?

TR: Those are the characteristics of samsara. Complete confusion, being trapped, being exploited, having your body torn apart, having parts of yourself eaten up, being stabbed, being dumped in shit, being run over by a railroad train, being poisoned to death, being stomped on, and all kinds of images. Those are the images of samsara. They say that the worst thing that could happen to you is being in samsara, that you will be completely annihilated in all kinds of ways—intellectually, spiritually, and socially; that you are the lowest of the lowest of the low. That's samsara. There's no fun in it.

Student: Is Vajrayogini an aspect of Tilopa and vice versa?

Trungpa Rinpoche: Vajrayogini is Tilopa's sister. She's a saleswoman who awakens Naropa. It's like in Mexico you might find a boy who shines your shoes, and as he does it, he says, "Would you like to come and visit my sister's shop?"

FIVE

Mahamudra

BEFORE WE DISCUSS Naropa's experiences with Tilopa further, we have to understand the meaning of mahamudra properly. So far, we have only a very rough sketch of that experience. In our earlier discussion of continuity, we discussed it as starting from the level of the hinayana realization of pain and then going on to the shunyata experience. Then from the shunyata experience of emptiness, we are led to mahamudra. The sense of continuity there is rediscovering one's basic ground; the mahamudra experience could be described that way. Having had all the illusions and hallucinations removed by the experience of shunyata, there is a sense of extraordinary clarity. That clarity is called mahamudra.

Mahamudra is a Sanskrit word. *Maha* means "big, great," and *mudra* means "symbol." But *maha* doesn't mean "big" in a comparative sense: something bigger compared to something smaller. It is not based on a dichotomy. It is simply that such clarity as this is beyond measure. There is no other clarity like this. It is fullness; it is without association in the sense that this experience is full in itself. And the sense in which *mudra* means symbol again has nothing to do with analysis or examples; rather the thing itself is its own symbol. Everybody represents themselves and everybody is a caricature of themselves. There is that sense of a humorous aspect, a caricature aspect, as well as everything having its own basic fullness. You represent yourself not by name but by being. So there is a sense of completion.

The mahamudra experience has been compared to the experience of

247

a young child visiting a colorful temple. He sees all kinds of magnificent decorations, displays, rich colors, vividness of all kinds. But this child has no preconception or any concept whatsoever about where to begin to analyze. Everything is overwhelming, quite in its own right. So the child does not become frightened by this vivid scenery and at the same time does not know how to appreciate it. It is quite different from a child walking into a playroom full of toys, where his attention is caught by a particular toy and he runs right over and starts playing with it. A temple—a highly decorated, colorful temple—is so harmonious in its own right that the child has no way of introducing his fascination from one particular standpoint. The experience is all-pervasive. At the same time, it is perhaps somewhat overwhelmingly pleasurable.

So the mahamudra experience is vividness, vividness to such an extent that it does not require a watcher or commentator; or for that matter, it does not require meditative absorption. In the case of shunyata, there is still a sense of needing a nursing process for that experience; it is not only that the sitting practice of meditation is required, but there is a sense of needing a registrar to record your experience in a memory bank. The very idea of emptiness is an experience, even though you may not have an experience*r* as such, since the whole thing is totally open and nondualistic. But even the very sense of nonduality is a faint stain, a very subtle, transparent stain. On the shunyata level, that stain is regarded as an adornment, like putting a varnish over well-finished wood. It is supposed to protect the wood from further stains of dirt or grease, to keep it looking fresh and new, to preserve the newness of this well-finished wood. But in the long run, that clear varnish becomes a factor that ages the new look of this fresh wood. It turns yellow and slowly begins to crumble, and scratches begin to show much more in it than they would in the original wood. So the nonduality becomes a problem in the shunyata experience.

In the experience of mahamudra, even the notion of nonduality is not applied or is not necessary. Therefore, it has been said in the scriptures that the only definition of mahamudra you can use is "unborn" or "unoriginated." Or again, often the mahamudra experience is described in terms of coemergent wisdom—that is, born simultaneously rather than born with the delays of process. This refers to confusion and realization existing simultaneously, as opposed to confusion coming first and then realization taking over and cleaning out the confusion. In the maha-mudra, confusion and realization are simultaneous, coemergent.

The eternally youthful quality of the mahamudra experience is one of its outstanding qualities. It is eternally youthful because there is no sense of repetition, no sense of wearing out of interest because of famil-iarity. Every experience is a new, fresh experience. So it is childlike, inno-cent and childlike. The child has never even seen its body—such a brand-new world.

Another term for mahamudra, used by Rangjung Dorje and other great teachers, is "ordinary consciousness." Experience ceases to be ex-traordinary. It is so ordinary—so clear and precise and obvious. The only thing that confuses us and prevents us from realizing this experience is its ordinariness. The ordinary quality becomes a kind of barrier, because when you look for something, you don't look for the ordinary. Even in the case of losing a pair of glasses that you are completely used to. When you lose them, the glasses become a very interesting object. They imme-diately become an extraordinary thing, because you've lost them. You begin to imagine: "Could they be here? Could they be there?" You shake all the cushions, you move all the chairs and tables, and you look under-neath the rugs. It becomes an extraordinary case. But the glasses are an ordinary thing.

In that way, mahamudra is self-secret because of its ordinariness. Or-dinariness becomes its own camouflage, so to speak. It has also been said that mahamudra cannot be expressed, that even the Buddha's tongue is numb when it comes to describing mahamudra. And it's true. How much can you say about ordinary things? And the more you see that it is very ordinary, the more that becomes an extraordinary case, which creates a further veil.

The experience of mahamudra is also somewhat irritating, or even highly irritating, because of its sharpness and precision. The energies around you—textures, colors, different states of mind, relationships—are very vivid and precise. They are all so naked and so much right in front of you, without any padding, without any walls between you and "that." That nakedness is overwhelming. Although it is your own experience, we often find that even when you have only a small glimpse of mahamu-dra experience, you want to run away from yourself. You look for pri-vacy of some kind—privacy from yourself. The world is so true and naked and sharp and precise and colorful that it's extraordinarily irritating—let alone when other *people* approach you. You think you can avoid them, run away from them physically, put a notice on your door, or take a trip to an unknown corner of the world. You might try to dissociate yourself from the familiar world, run away from your home ground, disconnect your telephone. You can do all kinds of things of that nature, but when the world begins to become *you* and all these preceptions are *yours* and are very precise and very obviously right in front of you, you can't run away from it. The process of running away creates further sharpness, and if you really try to run away from these phenomena, they begin to mock you, laugh at you. The chairs and tables and rugs and paintings on the wall and your books, the sounds you hear in your head, begin to mock you. Even if you try to tear your body apart, still something follows you. You can't get away from it. That is why it is called the ultimate nakedness. You begin to feel you are just a live brain with no tissue around it, exposed on a winter morning to the cold air. It's *so* penetrating, so irritating, and so sharp.

It is a fundamental and very profound irritation. The irritations we discussed before are relatively simple and seem to be ordinary ones. The irritation of the mahamudra experience is very insulting in many ways, disconcerting. That is why the experience of mahamudra is also referred to as "crazy wisdom." It is a crazy experience, but not exactly ego madness. It's wisdom that has gone crazy. The element of wisdom here is its playfulness, humorousness, and sybaritic quality. Even though you are irritated and naked and completely exposed without your skin, there is a sense of joy or, more likely, bliss.

One of the definite characteristics of the Buddhist tantra, on the mahamudra level at least, is not running away from sense pleasures, but rather identifying with them, working with them as part of the working basis. That is an outstanding part of the tantric message. Pleasure in this case includes every kind of pleasure: psychosomatic, physical, psychological, and spiritual. Here, it is quite different from the way in which spiritual materialists might seek pleasure—by getting into the other. In this case, it is getting into "this." There is a self-existing pleasurableness that is completely hollow if you look at it from the ordinary point of view of ego's pleasure orientation. Within that, you don't actually experience pleasure at all. All pleasure experiences are hollow. But if you look at it from the point of view of this nakedness, this situation of being completely exposed, any pleasure you experience is full because of its hollowness. On the mahamudra level, pleasure does not take place through the pores of your skin, but pleasure takes place on your very *flesh* without skin. You become the bliss rather than enjoying the bliss. You are the embodiment of bliss, and this contains a quality of your being very powerful. You have conquered pleasure, and pleasure is yours. One doesn't even have to go so far as to try to enjoy pleasure, but pleasure becomes self-existing bliss.

In this way, every experience that might occur in our life—communication, visual experience, auditory experience, consciousness, anything that we relate to—becomes completely workable, highly workable. In fact, even the notion of workability does not apply. It's yours. It is *you*, in fact. So things become very immediate.

This is what is often called vajra pride. Pride in this case is not arrogance, but is nondualistically self-contained. You are not threatened by your projections or projectors, but you are there, and at the same time, everything around you is you and yours.

It took a long time for Naropa to realize that. Having visited the freak show, he failed again. Finally, at the last moment, when he thought of killing himself and was just about to relate with the totality of himself, *finally* then he experienced that penetrating pain in himself. He thought that maybe if he eliminated his body, he might be able to relieve that pain. At that point, Tilopa finally appeared. Through the twelve tortures that Naropa went through (with the help of Tilopa), sometimes he understood this nakedness, experiencing it fully, totally, completely, and sometimes he didn't understand it and instead tripped out into the highest spiritual mishmash. The perfect example is when Tilopa put sharpened pieces of bamboo between his nails and his fingers, put little flags on the ends of the pieces of bamboo, and asked Naropa to hold them up into the wind. That exemplifies (through the medium of pain, of course) how real the nakedness could be if it were blissful.

That seems to be a very powerful message for us. Mind you, we are not going to practice that very exercise with every student, but that is an example of what the process is like. How many times can the guru tell a person, "Come out! I know you're there! Be naked!" A student might decide to take off his clothes and say, "Okay, I'm naked," but that's not quite it. We have to say, "There's more nakedness. Come on, do more than that. What else can you do?"

Particularly, a scholar like Naropa has enormous hang-ups. Receiving

instructions from a mahayana teacher requires only simple devotion, reducing oneself to an infant and asking the guru to act as the baby-sitter.
But on the vajrayana level, the student-teacher relationship demands
more than that. It is a process of training the student as a warrior. At
first, a warrior teacher does not use a sword on you. He uses a stick and
makes you fight with him. Since the student's swordsmanship is not so
good, he gets hurt more than he is able to hurt the master. But when
the student gains confidence and begins to learn good swordsmanship,
he is almost able to defeat his own teacher. Then, instead of a stick, it
becomes a sword. Nobody really gets killed or hurt, because all the levels
of communication take place within the realm of the rainbow or mirage
anyway. But there is a training period. A learning process takes place,
which is very immediate and very powerful and very necessary.

On the hinayana level, the teacher is a wise man. On the mahayana
level, he is a physician/friend, a spiritual friend. On the vajrayana level,
the student-teacher relationship is similar to that in the martial arts. You
could get hurt severely if you are too tense. But you could also receive
a tremendous—almost physical—message. The message is not verbal or
intellectual. It is like a demonstration of putting tables and chairs together. The teachings come out of the world of form, the real world of
form. The teachings consist of colors and forms and sounds rather than
words or ideas.

This is what Naropa was going through—the physical teachings,
which are real and direct and obvious. And they are personal, highly
personal. Each time we come closer to tantra in the journey through the
yanas, the relationship to the teacher changes and becomes more and
more personal. The teacher acts as his own spokesman but also as the
spokesman of the vivid and colorful world that you are part of. If you
don't have the experience of winter, you have to take off your clothes
and lie in the snow at night. That way, you will learn a very good lesson
on what winter is all about that doesn't need words. You could read a
book about it, but it doesn't mean very much unless you have that very
immediate and direct experience—which is frightening, very powerful.

Somehow we are unable to have an experience of this nature without
going through the basic learning process that enables us to handle that
kind of experience. Therefore, the three-yana principle is very important—the gradual process from hinayana to mahayana to vajrayana. This

process makes it all make sense. Without it, it does not make any sense; it is just training in masochism.

There's a story about a certain workshop that took place in this country, I don't remember exactly where. It was supposed to be a workshop in self-exposure, and anybody interested in that workshop could just pay their money and come in, without having the faintest idea what it was all about. They were invited to eat dinner together. There was beautifully prepared food and nice china and a nice tablecloth and candlelight and everything. They ate their food and they drank their wine. Then, at the end of the meal, everybody was supposed to break their plates and glasses and chop up their tables and chairs. That was the workshop. What does it mean? Of course, it might mean a lot if you really know what it is all about. But on the other hand, if you just saw that advertised in the newspaper and decided to go to it because you thought it was a groovy thing to do—you'd never done *that* before—it wouldn't mean very much. You might feel uncertain how much you should talk to the others about the experience. You might feel slightly awkward and, at the same time, released or something or other. But on the whole, it would make no sense if there were no training process behind it.

Vajrayana is also very powerful, but you can't just come in and do the workshop of the twelve trials of Naropa. It doesn't mean anything without basic training in mindfulness, awareness, groundlessness, and fearlessness. In that sense, tantra is a very dangerous thing. At the same time, it is very powerful, and every one of us can do it. Other people have done so. Actually, we don't have to be such great scholars as Naropa was. As long as we are interested in using our intellect and our intuition, we can do it. Mahamudra is possible as long as we have some basic training in relating with ourselves. We have to learn fearlessness that is without hesitation but is not based on blind faith. If we have a logical mind, a scientific mind full of suspicion, that is good.

Student: Why do you tell us all this? I find this kind of explosion quite frightening.

Trungpa Rinpoche: That's good. It means you're beginning to feel it.

S: Yes, I am.

TR: That's good. It's not up to me to keep this a secret. You might develop your own self-secretness, your own way of keeping it a secret from yourself. But if you're afraid, that means something is cooking. That's good to hear.

Student: Is mahamudra the first point at which the idea of samsara and nirvana ceases to apply? Or does that happen back with shunyata?

Trungpa Rinpoche: In shunyata, there is the idea of the nonduality of samsara and nirvana, but there is still a sense of this being sacred. In mahamudra, there is definitely nonexistence of samsara and nirvana.

Student: You said that at the point in the student-teacher relationship where sticks are exchanged for swords, all communication takes place in a rainbow realm. I was wondering if you could explain that a little more.

Trungpa Rinpoche: At the point where you pick up swords, there is no gain and no loss. At the level of using sticks, there may be still gain and loss, but when you pick up the swords, there's no gain and no loss.

S: Couldn't it be a very great loss if you got your head cut off?

TR: Well, your head is not particularly a concern here. The point is that you become a highly skilled dancer. You and the teacher can still play together even if you have no head. That's what I mean by rainbow.

S: How is that a rainbow?

TR: That's the rainbow. The teacher can still train a student without a head, or a student can learn without the head that's been chopped off. The physical, literal situation does not apply there anymore. It's as transparent as the rainbow, yet it is still colorful and vivid.

Student: You said that in the shunyata experience, ego is still a problem. Is the ego still a problem in mahamudra?

Trungpa Rinpoche: In the mahamudra experience, ego is not a problem, but the memory of the previous yana is a problem. You have to recover from the hangover of the previous medicine you were taking.

S: The previous medicine was shunyata?

TR: Yes. It works that way throughout the rest of the yanas. Throughout the tantric yanas, it works that way.

S: So in the shunyata experience, there is still an element of duality between ego and—

TR: An element of nonduality. That's the problem.

S: Oh, yes. I see.

Student: What's the difference between the pain we experience at first and the pain we experience in mahamudra?

Trungpa Rinpoche: The difference is that this pain is much, much more real. It is direct pain that is beyond any neurosis. The other one is seeming pain, psychosomatic pain.

S: You mean earlier on you don't get into the pain?

TR: That's right.

Student: You said at one point that ego is pain and pain is ego. If you lose your ego, how can you experience pain?

Trungpa Rinpoche: The absence of ego is pain still. You still feel the absence of ego, nonduality.

S: So that's still an experience.

TR: That has been compared to an empty perfume bottle. You can still smell the perfume.

Student: You said that mahamudra was unoriginated, but then you said that confusion and realization come about at the same time. It sounds like something is originating.

Trungpa Rinpoche: Well, they don't help each other; they don't ferment each other. They are just unoriginated; they come out of nowhere.

Student: Does the bodhisattva ideal of service to other sentient beings extend over into vajrayana?

Trungpa Rinpoche: Basically, yes; but on the vajrayana level, it is less pious and more immediate. On the mahayana level, there is still a notion of doing good.

Student: Could people experience mahamudra through taking acid? It seems to me that that is possible, but as you said before, without the proper preparation, it wouldn't make any sense.

Trungpa Rinpoche: You said it. You see, the mahamudra experience has nothing to do with being high. It's very real and direct. You are no longer under the control of the other. You are just yourself, very simply. But any kind of hallucinogenic experience has a sense of the other.

S: You mean memory, comparison to other experience?

TR: Yes.

Student: You said that mahamudra pain was without neurosis, and you also said that in the rainbow realm you could cut your head off and still learn. I am a little confused about what is going on here. What is direct pain at that level? Can it be talked about?

Trungpa Rinpoche: Pain from having your head chopped off. You have no head, right? But you still have a headache. That kind of pain.

S: Is that physiological or psychosomatic?

TR: Well, obviously psychosomatic. When I talk about your head being chopped off, I do not mean that the vajrayana master and his student would literally have swordplay. That's a figurative thing. That pain is very immediate pain. When you have no head, you still get a very painful headache. It becomes very penetrating.

Student: You were talking about the relationship between master and student in the vajrayana being personal. I was wondering how one makes it get personal.

Trungpa Rinpoche: The whole style of teaching is personal. The teacher minds your business forever. It's not necessarily a matter of the teacher's physical presence, having a constant relationship with your teacher physically present. But whenever the teaching is given to you, the means, methods, and techniques of conveying the teaching are very personal.

Student: Is it that on the vajrayana level, you yourself become an embodiment of your spiritual friend?

Trungpa Rinpoche: It's more that the guru is like a pill that you swallow that always remains in your stomach. Either it could poison and kill you on the spot, or it could grant you everlasting life. It's very personal. One of the basic principles of the vajrayana is what is called the samaya vow. The guru sows a seed in you which is part of himself, and you have that seed in you, and the guru has remote control of that seed.

Student: In Naropa's acts of self-denial, there is that repeated formula in which Tilopa says something like, "If I had a disciple wanting instruction, he would (for example) jump into the fire." Then Naropa does it and almost gets killed every time. I don't understand why he does that. Is it that he is still clinging to his ego?

Trungpa Rinpoche: It's something more than ego. It's that he has to become more naked. He is still not unmasking enough. It's more a process of stripping than of giving up ego—which he has already done anyway. Each one of his acts seems to be an enormous example of surrendering ego. But after surrendering his ego, he also has to unmask properly.

Student: You said that the mahamudra experience is irritating because of its nakedness, very irritating. Then later you said that in the mahamudra realm, you are bliss. My approach may be very dualistic, but for me, irritation and bliss don't go together.

Trungpa Rinpoche: Irritation happens at the level when you are still ambitious, when you are first committing yourself to the mahamudra path and you are beginning to see new views of the world. Seeing new views is very irritating. It's like, in the middle of a sunny day in Greece, taking off your dark glasses. The glare is so irritating to your eyes. And that's the first experience. But then you get used to it, and you learn to perceive things without distortion. And that becomes bliss. So it's a gradual process. Irritation comes first. Things are so close to heart, so immediate. Then you become used to it and develop confidence. Then the whole thing becomes bliss.

Student: How is assimilating the teacher as a pill or a seed different from taking a drug? How do you get rid of the sense of the teacher as the other?

Trungpa Rinpoche: Well, drugs don't last very long, and the teacher lasts your whole life.

S: But is the sense of the teacher always there?

TR: Until you become a teacher yourself.

Student: Are the other visions that Naropa had after the old lady's shadow fell on his book and before he met Tilopa also manifestations of shunyata?

Trungpa Rinpoche: Yes. Very much so.

S: But it seems that they're so concrete, that their whole point is somehow this concreteness. How is that connected with shunyata as emptiness?

TR: It's because of its fullness. The fullness does not allow any room; therefore, that frozen space could be called empty space.

S: Then how does that fullness lead into the fullness of mahamudra?

TR: Mahamudra is very sharp, not just full alone. It's colorful.

Shunyata fullness is rather gray and transparent and dull, like London fog. But the mahamudra experience of fullness is humorous; it is also the fullness of little particles dancing with each other within the fullness. It's like a sky full of stars and shooting stars and all the rest—so many activities are taking place.

SIX

The Levels of Mahamudra

THERE ARE DIFFERENT levels of mahamudra, which are related to different levels of clarity. Clarity here means confidence and fearlessness, rather than being a purely phenomenological quality.

According to the Buddhist approach, advancement toward enlightenment does not come from insight alone but also from skillful means. On the bodhisattva path, a powerful skillful means is the practice of the six paramitas—working with other sentient beings. In the vajrayana, exchange with the world is also a means of development. That seems to be a general pattern. In the vajrayana experience of mahamudra, first one develops one's basic sanity, and having done that, the only way to grow up and mature further is through further openness to the world. That is one of the important elements.

In order to relate with the world, one has to develop confidence. In order to develop confidence, one has to have some level of identification with one's basic being. As a result, at this stage, the five buddha principles become very prominent. One begins to develop an affinity with a particular buddha principle through receiving an abhisheka, or initiation, from a vajra master, that is, a vajrayana teacher. That vajra master, or teacher, teaches one how to conduct oneself as a real practitioner of the vajrayana. He is also the example one can follow. The key point is the meeting of his mind and your mind, together with the mutual discovery of a particular mandala. In this case, the mandala is a host of deities, which are associated with one's basic being. That is to say, the deities represent your type of energy rather than being divine beings who are external separate entities or even internal separate entities. At the moment of the discovery of this mandala, your own basic beingness is discovered in an enlightened form—the Jack-ness or the John-ness of you. Your basic beingness is seen in an enlightened form, in a mahamudra form. You begin to see that. You develop, not fascination, but an identification with such principles, which have your own particular characteristics, which are those of a particular buddha family: vajra, ratna, padma, karma, buddha.

The point of this is realization of the sacredness of the universe and of yourself. There are different ways of viewing sacredness. One might think, "The world is sacred because it was created by God and the mysteriousness of God, and His power and all-pervasiveness are beyond mind's measure." They boggle the mind, they're beyond our limited capacity. And because they are beyond the measure of our small mind, they should be regarded as divine principles. Since we don't have the power or the knowledge to make a rock, since we couldn't invent planets or create the four seasons, since that is beyond our control and reflects such power, it is unthinkable and therefore sacred. No one could conquer this large Conductor of the universe. Only God is on that level. By associating with this great principle, you might be helped to become one with it, but that is questionable; it depends on how good you are.

Another approach to sacredness might also be connected with meditative absorption. If you succeed in developing meditative absorption, you tend to get an ineffable experience of something-or-other. You can't name it. It is associated with divine power. One connects it with how He created the universe. It's beyond words, beyond concept.

The approach of vajrayana Buddhism to sacredness has a different quality. It is not so much a matter of things being big and enormous and beyond the measure of one's thought; rather it has to do with things being so true, so real, so direct. We know a fire burns. We know the earth carries us. We know that space accommodates us. All these are *real* facts and so obvious. Obviousness becomes sacredness from the point of view of vajrayana. It is not that things are sacred because they are beyond our imagination, but because they are so obvious. The magic is simplicity. Winter gets cold, summer gets warm. Everything in every situation has a little magic. If we forget to eat, we get hungry. There is a causal aspect, which is the truth. So in this case, the sacredness is a matter of truth, of the obviousness of the whole thing.

This has nothing particular to do with how things happen to be *made,* but rather how they *are.* There's no reference to the past in vajrayana, no concern with the case history of things or with chronology. The concern is with *what is.* When we look at things as they are on a very simple and ordinary level, we find that they are fantastically, obviously true, frighteningly true. Because of their quality of being true and obvious, things are sacred and worth respecting. This kind of truth reveals falsity automatically. If we are slightly off the point, we get hit or pushed or pulled. We get constant reminders, constant help. It's that kind of sacredness.

Another part of sacredness is a sense of well-being, which is a very interesting thing. It is a very typical characteristic of the vajrayana approach. This sense of well-being has to do with the fact that although you might be awestruck by the penetrating truth and obviousness of things, at the same time, in spite of this awesome quality, there is no sense of threat. There is a sense of courtship, of a love affair between the obviousness and you perceiving it.

The obstacle to this well-being is naiveté or mindlessness. Things are taken for granted; things are never questioned, never looked at. The sense of well-being has a quality of appreciation. You appreciate that you possess, or are in, such a beautiful universe, that the universe is part of you and you are part of it.

The mahamudra experience of clarity and sharpness allows us to develop a new attitude in which things are never taken for granted, in which every moment is a new experience. With that sense of sacredness, of well-being, one begins to rediscover the universe. Since this is not a fantasy but a real experience, it cannot be destroyed. As much doubt as comes up, that is how much clarity shines through. Because of this, this experience is called *vajra,* a Sanskrit word which means "adamantine" or "indestructible." Even the threat of defeat of this vajra quality is used as fuel for it to maintain itself. Therefore, it is constantly indestructible, imperturbable.

In the vajrayana practice of performing the sadhanas of the particular yidams who are appropriate to you that were given to you by your teacher, you identify with the iconographical representation of a yidam. Identifying with the iconographical details is no longer a problem, because you know the basic characteristics of the deity, and you have a sense of that in your mind already. Probably we would have no problem at all visualizing Uncle Sam, because we know what Uncle Sam represents. The image is very vivid. It is a similar kind of thing when you are given the practice of a particular deity and mandala. If you have a complete and thorough understanding of it, then it is no longer foreign or alien but easy to recognize and identify with.

Still, visualization is very tricky. It is not just fingerpainting your imaginings in your mind. It's getting into the spirit of what you're visualizing. Take as an example visualizing Broadway in New York City in the early evening. You close your eyes and begin to see yellow cabs and other traffic and neon lights and buildings and people walking. You visualize it completely. You don't actually have to visualize it; you just switch your mind to it and automatically you are there. You feel as though you are in New York City already, so you don't have to pay too much attention to details. You don't have to think about how many lampposts there are on Broadway or what color the neon lights are, particularly. You just get a sense of the general proportions and the general climate.

So that's the approach to visualization, rather than imagining an alien-looking guy with three heads and twelve arms, who turns into something plastic rather than a deity. Because if you don't have a real sense of who the deities are and what they represent, then visualization becomes just a child's game.

In tantric practice, there is the notion that sights, sounds, and consciousness turn into the expressions of those deities. Sight, or visual objects, become part of the realm of the deity, and sounds become the deity's mantra, and the thought process, or consciousness, becomes the wisdom of the deity. This does not mean that everybody appears dressed up as a deity, and that everyone's conversations are in the form of mantra, and that everybody's mind is blissed out. Rather, what you see has the quality of a particular deity. The principle is all-pervasive because it is your principle. You can't see any other world than your world, and sight, sound, and thought process become a part of that style. Then it becomes very vivid. At a certain point, even if you would like to forget about this or it becomes too much for you, it still follows you. That awareness comes back to you by itself rather than your having to try to be aware of it. This kind of identification with your basic principle, the awakening of your basic principle, is the starting point for developing confidence at the beginning. This is very important, extraordinarily important.

When you have achieved this confidence and dignity, the awareness is not constant all the time, but hundreds of flashes of awareness happen to you instantaneously. At that point, probably it is time to extend your practice out into relating with your exterior, with your expressions. So far, you have been working with your *impressions*, with your interior. Now you are going to work outward into the exterior, which is composed of all kinds of states of being. The first thing is to arouse energy. At that point, you still have all kinds of neurotic leftovers remaining, so you have to have a way of utilizing those leftovers as part of the energy. You also have to destroy any sense of preserving your perceptions of sight and sound and so on. Destroying that sense of preservation is a giving-away process.

This is where the first dharma of Naropa, called tumo, comes in. You may have heard of this. It does not simply mean developing central heating within your body so that you don't have to depend on warm clothes. It's not quite as utilitarian as that—or as cheap as that. *Tumo* is a Tibetan word that means "wrathful one." *Tum* means "wrath" or "anger"; *mo* is a feminine ending, so it is "female wrathful one." This is related to what is called *chandali* in Sanskrit, which is "flame" or "energy." But one cannot develop the physical effects of this practice until one has conquered or destroyed the sense of preserving one's being. One is consumed by this flame of chandali, which has no compassion, that goes in only one direction. Because it *is* compassion, it does not require any extra compassion. It is an all-consuming flame.

Then one does get the physical result of not being at the mercy of the elements. If you are in a hot country, you feel cool. If you are in a cool country, you feel warm. But that seems to be beside the point. The point here is dealing with the tension that one builds up within one's being, a psychosomatic tension that creates a sense of weakness. The body becomes such a big deal that one does not want to endure even the smallest discomfort. There is tremendous fear involved. Even the littlest discomfort brings enormous panic, particularly when you begin to think that you can't renew the body, you can't get further supplies to keep yourself happy. So there's a sense of panic, which is the cause of tension. One becomes very tight; psychosomatically, one's whole body becomes one lump of muscle. This makes one very vulnerable to the elements—the psychosomatic or the physical elements. This sense of tension—or anger—creates enormous unnecessary suffering.

Then there is the next dharma of Naropa, realization of the illusory body. Having disowned one's body, having conquered one's sense of possessiveness toward one's body, one's being, one's ego, then one begins to mingle oneself with the rest of the mirage of sounds, colors, shapes, energies, emotions—everything. Mingling with that is the practice of illusory body. It's a kind of celebration. Constantly, there is joy, a dance taking place. It's not to maintain your thing, but to celebrate.

Then there is the next dharma, dream. This is not necessarily dream at the level of sleep. It is the dreams that we have all the time in our lives, the fantasies and real experiences of our life during the day, the fantasies and thought processes that make our life like it is happening in Disneyland. The search for entertainment is an important aspect of the dream activity. If you realize the dream as dream, then there is no entertainment. But that does not necessarily mean depression. Entertainment is the sense of getting your money's worth, so to speak, or your energy's worth. But if we realize dream as dream, the whole approach to life becomes less businesslike, but at the same time very practical. Relating with friends, relatives, the business world, enemies—all these experiences become more real. Generally we think of dreams differently; we think of dreams as something unreal and of something that is not dreams as real. That seems to be a misunderstanding. The point of the dream yoga is to free oneself from the Disneyland-like quality, which is our regular day life, and replace that with dream experience, which is real life. From that point of view, if one could live completely in the dream world, that would be much more real and pragmatic and efficient and complete than the so-called nondream world.

Luminosity is the next one, light. That is a further elaboration of the intelligence one should develop in the *real* dream state, in which you don't dream but you live properly. There is a sense of panoramic awareness. You are certain about how things function. There is the confidence that we have already developed: the sense of real, genuine understanding and awareness, which is the absence of threat. That is the experience of luminosity.

The next one is called *phowa* in Tibetan, which literally means "pass out" or "eject." In this case, it's more likely "eject." This means that you are capable of making your consciousness step outside of your body when the time comes. Or your consciousness can enter into another body when the time comes. This again means cutting through a lot of possessiveness toward one's body, particularly the desire for possessions and entertainment. One has to have the power to remove clingings. You can step out in the middle of your meal; before you finish your sentence, you can step out. You don't have a chance to finish your pun or to finish your dessert. You have to leave things behind, which can be very scary and very unsatisfying.

The last one has to do with sleep.[1] There was an Indian siddha called Lavapa who fell asleep for twelve years by the side of the main highway running through his city. At the end of twelve years, he had realized mahamudra completely. Sleep is both literal and symbolic here. Symbolically, there is the sense that the samsaric state is a state of deep sleep. Also, physical sleep is a state of complete unconsciousness before dreams arise. The idea is to develop complete awareness, or better in this context of mahamudra, a state of wakefulness. When you're awake, you don't have to make a point of being aware, because you are constantly awake in any case. You can do other things along with that. That is the real example of mahamudra; mahamudra is like being awake; you don't have to maintain your practice or state of wisdom. Everything functions simply and naturally within the process of being awake.

Traditionally, after completing the six dharmas of Naropa, a person begins to practice hatha yoga—pranayama and so forth. The final outcome of the yoga practices is that you learn to perform miracles. Relating with the body in a certain way is very magical. Thus, it is regarded as very dangerous to introduce hatha yoga, or playing with your breath or whatever, at too early a stage. You still don't have intelligence, awareness, and confidence functioning in a coordinated way. Everything is not synchronized properly. The danger and the strain come when this synchronization does not exist but you are still pushing to achieve.

The notion of miracle is very interesting. Here, miracle is something very basic. It has to come about through the karmic situation, what is going on in your life and in the life of your country. Certain very powerful coincidences take place, and you might become the instigator of them. But if your action is not attuned to the karmic situation, things will go wrong. For instance, if you have the magical power to produce anything you want, the obvious first thing you might do is produce lots of banknotes. But that would create a strange fluctuation in the economic world. The banknotes you've produced won't have been registered properly; though they are seemingly real, they are actually fake.

Your action becomes criminal. Somehow the whole thing has to work with the karmic situation that exists in your country. You can't oversaturate the market. So a miracle is not one-sided in character. It is a mutual creation of you and the situation in the country. The country's energy and yours become the instigator.

The idea of hatha yoga practice is also to relate with the elements properly, make friends with them—the physical elements as well as the psychological elements. In other words, the vajrayana process is getting to know the world in the fullest possible way. By doing that, you will be able to work with other people and help them, because they are part of this universe, and they have their connections to the elements as well.

Student: Can you say anything more about stepping out, which you spoke of in connection with phowa practice?

Trungpa Rinpoche: It's being willing to leave. Things are half-finished, and there is a desire to finish them. You have a sense of openness that gives you the power to step out anytime you wish. That can also extend to being able to step out of your body, leave your body whenever you wish. But the situation has to be right. You can't practice phowa if you're freaking out and regarding it as a suicidal thing. In that case, you would still be kept in your body, because you would have a sense of imprisonment. The greater your sense of imprisonment, the more surely you will be kept in your body. So it would not work if you approached it suicidally. It's a sense of letting go.

S: Is it to be practiced at the time of death?

TR: Yes, but not only. It should have implications in all directions.

Student: Rinpoche, you seem to be saying that visualization of buddhas and yidams should only be done after realization of shunyata.

Trungpa Rinpoche: I wouldn't say complete realization, but the person should have practice in shunyata first, know how to perceive the world on the shunyata level first.

S: It seems to me that other Tibetan teachers give visualization practices to new students. Why would they do that?

TR: In Tibet, most serious practitioners would automatically enter vajrayana immediately. But theoretically they already have some training in the basic practice of meditation. A lot of Western students come to teachers in what is seemingly the same faithful, devoted fashion as Tibetans, but they have no training behind them. So it seems to be premature to start them with vajrayana practices, when they have not even realized the meaning of suffering or of the four noble truths. They can't just start with visualization.

There is another problem with Western practitioners. Whether they consider themselves Christians or followers of the theistic tradition or not, still their general thinking pattern, their fundamental way of carrying their mind about in this world on the spiritual level, is still based on the theistic tradition. A lot of people may have reservations about believing in an external god and things like that, but still their basic approach goes along with a theistic attitude. Then if they visualize another god, that doesn't sort anything out for them at all. It just reinforces their national ego or religious ego, which they immediately associate with this. Somehow it just becomes an extra burden rather than an approach toward freedom.

Student: Isn't it what you call "idiot compassion" to start students with vajrayana practices? It seems to make so much more sense to begin with the hinayana and mahayana approach of moment-to-moment compassion toward your own mind.

Trungpa Rinpoche: I think so, yes. Generally, I think we have a kind of social problem here. When Western students come to study with Eastern teachers, they are regarded as special guests, because they come from the land that invented airplanes, motorcars, radios, and other fantastic things of all kinds. There is already something special about them; they have their passport by birth. This is particularly true for Tibetans, for instance. In Tibetan, the word for "foreigner" is not at all derogatory. It has a sense of the exotic. Foreigners are not regarded as barbarians at all, but are thought to be very smart and have powerful minds. As a Tibetan, you might think that one American visitor in your monastery could build airplanes for you if you wanted, or motorcars, fountains, electric plants, or anything. Westerners are considered all-knowing, omniscient. Although they may not actually have any knowledge at all, because of that kind of credential, they are put in the category of special guests, which is actually quite close to idiot compassion. The hard-core ego or neurosis they in fact carry calls for much more training.

Student: There are literally thousands of people in the West practicing hatha yoga. Are these people making a mistake? Are they not prepared for hatha yoga?

Trungpa Rinpoche: If you relate with hatha yoga on a hinayana level, like instead of just sitting cross-legged and meditating, then it seems to be okay. A lot of people approach it as just a gymnastic thing. But if they begin to play with psychophysical energy with a semi-tantric approach, as in kundalini yoga, for instance, then it tends to become very dangerous.

Student: I don't understand what you said about miracles. It seems to me that even if you were thrown into jail for producing money out of thin air, it would still be a miracle.

Trungpa Rinpoche: It would be criminal. You are not helping the karma of the country. You are creating more unemployment and more pain, which cheapens the energy, green energy.[2] Producing money is an insult to the mandala.

Student: Is the idea of the dream yoga to realize how completely the world you perceive is made out of your own projections? Is it that once you realize that and relate to it enough, you're really being more realistic?

Trungpa Rinpoche: That's right, yes.

Student: What do you mean by a *real* dream state?

Trungpa Rinpoche: This, the way we are now. You are asleep.

Student: What form does the intelligence that develops into mahamudra take at the hinayana and mahayana levels?

Trungpa Rinpoche: The hinayana level of intelligence is mindfulness. I suppose we could say that the prajna level that comes then is awareness, which is greater than just being mindful of particular things. Mindfulness is also very intelligent, but that intelligence is not as great as awareness. Mindfulness is sometimes called "recollection" (*smriti* in Sanskrit), which does not mean recollecting the past, but recollecting what is happening here now. In the actual, real, final prajna, awareness becomes all-pervasive. You don't have to project in any particular direction or from any particular angle. It is everywhere. But still there is a sense of pulsation, of flash and spread, flash and spread. It isn't a constant thing.

S: What changes that causes the mindfulness to progress to awareness?

TR: Awareness develops because mindfulness begins to see things so precisely and clearly that the things begin to put out radiations of awareness, rather than just being the objects you're being mindful of. That permeates. It is an opening. For instance, if you look at a candle, you begin to see not only the candle but also the light that candle is reflecting at other objects. Your vision becomes much greater. That brings intelligence into another area. Awareness is not only awareness of things, but also awareness of space everywhere. You cannot develop such awareness without first developing mindfulness of things.

Student: Are the six dharmas of Naropa meditation practices?

Trungpa Rinpoche: They are a kind of meditation practice, I suppose you could say, but they have more to do with relating with the activity of your life; they are more on the level of meditation in action. Of course, there are certain techniques for developing the six dharmas, different tricks, so to speak—visualizations and mantras and so on. But the general idea is that you do those as a preparation, and the actual practice happens in your everyday life situation.

Student: You described various views of sacredness. It seemed on the whole that one had to do with God and the other one was the vajrayana approach. I was wondering whether one of these applied to the mahayana idea of sacredness, or if that was still another outlook. It seems to me that traditionally there's such a strong element of devotion and sacred richness in it that mahayana almost sounds like Catholicism.

Trungpa Rinpoche: I think the mahayana is much closer to the theistic approach, definitely, because it has a sense of greatness and it emphasizes performing transcending actions—which is still related with size. The vajrayana no longer relates to size; it relates to qualities. The mahayana is the "big vehicle." The vajrayana is the "diamond vehicle"; it could be big or small.

S: There's something confusing about the emphasis on grandioseness in the mahayana, since it's essential teaching is shunyata. I would have thought shunyata would cut through the grandioseness as pretentious.

TR: Well, it should cut, but somehow it doesn't entirely. Therefore, mahayana can lead into vajrayana. It's not so much that the grandioseness is cut down, but the grandioseness doesn't exist, so the whole setup begins to fall apart. That's the trick. This particularly happens in the later stages of the mahayana, like the eighth, ninth, and tenth bhumis. Definitely by the tenth bhumi there is no viewer anymore.

S: And the grandioseness—

TR: Just dissolves into dharmakaya. Like a car without a driver goes to the dump.

Student: Do you have to be a trickster to get enlightened? It seems there are a lot of tricks involved.

Trungpa Rinpoche: I should say so, yes.

Student: At this vajrayana level, where do reference points come in, if they come in at all?

Trungpa Rinpoche: The energies. In vajrayana, the reference point is not regarded as bad, but it is the way of accentuating the play of phenomena.

Student: But is there a reference point?

Trungpa Rinpoche: There is a vajra reference point rather than an ordinary reference point, which is wisdom.

Student: Why would you accentuate the play of the ordinary?

Trungpa Rinpoche: You are not doing it. Phenomena as they are accentuate themselves.

S: I see.

TR: That's it!

Student: How does the idea of a person having an aim fit in, or is that gone by this time?

Trungpa Rinpoche: An ordinary student might still have a sense of struggle, but in moments when flashes take place, when realizations take place in his state of mind, there's no aim. You remember the idea of ordinary mind we were talking about? The ordinariness? That's it.

Student: It's almost as if you and energy or you and the universe, or whatever you want to call it, are the same.

Trungpa Rinpoche: It's very simple. It's so simple. And there's a sense of well-being, so no ambition is involved, except entertaining oneself constantly—which the entertainments do for you, rather than your having to order them.

Student: And compassion kind of comes in naturally.

Trungpa Rinpoche: Yes. When you're lighting incense in your room, which clears the air, that's the compassion. It makes things workable, pleasant to be.

Student: Why is the illusory body called illusory body?

Trungpa Rinpoche: It's the same idea as the dream. This is a dream.

S: Oh, maybe I didn't understand right. I thought if one realized the illusory body, that was being more real.

TR: That's what I mean. It's the same as the dream. This is a dream, which is real. More real than the ordinary sleeping dream, than the dream dream.

S: This is a real dream.

TR: Yes, this is a real dream.

S: That means there is reality.

TR: There is reality, sure. And there is unreality at the same time.

S: The unreality is the dream.

S: Is not the dream. The real dream is reality. And the real illusion is the real thing. In other words, the mirage is the real water. You know, when you see a mirage in the desert—a lake with palm trees? That's real. You may not find it when you get there, when you want to have a drink of water, but still it's real.

S: If you're in the desert, though, you have to distinguish between the real oasis and the fake one.

TR: That's what I mean. That's what I mean, yes.

Student: How does the realization of the illusory body connect with that?

Trungpa Rinpoche: You are able to see real things, things that shimmer, change energy, shift patterns.

S: Like a mirage?

TR: Like a mirage; like you and I looking at each other now. That's the real illusory body. I change and you change, this way and that way. But it's a real change.

S: Then an unreal change would be if you were hallucinating.

TR: Yes.

Student: Could you say that real doesn't apply to anything particular, but we're just talking about clearing perception?

Trungpa Rinpoche: Clearing perception, yes. It's catching yourself, fragments of yourself, assembling this particular perception. That's the illusory body.

S: Learning how to spot that.

TR: Learning how to spot that, yes.

S: How to spot that detail and even make use of it?

TR: Yes.

S: And still keep track of it as an illusion.

TR: Yes. And very sanely.

S: So actually it's a very real energy.

TR: You've got it . . . I think.

Student: Are you saying there's a message involved in your perception at that point?

Trungpa Rinpoche: Not really messages. That's secondary. Third-hand. But this is *first*-hand. Even zero-hand.

Student: I still don't understand the relationship between the mirage and the reality.

Trungpa Rinpoche: The mirage *is* reality. It's a real mirage.

S: There's no fake mirage, then.

TR: No. It's very real.

S: That doesn't quite accord with my understanding of mirage, or at least what I was taught at school.

TR: What did they say?

S: A mirage is something you think is there and it's not.

TR: Well, that's it!

S: That's reality?

TR: That's reality.

S: So if I see a mirage, say of an oasis, the mirage is real, but the water, the palm trees, and the coconuts are not real.

TR: That's right, yes. I think you've got it.

S: Is a memory a mirage in that sense?

TR: Yes, precisely. That's a good question.

Student: Are you saying that to see the mirage as a mirage is to see reality?

Trungpa Rinpoche: That's the first thing. There is a song about that in the book, actually. It's in the section about Marpa meeting Naropa. Could somebody read that?

Student [reads poem from p. 101]:

> The sky-flower, the Daka riding on the foal
> Of a barren mare, the Oral Transmission,
> Has scattered the hairs of a tortoise, the ineffable,
> And with the poke of a hare's horn, the unoriginated,
> Roused Tilopa in the depth of ultimate reality.
>
> Through the mute Tilopa, the ineffable resisting all
>   attempts at communication,
> The blind Naropa became free in seeing Truth which is no
>   seeing.
> On the mountain of the Dharmakaya which is the ultimate,
>   the deaf Naropa,
> The lame Mati (Mar-pa) ran in a radiant light, which neither
>   comes nor goes.
> The sun and moon and dGyes-pa-rdor-rje—
> Their dancing is one-valueness in many.
> The conch-shell has proclaimed its fame in all directions,
> It has called out to the strenuous, who are worthy vessels
>   for instruction.
> The focal points, Chakrasamvara—the world
> Is the wheel of the Oral Transmission:
> Turn it, dear child, without attachment.

Trungpa Rinpoche: We should end our seminar here. I think you should read this song again and again if you can. It makes enormous sense. The translation is the best we have so far, and Dr. Guenther's very genuine effort has become a very valuable medium. He doesn't try to put in his own ideas. He tries to present the translation directly, as it is, which lays very important groundwork for us. Obviously, we have to discuss more about mahamudra and this mirage and so forth.

Notes

PART ONE

Chapter 1. Naropa and Us

1. Abhayakirti (Tib. 'Jig-med grags-pa), according to Guenther, "was the name which Naropa had when he renounced his post of abbot at Nalanda and set out in search of his Guru." Literally, the name means "renowned as fearless."

Chapter 2. Genuine Madness and Pop Art

1. *Ku-su-li-pa* is a Tibetan term, often also appearing as *kusulu,* describing a yogi who has reached such a level of simplicity that he only has thoughts concerning three things: eating, sleeping, and eliminating.

2. "*Lohivagaja* seems to be the Tibetan transcription of a Prakrit sentence which in Sanskrit might have been *rohita avagaccha,* 'fish go away!'" (Guenther's note, *The Life and Teaching of Naropa,* p. 35).

3. G. I. Gurdjieff was a well-known teacher of Greek-Armenian origin who taught his own system of spirituality in eastern and western Europe and the United States in the first half of the twentieth century. The Vidyadhara adopted Gurdjieff's notion of "idiot compassion," a "feel-good" approach of seeming kindness that actually contributes further to delusion and weakness.

PART TWO

Chapter 2. Giving Birth to Intellect

1. Don Juan is the sorcerer and spiritual teacher of the Yaqui Indian tribe of northern Mexico described in the many books of Carlos Castaneda.

Chapter 4. Beyond Shunyata

1. "Emptiness being form": This is a reference to the *Heart Sutra*, or *Sutra of the Heart of Transcendent Knowledge* (Skt. *Mahaprajnaparamitabridaya-sutra*). A key line in this sutra is "Form is no other than emptiness; emptiness is no other than form." This line is sometimes interpreted, as by the questioner here, as indicating two stages in the understanding of shunyata, or emptiness. In the first, the practitioner realizes that forms have no essence that makes them ultimately real and thus are "empty." This understanding may be associated with a tendency to reject or withdraw from the world. In a further stage, the practitioner realizes that it is the nature of emptiness to appear as form. This may prompt the fully realized person's return to the world. This analysis of shunyata is particularly stressed in Zen.

Chapter 6. The Levels of Mahamudra

1. "The last one has to do with sleep": The six dharmas of Naropa are usually listed as: (1) inner heat (Tib. *tumo*), (2) illusory body (*gyulü*), (3) dream (*milam*), (4) luminosity (*ösel*), (5) transference (*phowa*), (6) bardo, or in-between state. Though these may be given in a different order, the editor has no explanation for why the Vidyadhara chose to expound the last one as he does here.

2. "Green energy": Playing on the color of American banknotes, the Vidyadhara sometimes half-jocularly referred to money as green energy.

From

THE LIFE OF MARPA
THE TRANSLATOR

Seeing Accomplishes All

TSANG NYÖN HERUKA

*Translated from the Tibetan
by the Nālandā Translation Committee
under the direction of
Chögyam Trungpa*

Preface

I T IS MY GREAT PRIVILEGE and honor to present the life of Marpa the Translator. The life of Marpa is a great example of how the Tibetans of ancient times brought the buddhadharma from India to Tibet. It shows how the Tibetans conducted themselves on their journeys and how much hardship they went through to bring the teachings to Tibet. So Marpa was not purely a translator who translated from Sanskrit to Tibetan, but he actually brought Buddhism to Tibet.

Marpa is one of the great saints in the Buddhist tradition of Tibet. He was a scholar and a practitioner as well as a very practical person, being a farmer and householder. It seems that we don't have any equivalent of him in modern days. Today, you are either a scholar who translates from one language to another, or you are a devotee of a guru who is supposed to transmit the essence of the teachings he has studied. In the West, many scholars would agree that you become either a practitioner or a scholar; you can't be both. If you are a practitioner, you lose your "objective" viewpoint, and if you are a scholar, you lose the heartfelt magic. From that point of view, there is no hope of combining the two. But here, in the life of Marpa, we have a unique story that has been handed down from generation to generation of how translation and practice can be brought together.

The Tibetans, Chinese, and Japanese throughout history have both translated and practiced, and in these cultures, the belief is that if you don't practice, you can't translate accurately. Therefore, practice and translation go hand in hand. There is no particular bias to either side;

rather, the idea is that if you have personal experience of the basic logic or dharma of the teachings, you are in a better position to translate accurately with feeling. We could say that this approach is like a human being singing, as opposed to a computer making the same sound. A computer might be a technically good singer, but we still prefer the human voice.

We hope that presenting Marpa's life and his life example—how he brought Buddhism to Tibet—will be of some use to those who are practicing Buddhism, as well as to those who are purely interested in how Buddhism comes from one culture to another. In turn, at this point, we have a further translation happening, in that Buddhism and Buddhist literature are being translated into the English language. We have done this translation in the hope that it may be able to cross the cultural gap and enlighten people through the profound and powerful messages that come across in the example of Marpa's activity. Hopefully, this work could now be translated into other European languages, as well as Chinese and Japanese.

The working style of translation that we have adopted is to combine precision and accuracy with a certain sense of devotion. Because of this, we have had no need to add anything new or omit anything as irrelevant. Working in this way, we have also found that translating together as a committee is most enjoyable.

I would like to invite the readers to share in what we have found. I am so pleased that we are able to present this work. What we have discovered could be equally yours.

Translator's Colophon

Like a sword slashing through water
One sees mahamudra
And attains the teachings of the formless dakinis.
This indeed is your kindness, Marpa the Translator.

Though enveloped by the darkness of maras,
One sees the luminosity of the Great Eastern Sun
And discovers the sun of insight transcending mind.
This indeed is your kindness, Marpa the Translator.

The view arises free from bias,
Meditation arises free from grasping,
Action arises free from hesitation—
This indeed is your kindness, Marpa the Translator.

If we did not have you, Marpa the Translator,
The hearing lineage could not pervade everywhere.
Whenever your life example is heard,
Darkness in the mind of this little one, Chökyi Gyatso,
Is always dispelled.

By the power of propagating your life example,
This kalpa of plague, war, and famine is pacified.
In the great bliss of That
May all beings without exception

Enjoy this feast offering
Together with you, Vajracharya Marpa,
And may all attain enlightenment.

This was written on May 10, 1982, by Chökyi Gyatso, the eleventh Trungpa at the Kalapa Court within the dharmic sphere of Karma Dzong.

From

THE RAIN OF WISDOM

The Essence of the Ocean of True Meaning

BRINGING THE RAIN OF WISDOM

THE SPONTANEOUS SELF-LIBERATION

THE BLAZING GREAT BLISS

THE QUICK PATH TO REALIZATION
OF THE SUPREME SIDDHI

The Vajra Songs of the Kagyü Gurus

Translated by the Nālandā Translation Committee
under the direction of Chögyam Trungpa

Nālandā Translation Committee

Chögyam Trungpa, Director
Lama Ugyen Shenpen
Loppön Lodrö Dorje Holm
Larry Mermelstein, Executive Director

David Cox
Dana Dudley
Christine Keyser
Sherab Chödzin Kohn
Robin Kornman
Jud Levinson

John Rockwell, Jr.
Cathryn Stein
Ives Waldo
Scott Wellenbach
Gerry Wiener

Chökyi Gyatso, the eleventh in the succession of supreme Trungpa tül-kus, radiates like the sun all the precious teachings of the Kagyü in all the kingdoms of the world. This is evidence of his ability to incarnate according to his wish. Not only has he properly translated into English the realization songs of the great siddhas of the Practice Lineage, but in the western land of America, he has spread the teachings of the Kagyü in a hundred directions.

For the tenth-year anniversary celebration, I, the holder of the crown and title of the glorious Karmapa, proclaimed these good wishes of auspiciousness in the Tibetan Iron Monkey year, on the fifth day of the Vaishakha month, in the year 1980, on the good nineteenth day of the fifth month. Shubham

His Holiness the XVIth Gyalwa Karmapa
Dharma Chakra Centre
Rumtek
Gangtok Sikkim

Foreword

I AM VERY PLEASED to present this translation of *The Rain of Wisdom*, the *Kagyü Gurtso*. I feel highly inspired by the translation work that I and my students have done. I am realizing for the first time that the basically theistic English language has now been blessed by the Practice Lineages and is becoming a great medium for expressing the nontheistic, enlightened dharma. I and my translators have worked very hard and feel somewhat proud of what we have produced.

When I was eight my tutor recommended that I use the life of Milarepa as part of my reading practice. I remember clearly the illuminated manuscript of Milarepa's life that I used. Occasionally I would look at the illustrations and try to understand the contents. Reading this text not only improved my literacy, but aroused my feeling for the Kagyü tradition and my admiration of Milarepa's life and his asceticism.

I wept and laughed as my reading practice went on. Sometimes my tutor thought that I was weeping because I missed my mother, or because I was trying to get out of the harsh discipline that was part of my training. I used to tell him, "No, I'm crying because of what I am reading." So this reading had a profound effect on me. In fact, reading this book inspired me to compose beginning-level songs myself, which at that point I did by trial and error.

The sense of dedication and exertion that is expressed in the life examples and songs of our Kagyü forefathers is something one can never forget. The Practice Lineage of the Kagyü tradition inspires one to become fully involved in a heartfelt connection with the teachings. From my childhood until the present day, each time I open *The Rain of Wisdom* and read a few passages it makes me appreciate the hardships that our forefathers endured for the sake of future generations such as ourselves.

The Kagyü tradition is said to be the most stubborn and honest in following its heritage. We take delight in our heritage. Doubt, challenge, hesitation—in brief, any form of second thoughts—are not regarded as obstacles, but rather as fuel to push us further and cause our devotion and heartfelt longing to blaze, to increase our intense desire to follow the example of our forefathers. So we, as Kagyüs, have thrived on the transmissions of our forefathers, and sustained and nourished ourselves in reading and reciting their vajra songs along with their life stories.

As for myself, the older I get, the more of a Kagyü person I become. Aging in this way is wonderful. My thanks and appreciation to the fore-fathers.

Because of the destruction of Tibetan tradition and the disruption of the Kagyü dharma by the recent Communist takeover of Tibet, out of humble duty and with the inspiration of the Practice Lineage, I have accomplished some small deeds to enable the Practice Lineage to be kin-dled further. Here in North America and the Western world, a group of sincere students has gathered around me—dedicated practitioners who are free from arrogance, students who do not lean on their Kagyü reli-gion in order to glorify their individual egos. I am immensely thankful to my students, particularly my Vajra Regent, Ösel Tendzin, and to the guidance of my own teacher.

Needless to say, I am thankful to the splendor and magnificence of His Holiness the sixteenth Gyalwa Karmapa. His manifestation and exis-tence are so fortunate and powerful for us in this dark age. The propaga-tion of the Kagyü dharma is always within his empire. The brilliant sunshine of His Holiness's kindness, as well as that of Khyentse Rinpoche and Dudjom Rinpoche, has encouraged me in continuing my teaching in the Western world. Through their kindness they have acknowledged my transformation from a pebble to gold, and they have given me fur-ther responsibility as vajrācārya and vidyādhara in the modern world, so that I can teach continuously and further the dharma of the Practice Lineages.

Nonetheless, even with such encouragement from the present lin-eage fathers and my devoted students, I have been left out in the cold as full-time garbageman, janitor, diaper service, and baby-sitter. So finally I

alone have ended up as captain of this great vessel. I alone have to liberate its millions of passengers in this dark age. I alone have to sail this
degraded saṃsāric ocean, which is very turbulent. With the blessings of
the lineage, and because of my unyielding vow, there is obviously no
choice.

The readers of this book should reflect on the value and wisdom
which exist in these songs of the lineage in the following ways. First
there are the life examples of our forefathers to inspire our devotion.
There are songs which help us understand the cause and effect of karma
and so illuminate the path to liberation. There are songs which give instruction in relative bodhicitta, so that we can realize the immediacy of
our connection to the dharma. Some are songs of mahāmudrā and transmit how we can actually join together bliss and emptiness through the
profound methods of coemergence, melting, and bliss. Other songs
show the realization of Buddha in the palm of our hand.

Needless to say, these songs should be regarded as the best of the
butter which has been churned from the ocean of milk of the Buddha's
teachings. Reading these songs or even glancing at a paragraph of this
literature always brings timely messages of how to conduct oneself, how
to discipline oneself, and how to reach accomplishment. Furthermore,
these songs are very pithy and direct. Their wisdom is both old and new.
It is old because it is a tradition of twenty-five hundred years; it is new
because it directs itself to one's very moment of mind, at this very
second.

These songs should not be regarded as ordinary poetry, as a purely
literary endeavor. They are the insight of our forefathers, conceived, described, and proclaimed. The reason we refer to them as songs is because
they are based on the melody of circumstance, and on meditative experience. They are cosmic onomatopoeia, the best expression of sanity. Traditionally they are known as vajra dohās.

These vajra dohās of the Kagyü forefathers are read annually in the
celebration of the parinirvāṇa of Milarepa by a group of students who
have accomplished the preliminary discipline of entering into Buddhism,
taken the vow of benevolence of the bodhisattva path, and also glimpsed
the power of vajrayāna, so that they are not fearful, but further inspired.
Students are also advised to read this book for instructions when their
life is filled with disruption and uncertainty and neurosis. Even reading
only one passage is better than going to a psychiatrist or taking a dose

of aspirin. This is not a myth: from my personal experience these songs do provide a kind of staircase of liberation. They actually enable us to interrupt our perpetual subconscious gossip, awaken ourselves on the path, and energize ourselves so that we can help others.

The songs of Tilopa point out the indivisibility of saṃsāra and nir-vāṇa so that whatever arises is neither rejected nor accepted and we can recognize naked and raw coemergent wisdom on the spot. The songs of Nāropa bring realization of one taste, so that pain and pleasure are no longer connected with hope and fear. The songs of Marpa Lotsāwa de-scribe how to establish a relationship with saṃsāric society, when to join in and when to transcend. These songs of the great Lotsāwa instruct us in going beyond our body and mind neurosis, so that we can realize the unity of synchronized mind and body and thus become great warriors.

The songs of Milarepa tell us how we can free ourselves of both lone-liness and claustrophobia through the extraordinary ascetic exertion of joining together nāḍī, prāṇa, and bindu. The songs of Gampopa inspire us in the supreme samādhi that quells neurotic tendencies. As it is said in the *Samādhirājasūtra*, by achieving ultimate śamatha-vipaśyanā and re-alizing the great bliss, we can follow all the stages of the path. The songs of the Karmapas enable us to transcend hope and fear. Through total devotion, the blessings of auspicious coincidence are realized, so that we become genuine dharmic people.

The songs of other lineage holders point out to us the guru in our mind as one taste, and emptiness and compassion as a way to soften ourselves into decent human beings. They arouse in us the realization that the cause and effect of karma is inevitable and bring the revulsion and renunciation that come from seeing that the saṃsāric scheme is fu-tile and impermanent. Many of these songs act to clear obstacles and generate exertion in practice. According to tradition, each lineage holder has composed hundreds of thousands of songs of this nature. Some of these songs that were recorded appear in this particular text.

The essence of all the songs can be epitomized by the four dharmas of Gampopa. These are: (1) one's mind becomes dharmic; (2) that dharma practice becomes path; (3) in following that path, confusion is removed; (4) having removed confusion, everything dawns as wisdom.

The first dharma is the ground, where our mind becomes dharmic so that we and the dharma are no longer separate entities. We develop true renunciation and have a sense of revulsion towards saṃsāra. The second dharma is the path. When our mind goes along with the dharma, the dharma becomes path, and any obstacles, whether extreme or ordinary, become a part of our journey. The third dharma is the fruition. As the journey is taking place, the process of the journey liberates us from confusion and anxiety. We are delighted by our journey and we feel it is good. The fourth dharma is the total vision. When we are able to overcome confusion and anxiety, even our anxiety is not regarded as anti-dharma or antipath. Cosmic wakefulness takes place.

So to begin with, the lineage songs are genuine and precise. Then, because of their genuineness, we find them powerful and helpful. And because we can follow them easily, insight does not come as an unusual climax; it is simply the natural and obvious clarity of wakefulness. In this way Kagyü dharma is good and genuine. We are so privileged to be in the world of the Kagyü dharma.

I dedicate this book, *The Rain of Wisdom,* and its translation to all sentient beings without exception. May they benefit by it—those who oppose the Kagyü dharma of Vajradhatu as well as those who join in. Without exception, anyone who has had the slightest contact with our Kagyü dharma, whether with positive or negative reactions, is bound to become liberated.

With my humble duty, I remain a mere speck of dust. Since the fore-fathers wish to burden me with the responsibilities of a vajrācārya and vidyādhara, I remain a humble servant of the Practice Lineage.

The Vidyādhara,
Vajrācārya the Venerable Chökyi Gyatso,
the Eleventh Trungpa
March 4, 1980

ঽ৲ৎ

The Songs of Chögyam Trungpa

The Spontaneous Song of the White Banner

L AST NIGHT I DREAMT my only father guru, Padma Tri-me, was
carrying a white banner, marked with a blue HŪM, that fluttered in
the wind. He was mounted on a unbridled white horse, riding on the
surface of the ocean. As I awoke, with bittersweet memory, I wrote this
song of recollection:

> Incomparable father, lord guru:
> When you are riding the white horse of dharmatā
> You are not daunted by the waves of relative truth;
> With genuine penetrating insight,
> You fly the banner of self-existing HŪM.
>
> When you fly in the space of bliss and emptiness
> Your bearing is that of a white garuḍa;
> You are not daunted by extreme views;
> As you soar, all appearances are the hundred dances of
>   dharmakāya.
>
> When you reside in the palace of the Practice Lineage
> Your bearing is that of Vajradhara;
> You sing the songs of mahāmudrā;
> The three worlds are filled with holders of the ultimate
>   lineage.

When you are in the highlands of fearlessness
Your bearing is that of a high glacier peak;
The snowstorm of wisdom is all-pervasive;
You court the white clouds of compassion.

When you roam in the jungle of saṃsāra
Your bearing is that of a tiger;
You bite off the head of the beast of ego-fixation;
You consume the innards of hope and fear.

Remembering your bearing, father,
I, your son, wake from a dream into bliss and emptiness.
This gaṇacakra of supreme mahāmudrā—
How delightful is this glorious perpetual enjoyment!
May this song of one taste, the music of realization,
Liberate the beings of the three worlds.

The Spontaneous Song of Entering into the Blessings and Profound Samaya of the Only Father Guru

Śrī Heruka, the unchanging vajra mind,
The primordial buddha, all-pervading, the protector of all,
Padma Tri-me, you are the lord, the embodiment of all the
    victorious ones.
You are always reflected in the clear mirror of my mind.

In the space of innate ground mahāmudrā,
The dance of the self-luminous vajra queen takes place,
And passion and aggression, the movements of the mind,
    become the wheel of wisdom;
What joy it is to see the great ultimate maṇḍala!

The confidence of the unflinching youthful warrior
    flourishes,
Cutting the aortas of the degraded three lords of
    materialism

And dancing the sword dance of penetrating insight;
This is the blessing of my only father guru.

Inviting the rays of the waxing moon, Vajra Avalokiteśvara,
The tide of the ocean of compassion swells,
Your only son, Chökyi Gyatso, blossoms as a white lotus;
This is due to the limitless buddha activity of my guru.

In the vast space of mahāśunyatā, devoid of all expression,
The wings of simplicity and luminosity spread
As the snake-knot of conceptual mind uncoils in space;
Only father guru, I can never repay your kindness.

Alone, following the example of the youthful son of the
    victorious ones,
Riding the chariot of the limitless six pāramitās,
Inviting infinite sentient beings as passengers,
Raising the banner of the magnificent bodhisattvas,
I continue as your heir, my only father guru.

Like a mountain, without the complexities of movement,
I meditate in the nature of the seven vajras,
Subjugating Rudra with the hundred rays of deva, mantra,
    and mudrā,
Beating the victory drum of the great secret vajrayāna,
I fulfill the wishes of my only father, the authentic guru.

In the sky of dharmadhātu, which exhausts the conventions
    of the nine yānas,
Gathering rainclouds thick with the blessings of the ultimate
    lineage,
Roaring the thunder of relentless crazy wisdom,
Bringing down the rain that cools the hot anguish of the
    dark age,
As I transform existence into a heavenly wheel of dharma,
Please, my only father, authentic guru, come as my guest.

The Dohā of Sadness

The rain of the jñāna-amṛta of the ultimate lineage,
Always uncorrupted, you skillfully bestow upon my heart.
The only father guru, remembering you constantly,
I, Chögyam, your little son, remain in sadness.

In devotion firm as an unchanging mountain,
Truly seeing you alone as the Buddha,
Free from conventions of young or old,
In foreign lands, in sadness, with reverence,
I survive by the amṛta of your blessings.

In the spotless mirror of mind,
Enjoying the dance of self-liberated yogic discipline,
Listening to the sad dohā,
I, Chögyam, the little child, am dying of sadness.

Tormented by the hot rays of the fire of passion,
Having completely burned up the fuel of ālaya,
I have exhausted grasping for sophistries of liberation and
    confusion.
Isn't this the kindness of the only father guru.

By the sharp blade of the weapon of aggression,
Thoroughly piercing the fixation of mind,
I have discovered the nature of penetrating insight;
My only father, you are very kind.

In the dark narrow gorge of delusion,
Having aroused a hundred thousand turbulent waves of
    dharmatā,
Free from accepting and rejecting, thoughts of I and other,
Isn't this the kindness of the only father guru.

You, my only father guru, have gone far away.
My vajra brothers and sisters have wandered to the ends of
    the earth.

Only I, Chögyam, the little child, am left.
Still, for the teachings of the profound and brilliant Practice
    Lineage,
I am willing to surrender my life in sadness.

The Dohā of Confidence
Sad Song of the Four Remembrances

As I look constantly to the Great Eastern Sun,
Remembering the only father guru,
Overwhelming devotion blazes like a bonfire—
I, Chökyi Gyatso, remain alone.

Having been abandoned by my heart friends,
Though my feverish mind feels great longing,
It is joyful that I am sustained by this great confidence
Of the only father guru and the Great Eastern Sun.

Having seen the beauty of a mist covering the mountain,
The pines moving gently in the wind,
The firm power of rock-hard earth,
I am constantly reminded of the splendor and beauty
Of the only father guru and the Great Eastern Sun.

Wild flowers extend everywhere
On mountain meadows filled with the sweet smell of
    fragrant herbs.
Seeing the gentle deer frolicking from place to place,
I constantly remember the compassion and gentleness
Of the only father guru and the Great Eastern Sun.

Fighting enemies in the chasm of love and hate,
Having sharpened the weapon's point of joy and sorrow,
    hope and fear,
Seeing again and again these cowardly hordes,
I take refuge in the sole confidence
Of the only father guru and the Great Eastern Sun.

Fatherless, always dwelling in foreign lands,
Motherless, not hearing the speech of my own country,
Friendless, tears not quenching my thirst,
Remembering the warriors of the father and mother
    lineages,
I live alone in the sole blessing
Of the only father guru and the Great Eastern Sun.

༄༅། །ཡང་དྲི། གསལ་སྟེ་ཀྱི་ཡལ་ཝ་ཐག་ཝ་འདུ། རི་ཡོ་ཀོ། །ཡི་ཡ་ཐི།
རུག་ཝ་ཡལ་ཝ་འགོ་ཡ་ཝ་ཡིན།། ཤ་ར་ཝ་འདྲི་ཀ་ཡོ།། ཡི་ཀ་སྒྲུ་ཁེ་ཡ་ཏི།
ཟ་ག་ཀ་ལ་ཡི་འབི་ཇེ་ཏུ་ཝ་ཁ་ཝ་ཏི་ཡི།། ཆུ་ཀྱི་ཡ་ཁེ་ར་ཆི་ཡ་ཡི་ཡ་འཁུ།
།། ཆུ་ཀྱི་ འཇི་ར་ར་ཝ་འགེ་ཝ་ཀ་འཆེ་ཝི་ཡི།། ཁེ་ཡུ་ར་ཡེ་ཝ་ཡི་ཀ་ཡ།।
ཟ་ཝ་ཡུ།། ཆུ་ར་ར་ཀ་འཇི་ཇུ་ཀྱི་ཁ་ཡ་ཝ་ཆི་ཐི་ཡ་ཇུ་ཡ།། ཟ་ག་ཝ་ལ་འདི།
ཟེ་ཀི་ཆེ་ཝ་ཅུ་ཇ་ལ་ཆི་ཝ་ཡ།། །ཀོ་ཀ་ཆེ་ཝ་ལ་ཆུ་ལ་ཡ་ཐུ་ཝ་ཐ་ཡུ།།
ལི་རེ་ཟི་ཀྲུ་ཝ་ཇུ་ཡི་ཝ་ཆུ་ཝ་ཀ་ཡེ།། །ཆུ་ཀ་ཆོ་ལ་ར་ཅི་ག་ཐེ།
།ལ་ཡ་ཝ་ལ་ཡ།། ཤ་སྒྲུ་ཏེ་ཀ་ནེ་ཀི་ན་ཡུ་ལ་ཝ་ཏུ་ཀ་གྱུ་ར་འཆེ་ན། ཆེ་ཀུ་ཝ་ལ།
ག་ལེ་ཡི་ཆུ་ན་ཇུ་འཆེ་ཀྱི་ཡོ་ཀི་ཝི་ཡི།། །ཅི་ག་ཝ་ལ་ཝ་ལ་འཆེ་ཇུ་ན་ཇུ་འཆེ་ར་འདེ་
ར་ཝ།། ག་ཀ་ཝ་ལ་ཏུ་ཝ་ཀི་འཆེ་ན་ཇུ་འཆེ་ཡི་ར།། ཆེ་ཡི་ཀ་ཡེ་ཆི་ར་འཆེ་ཇུ་ར།
ཟུ་ཆི་ཝ་ཇུ་ར་འཆེ་ན། ཀ་ཡ་ལ་ཆོ་ར་ལ་ཡུ་ན་ཀི་ར་ན་ཟ་ཝ་ལ་ཝ་ཆི་ཝ་ཡ།། ཟ་ན་ཀ་ཡེ་འཆེ་ཝ
ཆེ་ཝ་ཆི་ཆི་ན་ར་ཀུ་ཡ་ན་ཀ།། །ཆུ་ཇུ་འཆུ་ཝ་ཡ་འཇི་ཆུ་ཝ་ལ་ཆ་ཏེ་ཡི་འཆུ་ར།
འཇི་ར།། ལ་ཆོ་ཝ་ལ་ཕུ་ཝ་ལ་ཆུ་ཝ་ཡ།། འཆུ་ན་ཝ་ཆ་ར་ན་འདི།། ཀུ་ཇ་ཕུ་ཡ།།
།ག་ཡ་ཝ་ལི་ཆི་ཝ་ལ་ཡ་འཆི།། ཁ་ལ་ཆོ་ཟི་ར་ཀ་ལུ་ལ་ཆི་ཆི་འཇི་ཆུ་ར།། ཡེ་ཡ།
ཀུ་ཝ་ཆ་ན་ཇུ་འཆེ་ནི་ཡོ་ཁ་ལ་ཝ་ཆུ་ར་འཆེ་ན   ཆི་ཝ་ཆེ་ར་ཝ་ལ་འཇི་ཆི་ཆི་ཝ་ལ་ཡུ།།
ཝ་ག་ལ་འཆུ་ར་ནེ་ཏེ་ཀི་ན་ལ་ཡ་ལུ་ཇུ་ཡ་ལ་ཆི་ཝ་ཆི་ཆུ་ལ་ཆི་ཝ་ར་ཟ་ཇུ་ར་ཀི་ཆི་ཝ་ཡ།།
ཆེ་ཡི་ལ་ལ་ཆུ་ལ་ཝོ།།

ཟར་ཀ

Colophon

Ah ho! Precious Kagyü, forefather of a hundred siddhas,
You are the amṛta which dispels the mind's suffering.
You alone are the guide who leads one on the path of
 liberation.
What joy that your profound brilliant wisdom has entered
 my heart!

This little one was born as your great-grandson
And is sustained by your blessings alone.
Grant your blessings so that I may attain the siddhi of being
 inseparable from you
And be able to liberate all beings as you do.

From the ocean of your spontaneous profound secret vajra
 songs,
Taking a small drop of its true meaning,
I have translated, edited, and published this in the English
 language.
May the stupid meditators be awakened from the sleep of
 ignorance;
May the attacks of the logicians with their sophistries be
 vanquished.

In the space of the ground mahāmudrā of luminous
 emptiness,
Traveling on the path mahāmudrā of luminous insight,

In the fruition mahāmudrā of luminous bliss—
May all the beings of the three realms be liberated.

May the plague, famine, and war of the dark age be pacified.
May the dharma sun of the three yānas eternally rise.
May the golden victory banner of the Practice Lineage be
   raised in a hundred directions.
May the authentic gurus live a hundred kalpas.
May all enjoy the perfect holy dharma.
May they attain the dharmakāya of the lord guru
   Vajradhara,
The mahāmudrā of devotion.

*This was written at the dharma assembly of Vajradhatu by Chökyi Gyatso
[Chögyam Trungpa], who throughout many lives has been a servant of the precious Kagyü.* MAṄGALAM.

SELECTED
WRITINGS

The Sadhana of Mahamudra

Which Quells the Mighty Warring of the
Three Lords of Materialism and Brings
Realization of the Ocean of Siddhas
of the Practice Lineage

SELECTIONS FROM A
TANTRIC LITURGY

T HIS IS THE DARKEST HOUR of the dark ages. Disease, famine, and warfare are raging like the fierce north wind. The Buddha's teaching has waned in strength. The various schools of the sangha are fighting among themselves with sectarian bitterness; and although the Buddha's teaching was perfectly expounded and there have been many reliable teachings since then from other great gurus, yet they pursue intellectual speculations. The sacred mantra has strayed into Bön, and the yogis of tantra are losing the insight of meditation. They spend their whole time going through villages and performing little ceremonies for material gain.

On the whole, no one acts according to the highest code of discipline, meditation, and wisdom. The jewel-like teaching of insight is fading day by day. The Buddha's teaching is used merely for political purposes and to draw people together socially. As a result, the blessings of spiritual energy are being lost. Even those with great devotion are beginning to lose heart. If the buddhas of the three times and the great teachers were to comment, they would surely express their disappointment. So to enable individuals to ask for their help and to renew spiritual strength, I have written this sadhana of the embodiment of all the siddhas.

NAMO
Earth, water, fire, and all the elements,
The animate and the inanimate, the trees and greenery and
    so on,
All partake of the nature of self-existing equanimity,
Which is quite simply what the Great Wrathful One is.
In the spontaneous wisdom of the trikaya
I take refuge with body, speech, and mind.
In order to free those who suffer at the hands of the three
    lords of materialism
And are afraid of external phenomena, which are their own
    projections,
I take this vow in meditation.

.   .   .   .

HUM HUM HUM
In the boundless space of suchness,
In the play of the great light,
All the miracles of sight, sound, and mind
Are the five wisdoms and the five buddhas.
This is the mandala which is never arranged but is always
    complete.
It is the great bliss, primeval and all-pervading. HUM
It is boundless equanimity, which has never changed.
It is unified into a single circle beyond confusion.
In its basic character there is no longer any trace
Of ignorance or of understanding.
Nothing whatever, but everything arises from it.
Yet it reveals the spontaneous play of the mandala.

HUM HUM HUM
My whole being is Dorje Trolö
And my form is Karma Pakshi,
My speech is Mikyö Dorje
And my mind is Rangjung Dorje.
With that unwavering conviction
Fearlessly enjoy the mahamudra
And attain the experience of maha ati.

HUM HUM HUM
. . . .

O Karmapa, lord and knower of the three times,
O Padmakara, father and protector of all beings,
You transcend all coming and going.
Understanding this, I call upon you—
Give thought to your only son.
I am a credulous and helpless animal
Who has been fooled by the mirage of duality.
I have been fool enough to think that I possess my own
    projections,
So now you, my father, are my only refuge;
You alone can grasp the buddha state.
The glorious copper-colored mountain is within my heart.
Is not this pure and all-pervading naked mind your dwelling
    place?
Although I live in the slime and muck of the dark age,
I still aspire to see it.
Although I stumble in the thick, black fog of materialism,
I still aspire to see it.

The joy of spontaneous awareness, which is with me all the
    time,
Is not this your smiling face, O Karma Padmakara?
Although I live in the slime and muck of the dark age,
I still aspire to see it.
Although I stumble in the thick, black fog of materialism,
I still aspire to see it.
At glorious Taktsang, in the cave
Which can accommodate everything,
Samsara and nirvana both,
The heretics and bandits of hope and fear
Are subdued and all experiences
Are transformed into crazy wisdom.
Is not this your doing, O Dorje Trolö?
Although I live in the slime and muck of the dark age,
I still aspire to see your face.
Although I stumble in the thick, black fog of materialism,
I still aspire to see your face.

The corpse, bloated with the eight worldly concerns,
Is cut into pieces by the knife of detachment
And served up as the feast of the great bliss.
Is not this your doing, O Karma Pakshi?
Although I live in the slime and muck of the dark age,
I still aspire to see your face.
Although I stumble in the thick, black fog of materialism,
I still aspire to see your face.

In the boundless space of nonmeditation
He who performs the great dance of mahamudra
Puts a stop to thoughts
So that all acts become the acts of the guru.
Is not this your doing, O Tüsum Khyenpa?
Although I live in the slime and muck of the dark age,
I still aspire to see your face.
Although I stumble in the thick, black fog of materialism,
I still aspire to see your face.

When the current of thoughts is self-liberated
And the essence of dharma is known,
Everything is understood
And apparent phenomena
Are all the books one needs.
Is not this your doing, omniscient Mikyö Dorje?
Although I live in the slime and muck of the dark age,
I still aspire to see your face.
Although I stumble in the thick, black fog of materialism,
I still aspire to see your face.

The kingdom of no-dharma, free from concepts,
Is discovered within the heart.
Here there is no hierarchy of different stages
And the mind returns to its naked state.
Is not this your doing, O Rangjung Dorje?
Although I live in the slime and muck of the dark age,
I still aspire to see your face.

Although I stumble in the thick, black fog of materialism,
I still aspire to see your face.

The father guru, the embodiment of all the siddhas,
Is all-seeing and all-pervading.
Wherever you look, his transparent body is there,
And the power of his blessing can never be diminished.
Although I live in the slime and muck of the dark age,
I still aspire to see his face.
Although I stumble in the thick, black fog of materialism,
I still aspire to see his face.
Living, as I do, in the dark age,
I am calling upon you, because I am trapped
In this prison, without refuge or protector.
The age of the three poisons has dawned
And the three lords of materialism have seized power.
This is the time of hell on earth;
Sadness is always with us
And unceasing depression fills our minds.

The search for an external protector
Has met with no success.
The idea of a deity as an external being
Has deceived us, led us astray.
Counting on friends has brought nothing
But sorrow and insecurity.
So now I have no other refuge
But you, Karma Pakshi, the lotus-born.

Think of us poor, miserable wretches.
With deep devotion and intense longing
I supplicate you.
The time has come for you to arouse yourself and do
    something.
The tradition of meditation is waning
And intellectual arguments predominate.
We are drunk with spiritual pride
And seduced by passion.

The dharma is used for personal gain
And the river of materialism has burst its banks.
The materialistic outlook dominates everywhere
And the mind is intoxicated with worldly concerns.
Under such circumstances, how can you abandon us?
The time has come when your son needs you.
No material offering will please you
So the only offering I can make
Is to follow your example.

.   .   .   .

When the wild and wrathful father approaches
The external world is seen to be transparent and unreal.
The reasoning mind no longer clings and grasps.
It is wonderful to arrive in your domain
In the pure land of the blazing mountain
Where every experience is full of joy.
Hey ho, the happy yogi!

Every movement of the mind
Becomes bliss and emptiness;
All polarity disappears
When the mind emerges into nakedness
This is the mandala in which
The six senses are self-liberated.
On seeing your face I am overjoyed.
Now pain and pleasure alike have become
Ornaments which it is pleasant to wear.

The experience of joy becomes devotion
And I am drunk with all-pervading blessings.
This is a sign of the merging of mind and guru.
The whole of existence is freed and becomes the guru.
When such blessings descend, your son's depression
Is entirely liberated into blissfulness.
Thank you, great Karmapa! Thank you, father Padmakara!
There is no separation between teacher and disciple;
Father and son are one in the realm of thought.

Grant your blessings so that my mind may be one with the
dharma.
Grant your blessings so that dharma may progress along the
path.
Grant your blessings so that the path may clarify confusion.
Grant your blessings so that confusion may dawn as
wisdom.

Joining Energy and Space

COMMENTS ON *THE SADHANA OF MAHAMUDRA*

T HIS IS A VERY CONFUSED WORLD, a corrupt world at many levels. I'm not particularly talking about the Orient versus the Occi-
dent but about the world in general. Materialism and the technological
outlook no longer come from the West alone; they are universal. The
Japanese make the best cameras. Indians make atomic bombs. So we can
talk in terms of materialism and spirituality in the world at large.

We need to look into how we can overcome spiritual materialism,
not just brushing it off as an undesirable but inevitable consequence of
modern life. How can we actually work with the tendencies toward spiritual and psychological materialism in the world today, so that we can
transmute them into living, workable, enlightened basic sanity?

I wrote *The Sadhana of Mahamudra*, a tantric liturgy, in Bhutan in 1968
in Tibetan, and then it was translated into English. My situation at that
time was unusual in that I was in a position to see both the English and
the Bhutanese cultures together, which was seeing the West and the East
together as well. I have been in the United Kingdom for about five years,
and I had experienced that world fully. When I returned to Asia, Bhutan
in this case, I rediscovered characteristics that were quite familiar to me
from my earlier life in Tibet. At the same time, the contrast between
East and West was very powerful.

I asked the Queen of Bhutan, who was my hostess, whether I could
do a short retreat at the Taktsang Retreat Center, at the site of the cave
where the great Indian teacher Padmasambhava—who brought Buddhism to Tibet—meditated and manifested in his crazy-wisdom form,
which is called Dorje Trolö. Being at Taktsang was not particularly im-
pressive at the beginning. In fact, the first few days were rather disap-

pointing. "What is this place?" I wondered. "Maybe this is the wrong place. Maybe there is another Taktsang somewhere else, the *real* Taktsang."

As I spent more time there, however, I realized that the place had a very powerful nature. Once you began to click into the atmosphere there, it had a feeling of profound empty-heart. The influence of the Kagyü tradition, the practice lineage, was very strong there. At the same time, there was a feeling at Taktsang of austerity and pride and the wildness from the Nyingma tradition. When I started to feel that, the sadhana came through without any problems. I felt the presence of Dorje Trolö from the Nyingma tradition combined with Karma Pakshi from the Kagyü lineage. At first, I told myself, "You must be joking. Nothing is happening." But still, there was immense energy and power.

The first line of the sadhana came into my head about five days before I wrote the sadhana itself. It kept coming back into my mind with a ringing sound: "Earth, water, fire, and all the elements . . ." Finally I decided to write that passage down, and once I started writing, it took me about five hours to compose the whole thing.

The basic vision of the sadhana is based on two main principles: space and energy. Space here refers to maha ati, or dzogchen, the highest level of Buddhist tantra in the Nyingma tradition. The energy principle, or mahamudra, is also a high level of experience in the Kagyü tradition. *The Sadhana of Mahamudra* strives to bring space and energy together, and through that, to bring about understanding and realization in the world. Even the wording of this sadhana, how each sentence is structured, is based on trying to bring together the mahamudra language with the ati language in a harmonious way.

Underlying both mahamudra and maha ati is the practice of surrendering, renunciation, and devotion. You have to surrender; you actually have to develop devotion. Without that, you can't experience the real teachings. However, in the Buddhist tradition, devotion is not admiring somebody because he or she has great talent and therefore would be a good person to put on your list of heroes. Ordinarily, we may admire people purely because they seem to be better at something than we are. We think we should worship all the great football players or great presidents or great spiritual teachers. That approach, in this case, is starting out on the wrong footing.

Real devotion or dedication comes from personal experience and connection. The closest analogy to devotion that I can think of would be the way you feel about your lover, who may not be a great musician or a great football player or a great singer. He may not even be all that great at keeping his domestic life together. But there is something about the person, even though he doesn't fit any of the usual categories of heroes. He is just a good person, a lovable person who has some powerful qualities in himself.

Love seems to be the closest analogy. At the same time, with real devotion, there is something more to it than that. As we said, the object of devotion, the guru, is not so much an object of admiration, not a superman. You don't expect everything to be perfect. You simply realize that a love affair is taking place, not at the level of hero worship or even at the wife or husband level. Something else is taking place, at ground level, a very fundamental level that involves relating with your mind and your whole being. That something else is difficult to describe, yet that something else has immense clarity and power.

Another aspect of the sadhana is crazy wisdom, which is an unusual term. How can craziness and wisdom exist together? The expression "crazy wisdom" is not correct, in fact. It is purely a linguistic convention. Wisdom comes first, and craziness comes afterward, so "wisdom crazy" would be more accurate. Wisdom is an all-pervasive, all-encompassing vision or perspective. It is powerful, clear, and precise. You have no bias at all, so you are able to see things as they are, without any question. Out of that, the craziness develops, which is not paying attention to all the little wars, the little resistances, that might be created by the world of reference points, the world of duality. That is craziness. "Wisdom crazy" involves a sense of tremendous control, vision, and relaxation occurring simultaneously in your mind.

The lineage of *The Sadhana of Mahamudra* is the two traditions of immense crazy wisdom and immense dedication and devotion put together. The Kagyü, or mahamudra tradition, is the devotion lineage. The Nyingma, or ati tradition, is the lineage of crazy wisdom. The sadhana brings these two traditions together as a prototype of how emotion and wisdom, energy and space, can work together.

The Tibetan master Jamgön Kongtrül the Great first brought these two traditions together about two hundred years ago. He developed a deep understanding of both the ati and the mahamudra principles, and he became a lineage holder in both traditions. He developed what is called the Ri-me school, which literally means "unbiased."

Joining mahamudra and maha ati is like making tea. You boil water, and you add a pinch of tea leaves. The two together make a good cup of tea. It makes a beautiful blend, an ideal situation. Quite possibly it's the best thing that has happened to Tibetan Buddhism. It's a magnificent display of total sanity, of basic enlightenment. It displays the ruggedness and openness, the expansiveness and craziness of both traditions together. My personal teacher, Jamgön Kongtrül of Sechen, was the embodiment of both traditions, and he handed down the teachings to me.

The language used in the sadhana reflects both the highest level of devotion and the highest level of wisdom combined. Karma Pakshi, who is the main figure in the sadhana, was one of the Karmapas, the head of the Kagyü lineage. He was also a crazy-wisdom teacher within his lineage. In *The Sadhana of Mahamudra* he is regarded as the same as Padmasambhava, who was the founder of the Nyingma lineage, the oldest Buddhist lineage in Tibet. It was Padmasambhava, also called Padmakara, who introduced the Buddhist teachings to Tibet, and he was also a tantric master. My purpose in writing the sadhana was to build a bridge between their two contemplative traditions.

The sadhana is composed of various sections. At the beginning is taking refuge, committing yourself to the Buddhist teachings and taking the bodhisattva vow to help others. The first section also creates an atmosphere of self-realization or basic potentiality, which is an ongoing theme in the sadhana. In tantric language, it is called "vajra pride." Your basic existence, your basic makeup, is part of enlightened being. You are already enlightened, so you need only recognize and understand that. The next part of the sadhana is the creation of the mandala, or the world, of Karma Pakshi and Padmasambhava, who are embodied together. Several of the other great teachers in the Kagyü lineage are also included in this visualization.

Next is the supplication section, which describes our own condition, which is "wretched" and "miserable." We are surrounded by a "thick, black fog of materialism," and we are bogged down in the "slime and muck of the dark age." It's like the description of an urban slum. There is so much pollution, dirtiness, and greasiness, not only in cities but throughout the country. "The slime and muck of the dark age" also has a metaphysical meaning. It has the connotation of an overwhelming environment that we are unable to control. We sense the world's hostility and aggression, as well as its passion. Everything is beginning to eat us up. "The thick, black fog of materialism" refers to the basic or fundamental problems with that environment.

The next passage is about our disillusionment with that world of spiritual materialism. It reads, "The search for an external protector has met with no success. The idea of a deity as an external being has deceived us, led us astray." There are all kinds of spiritual materialism, but theism seems to be the heart of spiritual materialism. In the sadhana, we are trying to reintroduce the style of the early Buddhists, the purity of the Buddhism which first came to Tibet. We are trying to turn back history, to purify ourselves, to reform Buddhism.

Theistic beliefs have been seeping into the Buddhist mentality, which should be nontheistic, and that has been a source of corruption and other problems. There has been so much worship and admiration of deities that people can't experience the awakened state of mind; they can't experience their own sanity properly. In fact, I wrote *The Sadhana of Mahamudra* because such problems exist both within and outside of the Buddhist tradition. Indeed, the spiritual scene all over the world is going through that kind of corruption. The whole world is into fabricating its spiritual mommies and daddies. So the purpose of the supplication is to awaken people from such "trips." At that point, inner experience can arise.

The last theme is the idea of merging one's mind with the guru's mind. It's not that the guru is a deity that you bring into your heart, with whom you become one. It's not like artificial insemination. It is very personal and spontaneous. You are what you are, and you realize that your own inspiration exists in the teacher's intelligence and clarity. With that encouragement, you begin to wake up. You begin to associate yourself completely with the dharma; you identify completely with the dharma; you become one with the dharma. As it says in the sadhana, "Grant your blessings so that my mind may be one with the dharma." You no longer depend on any external agent to save you from your misery; you can do it yourself. That is just basic Buddhism. It could be called the tantric approach, but it's just basic Buddhism.

HUM

AN APPROACH TO MANTRA

Homage to the guru, yidams, and dakinis!

> When I hear the profound music of HUM
> It inspires the dance of direct vision of insight.
> At the same time my guru presents the weapon
>   which cuts the life of ego,
> Just like the performance of a miracle.
> I pay homage to the Incomparable One!

One must understand the basic usage of mantra in the teachings of Buddha. Whether it is in the form of mantra, dharani, or a single syllable, it is not at all a magical spell used in order to gain psychic powers for selfish purposes, such as accumulation of wealth, power over others, and destruction of enemies. According to the Buddhist tantra, all mantras and other practices, such as visualizations, hatha yoga, or any other yogic practices, must be based on the fundamental teaching of Buddha, which is the understanding of the four marks of existence: impermanence (anitya), suffering (duhkha), void (shunyata), and egolessness (anatman.)

In this connection, it should be pointed out that in contrast to Hindu tantra, Buddhist tantra is based on shunyata and anata. The concept of shunyata is quite easy to relate to the whole content of tantra, as in mahamudra experience, and that of anata is most essential. Some Western scholars mistakenly identify the preparation of mandalas and the countless divinities with the Hindu tradition, as if it were an umbrella under

317

which all other Indian religions might be found. Although some Vedantic mystics might claim their experiences to be the same as mahamudra, there is an essential difference, for the herukas and all the other divinities in Buddhism are not external. In other words, they are aspects of the awakened state of mind, such as Avalokiteshvara representing the compassionate aspect of buddha nature.

There are various mantras connected with these bodhisattvas and herukas which help to achieve, for example, the essence of compassion, wisdom, or energy. In this essay we are discussing the single syllable HUM. Hum is the sound connected with energy, and is most profound and penetrating. This mantra was used by Guru Padmasambhava in his wrathful aspect in order to subdue the force of the negative environment created by minds poisoned with passion, aggression, and ignorance. HUM is often the ending of certain mantras used to arouse the life energy.

Before chanting the sacred music of HUM, it is necessary to consider the relationship of teacher and pupil. There must be oral transmission. The pupil should not choose a teacher at random, for unless the teacher belongs to a spiritual lineage, he may be able to give a mantra but he will not be able to transmit its power. With a strong karmic bond between teacher and pupil, the pupil should be inspired with an unwavering conviction of trust in the teacher's spiritual quality. Whatever difficulties the pupil might continually have to undergo and whatever sacrifices he might have to make, his devotion must remain constant until he is able to surrender his ego. If he fails to do this, he will not be able to experience the sacred music of HUM, he will not be able to develop understanding of its profound meaning, and he will not be able to develop the transcendental siddhi.

When a beginner chants the sacred music of HUM, he might find some temporary benefits; for example, his mind might become quiet and irritating thoughts might be eased. This is because HUM is composed of HA, ॅ, U, ॖ, and M ॗ. Ha expels the impure air from the lungs, U releases the most irritating thoughts through the mouth, and M clears the remaining thoughts through the nose.

As mentioned in yogic texts, prana (breath) is like a horse, the nadis (channels) are like roads, and the mind is the rider. In this way, using prana, tension is released and any psychological disturbance may be relieved, but only as a temporary measure.

For advanced meditators, the syllable HUM is a means of developing the five wisdoms. H 𑀲 is the mirrorlike wisdom, clear and continuous. A 𑀲 is the wisdom of equanimity, panoramic awareness. U 𑀲 is the wisdom of discriminating awareness, awareness of details. M 𑀲 is all-accomplishing wisdom, effortless accomplishment of all actions. A 𑀲 is the wisdom of all-encompassing space (dharmadhatu), the ground from which all things originate and to which they return.

The meditator will not find these wisdoms in an external source but, rather like the spark which bursts into flame when fanned by the wind, he discovers them within himself.

HUM is the seed syllable of all herukas in the four orders of tantra (kriya, upa, yoga, and anuttara which includes ati). The herukas originated with the subjugation and transformation of the Rudra of ego. The absence of ego is shunyata. In the vajrayana, shunyata or voidness is expressed in terms of fullness, as in the line of the *Heart Sutra* which says "form is emptiness, and the very emptiness is form." Therefore this form has tremendous energy which is simply what the five wisdoms are.

HUM is referred to in many texts as the sonorous sound of silence. HUM represents that state of meditation when awareness breaks out of the limits of ego. It was by that force of HUM that the fortress of Rudra was reduced to dust. HUM may be regarded as the fearless utterance of a warrior shooting his arrow in the battlefield. HUM is sometimes referred to as the mantra of the Vajrakilaya Mandala of the high tantra school. First, it is the dagger of beyond-thought, which stabs with deadly accuracy into the heart of dualistic thoughts. Second, it is the dagger of luminous transcendental insight, which pierces the heart of confused darkness. Third, it is the dagger of the state of nonmeditation, which pierces the heart of thought-formed meditation, so that the meditator is delivered from subject matter. Fourth, it is the dagger of complete devotion to the all-pervading guru, which stabs to the heart of hopes and fears so that the teacher and pupil become inseparable. These four penetrations of HUM are described in the text of the anuyogatantra.

Guru Padmasambhava said that when you sing the crescendo music of HUM and let go of all thoughts, the ultimate meditation experiences are the echo of this music. Also, HUM is referred to as the concentration of all blessings and energy. Etymologically speaking, the Sanskrit word *HUM* means "gathering together." HUM is not a magic spell to increase the power of ego, but it is concentrated power devoid of ego. HUM combined with complete devotion is like an arrow piercing the heart—it takes the form of the memory of the guru. Also the abrupt experience of cutting through all thoughts is the action of HUM. Therefore HUM is the energy of universal force which transcends the limitations of ego, or rather, pierces through the wall of ego.

I hope that the people who practice *The Sadhana of the Embodiment of All the Siddhas* [*The Sadhana of Mahamudra*] will study this essay very closely. May we all unite in the crescendo of HUM and liberate all sentient beings into the oneness of HUM.

Explanation of the Vajra Guru Mantra

IN THE VAJRAYANA TRADITION, which deals with energy, one speaks of three principles: body, speech, and mind. Body corresponds to matter, and mind to thoughts and space. Speech is that which links them together, which is energy. Meditating on the sound of mantras is one of the traditionally known ways of relating to this energy. The mantra creates an environment, a living environment of energy. This particular mantra, OM AH HUM VAJRA-GURU-PADMA-SIDDHI HUM, can be used in this way.

Generally, when a yogi recites a mantra, he or she does not think out intellectually the meanings of the Sanskrit words. In Tibet, and also in China and Japan, whenever a mantra has been introduced as a part of tantric teachings, it has been left in the original Sanskrit in order not to invite conceptualized translations of meaning. You just feel the sounds.

It is the same with colors. When you see a color, that color means something spiritually. When you hold a rock, that also means something spiritually as well as just physically. This kind of direct link, this direct feeling with nature, also takes place with sounds.

For instance, take the word OM. OM consists of three sounds. The first is AH, the sound of space, the sound of basic background. When you pronounce AH, it comes straight from the heart, a sort of hollowness and openness. The next sound is OH, which is the basic space being seen in terms of manifestation of energy from the AH. The energy begins to be formulated into something. Then M is the final manifestation into form, like giving birth. So OM represents open space and energy, communication out of open space and energy, and then the solid, vivid, colorful, phenomenal world, all of which is creation—OM.

In this Vajra Guru mantra, we have at the beginning OM AH HUM. OM is the creation of form. AH is the same as at the origin of the OM—speech, sound. AH is supposed to contain all speech. Also emotive utterances of any kind—laughter "HA HA" or crying "HOO HOO"—all are contained in the word AH. Babies first say "AH." The primal first vowel AH represents emotions and communication. HUM is piercing, penetrating. It represents the penetrating quality of mind, thought, intelligence.

Vajra means "indestructible." It is historically a synonym for diamond, a celestial diamond, the scepter of certain mythological gods. Next is Guru, Vajra Guru—indestructible guru or teacher. There are three aspects of the guru: the guru as superior, the teacher; the guru as spiritual friend; and the guru as environment. As the superior teacher, he is the one to whom you open yourself completely, surrender yourself, expose the negative and raw and rugged quality of the ego without hesitation, without being ashamed. It is surrendering in order to receive knowledge, becoming an empty vessel so that there is something to fill, something into which to pour the spiritual nectar. And the guru has the aspect of friend, because you must be able not only to surrender but to communicate. This is communication as equals, friends. You can communicate with the guru as a friend, meeting on the ground of friendliness, which is the open space of meditation. This is the meeting of two minds. Your mind is open to the open space, and the guru's mind is open to the open space. That is the way of making your mind one with that of the guru.

The guru as environment is related to the idea of all-pervading energy. The happenings of life are manifestations of energy. This energy in the situations of life is a very powerful teacher. If you go too far, in the sense of not being receptive enough to learn from the experience of life, if you ignore this experience and go too far with the extreme emotional excitement of ego, then sooner or later you are going to be pulled back. This might take the form of accident, illness, or disaster—any sort of chaos. Whereas if you are able to see the first signal that you have lost touch with the life situation as teacher, then you will be able to tune yourself back into it. That is guru as environment.

Padma means "lotus" in Sanskrit. It symbolizes compassion. The unshakable guru also grants the energy of compassion. Compassion grows within passion—desire, attachment. But that desire and attachment has now lost its clinging, the possessiveness of ego. Compassion creates more open space of communication. The lotus is grown in mud, but it itself is clean and pure, unaffected by the mud of possessiveness. Passion could be said to be imposing our desire on someone else, some other things, or on ourselves. Compassion is the opposite of that. Instead of imposing, you create space, you welcome the possibilities of love, the possibilities of exchange in the warmth of communication. In that way, you are able to help other people to help themselves. Compassion is inspiring other people as well as helping them. If you inspire them, then they will be helped, either physically or psychologically.

Siddhi is a Sanskrit word which means "miraculous power" or "energy." It is possible to perceive the play of energy as miraculous. When we speak of miracles, it does not mean such a thing as fire turning into water or the world turning upside down. Rather, a miracle is something happening unexpectedly, some situation developing unexpectedly. There will always be a scientific explanation. A miracle need not be illogical. It could be highly logical, highly scientific. But nonetheless it takes the form of an apparent accident. For example, our meeting here together could be called a miracle. Why did I alone have to come from Tibet, and why did you all have to be here? So a siddhi is a miracle in the sense of the sudden coming together of situations, assuming the guise of "accident."

HUM as the last syllable in the mantra is similar to the HUM at the beginning, but it has the slightly different sense in this case of gathering energy. It is like the piercing through of an arrow, gathering energy in one-pointedness, penetrating. This is the penetrating quality of peace, related to its indestructible quality, and the penetrating quality of nowness: that which cuts right through the layers of ignorance and duality, passion, and desire. It cuts right through, penetrates right through—HUM—the sound of gathering together or penetration.

So taking the mantra as a whole, it is something like: "Indestructible guru, vajra guru, vajra teacher, vajra friend, please grant the miracle of compassion at this very moment, at this very point," which is HUM. This mantra is based on what is called the "mantra of the guru," which is one of compassion and devotion, devotion in the sense of openness, as already mentioned in connection with the guru. In other words, the penetration of the awareness of the indestructible quality of the guru must open one's heart, pierce through one's heart and open it, open the closed, conceptualized, and confused boundary of ego and grant the miracle power of compassion, ultimate communication.

Foreword to

THE TORCH OF CERTAINTY

T HE SPIRITUALITY OF BUDDHISM is a nontheistic one. It deals with the ways and means of attaining enlightenment, discovering buddha within through the aid of great teachers and the diligent practice of meditation. It has always been emphasized that one does not purely practice the dharma, but one becomes the dharma.

The teachings of Buddha are divided into three sections: hinayana, mahayana, and vajrayana. They should be methodically practiced in this order. If one does not begin at the beginning, there is a danger of provoking further confusion, of viewing practice as entertainment, which only causes greater arrogance and neurosis.

The pattern of the practitioner's progress through the three yanas is as follows: First, one develops extreme exertion in uncovering one's own neurosis. This one-pointed mindfulness brings the sense of one's actual human quality. The second stage is marked by gentleness, allowing one's energies to expand and be shared with the rest of sentient beings. Finally, one develops fearlessness and a sense of joy and penetrating insight, filled with immense devotion to the lineage and one's root guru. This text, dealing with the preliminary practices of the vajrayana discipline, belongs to the third category.

I am very pleased that this authentic torch of certainty is available to those who are inspired to follow the vajrayana path. It was written by Jamgön Kongtrül the Great, whose reincarnation, Jamgön Kongtrül of Sechen, was my root guru. Those who are deeply inspired by this book should receive oral transmission from a living lineage holder. They should have a strong foundation in hinayana and mahayana as a prelude to entering the path of vajrayana. This is the way which has been taught.

Judith Hanson has put a great deal of energy and devotion into the translation of this text. The fruition of her effort is evidence of her karmic link with the Kagyü tradition.

Practice of the Four Foundations:
An Interview

Before beginning a meditation session, the practitioner excludes all distractions. He may then set up an icon of the visualization used in that practice, for example, an image of Vajrasattva, a picture of the refuge tree, and so on.

Actual practice of the four special foundations involves the practitioner in an intense drama combining physical, verbal, and mental acts. As he chants each section of the liturgy, he visualizes the scene described in it, considers the significance of the prayers, and performs the ritual acts indicated. During all of this, he tries to focus his attention exclusively on the ritual.

To complete the practice, he must perform each of the four special foundations 111,111 times. Since taking refuge also includes 111,111 full prostrations, the total is 555,555. Hence, the practice is commonly called the "five-hundred-thousand."

The following interview [May 18, 1976] with a leading teacher of Tibetan Buddhism focuses on the practice of the four foundations and its significance for modern students of Buddhism.

—Judith Hanson in *The Torch of Certainty*

INTERVIEW WITH CHÖGYAM TRUNGPA RINPOCHE

Question: What are the four special foundations, and how do they fit into the whole scheme of Buddhist practice?

Chögyam Trungpa Rinpoche: Every type of spiritual discipline, craft, or educational system has its beginning, middle, and concluding levels. The four foundations (*sngon 'gro*, literally "prelude") are the beginning of the vajrayana discipline. Of course, the vajrayana is not the first but the third level of Buddhist practice, to be preceded by the hinayana and mahayana. But those who begin the vajrayana discipline do so with the four foundations.

According to tradition, the foundation practices require a lot of preparation. In the early days in Tibet, people had to have a great deal of training before practicing the foundations. This included basic training in tranquillity and insight meditation (*zhi gnas* and *lhag mthong;* Skt. *shamatha* and *vipashyana*), as well as some training in the mahayana, which included formally receiving the bodhisattva vow, and so on.

Q: What is the function of each of the four special foundations?

CTR: The four special foundations are an evolutionary process in which each event has a definite place. They could be connected with the four dharmas of Gampopa. In taking refuge, your mind begins to follow the dharma, which is the first dharma of Gampopa. Your attitude toward yourself and toward everything in your life becomes connected purely with dharma practice. There is no longer such a thing as a division between sacred and profane.

To begin to practice, you must first "give in" to the dharma completely. This is accomplished by doing prostrations, a process of complete surrender, of definite commitment. I don't think anyone can begin vajrayana practice without that.

When you take the bodhisattva vow, having decided to go and having bought your ticket, you actually begin the journey—bodhichitta and the bodhisattva path. This is related to the second dharma of Gampopa, which is that your dharma practice can actually win success on the path.

When you do the Vajrasattva practice, having already surrendered, you have to purify and further acknowledge what you have surrendered. All the impurities must be purified.

After purification, something still remains—the pure person, which might contain some stain of arrogance, some stain of existence. In the mandala practice, you actually give everything, including the pure person. You offer this—the giver—as well as all the offerings, at which point, in a sense, you no longer exist.

By the time you reach the guru yoga practice, you are psychologically ready to identify with your guru, and immense devotion is born in your mind. This is connected with the third dharma of Gampopa, which is that, in following the path, confusion could be clarified. The actual transformation of confusion into wisdom, the fourth dharma of Gampopa, is receiving abhishekas and practicing various sadhanas. This is the main part of the vajrayana discipline, which comes much later.

Q: In what ways, if any, will the manner of practicing the four foundations here in the West differ from that followed in Tibet? Will Westerners find the foundations easier or more difficult to practice?

CTR: Because of the cultural differences, the practice of the four foundations will be somewhat different for Western students. Since they are not completely familiar with the cultural background of Buddhism, when they try to practice the foundations, they will encounter some cultural gaps which they will have to overcome. We must try not to impose the Tibetan tradition on them but to present them with the basic "mind's work" of the teachings.

One problem in the West is that people are accustomed to focusing on their bodies. The whole society is based on comfort. Western students practicing the foundations make a big issue of their aches and pains and tend to get very attached and exaggerate them.

An important difference is that Western students need a lot more prior training in the hinayana and mahayana so that they will know what they are doing when they practice the foundations. Since they lack the cultural background of Tibetans, when introduced to the foundations they will not be ready to jump into the practices immediately, and they may see them as alien, as some sort of a gimmick. We cannot respond to their doubts by telling them to shut up and have faith. To help them overcome these doubts, we must train them in tranquillity and insight meditation much more thoroughly than was done in Tibet. Apart from these, I don't see any particular differences.

Q: Before an individual practices the four special foundations, what should he study and/or practice first?

CTR: As I have said, before he tries to practice the foundations, an individual must be thoroughly trained in tranquillity and insight meditation. In addition, he must be familiar with the basic teachings of Buddhism—such as the four noble truths, six perfections, and five skandhas—so that when he is introduced to the vajrayana via the four foundations, it will not seem like a foreign product.

Q: What type of person should practice the four foundations?

CTR: It doesn't matter. Any type of person can do these practices.

As long as an individual has become involved in tranquillity and insight meditation, his personality has begun to dissolve somewhat. By the time he gets involved in the vajrayana through the foundations, he is no longer a "type of person," particularly—he is already there!

Q: What role does the guru play in guiding an individual through practice of the foundations before, during, and after completion of the practices? What is the nature of the guru-disciple relationship?

CTR: A person who is practicing the vajrayana discipline should have some notion of what is known as the "vajra master" or root guru who instructs us in the vajrayana. In each of the three yanas, the teacher has a different role. In the hinayana, he is the elder (Skt. sthavira), or wise man. In the mahayana, he is the good spiritual friend (Skt. kalyanamitra). In the vajrayana, he is the master—almost a dictator—who tells us what to do. The relationship must be very strong, definite, and direct—one of great devotion.

When you practice the foundations, your prostrations are directed toward your root guru as Vajradhara in person. If your relationship with your guru is not very strong, this practice will be very feeble.

In these practices, Vajradhara has two aspects. The first, the dharmakaya or primordial aspect of Buddha—the awakened state of mind or the general existence of full enlightenment without any obstacles, obscurities, or definitions—is the Vajradhara at the head of the lineage [i.e., the top of the refuge tree]. The second aspect of Vajradhara is that very concept, transplanted into your personal root guru. So your root guru is the Buddha in person, not only in the sense of a nirmanakaya like Gautama Buddha, but Vajradhara himself—the complete Buddha. So the reference to Vajradhara is tied up with the notion of trust and faith in your root guru.

It has been said that the guru's body is the sangha, his speech is the dharma, and his mind is the Buddha. In this case, Buddha has three aspects: nirmanakaya, sambhogakaya, and dharmakaya. So the guru buddha includes the whole thing.

Of great importance in the guru-disciple relationship is the samayabond (dam tshig), the commitment established between you and your guru once you have undertaken the vajrayana discipline. Although you may not yet have received any empowerments from him, once you have taken him on as your vajrayana teacher, the commitment has already been made and the bond established absolutely. There is no such thing as a mediocre samaya-bond.

Commitment to your guru and his teachings is very necessary; it gives you some guidelines for your life. Without that commitment, you might begin to make up your own version of the dharma, your own edition of the teachings, and sooner or later what you will get back is just your own ego version of the teachings. So the idea of commitment here is total surrendering, complete surrendering. You don't edit your own version of the dharma anymore.

The commitment allows you to receive the pure teachings undiluted by the influence of ego. Commitment keeps the teachings clean, pure, and workable, so that the actual teaching, the teaching in its pure form, works for you. Maybe the teacher might be pure, and the teachings might be pure, but if you don't commit yourself properly, then you end up putting a part of yourself into the teachings, and you don't receive the pure thing. It's like drinking out of a dirty cup.

If a student tries to practice the foundations without a guru's guidance, probably nothing will happen, except that his confusion will increase. It will be a waste of time.

Q: What is the importance of the mahamudra lineage for one who is practicing the foundations?

CTR: The lineage is very important for the practitioner. Each teacher in the lineage had his particular skillful way of teaching. Each has contributed a great deal to the wealth of the Kagyü tradition. Each one's life is a perfect example for us to study. Each one has left behind and passed on his experiences to us.

The lineage shows us that "it can be done"—even by us! It makes us aware that the teachings represent not one but many lifetimes of work. Each teacher sacrificed a lot, went through a great deal of personal hardship, and finally attained enlightenment. Belonging to this lineage makes us very rich and full of enlightenment wealth. Being part of this family gives us immense encouragement and also a sense of validity [regarding that which we are trying to practice]. We realize that the teachings we now receive have come down from all of them.

The lineage also enables us to place ourselves within a certain geography. We have happened upon somebody who has opened up the whole thing for us—like a gigantic rain descending on us!

Q: What is the significance of the physical, verbal, and mental techniques used in practice of the four foundations?

CTR: Prostrations originally came from the Indian tradition where you make a gesture of reverence to somebody higher than you. The idea of prostrations is that you have found somebody who is utterly worthy for you to open to, completely. So you fall on the ground and touch your forehead at his feet. Then you find something more to do, which is called ninefold prostrations, where nine joints of your body are completely on the ground. That's the final idea of prostrations, which is much more elaborate and definite; physically, you are really doing something.

In the mandala practice, you are offering your wealth and yourself at the same time. You feel happy that you can walk on earth, you feel that the earth is yours, in some sense, and you just give all that in the form of piles of rice.

Mount Meru, the four continents, and so on, which are represented by the piles of rice, comprise the traditional universe derived from Hindu mythology. This is strictly a cultural phenomenon: in those days, the universe consisted of that. In modern times, we might offer the solar system and so on. The basic idea is that you are giving the world you live in and also the symbols of work, sense perceptions, basically everything that is worthwhile.

The geography is meant to be discussed. I hope that some day a conference will be called by Buddhist leaders in which we can discuss the geographical aspects and come up with some solution.

When we chant the liturgy in all the foundation practices, we actually say it. In ordinary life when we are very involved with ourselves, we usually talk to ourselves. In this case, you actually *say* it, which makes it much steadier and more solid—something definite happens.

The mantras we chant in these practices are not regarded as the same as the mantras used in the more advanced sadhana practices. Here, it's still just a process rather than the actual, real mantras in higher forms of vajrayana. For example, the Vajrasattva mantra, which is a purification mantra, has one hundred syllables which contain the bijas for one hundred peaceful and wrathful deities. These are said in a certain way which invokes the essence which would be fundamentally, inherently pure. But it's still a superficial use of mantra here, in some sense.

Visualization, the mental technique used in all four foundations, is something that most people find very difficult to do. In vajrayana, visualization is called kye rim, or the developing stage of meditation. It is slightly different from how we normally think of visualizing. Ordinarily, we think of visualization as just daydreaming. In this case, it is taking the complete attitude of the deity, actually seeing it mentally, rather than purely daydreaming it. This requires prior training—basically, sitting practice, which is tranquillity and insight meditation. Even people who have undergone this training have a lot of difficulty with visualization. But you have to start with the teaching of nirmanakaya, rather than relating first to dharmakaya. You have to start with body and then work with mind. Otherwise it will be very difficult.

Traditionally, while students are going through the four foundation practices, they are also taught certain particular formless meditations which are connected more closely to the mahamudra principle. That is the notion of the fulfillment stage, or dzog rim, which is always recommended a great deal. There should always be the developing stage and the fulfillment stage together, visualization and formless meditation together. Without that, somehow the whole thing is like finger painting rather than actually doing it. There are different levels of formless meditation, of course. Students usually begin by borrowing the hinayana practice of tranquillity and insight meditation, and then out of that some glimpse of the mahamudra experience might occur. That seems to be very important. The idea is not to trust purely in the gadgets of the practices alone, but that there is something happening behind that. Some kind of unseen, unformed—I don't know what you'd call it. The incomprehensible is comprehended, with just a few glimpses. That has to happen. Traditionally that is done, and I did that myself.

Dzog rim or the fulfillment stage is a general term. There are different levels of dzog rim or formless meditation. From the hinayanist point of view, it would be shamatha and vipashyana, tranquillity and insight meditation. From the mahayanist's point of view, it would be maitri bhavana or something like that. From vajrayana, dzog rim is finally mahamudra. But you can't have that just suddenly given to you without previous training. That's why the basic training in shamatha and vipashyana is very important.

This idea of dzog rim or formless meditation is traditionally handed down from teacher to student. It's not talked about even in the commentaries. That's the company policy, so to speak. That is true for this text, *The Torch of Certainty*, as well. This commentary is very basic, direct, and written with a lot of heart, a lot of soul. It's nice that people can read it. At the same time, I feel that people shouldn't just pick up the book and try to practice without a teacher. We have to take some kind of measures to protect the teachings, so that they can be presented properly. I feel some concern about this, and I think the dharmapalas will be behind my shoulders, trying to mind my business: they always are.

Q: In what surroundings should the four foundations be practiced?

CTR: People have a problem deciding whether to practice in a group or alone. Generally, vajrayana practice should be done in groups. In the vajrayana, there is much more idea of sangha than in the hinayana or the spiritual brotherhood of the mahayana. In vajrayana, the concept of the vajra sangha is very important and very necessary. Actually, people might practice the four foundations in groups together or by themselves. It doesn't make that much difference. The main point is that you can't expect ideal surroundings; there would be no such thing, particularly, as ideal surroundings. People can't afford to take a whole year off from work, and they have their families and so on. Of course, in Tibet in the monasteries, we had retreat centers, and we practiced quite a lot together. [To work with this situation here] I have some of my students practice the foundations in groups. We have set up prostration shrine rooms, Vajrasattva mantra shrine rooms, and mandala shrine rooms. The basic principle of practicing together is what's known as the vajra feast: once you join the vajrayana discipline, there should be no holding back of yourself; everything should be shared together. It's also a question of transmitting the insight that comes out of group practice, sharing that with your brothers and sisters in the dharma, rather than keeping it secret. It doesn't particularly have to be a group-encounter type of situation, but just feeling and being together. When people achieve an understanding of the fulfillment stage of meditation, or mahamudra, there are some psychological happenings that can actually be felt as well as said by the whole group. Everybody's prostrating together; you are in the same boat. The idea is that is should be more normal, definitely, rather than that you are doing some funny thing while your wife or husband and your kids are away.

Q: Must the four foundations always be practiced in the order in which they are presented in *The Torch of Certainty?*

CTR: The order should be kept the same. Each stage prepares for the next, and they become increasingly more subtle until you reach guru yoga, which is complete devotion to the guru. Having evolved to this level, you are prepared to receive abhishekas.

Q: If an individual loses interest in the practice, should he stop and wait for the inspiration to return or keep practicing?

CTR: Losing interest in the practice is a symptom of not having enough training in tranquillity and insight meditation. Training in tranquillity and insight makes you, first of all, very aware of your pain and your neuroses. It increases your mindfulness and enables you to begin to make friends with yourself. You learn how to be by yourself, with yourself. Without this training, you might easily become overwhelmed and put off by the physical exertion and mechanical aspect of these practices.

If a person finds himself put off and feels that he cannot continue the foundations, he should return to tranquillity and insight meditation and go back to the vajrayana discipline later on.

Q: What are the indications of successful practice?

CTR: Basically, you will be less arrogant and less opinionated.

Q: How does an individual know when his practice of the four foundations has been unsuccessful?

CTR: If you become more arrogant and opinionated, it means that you do not have enough compassion and sympathy and that something is wrong with your practice.

Q: What should a person do if he feels that his practice has been unsuccessful?

CTR: If an individual's practice is not working, this is because he approaches it as some kind of gymnastics, due to a lack of genuine renunciation. He is still blinded by the confused world. In order to begin to see clearly, the practitioner should return to tranquillity and insight meditation. This advice is not in conflict with that of the other rinpoches. The "four thoughts" are a contemplative discipline by which you develop disgust with samsara. If you practice tranquillity and insight as the basis of the whole spiritual journey, then the "four thoughts" will arise as a natural process.

The Practicing Lineage

O UR SUBJECT IS THE LINEAGE, or the line, of the Trungpas. The particular person sitting in front of you belongs to, or *is,* one of them—in fact, the eleventh one of them. We are not talking about the dynasty of a kingdom, and we are not talking about a family history, hopefully not. But we are talking about *how* the situation has evolved through the various Trungpas over the ages, up to the present situation.

The question is, what particular tradition is the line of the Trungpas associated with? To begin with, Buddhism, of course, and Tibet. What kind of Buddhist discipline? And connected with what particular locality of Tibet? We are forced to go back to the background story, which is connected with what is known as the teachings of the practicing lineage.

All of you are also part of that lineage. At this point, a lot of you have inherited it, a lot of you are just about to inherit it, and a lot of you are just beginning to dip into this particular tradition. That tradition, again, is called the practicing lineage.

There are four schools of Tibetan Buddhism. There is the old, or older, school; the medium, or middle, schools; and the new one. The old school is known as the Nyingma tradition. It is continuing the tradition of Padmasambhava, the great Buddhist adept, saint, yogi who introduced, or instigated—formally, officially—the teachings of Buddha into Tibet.

Then there are the medium, or middle, schools, which are two: the Kagyü and the Sakya. They came into the picture much later, presenting further Buddhist teachings from India. Then, the latest one, the newest one, the youngest one of all, is called the Geluk tradition.

The Geluk tradition is, we could say, completely and fully a Tibetan product of Buddhism, because it did not have any direct historical relationship to Indian Buddhism. By that time, Indian Buddhism was already far gone and slowly dying out, due to the Mogul invasions of India. Most of the Buddhists in India were persecuted or had gone underground. A lot of the monasteries were attacked because the Mogul troops thought that people wearing uniforms must be soldiers. So monks were killed and monasteries were completely destroyed.

The Islamic tradition, particularly, doesn't believe in deifying any idols. They believe that any kind of images representing the truth shouldn't be anthropomorphic. Consequently, the Moguls destroyed a lot of statues, wiping out evidence of Buddhist culture, as much as they could. Still, these days, from excavations taking place in India, we are finding Buddhist temples and stupas and images. But they have received a token Mogul seal on them: either the statue is without a nose or without ears or fingers as a mark of disapproving of anthropomorphic images being deified.

The practicing lineage, to get back to the subject, is one of the middle schools, which came after the old, or ancient, school. It developed through various Tibetan masters, scholars who visited India and received teachings there and then established their particular situations. Namely, there was the famous translator-saint Marpa, who visited India three times and brought the teachings to Tibet. And his disciple Milarepa was the greatest yogic poet of Tibet, or shall we say, more likely, singer-poet, or the first Tibetan blues singer. And then there was Gampopa and so forth. The lineage of the Kagyü, the practicing lineage, at this point consists of something like thirty-six generations—up to the present Trungpa, whoever he might be!

The meaning of the practicing lineage is important for you to understand before we can understand the rest of the story, so to speak. The practicing lineage is a term that was developed particularly by Milarepa. Previously, the tradition was known as the Lineage of the Sacred Word, which is actually a phrase that we are using again these days. In the Kagyü tradition, *ka* means "logos," or "sacred word," "command," "truth." *Gyü* means "thread," or "continuity," which is close to the idea of lineage—continuity. In Milarepa's time, the Kagyü tradition became known as *drubgyü*, *drub* meaning "practice," and *gyü* meaning "lineage," "line."

The practicing lineage places a lot of importance on the need to practice, sit, meditate a lot. Without practicing, without understanding the meaning of practice, no *real* communication takes place in your understanding of Buddhism, buddhadharma.

It is also equally important to have a great deal of devotion to your teacher, who actually embodies the symbolism or the concept of practice. The guru himself or herself has already achieved a high degree of enlightenment through practice. Moreover, the guru is the only person who can actually push you and who can be a heavy-handed friend, who can actually make you sit a lot and go beyond your slothfulness and laziness. If you want to boycott anything, only the guru can push you and make you sit a lot, practice a lot.

Theoretically, a cosmic guru could send you blessings and encouragements through your particular psychic antenna, and he might tell you all kinds of stories and send you all kinds of messages. Such things are regarded as very fishy according to the practicing lineage. We can always reinterpret them according to our own desires. To begin with, our own interpretations, received through our antennae, are not so substantial. But on top of that, we can actually reinterpret things according to our liking.

So it is necessary to have an earthly person, born and raised on his planet Earth, to begin with. You need someone who regards himself or herself as a human being, who would like to share the love and hate, and sweet and sour, and hot and cold of this particular world. Someone who can speak to you on a man-to-man basis, who acts as a mirror reflection, in some sense, and also provides real, genuine communication, independent of politicking or overindulgence in charitable kindness or obsession with masochistic trips: free from all those. Someone who is somewhat sensible, reasonable, but at the same time unyielding. Traditionally, we call this a "wise person," somebody who can't be persuaded to buy your side or your trip. Somebody who can actually be clear about the whole thing. Somebody who buys your story with a pinch of salt, but at the same time, is kind and friendly—to a certain extent. Such a person is the teacher, who then teaches you to practice a lot, sit a lot.

The basic teachings of Buddha are based on understanding what we are, who we are, why we are. When we begin to realize who we are, what we are, why we are, then we begin to realize why we are *not,* who we are *not,* what we are *not.* We begin to realize that we don't have basic, substantial, solid, fundamental ground that we can exert anymore.

We begin to realize that our ideas of security and our concept of freedom have been purely phantom experiences.

We would like to use the spiritual discipline and traditional wisdom to fit into our own particular pigeonhole, our own desires. We usually want to glorify ourselves by collecting stories and wisdom from every worthy person. We would like to meet lots of people who are seemingly worthy people, according to our own judgment, and collect all of those stories and re-edit them according to what we want, constantly. When you begin to do that, you develop your own version of freedom, which is "I would like to become a greater version of myself, spiritually uplifted, and so forth. I might even have a place in social situations, be known as an important wise person, so that people will come to me and consult me." We have those kinds of desires. We are not really interested in developing spiritually; we are more interested in evolving politically in the name of spirituality. Such a situation is known as "spiritual materialism." There is a book about it. [*Laughter. Chögyam Trungpa was referring to his own book* Cutting Through Spiritual Materialism.]

The practicing lineage teaches us that we have to get rid of those ego-centered conceptualized notions of the grandiosity of our own development. If we are truly involved with spirituality, we are willing to *let go* of trying to witness our own enlightenment, the celebration of our enlightenment. We have to learn to be willing to die, to subside. This particular "me" that wanted to attain enlightenment has to go away. When that happens, then you actually attain enlightenment. So one can't watch one's own burial, in other words.

In order to shed the ego, in order to understand that particular principle, we have to practice a lot, sit a lot. We have to *experience* a lot. We might have some intellectual, analytical understanding, but even that understanding has to be based on an intuitive experience of the practice situation. Without that, we can't develop at all. We are simply creating further schemes, expanding further schemes of our own grand plans of a spiritual ego trip, spiritual materialism, and so forth.

Throughout the lineage of the practicing tradition, every one in the lineage has been extremely sarcastic and critical of the current scenes taking place around them. They were extremely critical of the name of the dharma. We could say that the practicing lineage is the guardian of the buddhadharma, not only in Tibet alone but in the rest of the world. Someone should at least have a critical view of how things should hap-

pen, how things shouldn't happen. That particular sharp vision, traditionally known as prajna vision, is very important. And that is a very
lively situation, a living situation, which still is up-to-date. In fact, that is
why we are here.

The practicing lineage is the most pure and is unhampered by all
kinds of spiritual materialism. Instead of just viewing this lineage from a
purely historical point of view, we should realize that this can take place
in ourselves. How we have come to be, to practice, our particular basic,
general background is that we would like to become a richer and more
conscious person, a highly evolved person. That is why we are interested
in spiritual practice. But those trips are known as real *trips*. Those trips
are questionable. And such trips require a very heavy critical dosage of
the practicing lineage message, so that we could at least be woken up
from our naiveté, our confused attitude about spirituality, and our attempts to pollute the spiritual world of the twentieth century.

The Mishap Lineage

WE COULD GO FURTHER in understanding the meaning of the contemplative tradition and why the tradition that I come from, the practicing lineage, or the Kagyü, does exist. It is not just an accident or a matter of chance. Rather, the whole thing is somewhat planned or programmed to the extent that there is an intelligent awareness or a vision at work, of how a practitioners' lineage can exist and continue.

As far as that vision is concerned, it is a prolonged sense of commitment to humanity and to working with the neurosis of humanity. The practicing lineage is not based on practitioners locking themselves up in their meditation cells so that they become social nuisances. But practitioners in our lineage also work with their commitment to their teacher and with surrendering, openness, and devotion—as well as with commitment to the rest of the world, all sentient beings.

Usually, when we practice some kind of discipline and we begin to teach that discipline to others, we tend to present a great deal of qualifications and credentials, hoping that they will carry us a long way. After that, we just say what we have to say, which is quite short and maybe presented with the pretense of some kind of wit, which is based on not having enough confidence in oneself. So the whole thing short-circuits. That is the usual style of presentation for somebody without any background or lineage. Traditionally, that has been a problem. But in this case, borrowing the name of the lineage is not so important in order to reach people. It is not so much providing one's credentials or using them as one's own decorations. Rather, the point is to tell people that their lineage had good forefathers and that there is a good background, a good lineage, behind them. So it is a trustworthy situation.

Similarly, the Kagyü tradition has developed more pride in an individual's practice and less quotation from the lineage as a reference point.

People relate with practice much more closely, but not in the Ram Dass fashion, which is a mutual confession. "I'm messed up; you're messed up; so let's meet together and have a nice time and talk it over." But in this case, let us meet each other in the spirit of the practitioners' lineage.

Let us encourage each other to sit, let us practice together. Let us encourage each other properly, fully, thoroughly, so that we can inspire ourselves in the spirit of *awake* rather than in the spirit of confusion.

When that begins to happen, there is lots of room to expand. Traditionally, it is said that the Kagyüs and the goats like to preside over rocky mountains. And Gelukpas and horses like to roam around in the fields. That is an interesting saying. The reason why we would like to preside over rocky mountains is partially that we are mountain freaks, traditionally, geographically. Partially we would like to approach things from the hard-core practitioner's angle—in a very personal style.

You may ask, "If your particular tradition is so interested in locking yourselves up in caves and practicing by yourselves, how is it possible to expand your administration? How can administration and expansiveness take place all together?" That's a very interesting point, which you should understand. It's a very important point here. Although the Kagyüpas like to live in the rocks in the mountains, they don't particularly make a nest in the mountains, the rocks, and the caves. They conquer the mountains and the rocks. They don't regard their caves as hippie pads where they could indulge themselves or as apartments. You have no idea what goes on in the rest of the apartment building, but you have a nice little cave on the fifth or sixth floor, whatever. In this case, it is conquering the whole mountain.

Likewise, the Kagyüpas are known for conquering foreign territory. The rings of Kagyüpa expansion took place not only within the heart of Tibet alone, but the Kagyü also liked to live in the surrounding territories. The Kagyü established rings of expansion into Bhutan, Sikkum (which is a border of Tibet), and India. They also expanded into the Sing Jong province of China, into Mongolia and all the rest of the countries bordering Tibet. The Kagyü are not afraid of the cliffs or of the sheer drops of cultural misunderstanding that exist. If you jump from one culture to another, you may find that the next culture does not have any connections with you anymore. You find that jumping into another country is like jumping over another cliff. But the Kagyüpas never had fear about that. And likewise we are here. We are not afraid of foreign space. Foreign space is domestic space at the same time.

The expansion of the practicing tradition is interesting. It sheds light on Buddhism altogether, in some sense. The southern tradition of Buddhism had reservations about conquering the mountains. So the hinayana tradition went to the south, into Southeast Asia. The vajrayana tradition went to North India, crossing the barbarian lands. The Indians used to call Tibet the monkey land or the vampire land, the land of red-faced people who eat raw meat and drink raw milk, which was regarded by the Indians as a terrible thing to do. To have never known vegetables is absolutely terrible, from their point of view.

The Kagyü tradition also developed fearlessness in relating with their own bodies and minds, which we often find is a foreign situation as well. We are confronted constantly, again and again, with foreign territories, all the time. We are always faced with the unknown. Our death, our birth, our parents, our emotionality: everything is always a foreign country. And *that* mountain, *that* foreign territory is also conquered, as much as the physical geographical territory beyond Tibet has been conquered.

You might say this is such Kagyü chauvinism. I think that is true. But behind such chauvinism there is an immense sense of devotion. With that hard-core conquering of the mountains and conquering of foreign territory, there is, at the same time, also an immense sense of softness, of surrendering and sentimentality. The Kagyü tradition is based on sentimentality—of a higher level, of course. [*Laughter*] It is not so much the sentimentality of dreaming about one's mother's chicken soup when you're hungry or thinking about a well-made kreplach or Christmas pudding, for that matter.

An interesting thing develops by being emotional and hard core at the same time. We don't usually connect those things together. We don't usually smoke menthol cigarettes and Marlboros at once. [*Laughter*] But they could be blended together. That is what the Kagyü tradition is actually doing. The hard core of relating with the foreignness of foreignness of foreignness exists all the time in our life. You pay your landlord the rent, and you think that at least you can relax for a month. Suddenly, the landlord knocks on your door and says, "I want to kick you out, because you did such and such a thing. Otherwise, I'm going to call the police." Or you think that your love affair is going well. Suddenly, something comes up. Your lover has apparently not spoken out enough, and suddenly the pimple begins to burst. A big explosion takes place.

All kinds of things like that take place all the time in our life. We think we have settled or solved our most outrageous or outstanding problem. Whew. We try to relax. Then something else comes up and scares us. We might think that we know New York City completely, inside out— which street not to go on, which areas to avoid. But we get mugged on Fifth Avenue or in the United Nations building. That is always possible. Such things happen to us all the time. So we find that we can't actually relax to the extent we thought, and we can't be caught up, up in arms, completely all the time either. There's room for romanticism and there's room for working with foreign territory all the time as well.

The Kagyü tradition begins to teach us that. We experience, simultaneously, both situations together at once. *One* situation is *both* situations. Both situations means both romanticism and the threat from foreign territory. In romantic situations, usually you're settling down, helping yourself to something, lying back and enjoying the pleasure. That's romanticism. And foreign territory means being up in arms, watchful.

The Trungpas had the same experience as the Kagyüpa pioneers. In some sense, it was on a much lesser scale than Milarepa and Marpa and Naropa, but the Trungpas had a similar kind of experience constantly taking place. One of the Kagyü mystics once said, "Being in the Kagyü tradition, the Kagyü lineage, is like inheriting constant mishaps." [*Laughter*] Constant mishaps. That's true. If you are actually in contact with reality, and particularly if you are in control of reality, then you are in contact with completely constant mishaps. Because you are in contact and in control, therefore the mishaps begin to come to you rather than you bumping into them. They begin to come to you constantly. All the time these little things are taking place. Fantastic. [*Laughter*] Delightful. And it is that which makes everything very cheerful.

Take the story of Milarepa. He was told by Marpa to leave and go back to his home. He had finally been accepted by Marpa, who had made him his chief disciple and an important person, the only son of the lineage. Milarepa was completely fine, feeling extremely good. Then he went back home and everything was ruined, completely destroyed. That kind of mishap is always apropos of the practicing lineage, once you begin to have any association with the lineage. Milarepa found his house ruined, his mother enskeletoned inside. Nobody had even conducted a funeral service for her. His father was long dead and his aunt and uncle and everybody were up in arms and there were no friends—none at all. It was like returning to a completely haunted house, like the haunted house in Disneyland. Everything is shrieking and haunting, seemingly. Of course, for Milarepa this was not regarded as a ride, like in Disneyland. In Milarepa's case, it was real. One shrieking situation after another shrieking situation, one haunted situation after another haunted situation take place because you are on top of situations.

We would like to come face to face with a ghost. We hear stories about ghosts, and we would like to find out whether ghosts actually exist or not. If you are in a playful mood, ghosts don't appear, because they are not interested in haunting you at that point. Ghosts are only interested in haunting you when you are in a transitional period or else when you are on top of the situation. On the other hand, we are not talking about the reality of ghosts here. We don't want to get back into that psychic phenomenal world. That's another waste of time, on the other hand, of course. But ghosts will come to you. They come to you. [Laughter]

The practicing lineage is very much in contact with what's going on, virtually what is going on, actually what is going on, on the spot, on the dot, constantly. Interestingly, students in the Kagyü tradition have had less guidance from substantial phenomena, or the realistic world. In other words, they had less tutorship of people telling them how to do things or how not to do them. They had to take a chance all the time, constantly. But they have more commitment to their guru, their teacher. So they have more devotion at the same time, which is an interesting point. When you have completely signed on with a church or an existing club, the company pays for the damage. Or else you are completely abandoned. Between those situations, there is some sense of actual reality taking place. How much you are connected with reality somewhat depends on your degree of sanity. At the same time, your disconnection with reality also comes through. A message will come through very clearly, strongly, properly.

Before we get into too many details of the line of the Trungpa, I would like to lay the ground for you. I would like you to understand the difference between the practicing lineage and any other old lineage. So I will be interested in further feedback, such as your nightmares, your dreams, your thoughts about the whole thing. If you have any questions, you are welcome.

Allen Ginsberg: Coming to you interested in Buddhism, what we wind up with is *you,* in a sense, or with your particular specialty, rather than some larger maybe vaguer Buddhism. But really, then, it comes right down to yourself and your lineage—which is kind of a, often, a kind of nightmare. [*Laughter*] Is that the way it's supposed to be?

Chögyam Trungpa Rinpoche: That's good. That's great. That's good. I'm sure that, if you exchanged notes with Milarepa, he would say the same thing about his father, too. Maybe much more so.

Teachings on the Tulku Principle

THERE ARE SEVERAL TYPES of tulkus. The buddha on earth is one type of tulku. The images of Buddha are also known as tulkus, "tulkus of art." Another tulku is the tulku who continues to be reborn constantly in order to help beings on various levels. But the Tibetan tradition of discovering tulkus who are incarnate lamas, that somebody is the tulku of so-and-so, is a different kind of setup, in a sense. There are actually various types of incarnate lamas and various types of rebirth taking place. There is the tulku who incarnates before the previous incarnation has died, several months or even years earlier. And then there is what's called a "blessed tulku," in which the previous person chooses the person who is closest to him or blesses some passing bodhisattva who hasn't quite attained the highest of the bhumis. And he takes certain types of energy, or spiritual energy, which transcends ego anyway, and transfers it to the chosen person. That person then comes back as the incarnation of the previous person. Actually it is a different kind of ego; but at the same time, there is a spiritual continuity which takes place. Those are the various levels of incarnation.

Generally in Tibet, the blessed tulkus seem to be most prominent Such tulkus have to be raised and educated; they have to go through training and practice and everything. They have the element of realization; they have more potential of realization than just an ordinary person who has no push or encouragement and nothing injected into them. So these people have a great deal of potential. But they haven't quite realized it, so therefore they have to go through training, education, and everything. Then they begin to come up to the level of their previous incarnation because such spiritual energy has been put into them.

The reason why this is possible but that we ordinary people can't do it is because we believe ourselves to be one entity, in spite of philosophi-

346

cal indoctrination. So we find it very difficult to split our personality unless we become schizophrenic, which is the neurotic level, not a very pleasant or enlightened way of splitting oneself. So there may be a higher level of splitting personality, not into just one person, but many. Usually the body, speech, mind, quality, and action aspects of a particular being are transferred. So you have five types of tulkus, who particularly specialize in scholarship or contemplation, or are very active in propagating the dharma, and so forth. So the Dalai Lama, Karmapa, or any other tulkus we can think of seem to be generally the blessed-tulku type of personality. They are recognized by their predecessor and that person actually blesses that new ego of somebody who is already making some progress in some way. They encourage them or enforce them in a certain way so that the person can reincarnate as the next Karmapa or the next Dalai Lama. Therefore, such a person also has to study and go through various trainings. Otherwise, if everybody is already enlightened or if everybody has to begin all over again, it seems to give the wrong impression. If in each life you have to struggle all the time, it seems to contradict the perpetuating development of enlightenment.

Another question is what happens to those people who have already injected their essence and their wisdom into somebody else? What happens to the original people? Where do they go? It seems that those original people also come back to this world, not as the reincarnation of themselves particularly, but anonymously, incognito, so to speak. They come back as farmers or fishermen or businessmen or politicians or whatever. They don't necessarily have to come back into a Buddhist environment, particularly, because the teachings of enlightenment could be taught at any level. People can be helped at all kinds of levels. That seems to be the basic point. There are possibilities of meeting such people who never heard or thought about any form of the teachings of Buddha but who somehow are realized in themselves. And in such cases, some memories exist within them; they have some idea of their basic being. But there's no point in advertising that eccentricity, particularly if they're going to communicate with the ordinary world. So that seems to be the general setup.

Milarepa

A WARRIOR'S LIFE

T HE YOGI MILAREPA LIVED in Tibet during the eleventh century. A famous religious figure in the development of Buddhism, Milarepa is also one of the greatest folk heroes of the Tibetan people. In modern times, his life story and beautiful songs have become well known throughout the world. We might regard Milarepa's life as a mythical tale of a saint or a superhuman person, but there is another approach that we could take. During his own lifetime, Milarepa was considered to be such a highly developed person that many of his students felt that his achievement was far beyond their own abilities. Milarepa seemed to find his students' attitude both somewhat touching and amusing, and he would regard any modern deification in a similar manner. He always reminded his disciples that he came from a humble background and that he had achieved his understanding and realization of the dharma by a simple, straightforward process that was possible for any human being to follow—through the application of effort and devotion. He encouraged his disciples to do as he had done. For us, his life story is similarly an invitation to follow his example.

It is said that the path of dharma is good at the beginning, good in the middle, and good at the end. Good in this instance does not mean "ideal" or free from obstacles and suffering. Goodness is the quality of genuineness that we discover as practitioners of meditation. At the beginner's level, genuineness is applying wholehearted dedication and diligence to our practice. When we start out, it is necessary to apply one hundred percent effort to working with our confusion and developing the foundation of discipline. That kind of energy never ceases, but taking the first step in that direction is extremely important. In the middle, goodness or genuineness has to do with our relationship with our teacher, who is the embodiment of the genuineness that we are striving for. At this stage, surrendering to the teacher is the most important step we can take. So genuineness here takes the form of complete devotion.

At the end, genuineness means that we have completely identified with the teachings, so much so that we can no longer speak of any separation. We have overcome any form of self-deception, and we are completely ourselves. At this level, the quality of genuineness is relaxed and confident and extremely powerful, absolutely skilled in working with things as they are. The final attainment of genuineness is thus the embodiment of compassion, and it expresses itself as buddha activity. In Milarepa's life story we see the complete unfolding of these three stages.

This kind of development can also be described as the birth, training, and fruition, or attainment, of the warrior. It might seem odd to talk about Buddhist practitioners as "warriors," since buddhadharma is synonymous with nonaggression. Yet in the Buddhist scriptures, many of the great teachers and the Buddha himself are frequently described as great warriors.

A warrior, in this sense, is someone who is not afraid of himself or herself and who is also fully dedicated to wakefulness and to helping others. Not being afraid means being willing to acknowledge one's own confusion and suffering. The warrior sees that the anger, hatred, lust, jealousy, and ignorance in the world are enemies of wakefulness and compassion. He or she also sees that false beliefs about oneself and clinging to those beliefs are what generate the endless cycle of passion, aggression, and ignorance—the three poisons. So the illusion of ego is the warrior's fundamental enemy.

The tools of the dharmic warrior are discipline and dedication and, most importantly, gentleness, which is the essence of nonaggression. By joining these attributes with meditation and devotion to the teacher, the warrior forges an invincible weapon of compassionate action. Along the path, one encounters many obstacles of self-deception. One is bound to make mistakes, which are part of the learning process. The warrior must be willing to acknowledge his or her errors and to learn from them. What characterizes the warrior is the fearless energy to go forward, which he or she learns to join together with sanity and concern for the welfare of others.

Milarepa's life exemplifies the development and attainment of warriorship. His life began in very difficult circumstances. When Milarepa was only seven years old, his father died suddenly, and the family was left in the care of Mila's aunt and uncle. They were extremely cruel and scheming people, so much so that they treated the family as servants and stole the entire inheritance. Milarepa's mother had been known to her neighbors as a kind and generous woman, but when she found herself a servant in her own home, she could think of nothing but revenge. Her only thought for her son was that he might grow up to be a powerful person who could help her to reclaim the family's wealth and position.

As a loving and dedicated son, Milarepa felt that he should help his mother. As a first step, Milarepa left his village to study reading and writing. This was quite unusual for a person of his means, but he realized that without training he could do little. He proved to be a very good student, and his natural talent and energy thrived on his studies. He enjoyed this formal learning very much and might have continued his schooling, but his mother kept reminding him of their situation, and she urged him to apprentice himself to a teacher of black magic who could teach him spells to exact revenge on his aunt and uncle.

Milarepa joined a group of young men traveling in search of a tutor. He was quite curious about magic, as well as wanting to please his mother. He and his companions journeyed until they found a magician who was highly respected as a master of the black arts. When they arrived at the teacher's farm, each student made an offering and asked for instruction. While the others presented small gifts, Milarepa gave all of his possessions and offered his body, speech, and mind. The teacher accepted all of the travelers as his students. For the first year, he taught them only insignificant magic, such as little spells to make thunder and lightning. At the end of the year, the other students returned home, believing there was nothing further to learn. Milarepa remained, and for a second time, he requested that the magician teach him the black arts. The man was extremely impressed by his student's perseverance. He thought to himself, "Here is a student who sincerely desires to learn." He decided to teach him everything he knew and even thought about sending Mila to study with another magician who knew even more powerful spells.

Milarepa progressed swiftly in his studies of magic. He learned to control the natural energies around him and could call on guardian deities to carry out his commands. When he became confident of his strength, he turned his thoughts to his village and to the plight of his mother and sister. Using magical incantations, he called up giant scorpions as well the local deities and sent them to the home of his aunt and uncle. When the guardian deities returned, they carried with them the heads of thirty-five people who had been attending a wedding celebration in the house. The scorpions had uprooted the pillars of the house, causing the roof to collapse, killing everyone except Mila's aunt and uncle.

At this point, Milarepa had developed quite a lot of skill in working with the phenomenal world. Of course, his approach was extremely misguided. He had learned to combat violence with violence, which has been a crude strategy for working with our problems for a very long time. Mila had not yet understood that his own aggression could only breed further destruction and misery. So, although in some sense Milarepa had become accomplished and powerful, he had not yet learned how to actually help someone else. He had not yet discovered the greater power of the dharma or the truth of nonaggression, which transcends clinging to primitive beliefs about oneself or others. Without this clarity or insight of egolessness, his actions might bring some immediate relief or victory to his family, but ultimately they could only lead to further suffering. Ironically, the apparent source of Milarepa's suffering, his aunt and uncle, were left alive. Later in his life, they became important reminders of the futility of his aggression.

Milarepa knew that the villagers would be angry about what he had done and that the lives of his mother and sister would be endangered. So he used his magical powers again. This time, he conjured up a hailstorm that descended onto the fields in the village, destroying the crops and leaving huge gullies in the earth. The villagers realized that this was his work as well. Although they were still very angry, they were also afraid of Mila and left his family alone.

Mila had accomplished what he had set out to do, fulfilling his mother's desire for revenge, yet he didn't feel any satisfaction. In fact, he began to sense that there was something missing in his life. Milarepa's intent had been to master the arts of magic in order to avenge the wrongs done to his family. However, the most valuable qualities he had mastered were actually his sincerity, bravery, and resourcefulness. His belief in violence as a solution began to fall apart, but his sense of basic discipline remained. The degradation of his life and his own aggression began to dawn on him. He experienced great remorse for all the harm he had caused. Finally, it occurred to him that there might be another way to overcome evil and misery. His desire to discover such a path grew, and he began to think of finding a teacher who could show him this way.

At the same time, the magician became ill and, as his death approached, he began to repent of all the evil deeds he had committed in his life. When Milarepa shared his desire to find a teacher, the magician was overjoyed and told Mila that it would be an excellent idea for him to seek out the path to overcome suffering and the effects of karma accumulated through misdeeds. After promising the magician that he would dedicate himself to finding a teacher, Milarepa said his good-byes and went on his way. Although he had made many mistakes and had committed what we might call "crimes" while he was with the magician, at the same time, Milarepa had learned important lessons about himself and the world.

He traveled around looking for someone to study with and, at first, stayed briefly with a lama who promised him an easy path to complete enlightenment. Even in those days, almost a thousand years ago, such seductions were commonplace. Milarepa was told that he would gain amazing results if he would simply practice a particular meditation for a few days. He tried diligently for quite some time, but the practice had no effect. Finally, the lama realized that he couldn't help Milarepa. He suggested that he might study with a teacher known as Marpa the Translator, who seemed to be able to do something for particularly hard cases. The minute that Milarepa heard Marpa's name, he experienced intense longing. He knew nothing about this man, but he felt an immediate connection, so great that he set out right away to find him.

Milarepa reached the province of Lhotrak, where he had been told Marpa lived. He asked someone he met on the road if he knew where one could find the great teacher Marpa and his monastery. The man said, "Well, there is a farmer who lives near here, at Drowo Lung. He has a nasty temper and is fond of drinking beer. Some call him Lama Marpa, but I myself know nothing of that." Milarepa continued on his way. He passed a young boy on the road and asked him where he might find Marpa's house. The boy said, "You must be looking for my father. He sold all our wealth for gold and went to India. Now he has returned with many precious books. Today you will find him plowing the field."

Milarepa hurried down the road, filled with anticipation at the prospect of meeting his teacher.

When he saw Marpa working in his fields, Milarepa prostrated to him and offered his body, speech, and mind. Marpa said that, before he would accept Milarepa as his student, Mila must use his magical powers against Marpa's enemies in a neighboring valley. He assured Milarepa that this was religious work, so Milarepa agreed to help him, thinking that this would please his teacher. Using magical spells, he killed many men and destroyed their fields with hailstorms. Then he returned to Marpa's house and asked him for the teachings. Marpa, much to Milarepa's surprise, became furious. He said that he would be a fool to give any teachings to an evil magician. He drove Milarepa out of his house, telling him not to come back until he had restored the lives he had taken and the fields he had ruined.

Milarepa was shocked. He was confronted for the first time in his life with a completely uncompromising human being, someone who was totally unimpressed with his magical powers and impossible to seduce. Milarepa knew that he could not undo his crimes—he didn't have that kind of power. (Later, he discovered that Marpa did have this ability, for he restored the lives of those whom Milarepa had killed in his misguided desire to win approval. At this time, however, he did not know about Marpa's powers.) It seemed to Mila that his life had been useless. All of his own aggression came crashing down on him, and he felt wretched. He broke down and wept.

The next day, Marpa sent a messenger to bring Milarepa back to the house and told him not to be discouraged. He promised to initiate Milarepa into the teachings if first he would build a tower for Marpa's son. Following Marpa's instructions, Milarepa began to construct a round tower on the eastern corner of Marpa's land. When the structure was about halfway built, Marpa came by and told Milarepa to tear it down. He wasn't satisfied with the design and placement of the building. Then, he asked Milarepa to build a semicircular tower in the west. When it was half-finished, Marpa showed up and claimed that he had been drunk when he started this project, and he asked Milarepa to tear it down and to replace the stones where he had found them. Then Marpa told Milarepa to build a triangular tower. Milarepa asked his guru to consider carefully whether this was really what he wanted, so that his effort and Marpa's wealth would not be wasted again. Marpa assured him that he

true heartson and giving him initiation into the vajrayana teachings of Buddhism.

Milarepa remained with Marpa for several years. He stayed in solitary retreat in a cave above the farm for months at a time. His practice, like everything in his life, was marked by total conviction and sincerity. Because of his teacher's skill in working with him, his zealousness and steadfastness became a source of great accomplishment.

After he had been living at Marpa's farm and practicing for several years, one night Milarepa dreamed that his mother was dead and his sister had become a wandering beggar. He awoke in tears, thinking of his mother. The next morning he left retreat to ask Marpa's permission to return home. When he entered Marpa's room, the guru was still asleep. As Marpa opened his eyes, the sun was rising and a beam of sunlight touched his forehead. After listening to Milarepa's request, he reminded him of everything he had given up to practice the dharma. However, when Milarepa still wanted to go, Marpa realized that this journey was a necessary step on the path and he agreed to let him go.

Marpa understood his being asleep when Milarepa entered his room as a sign that, after this parting, he and Milarepa would not see one another again in this lifetime. He told Milarepa that the sun rising as he entered the room foretold that the Buddhist teachings would shine like the rays of the sun. The light falling on the guru's head meant that the teachings of Marpa's school, the Kagyü lineage of Tibet, would flourish.

Before he left, Milarepa was given several important transmissions from Marpa. A special celebration, a feast offering, was held, and Milarepa was empowered as a lineage holder in the Kagyü tradition. Marpa gave Milarepa an oral, or ear-whispered, transmission, which can only be passed down from one teacher to one disciple. He told Milarepa to guard this teaching more dearly than his life. Marpa instructed Milarepa to remain only briefly in his village. Then he should find isolated caves throughout Tibet where he could practice meditation in solitary retreat until he attained realization. The guru also gave Milarepa a scroll, telling him to read it only when he encountered a great obstacle in his practice. When Milarepa finally left, Marpa and Damema accompanied him partway down the road. When they finally said good-bye, it was with great sadness.

When Milarepa reached his home, he found everything just as he had seen it in his dream. He found his mother's bones lying in the ruins of

MILAREPA: A WARRIOR'S LIFE

their house. He seated himself on the bones and meditated there for seven days. Not surprisingly, the impermanence of life and the reality of death filled his mind. The futility of samsara, or confused existence, was overwhelming to him. Realizing the importance of meditation, he vowed to renounce the world of illusion and ego-clinging and to practice the dharma as his only occupation.

Following Marpa's instructions, Milarepa then left the village and went into solitary retreat, practicing in many caves throughout the countryside. When his food ran out and his clothing became tattered, rather than leave his cave to beg, he wore rags or went naked and ate nettles that he found nearby. He became quite emaciated, and his skin gave off a green glow from all the nettles in his diet. His body became covered with strange gray fuzz, and hunters passing by his cave ran away, fearing that he was a ghost.

Milarepa's asceticism has sometimes been described as self-mortification. However, Milarepa presents us with an example of genuine ascetic practice, which is not based on punishment but on complete adherence to discipline, not giving in to any samsaric corruptions of ego. A dharmic warrior, Milarepa had total dedication to his practice and to his teacher's instructions. Because wealth, fame, and even companionship no longer had a hold on him, his renunciation of these things was an expression of freedom and a celebration of simplicity.

Of course, Milarepa did experience loneliness during his solitary retreats and he missed his guru very much. Sometimes he became discouraged in his practice. However, he never lost his faith in his teacher, and he continued to follow the basic instructions he had been given: to meditate in isolation and to join all experiences together with his practice of meditation. In this way, the obstacles that he encountered eventually became the source of insight and inspiration. For example, Milarepa once returned to his cave to find it inhabited by a number of demons. He tried to subjugate them with a mantra, which had no effect, and then tried meditating on compassion and friendliness, which did nothing to pacify them. Several of them disappeared when he sang a song praising them and making offering to them as local deities. Several others departed when he sang a song expressing his confidence in the experiences and view of meditation. One particularly persistent demon only disappeared when Milarepa sang a song expressing his deepest realization and then surrendered to the demon by putting his head in its mouth. Over the years, Milarepa befriended and converted many of the mountain demons and gods—which from a modern perspective we might say represents conquering both our own internal fears and confusion as well as the local, environmental energies and preconceptions.

While he was in solitary retreat, Milarepa was visited by his sister, Peta; his scheming aunt; and his former fiancée. In the past, they had represented a world of struggle and grief. Initially, while he was in retreat, they tried to dissuade him from his ascetic life. His gentleness, insight, and dedication to his practice so impressed his aunt that she eventually became a yogic practitioner. His fiancée and his sister became devoted to him and brought him food and clothing.

Over the years, Milarepa had many encounters with those who passed near his cave. Hunters, animals, and others wandering in the wilderness became his disciples. Visitors frequently thought he was a wretched hermit when they first saw him, and they would bring him food and clothing out of pity. Many were converted to the path of meditation by the beautiful yogic songs that Milarepa sang, praising the teachings of dharma and pointing out the misery of samsaric life. Far from being a miserable person, Milarepa had tremendous appreciation for the beauty and richness of his environment and of his lineage.

After years of solitary meditation, Milarepa reached a great obstacle in his practice. Constantly in a state of hunger, he was experiencing such fluctuations of pain and pleasure that he found that he could not meditate. Unable to overcome these distractions, he finally opened the scroll that Marpa had given him. It contained instructions for his meditation and also advised him to eat good food at this time. He followed the teacher's advice, and his meditation became thoroughly accomplished. Recognizing that his realization was the fruition of many years of practice, he felt extremely grateful to all those who had provided him with food, clothing, and other provisions. At this time, he also recognized that the root of suffering and the root of liberation are in essence the same. Realizing this interdependence, he experienced great compassion and gratitude for all beings. When he realized that there was no longer any question of rejecting or accepting his experience, the final traces of ego were overcome. He understood the ultimate meaning of nonaggression: that there is no separation between oneself and others.

For the remainder of his life, Milarepa traveled throughout Tibet, meditating and spreading the teachings of the Buddha. Wherever he went, he accumulated disciples and was loved by the people. When he was eighty-four, he accepted a drink from a lama who was jealous of his reputation. He knew that it contained poison, but he felt that his life's work was complete. Before he died, he gave his final instructions to the assembled students. These are instructions that could benefit any of us today, as much as they did then. He said,

> When I die, there is no certainty that my body will remain in the form of a corpse. Don't build statues or stupas in my memory. Instead, raise the banner of meditation. Reject all that increases ego-clinging or inner poison, even if it appears good. Practice all that benefits others, even if it appears bad. This is the true way of dharma. Since life is short and the time of death unknown, devote yourselves wholly to meditation. Act wisely and courageously according to your innate insight, even at the cost of your life. In short, act in a way that you will not be ashamed of.

When Milarepa died, many miracles were reported. He was seen at the same time in many different places, and the air was filled with dakinis singing his praises. It is said that a shower of many-colored blossoms fell to the earth and that rainbows filled the sky. As he had predicted, his body did not remain but dissolved into a crystal stupa, which was carried off into space by the assembly of deities.

In the Shambhala teachings, it is said that the warrior whose way is complete achieves both temporal and spiritual victory, that his mind is beyond mind, and that he is the warrior of the warriors. In the Buddhist scriptures, it says that when the Buddha Sakyamuni was born from his mother's side, he took seven steps and proclaimed that in heaven and earth he was the World-Honored One. Whether we see them as literal or symbolic, the miracles that accompanied Milarepa's death are similarly a proclamation of his conquest over the corruptions of ego. He too was a world conqueror; his victory was a statement of the power of non-aggression.

There is a saying in the Kagyü tradition that the grandchildren will surpass the ancestors. Milarepa's teachings of complete sanity—which came from the Buddha Vajradhara, were passed down from Tilopa to Naropa to Marpa, and then were given to Milarepa—he in turn gave to Gampopa, who founded the monastic order of the Takpo Kagyü, which spread the teachings of the dharma to innumerable disciples. The order of the Karma Kagyü, to which I belong, began with the first Karmapa, Tusum Khyenpa, a disciple and heartson of Gampopa. As a lineage holder of this tradition, I am extremely grateful to Milarepa for giving us such a magnificent example of courage and wisdom to follow. Through the incorruptibility of his lineage, the teachings of the buddhadharma have been completely preserved and constantly renewed, so that the power of wakefulness continues to sound the great drum of dharma in the world today. I am pleased that we can fulfill the prophecy of our forefathers.

Milarepa

A SYNOPSIS

M ILAREPA WAS BORN on a farm in northern Tibet of a lower-
middle-class family. When his father died, his aunt took over the
farm and forced Milarepa, his mother, and his sister to work for her.
Milarepa's mother was very bitter about this suppression and urged him
to study black magic in order to seek revenge against her sister-in-law
and her relatives. And so Milarepa became an adept of the black arts.

He produced a hailstorm that completely destroyed all the fields belonging to his relatives except those rightfully owned by his mother. He
created a giant scorpion that uprooted the pillars supporting their house,
while a gay party went on within. The house collapsed, killing all except
his aunt, who was powerless to continue her domineering ways without
her family to reinforce her.

Seeing that the endless round of aggression, suffering, and pain would
never bring fulfillment, he decided to devote his energies to seeking enlightenment.

He set out to find a teacher and encountered considerable difficulty
in finding one. When he heard the name of the great guru Marpa the
Translator, he knew immediately that it was right. When Milarepa offered his whole being to him, Marpa said he would either support him or
give him teaching, but not both. Milarepa then undertook the building of
a great stone tower under Marpa's supervision in order to pay for his
teaching. This was still learning, but by situation rather than by formal
theoretical training.

Marpa expressed dissatisfaction with the tower and told Milarepa he
would have to tear it down and build another. He had to put all the
stones back where he had found them so as not to spoil the landscape.
Marpa caused him to build three towers in this way.

Many years later, when the last tower, nine stories high, was completed, Milarepa once again appealed to Marpa for the teaching. Marpa refused. Damema, Marpa's wife, was more sympathetic and secretly asked Marpa's chief disciple to teach Milarepa. This project failed because the disciple had no real link with Milarepa, so he joined an audience of disciples who were going to Marpa for a particular initiation. This also did not work because the gift that he brought to pay for the teaching had been kindly provided by Damema; Marpa angrily realized that it was already his own possession and he got up off his throne and chased Milarepa out.

Completely disheartened, Milarepa decided to commit suicide. Just at the crucial moment, a message arrived asking him to go to see Marpa, who offered to give him the teaching he longed for if Milarepa would give him an appropriate gift. Delighted, Milarepa set out with a begging bag to accumulate barley grain, which he exchanged for a copper cauldron. Marpa received him well but told him that the empty cauldron signified that his practice would be a severe one. He would often be without food and would suffer many other hardships. Marpa then gave him the teaching for which he had waited so long.

He went into retreat in a small cave near his guru's home where he stayed for some time. One day Marpa suggested that he return home to see his family. Milarepa found his house in ruins with his mother's skeleton in the doorway and his father's skeleton entombed within. The triangular barley field was overgrown with weeds, and everywhere it was desolate and ghostly. The death of his family brought him to the realization of the transitory nature of all existence. He passed the night there in great sadness and left the following morning with some of the family heirlooms that remained: some pages of gold-written manuscript. With this gift, he went to see the teacher who had taught him reading and writing. At this teacher's suggestion, he went to see his aunt. As soon as she saw her nephew approaching, she let loose her dog and chased him away with her tent pole.

Milarepa found a cave and stayed there to meditate, depending on nettles for nourishment. One day his aunt took him some food and told him that he should never go back to the farm as he had a bad reputation as a black magician and for neglecting his mother. But Milarepa had no more desire to connect himself with the past.

Later, his sister arrived and begged him to return to the world and shape his spiritual practice, more like the grand abbots of the surrounding monasteries. But he wished only to continue his solitary meditation.

One day while he was meditating, Milarepa suddenly felt hunger. Discovering that he had neither food nor fuel, he went out in search of wood and to gather nettles. A strong wind came up and blew his robe away. When he grabbed the robe, the wood blew away. Tired of his own ego-clinging, he ceased resisting and let the wind blow away his robe and the wood. Due to lack of food, he fell in a faint with the next gust of wind.

When he came to, he saw clouds coming from the direction of the Drowo Valley where his guru lived. Filled with longing to see Marpa Milarepa dedicated a song to him. The clouds stretched toward him and on the clouds appeared Marpa, riding on a snow lion. He reassured Milarepa that their spiritual link was a bond that would keep them together always. He told him to continue meditating.

Milarepa returned to his cave and found five demons with eyes as big as soup bowls and bodies as small as thumbs inside. One was preaching from Milarepa's seat while two others listened. Two more demons were preparing food. He made several attempts to vanquish them, but to no avail. Realizing then that they were creations of his own mind, he became confident and rushed at them. They shrank back and disappeared. . . .

. . . Marpa told Milarepa that he should go to meditate in a cave at Lapchi Snow Mountain. When he arrived there, the villagers welcomed him warmly, for they had heard of the powerful Yogi who always lived alone in remote places. They asked him to stay with them and teach them and begged him to rid one of their farms of the demons and ghosts that were plaguing it. He agreed to do so, for the farm was on the very mountain that Marpa had ordered him to go to.

When he arrived there, a great storm broke loose and lightning struck all around. The river burst its banks and created a vast lake. Milarepa made a gesture and the flood subsided. The demons shattered the mountains and created landslides. Milarepa once more subdued them. Then the demons came and threatened to tie him up and chop him into pieces. Milarepa expounded the teaching to them in song; their evil deed would beget more of the same and they would forever remain demons. They were all gradually subdued and became his disciples. Because

Milarepa overcame these obstacles, he experienced great spiritual growth. . . .

. . . Milarepa went to Nyanang to meditate in a cave. One night he heard a sound coming from a crevice next to where he sat. A beam of light shone through, in the midst of which appeared a red man on a black deer led by a beautiful woman. The man gave Milarepa a blow with his elbow, accompanied by a suffocating wind, and then disappeared. The woman became a red bitch, who immediately caught Milarepa by the foot. He realized that she was an apparition conjured by the she-demon Tra Simmo, so he sang to her,

> Should you not control your harmful thoughts and vicious
>   heart?
> If you do not realize that all things are merely of the mind,
> The endless apparitions of Namtog will never cease.
> If one realizes not that the mind-essence is void,
> How can one dispel the spirit of evil? [40]*

She disappeared, but still holding his foot, she replied to Milarepa,

> When you were engrossed in the practice of meditation,
> The powerful force of your habitual thoughts arose,
> It stirred your self-mind and aroused delusory
>   discriminations.
> If in your mind the discriminating thought "Enemy" has
>   ne'er arisen,
> How could I, Tra Simmo, afflict you? [42]

Milarepa told her that he was making fun of her, that he had no fear of her nor of anything else. Moved by his song, Tra Simmo released Milarepa's foot and sang,

> I roam the earth in this evil form,
> Desiring blood and flesh for food.

---

*All verses quoted are from *The Hundred Thousand Songs of Milarepa*, translated by Garma C. C. Chang (Boston: Shambhala Publications, 1999). © 1962 by the Oriental Studies Foundation.

I enter into the soul of whomsoever I encounter;
I incite the hearts of maidens, pretty and charming;
I madden with lust the blood of young men, strong and
    handsome.
With my eyes, I amuse myself watching all the dramas;
With my mind, I instigate cravings in all nations;
With my body, I incite people to excitement and
    restlessness. [45]

Milarepa told her to make a wish to be his disciple in the future. Great faith arose in her. She reappeared visibly and renounced her wrongdoings and swore before Milarepa that in the future she would never harm anyone and would protect all who meditate. Then she made obeisances to him and circumambulated him many times.

Then Milarepa sang,

Should one cling to the reality of visions,
He would be confused in his meditation.
If he knew not that all obstacles
Reveal the void, the manifestation of mind,
He would be misled in his meditation.
The very root of all confusion
Also comes out of the mind.
He who realizes the nature of that mind
Sees the great illumination without coming and going.
Observing the nature of all outer forms,
He realizes that they are but illusory visions of mind.
He sees also the identity of the void and form. [53]

. . . One day as Milarepa sat meditating in a cave on the border between Tibet and Nepal, he heard a dog barking in the distance. Sensing that some disturbance was on the way, he left the cave. He came to a huge rock and, pausing there, he became absorbed in meditation. A spotted deer ran up, badly frightened. Milarepa, taking pity on him, sang him a song about fear and hope. The deer was relieved of his pain and he lay down at Milarepa's feet. Shortly thereafter, a savage hunting dog ran up. Milarepa sang to her of hatred and greed, which greatly moved the dog.

She became completely subdued and lay down on the other side of Mi-larepa.

Thereupon a hunter, the owner of the dog, rushed up and shouted angrily at Milarepa. The hunter drew his long bow and shot an arrow at him. The arrow flew high of its target. Milarepa assured the man that he had plenty of time to shoot him and that he might first listen to his song. And so he taught the hunter that if he would conquer his own mind, then all his enemies in the outer world would disappear. The hunter suspected that Milarepa was a black magician because he had completely subdued the animals; he entered the cave and saw nothing but some inedible herbs. Finally overcoming all his doubts, great faith arose in the hunter. He offered Milarepa all his possessions and became one of his disciples. . . .

. . . At a certain stage, Marpa advised Milarepa to go to Gung Tang. Milarepa went there and found a cave. A young boy came to visit him and was overwhelmed by Milarepa's presence. He was an intelligent boy and though already well versed in Buddhist teachings, he asked Milarepa for further instruction. Milarepa agreed. The boy's mother and uncle be-came very angry because the boy had left them, so they sent him a pot on which a curse had been placed. As a result, the boy—Rechungpa—contracted leprosy. Some Indian Yogis passed and suggested that he go to their guru in India, who might be able to cure him. He went to India and was cured. Fearing that Milarepa was dead, he returned to the cave where he had left his guru. Milarepa sat within, meditating. When Re-chungpa asked about his health and welfare, Milarepa sang this song:

> I bow down at the feet of Marpa, the gracious one.
> Because I have left my kinsmen, I am happy;
> Because I have abandoned attachment to my country, I am
>   happy;
> Since I disregard this place, I am happy;
> As I do not fear the lofty garb of priesthood, I am happy;
> Because, I cling not to house and family, I am happy;
> I need not this or that, so I am happy.
> Because I possess the great wealth of dharma, I am happy;
> Because I worry not about property, I am happy;
> Because I have no fear of losing anything, I am happy;
> Since I never dread exhaustion, I am happy;

Having fully realized mind-essence, I am happy;
As I need not force myself to please my patrons, I am happy;
Having no fatigue nor weariness, I am happy;
As I need prepare for nothing, I am happy;
Since all I do complies with dharma, I am happy;
Never desiring to move, I am happy.
As the thought of death brings me no fear, I am happy;
Bandits, thieves, and robbers ne'er molest me,
So at all times I am happy!
Having won the best conditions for dharma practice, I am
    happy;
Having ceased from evil deeds and left off sinning, I am
    happy;
Treading the path of merits, I am happy;
Divorced from hate and injury, I am happy;
Having lost all pride and jealousy, I am happy;
Understanding the wrongness of the eight worldly winds, I
    am happy;
Absorbed in quiet and evenmindedness, I am happy;
Using the mind to watch the mind, I am happy;
Without hope or fear, I am ever happy.
In the sphere of nonclinging illumination, I am happy;
The nondistinguishing wisdom of dharmadhatu itself is
    happy;
Poised in the natural realm of imminence, I am happy;
In letting the six groups of consciousness go by
To return to their original nature, I am happy.
The five radiant gates of sense all make me happy;
To stop a mind that comes and goes is happy;
Oh, I have so much of happiness and joy!
This is a song of gaiety I sing,
This is a song of gratitude to my guru and the three precious
    ones—
I want no other happiness.

Through the grace of buddhas and the gurus,
Food and clothes are provided by my patrons.
With no bad deeds and sins, I shall be joyful when I die;

With all good deeds and virtues, I am happy while alive.
Enjoying yoga, I am indeed most happy.
But how are you, Rechungpa? Is your wish fulfilled? [111–112]

Rechungpa assured Milarepa that he was cured and wished to stay
with him. He received further teaching from Milarepa and in time attained realization. . . .

. . . One day Milarepa went toward Balkhu to meet Rechungpa, who
was returning from his second trip to India. Milarepa saw in a vision that
Rechungpa was suffering from pride. When they met, Rechungpa was
indeed thinking that Milarepa should return his obeisance because now
he was as great as Milarepa; he was in fact much more learned in theoretical Buddhist philosophy. Milarepa did not acknowledge Rechungpa's
feelings about this, but instead sang to him of the pitfalls of pride.

They proceeded along the road. Milarepa saw an old yak horn lying
by the side of the road and asked Rechungpa to pick it up and bring it
along as it might prove useful to them. Rechungpa thought that Milarepa was being miserly and didn't bother to pick it up. So Milarepa
picked up the yak horn and carried it himself. Suddenly a great storm
broke loose accompanied by violent hail. Rechungpa quickly covered his
head and didn't bother to take care for his teacher. When the storm
abated, he looked for Milarepa but could not find him. He heard Milarepa's voice coming from the yak horn. When he tried to pick the horn
up, it was too heavy. He bent down and looked into it and saw Milarepa
seated comfortably inside. His body was no smaller and the horn no
bigger than before. Milarepa sang to Rechungpa, inviting him to come
into the horn since he considered himself so accomplished. But when
Rechungpa tried to get into the horn, he could not even get his head and
hand in. Putting his mouth close to the horn, he sang a song of obeisance
to his guru.

Then Milarepa came out of the horn and gestured toward the sky.
The storm passed and the sun came out. . . .

. . . One day as Milarepa sat with his disciples, a young monk came
to see him. He prostrated and offered Milarepa sixteen ounces of gold
and a brick of tea. Milarepa said, "Gold and yogi don't agree with each
other. There's no stove to cook the tea, so take these things back and
use them for your own needs." He took a full skull cup of wine and
drank half of it, offering the rest to the young monk. Gampopa, the

monk, was reluctant to take it as it was against the precepts, but not wanting to upset the symbolical pattern, he drained the cup. Up until that time, Gampopa's training had been scholarly, so Milarepa gave him the initiation of the oral instructions and also the Cinnabar Mandala. Having seen successive visions in yogic practice, Gampopa became very excited and thought that each vision was the ultimate discovery. Milarepa, with his greater knowledge, guided him further so as to avoid all pitfalls. He finally accepted Gampopa as part of the lineage of transmission and made him his successor. He advised him to start the monastery of Gampo Lhari. Gampopa fulfilled all the instruction he had been given, and the monastery of eight thousand monks, half of them scholars and the other half in retreat in caves, became renowned. . . .

. . . In order to teach his disciples and some of his patrons, Milarepa one day performed some miracles. He flew into the sky and transformed his body from one to many and then retracted them back into one. He also preached in an invisible form. One of his disciples, Sevan Repa, also tried to fly. He held his breath but all he could do was to walk above the ground.

Another time, Milarepa became invisible to all who came to see him. Some people saw light; some saw a glowing lamp shining on his bed; some saw a rainbow, water, a bar of gold, or a whirlwind; others could not see anything.

> If there be obstacles,
> It cannot be called space;
> If there be numbers,
> It cannot be called stars.
> One cannot say, "This is a mountain,"
> If it moves and shakes.
> It cannot be an ocean
> Should it grow or shrink.
> One cannot be called a swimmer
> If he needs a bridge.
> It is not a rainbow
> If it can be grasped. [31]

The Art of Milarepa

THE TIBETAN TRADITION is sometimes referred to as "lamaism," but it is rather the tradition of the practice of meditation. "Lamaism" is a purely fanciful and inaccurate term most frequently associated with the idea of high priests performing magic. Fundamentally, Buddhist traditions in Tibet are no different from those of such countries as Ceylon, Burma, and Thailand. But at the same time, the prolonged peaceful and uninterrupted social situation in Tibet favored the thriving living tradition of its transmission of Buddhist wisdom.

Being geographically closer to India, Tibetans had the opportunity to watch and absorb the evolutionary process of Buddhism as the teaching grew from Sangharakshita's philosophy of Yogachara to the tantric crescendo in the period of Saraha, Naropa, and Kukuripa.

In the ninth century, tremendous enthusiasm for the secret practice of Buddhist yoga developed in the great universities of Nalanda and Vikramanshila. The secret practices inspired great pandits like Naropa and Saraha to a more thorough and rugged level of receiving teachings and of practicing them. One of the songs of Saraha says "up to now I was the perfect bhikshu, the complete bhikshu." At this time, great pandits began to leave the security of the monasteries in search of wild yogis such as Tilopa and Kukuripa. They did this at the expense of their previous way of life. They had to give up vegetarian diets, monastic vows (such as the twelve repentances of Naropa), and other ascetic practices.

The problem for Tibetan devotees who wanted to translate and receive teachings from Indian yogis was how to approach such outlandish people and what criteria to use in relating to them. Marpa was one of the adventurous people who went in search of the yogis. He was willing to throw his store of gold (which he had saved for the journey) into the Bengali jungle and to do other crazy things, including being willing to sacrifice his own life for the sake of receiving the teachings. Although Marpa was a solid, stable Tibetan scholar and farmer, his faith and romantic notion of Indian tradition led him to this point. But having received the teachings, he found that the only way to communicate them to other Tibetans was as himself, as a very earthy person, rather than to make himself over into a replica of Naropa and Kukuripa.

Marpa taught people in his spare time for he was mainly occupied with plowing the fields, harvesting, and taking care of his seven children. Probably he even had to care for another dairy farm up in the mountains. The pattern developed that he generally had other householders and farmers interested in his teachings. Pilgrims, travelers, and mendicants flocked to visit Marpa's farm. Milarepa was an exception, for he was inspired to stay.

Mila was his family name, but he was known as Tuchen, the great powerful one, because of his reputation as a black magician able to kill his enemies by conjuring great scorpions to uproot the structures of their houses. Such success with his powers and subsequent guilt and conflict led him to seek Marpa, but merely unburdening himself was not the way to communicate with his teacher.

Milarepa was forced to relate to his own body by undergoing all sorts of extremely difficult physical work and suffering in payment for receiving teaching. Marpa said, "I cannot promise you food, lodging, and teaching. Either you seek food and lodging elsewhere and I give you teaching, or I provide food and lodging and you receive teaching elsewhere. But in any case, if you want to receive teaching, you will have to present a gift." Finally, Milarepa was accepted with the provision that he build a certain tower for Marpa. But Milarepa thought that he should receive the teachings on the basis of his workmanship as a kind of exchange. However, his anxiety and restlessness presented more problems than he realized, for in order to receive teaching, he had to give up not only all expectation, but also wanting to be free from the conflicts and guilts of his previous wrongdoings. This was, in a way, the gift he had to give.

Milarepa was led to believe that he was not worthy of receiving the teachings in his lifetime, so he gave up all hope—which it was necessary for him to do—not only psychologically but literally as well, for he decided to commit suicide. At that moment, when expectation and a sense of wanting to be saved did not exist in him anymore, he was accepted into the abhisheka circle and was able to receive teachings. He practiced diligently for the next six years.

Marpa realized that Milarepa had to relate to his unfinished karmic debts and to have the experiences of working them out, and so he encouraged him to return to his homeland. Perhaps until this point, the teachings were to a great degree only theoretical, except for the presence and word of Marpa which had naturally made a deep impression on Milarepa. But it was not until he met with disappointments and the desolate situation of his home village, that he was really connected to the teachings.

The rich, fertile barley fields were overgrown with weeds. The family scripture—the *Prajnaparamita Sutra*—had been blown over the neglected fields by the wind. His relatives hadn't touched the property because they thought it was bewitched by Milarepa's magical powers. His sister had become a beggar and his mother had died. Using the bones of his mother's skeleton as a pillow as he lay in the derelict mansion of the Mila family, Milarepa was thrust into the literal application of the teachings.

After some searching in his homeland of western Tibet, Milarepa found a cave in the Red Rock Castle Mountain of the Garuda. There, living purely on a diet of nettles, the loneliness and sense of freedom were like having pain and pleasure simultaneously. In a way, the loneliness that Milarepa felt was very romantic and inspiring. There was a sense of support from the whole lineage behind him. It was a kind of love affair with the desolate mountains. Naturally, there was a sense of longing and need for comfort from Marpa. Intoxicated by the beauty of aloneness: "He went out. But when he had gathered a handful of twigs, a sudden storm arose, and the wind was strong enough to blow away the wood and tear his ragged robe. When he tried to hold the robe together, the wood blew away. When he tried to clutch the wood, the robe blew apart. [Frustrated] Milarepa thought, 'Although I have been practicing the Dharma and living in solitude for such a long time, I am still not rid of ego-clinging! What is the use of practicing Dharma if one cannot subdue ego-clinging! Let the wind blow my wood away if it likes. Let the wind blow my robe off if it wishes!' Thinking thus, he ceased resisting. But, due to weakness from lack of food, with the next gust of wind he could no longer withstand the storm and fell down in a faint."*

---

*This and subsequent quotations are from *The Hundred Thousand Songs of Milarepa*, translated by Garma C. C. Chang. (Boston: Shambhala Publications, 1999). © 1962 by the Oriental Studies Foundation.

At that very moment, intense emotion manifested itself as a vision of Marpa riding on a white snow lion in the clouds. Gazing at the distant sky, Milarepa sang this song:

> Though in my deepest faith and veneration
> I have never been apart from you,
> I am now tortured by my need to see you.
> This fervent longing agonizes me,
> This great torment suffocates me.
> Pray, my gracious Guru, relieve me from this torment.

Because of absorption and unshakeable faith, he heard the voice of Marpa saying, "Powerful one, my son, why with such deep emotion did you call to me so desperately? Why do you struggle so? Have you not an abiding faith in your Guru and Yidam. Does the outer world attract you with disturbing thoughts? Do the Eight Wordly Winds howl in your cave? Do fear and longing sap your strength?"

This was the moment of a great lesson. The pleasure of the vision of the guru had to be accompanied by the pain of hidden neurosis. And so, as Milarepa returned to the cave, he confronted his own projections which manifested themselves as demons, the living portrait of aggression. Trying to subjugate them by mantric spell did not work; theoretical understanding, that is, regarding everything as one's own mind in a naive attitude, didn't do the trick; finally, a nondualistic attitude, that of welcoming any threatening projections of mind, dissolved them.

Milarepa's experience of practicing yogic teachings had gone through different phases; first the romantic notion of Marpa and then the heroic attitude of asceticism had to be used up. Milarepa discovered that he had made a commitment from which there was no stepping back. There was not only his commitment to the teachings but also a commitment to others. He had to learn to communicate with ordinary people who had not gone through the same experiences as himself. People began to discover that there was an extraordinary quality about Milarepa, a steadfast wildness, a quality of relating to basic sanity rather than to convention.

Nevertheless, he remained an ascetic because that physical situation had become part of his makeup. Since he was true to himself, he had no relative concept of other living styles and did not compare himself to others. Although he taught people with many different lifestyles, he had no desire to convert them and so remained true to his own style, even though the "trip" aspect had worn away.

Milarepa often mentioned how joyful it is that the phenomenal world can be seen as scriptures, "so I don't have to become a bookworm." The way he related to every situation in his life coincided with the teaching rather than being a result of a calculation in terms of the doctrine. This is ultimate yoga, where every happening is seen in the spectrum of the mandala. It is clear perception of anuttara yoga which can also be expressed in terms of mahamudra.

On the other hand, Milarepa, in the inspiration of his songs, did not romanticize the living quality of nature but just stated the facts of the natural occurrence in the situations of the moment.

> In the West, in the Ma Pam ocean, blue and vast,
> The Tangkar Nya (white-bellied fish) brings prosperity;
> She is the supreme dancer of the water-element,
> In a marvelous way she rolls her eyes.
> When she seeks delicious food,
> Do not harm her with a fish-hook!

Milarepa was not regarded as a poet from the scholarly point of view. At that time, Tibetans cultivated the Indian style of poetry which is long-winded and full of synonyms, its imagery involved with *Ramayana* and *Mahabharata* myths. But the ruggedness of Milarepa's literal poetry is comparable to the koan quality in the Zen tradition—purely stating the facts. The implications behind the facts are merely a shadow.

This mahamudra quality of literalness and simplicity in Milarepa's songs is thought-provoking. A simple person speaks a simple language as in the following song:

> If there be obstacles,
> It cannot be called space;
> If there be numbers,
> It cannot be called stars.
> One cannot say, "This is a mountain,"
> If it moves and shakes.
> It cannot be an ocean
> Should it grow or shrink.

One cannot be called a swimmer
If he needs a bridge.
It is not a rainbow
If it can be grasped.
These are the Six Outer Parables.

The practicality of Milarepa's wisdom is ageless because somebody experienced something and actually expressed it in the literal sense. His inspiration continues, without any conflicts. His teaching of mahamudra is liveable. Ordinary people like ourselves can keep up with the ruggedness and simplicity. This simplicity is applicable to the situation of transcending neurotic mind by using domestic language. It becomes profound without pretense, and this naturally provokes the actual practice of meditation at its simplest level and allows us to perceive the colorful and dramatic experiences of life.

GLOSSARY

THE DEFINITIONS given in this glossary are particular to their usage in this volume and should not be construed as the single or even most common meaning of a specific term.

abhisheka (Skt., "anointment"): A ceremony in which a student is ritually introduced into a mandala of a particular tantric deity by a tantric master and is thus empowered to visualize and invoke that particular deity. The essential element of abhisheka is a meeting of minds between master and student.

arhat (Skt., "worthy one"): One who has attained the highest level of hinayana.

ati (Skt., "great perfection"): The primary teaching of the Nyingma school of Tibetan Buddhism. This teaching is considered the final statement of the fruition path of vajrayana. It is called "great" because there is nothing more sublime; it is called "perfection" because no further means are necessary. According to the experience of ati practitioners, purity of mind is always present and needs only to be recognized.

Atisha Dipankara (980/90–1055 CE): A Buddhist scholar of royal family who particularly systematized the method for generating enlightened mind.

bhikshu (Skt.): Beggar; monk; male member of the Buddhist sangha who has entered homelessness and received full ordination.

bhumi (Skt., "land"): Each of the ten stages that a bodhisattva must go through to attain buddhahood: (1) very joyful; (2) stainless; (3) luminous; (4) radiant; (5) difficult to conquer; (6) face-to-face; (7) far-going; (8) immovable; (9) having good intellect; and (10) cloud of dharma.

bodhisattva (Skt., "awake being"): Someone who has completely overcome confusion and dedicated his or her life and all of his or her actions to awakening or liberating all sentient beings.

bodhisattva path: Another name for the mahayana.

buddha families: The mandala of the five buddha families represents five basic styles of energy, which could manifest dualistically as confusion or nondualistically as enlightenment. The enlightened mandala is portrayed iconographically as the mandala of the five tathagatas, or victorious ones. All experience is said to be colored by one of these five energies. The central, or buddha, family represents ignorance which can be transformed into the wisdom of all-encompassing space. In the east is the vajra family, representing aggression, which can be transformed into mirror-like wisdom. In the south is the ratna family, representing pride, which can be transformed into the wisdom of equanimity. In the west is the padma family of passion, which can be transformed into discriminating awareness wisdom. And in the north is the karma family of envy, which can be transformed into the wisdom that accomplishes all action.

buddha nature: According to the mahayana view, the true, immutable, and eternal nature of all beings. Since all beings possess this buddha nature, it is possible for them to attain enlightenment and become buddhas, regardless of what level of existence they occupy.

buddha principles: *See* buddha families.

buddhadharma (Skt.): The Buddha's teaching; Buddhism.

crazy wisdom (Tib. *yeshe chölwa*): Primordial wisdom that radiates out spontaneously to whatever situation is present, fulfilling the four enlightened actions of pacifying, enriching, magnetizing, and destroying. Crazy wisdom goes completely beyond convention. Thus, though the crazy-wisdom person's behavior may appear mad or outrageous to others, he or she always automatically destroys whatever needs to be destroyed and nurtures whatever needs to be cared for.

dharmakaya (Skt.): One of the three bodies of buddhahood. The dharmakaya is enlightenment itself, wisdom beyond any reference point—unoriginated primordial mind, devoid of content.

duhkha (Skt., "suffering"): *Duhkha satya*, "the truth of suffering," is the first of Buddha's four noble truths. The term refers to physical and psychological suffering of all kinds, including the subtle but all-pervading frustration we experience with regard to the impermanence and insubstantiality of all things.

hinayana (Skt.): The "lesser vehicle," in which the practitioner concentrates on basic meditation practice and an understanding of basic Buddhist doctrines such as the four noble truths.

jnana (Skt.): The wisdom activity of enlightenment, transcending all dualistic conceptualization.

Kagyü (Tib., "command lineage"): One of the four principal schools of Tibetan Buddhism. The Kagyü lineage is known as the practice or practicing lineage because of its emphasis on meditative discipline.

karmamudra (Skt.): A tantric practice using a consort as an object of meditation and devotion, seeing union with him or her as the embodiment of nondual wisdom.

mahamudra (Skt., "great seal/symbol/gesture"): The central meditative transmission of the Kagyü lineage. The inherent clarity and wakefulness of mind, which is both vivid and empty.

mahayana (Skt.): The "greater vehicle," which emphasizes the emptiness (shunyata) of all phenomena, compassion, and the acknowledgment of universal buddha nature. The ideal figure of the mahayana is the bodhisattva; hence, it is often referred to as the bodhisattva path.

mandala (Skt.): A total vision that unifies the seeming complexity and chaos of experience into a simple pattern and natural hierarchy. The Tibetan translation, *khyilkhor*, literally means "center and surroundings." A mandala is usually represented two-dimensionally as a four-sided diagram with a central deity, a personification of the basic sanity of buddha nature. Three-dimensionally, it is a palace with a center and four gates in the cardinal directions.

Manjushri (Skt., "He Who Is Noble and Gentle"): The bodhisattva of knowledge and learning; usually depicted holding a book and the sword of prajna.

mantra (Skt.): Mantras are Sanskrit words or syllables that are recited ritually as the quintessence of various energies. For instance, they can be used to attract particular energies or to repel obstructions.

mindfulness: To practice mindfulness in Buddhism means to bring attention to bear on all activities—including everyday, automatic activities such as breathing and walking. Mindfulness is associated in meditation with the practice of shamatha, which is based on paying attention to the breath and labeling thoughts as thinking, so that one experiences the basic space of mind.

Nagarjuna (second/third century): A great Indian teacher of Buddhism, the founder of the Madhyamaka school of Buddhist philosophy. He contributed greatly to the logical development of the doctrine of shunyata; was the author of many key texts; and, in legend, was the guru of various important Buddhist teachers who lived centuries apart.

nirmanakaya (Skt., "emanation body," "form body," or "body of manifestation"): Communication of awakened mind through form—specifically, through embodiment as a human being.

nirvana (Skt.): The idea of enlightenment according to the hinayana. It is the cessation of ignorance and conflicting emotions and therefore freedom from compulsive rebirth in samsara.

pandit (Skt., "scholar"): A scholar or learned person who studies and interprets sacred texts as an intellectual activity.

paramita (Skt., "that which has reached the other shore"): The six paramitas, or "perfections," are generosity, discipline, patience, exertion, meditation, and knowledge.

prajna (Skt., "transcendental knowledge"): Prajna, the sixth paramita, is called transcendental because it sees through the veils of dualistic confusion.

pranayama (Skt.): A form of yoga practiced in the vajrayana, which involves working with the illusory body by means of controlling mind, breath, and body.

Rangjung Dorje (1284–1339): The third Karmapa, spiritual leader of the Karma Kagyü lineage.

Rudra (Skt.): Originally a Hindu deity, an emanation of Shiva. In the vajrayana, Rudra is the personification of the destructive principle of ultimate ego. Traditionally, Rudra was a student who perverted the teachings, eventually killing his guru. Rudrahood is the complete opposite of buddhahood.

sadhana (Skt.): A ritual text, as well as the accompanying practice. Ranging from very simple to more elaborate versions, sadhanas engage the mind through meditation, the body through gestures (mudras), and the speech through mantra recitation.

samaya (Skt., "coming together"): The vajrayana principle of commitment, whereby the student is bound completely to the discipline, to the teacher, and to his or her own sanity.

sambhogakaya (Skt., "enjoyment body"): The environment of compassion and communication linking the dharmakaya and the nirmanakaya.

samsara (Skt., "journeying"): The vicious cycle of transmigratory existence. It arises out of ignorance and is characterized by suffering.

Saraha (ninth century CE): An Indian teacher referred to in Tibetan texts as "Great Brahmin." Tradition has it that he was born 336 years after the Buddha's death and that he was the spiritual master of Nagarjuna.

shunyata (Skt., "emptiness" or "void"): A completely open and unbounded clarity of mind.

siddha (Skt., "perfect" or "complete"): One who possesses siddhis, or perfect abilities. There are eight ordinary siddhis: indomitability, the ability to see the gods, fleetness of foot, invisibility, longevity, the ability to fly, the ability to make certain medicines, and power over the world of spirits and demons. The single "supreme" siddhi is enlightenment.

skandha (Skt., "group," "aggregate," or "heap"): Each of the five aggregates, which constitute the entirety of what is generally known as "personality." They are form, sensation, perception, mental formations, and consciousness. These are frequently referred to as "aggregates of attachment," since (except in the case of arhats and buddhas) craving or desire attaches itself to them and attracts them to itself; thus, it makes of them objects of attachment and brings about suffering.

skillful means: *See* upaya.

spiritual materialism: "Walking the spiritual path properly is a very subtle process; it is not something to jump into naively. There are numerous sidetracks which lead to a distorted, ego-centered version of spirituality; we can deceive ourselves into thinking we are developing spiritually when instead we are strengthening our egocentricity through spiritual techniques. This fundamental distortion may be referred to as spiritual materialism" (Chögyam Trungpa).

tantra (Skt.): A synonym for *vajrayana*, the third of the three yanas of Tibetan Buddhism. Tantra means continuity and refers both to the root texts of the vajrayana and to the systems of meditation they describe.

trikaya (Skt., "three bodies"): The three bodies of buddhahood. The dharmakaya is enlightenment itself, wisdom beyond any reference point— unoriginated primordial mind, devoid of content. The sambhogakaya is the environment of compassion and communication. The nirmanakaya is the buddha that actually takes form as a human, who eats, sleeps, and shares his life with his students.

Tripitaka (Skt., "three baskets"): The canon of Buddhist scriptures, consisting of three parts: the Vinaya-pitaka, the Sutra-pitaka, and the Abhidharma-pitaka. The first "basket" contains accounts of the origins of the Buddhist community (sangha) as well as the rules of discipline regulating the lives of monks and nuns. The second is composed of discourse said to have come from the mouth of the Buddha or his immediate disciples. The third part is a compendium of Buddhist psychology and philosophy.

upaya (Skt.): Skill in means or method. **1.** The ability of a bodhisattva to guide beings to liberation through skillful means. All possible methods and ruses from straightforward talk to the most conspicuous miracles could be applicable. **2.** Skill in expounding the teaching.

vajrayana (Skt., "diamond vehicle"): The third of the three main yanas of Tibetan Buddhism. Vajrayana is also known as the sudden path, because it is claimed that through the practice of vajrayana, one can realize enlightenment in one lifetime.

Vajrayogini (Skt.): A semiwrathful yidam. She is red, with one face and two arms, young and beautiful, but enraged and wearing ornaments of human bones. She represents the transformation of ignorance and passion into shunyata and compassion.

vihara (Skt., "sojourning place"): A residence for monks, to which they can also retire for meditation.

vipashyana (Skt., "insight" or "clear seeing"): With shamatha ("tranquillity"), one of the two main modes of meditation common to all forms of Buddhism.

yana (Skt., "vehicle"): A coherent body of intellectual teachings and practical meditative methods related to a particular stage of a student's progress on the path of buddhadharma. The three main vehicles are the hinayana, mahayana, and vajrayana. These can also be subdivided to make nine yanas.

yidam (Tib., "firm mind"): The vajrayana practitioner's personal deity, who embodies the practitioner's awakened nature. Yidams are usually sambhogakaya buddhas.

SOURCES

"The Art of Milarepa." *Garuda II: Working with Negativity.* Barnet, Vt.: Tail of the Tiger, 1972, 12–16. © 1972 by Diana J. Mukpo.

Colophon by Chögyam Trungpa in *The Rain of Wisdom: The Essence of the Ocean of True Meaning.* Translated by the Nālandā Translation Committee under the direction of Chögyam Trungpa. Boston: Shambhala Publications, 1999, 290–92. © 1980 by Diana J. Mukpo.

Crazy Wisdom. Edited by Sherab Chödzin. Boston: Shambhala Publications, 1991. ©1991 by Diana J. Mukpo.

"Explanation of the Vajra Guru Mantra." © 2004 by Diana J. Mukpo. Unpublished article.

Foreword to *The Rain of Wisdom: The Essence of the Ocean of True Meaning.* Translated by the Nālandā Translation Committee under the direction of Chögyam Trungpa. Boston: Shambhala Publications, 1999, xi–xv. ©1980 by Diana J. Mukpo.

Foreword to *The Torch of Certainty* by Jamgon Kongtrul the Great. Translated from the Tibetan by Judith Hanson. Boston: Shambhala Publications, 2000, p. i. ©1977 by Judith Hanson and Shambhala Publications, Inc.

"Hum: An Approach to Mantra." *Garuda II: Working with Negativity.* Barnet, Vt.: Tail of the Tiger, 1972, 9–11. © 1972 by Diana J. Mukpo.

Illusion's Game: The Life and Teaching of Naropa. Edited by Sherab Chödzin. Boston: Shambhala Publications, 1994. ©1994 by Diana J. Mukpo.

"Joining Energy and Space." *The Shambhala Sun* 9, no. 5 (May 2001): 63–65, 70. © 2001 by Diana J. Mukpo. Excerpted and arranged by Carolyn Rose Gimian from material in *The Sadhana of Mahamudra Sourcebook* (Halifax: Vajradhatu Publications, 2000). © 1979 by Diana J. Mukpo.

"The Line of the Trungpas: Talk One, The Practicing Lineage." *The Shambhala Centre Banner* 11 (April 1997): 1, 15–16. © 1997 by Diana J. Mukpo.

"The Line of the Trungpas: Talk Two: The Mishap Lineage." *The Shambhala Centre Banner* 11 (June 1997): 1, 16–18. © 1997 by Diana J. Mukpo.

"Milarepa: A Synopsis." Unpublished article. © 2004 by Diana J. Mukpo.

"Milarepa: A Warrior's Life." Unpublished article. © 2004 by Diana J. Mukpo.

"Practice of the Four Foundations," in the introduction to *The Torch of Certainty* by Jamgön Kongtrül the Great. Translated from the Tibetan by Judith Hanson. Boston: Shambhala Publications, 2000, pp. 9–24. ©1977 by Judith Hanson and Shambhala Publications, Inc. The introduction contains interviews with Kalu Rinpoche and Deshung Rinpoche, as well as Chögyam Trungpa Rinpoche. Trungpa Rinpoche's answers have been excerpted from the larger document.

Preface to *The Life of Marpa the Translator: Seeing Accomplishes All* by Tsang Nyön Heruka. Translated by the Nālandā Translation Committee under the direction of Chögyam Trungpa. Boston: Shambhala Publications, 1995, pp. xiv–xv. ©1982 by Diana J. Mukpo.

Selections from *The Sadhana of Mahamudra: Which Quells the Mighty Warring of the Three Lords of Materialism and Brings Realization of the Ocean of Siddhas of the Practice Lineage* (selections), *The Shambhala Sun* 3 (May 2001): 66–69. Translated from the Tibetan by Chögyam Trungpa. © 1968, 1976, 1990 by Diana J. Mukpo.

The Songs of Chögyam Trungpa in *The Rain of Wisdom: The Essence of the Ocean of True Meaning*. Translated by the Nālandā Translation Committee under the direction of Chögyam Trungpa. Boston: Shambhala Publications, 1999, pp. 285–289. ©1980 by Diana J. Mukpo.

"Teachings on the Tulku Principle." *The Shambhala Sun* (May/June 1992): 25. © 1974 by Diana J. Mukpo.

Translator's Colophon from *The Life of Marpa the Translator: Seeing Accomplishes All* by Tsang Nyön Heruka. Translated by the Nālandā Translation Committee under the direction of Chögyam Trungpa. Boston: Shambhala Publications, 1995, 205–206. ©1982 by Diana J. Mukpo.

ACKNOWLEDGMENTS

MANY PEOPLE PLAYED A ROLE in the creation of the works by Chögyam Trungpa that appear in Volume Five of *The Collected Works*. Thanks
are due to Sherab Chödzin Kohn, who edited both *Crazy Wisdom* and *Illusion's Game*. Overall, Sherab has made a major and distinguished contribu-
tion to the published works of Chögyam Trungpa. His work as an editor
of Trungpa Rinpoche's material goes back to the earliest years that Rinpoche was in America and has continued up to the present day, spanning
more than three decades. Following Rinpoche's death in 1987, Sherab took
a leading role, along with Judith Lief, in editing material for the Dharma
Ocean Series. *Crazy Wisdom* and *Illusion's Game* were both edited for that
series, *Crazy Wisdom* being the first posthumous volume in the series.

While the contributions of the Nālandā Translation Committee are discussed in the introduction to Volume Five, it seems appropriate to thank
the members once again in these acknowledgments and to acknowledge as
well the ongoing efforts of all the many dedicated contemporary translators
who work on bringing the sacred texts and teachings of Tibetan Buddhism
into the English language. Without the benefit of good translations, Westerners would have a much more difficult time gaining a true understanding
of the Buddhist teachings. As practitioners, we would be in the dark, often
confused by the inability to practice these teachings in our native tongue.[1]

Chögyam Trungpa involved many of his Western students in the translation of material from Tibetan to English, even some who knew nothing
about the Tibetan language. This was the case with Richard Arthure, who

---

1. Some Tibetan teachers prefer to have their students practice texts in the original Tibetan. Even in these cases, however, a simultaneous translation is usually printed under-
neath the Tibetan, so that a Westerner will know the meaning of what they are chanting.

worked with Rinpoche on the translation of *The Sadhana of Mahamudra* in Bhutan in 1968, while knowing barely a word of Tibetan. Owing to Richard's training in and sensitivity to the English language and to his connection with Trungpa Rinpoche, the translation the two of them produced has survived the test of time. I also would like to acknowledge the efforts of Judith Hanson, who translated *The Torch of Certainty,* an important text of the Kagyü lineage on the practice of the four foundations, or the ngöndro. Her book, in addition to including the excellent interviews she conducted with Chögyam Trungpa and two other important Kagyü teachers, also provides an excellent resource for students embarking on the practice of ngöndro themselves.

For help in preparing Volume Five, I would also like to thank Larry Mermelstein and Scott Wellenbach of the Nālandā Translation Committee for their generosity in reading and commenting on the introduction to this volume and for helping me with Tibetan spellings in the manuscript. I would also like to thank the Shambhala Archives for preserving the articles written by Chögyam Trungpa. I found the unpublished articles that appear in Volume Five in the files at the Archives. As well, I would like to thank Kendra Crossen Burroughs, my editor at Shambhala Publications for *The Collected Works of Chögyam Trungpa.* In the beginning, Emily Hilburn Sell served as the editor for this project; Eden Steinberg helped in the editorial process as well. However, the project found its final editorial home with Kendra. She is a thoroughly delightful person to work with. I am always impressed by the level of detail to which she pays attention—seemingly quite effortlessly. That tireless approach to detail is so necessary for this project. Without her, I think I would have felt quite lost at times. I would also like to thank Peter Turner, the president at Shambhala, and Jonathan Green, the associate publisher, for their input and help in shaping the project in the early phases. And thanks to Helen Berliner for the index and to Dede Cummings, Steve Dyer, and Hazel Bercholz for the design of the book.

Of course, the primary "creator" of the material in Volume Five was Chögyam Trungpa himself. His teachings on lineage and devotion are certainly among his most important contributions to the development of Buddhism in the West. It is impossible to offer adequate thanks to him, both for the teachings themselves and for the personal example he provided—as both a devoted student and as a true and brilliant holder of his lineage. I also would like to thank his family, in particular Diana J. Mukpo, for their ongoing commitment to the publication of Rinpoche's dharma teachings.

A BIOGRAPHY OF
CHÖGYAM TRUNGPA

THE VENERABLE CHÖGYAM TRUNGPA was born in the province of Kham in eastern Tibet in 1939. When be was just thirteen months old, Chögyam Trungpa was recognized as a major tulku, or incarnate teacher. According to Tibetan tradition, an enlightened teacher is capable, based on his or her vow of compassion, of reincarnating in human form over a succession of generations. Before dying, such a teacher may leave a letter or other clues to the whereabouts of the next incarnation. Later, students and other realized teachers look through these clues and, based on those plus a careful examination of dreams and visions, conduct searches to discover and recognize the successor. Thus, particular lines of teaching are formed, in some cases extending over many centuries. Chögyam Trungpa was the eleventh in the teaching lineage known as the Trungpa Tulkus.

Once young tulkus are recognized, they enter a period of intensive training in the theory and practice of the Buddhist teachings. Trungpa Rinpoche, after being enthroned as supreme abbot of Surmang Monastery and governor of Surmang District, began a period of training that would last eighteen years, until his departure from Tibet in 1959. As a Kagyü tulku, his training was based on the systematic practice of meditation and on refined theoretical understanding of Buddhist philosophy. One of the four great lineages of Tibet, the Kagyü is known as the practicing (or practice) lineage.

At the age of eight, Trungpa Rinpoche received ordination as a novice monk. Following this, he engaged in intensive study and practice of the traditional monastic disciplines, including traditional Tibetan poetry and monastic dance. His primary teachers were Jamgön Kongtrül of Sechen and Khenpo Gangshar—leading teachers in the Nyingma and Kagyü lineages. In 1958, at the age of eighteen, Trungpa Rinpoche completed his studies, receiving the degrees of kyorpön (doctor of divinity) and khenpo (master of studies). He also received full monastic ordination. The late 1950s were a time of great upheaval in Tibet. As it became clear that the Chinese communists intended to take over the country by force, many people, both monastic and lay, fled the country. Trungpa Rinpoche spent many harrowing months trekking over the Himalayas (described later in his book *Born in Tibet*). After narrowly escaping capture by the Chinese, he at last reached India in 1959. While in India, Trungpa Rinpoche was appointed to serve as spiritual adviser to the Young Lamas Home School in Delhi, India. He served in this capacity from 1959 to 1963.

Trungpa Rinpoche's opportunity to emigrate to the West came when he received a Spaulding sponsorship to attend Oxford University. At Oxford he studied comparative religion, philosophy, history, and fine arts. He also studied Japanese flower arranging, receiving a degree from the Sogetsu School. While in England, Trungpa Rinpoche began to instruct Western students in the dharma, and in 1967 he founded the Samye Ling Meditation Center in Dumfriesshire, Scotland. During this period, he also published his first two books, both in English: *Born in Tibet* (1966) and *Meditation in Action* (1969).

In 1968 Trungpa Rinpoche traveled to Bhutan, where he entered into a solitary meditation retreat. While on retreat, Rinpoche received[2] a pivotal text for all of his teaching in the West, "The Sadhana of Mahamudra," a text that documents the spiritual degeneration of modern times and its antidote, genuine spirituality that leads to the experience of naked and luminous mind. This retreat marked a pivotal change in his approach to teaching. Soon after returning to England, he became a layperson, putting aside his monastic robes and dressing in ordinary Western attire. In 1970 he married a young Englishwoman, Diana Pybus, and to-

---

2. In Tibet, there is a well-documented tradition of teachers discovering or "receiving" texts that are believed to have been buried, some of them in the realm of space, by Padmasambhava, who is regarded as the father of Buddhism in Tibet. Teachers who find what Padmasambhava left hidden for the beings of future ages, which may be objects or physical texts hidden in rocks, lakes, and other locations, are referred to as tertöns, and the materials they find are known as terma. Chgyam Trungpa was already known as a tertön in Tibet.

gether they left Scotland and moved to North America. Many of his early students and his Tibetan colleagues found these changes shocking and upsetting. However, he expressed a conviction that in order for the dharma to take root in the West, it needed to be taught free from cultural trappings and religious fascination.

During the seventies, America was in a period of political and cultural ferment. It was a time of fascination with the East. Nevertheless, almost from the moment he arrived in America, Trungpa Rinpoche drew many students to him who were seriously interested in the Buddhist teachings and the practice of meditation. However, he severely criticized the materialistic approach to spirituality that was also quite prevalent, describing it as a "spiritual supermarket." In his lectures, and in his books *Cutting Through Spiritual Materialism* (1973) and *The Myth of Freedom* (1976), he pointed to the simplicity and directness of the practice of sitting meditation as the way to cut through such distortions of the spiritual journey.

During his seventeen years of teaching in North America, Trungpa Rinpoche developed a reputation as a dynamic and controversial teacher. He was a pioneer, one of the first Tibetan Buddhist teachers in North America, preceding by some years and indeed facilitating the later visits by His Holiness the Karmapa, His Holiness Khyentse Rinpoche, His Holiness the Dalai Lama, and many others. In the United States, he found a spiritual kinship with many Zen masters who were already presenting Buddhist meditation. In the very early days, he particularly connected with Suzuki Roshi, the founder of Zen Center in San Francisco. In later years he was close with Kobun Chino Roshi and Bill Kwong Roshi in northern California; with Maezumi Roshi, the founder of the Los Angeles Zen Center; and with Eido Roshi, abbot of the New York Zendo Shobo-ji .

Fluent in the English language, Chögyam Trungpa was one of the first Tibetan Buddhist teachers who could speak to Western students directly, without the aid of a translator. Traveling extensively throughout North America and Europe, he gave thousands of talks and hundred of seminars. He established major centers in Vermont, Colorado, and Nova Scotia, as well as many smaller meditation and study centers in cities throughout North America and Europe. Vajradhatu was formed in 1973 as the central administrative body of this network.

In 1974 Trungpa Rinpoche founded the Naropa Institute (now Naropa University), which became the first and only accredited Buddhist-inspired university in North America. He lectured extensively at the institute, and his book *Journey without Goal* (1981) is based on a course he taught there. In 1976 he established the Shambhala Training program, a series of seminars that present a nonsectarian path of spiritual warriorship grounded in the practice of sitting meditation. His book *Shambhala: The Sacred Path of the Warrior* (1984) gives an overview of the Shambhala teachings.

In 1976 Trungpa Rinpoche appointed Ösel Tendzin (Thomas F. Rich) as his Vajra Regent, or dharma heir. Ösel Tendzin worked closely with Trungpa Rinpoche in the administration of Vajradhatu and Shambhala Training. He taught extensively from 1976 until his death in 1990 and is the author of *Buddha in the Palm of Your Hand*.

Trungpa Rinpoche was also active in the field of translation. Working with Francesca Fremantle, he rendered a new translation of the *Tibetan Book of the Dead*, which was published in 1975. Later he formed the Nālandā Translation Committee in order to translate texts and liturgies for his own students as well as to make important texts available publicly.

In 1979 Trungpa Rinpoche conducted a ceremony empowering his eldest son, Ösel Rangdröl Mukpo, as his successor in the Shambhala lineage. At that time he gave him the title of Sawang ("Earth Lord").

Trungpa Rinpoche was also known for his interest in the arts and particularly for his insights into the relationship between contemplative discipline and the artistic process. Two books published since his death— *The Art of Calligraphy* (1994) and *Dharma Art* (1996)—present this aspect of his work. His own artwork included calligraphy, painting, flower arranging, poetry, playwriting, and environmental installations. In addition, at the Naropa Institute he created an educational atmosphere that attracted many leading artists and poets. The exploration of the creative process in light of contemplative training continues there as a provocative dialogue. Trungpa Rinpoche also published two books of poetry: *Mudra* (1972) and *First Thought Best Thought* (1983). In 1998 a retrospective compilation of his poetry, *Timely Rain*, was published.

Shortly before his death, in a meeting with Samuel Bercholz, the publisher of Shambhala Publications, Chögyam Trungpa expressed his interest in publishing 108 volumes of his teachings, to be called the Dharma Ocean Series. "Dharma Ocean" is the translation of Chögyam Trungpa's Tibetan teaching name, Chökyi Gyatso. The Dharma Ocean Series was to consist primarily of material edited to allow readers to encounter this rich array of teachings simply and directly rather than in an overly systematized or condensed form. In 1991 the first posthumous volume in the series, *Crazy Wisdom*, was published, and since then another seven volumes have appeared.

Trungpa Rinpoche's published books represent only a fraction of the rich legacy of his teachings. During his seventeen years of teaching in North America, he crafted the structures necessary to provide his students with thorough, systematic training in the dharma. From introductory talks and courses to advanced group retreat practices, these programs emphasized a balance of study and practice, of intellect and intuition. *Trungpa* by Fabrice Midal, a French biography (forthcoming in English translation under the title *Chögyam Trungpa*), details the many forms of training that Chögyam Trungpa developed. Since Trungpa Rinpoche's death, there have been significant changes in the training offered by the organizations he founded. However, many of the original structures remain in place, and students can pursue their interest in meditation and the Buddhist path through these many forms of training. Senior students of Trungpa Rinpoche continue to be involved in both teaching and meditation instruction in such programs.

In addition to his extensive teachings in the Buddhist tradition, Trungpa Rinpoche also placed great emphasis on the Shambhala teachings, which stress the importance of meditation in action, synchronizing mind and body, and training oneself to approach obstacles or challenges in everyday life with the courageous attitude of a warrior, without anger. The goal of creating an enlightened society is fundamental to the Shambhala teachings. According to the Shambhala approach, the realization of an enlightened society comes not purely through outer activity, such as community or political involvement, but from appreciation of the senses and the sacred dimension of day-to-day life. A second volume of these teachings, entitled *Great Eastern Sun*, was published in 1999.

Chögyam Trungpa died in 1987, at the age of forty-seven. By the time of his death, he was known not only as Rinpoche ("Precious Jewel") but also as Vajracharya ("Vajra Holder") and as Vidyadhara ("Wisdom Holder") for his role as a master of the vajrayana, or tantric teachings of Buddhism. As a holder of the Shambhala teachings, he had also received the titles of Dorje Dradül ("Indestructible Warrior") and Sakyong ("Earth Protector"). He is survived by his wife, Diana Judith Mukpo, and five sons. His eldest son, the Sawang Ösel Rangdröl Mukpo, succeeds him as the spiritual head of Vajradhatu. Acknowledging the importance of the Shambhala teachings to his father's work, the Sawang changed the name of the umbrella organization to Shambhala, with Vajradhatu remaining one of its major divisions. In 1995 the Sawang received the Shambhala title of Sakyong like his father before him and was also confirmed as an incarnation of the great ecumenical teacher Mipham Rinpoche.

Trungpa Rinpoche is widely acknowledged as a pivotal figure in introducing the buddhadharma to the Western world. He joined his great appreciation for Western culture with his deep understanding of his own tradition. This led to a revolutionary approach to teaching the dharma, in which the most ancient and profound teachings were presented in a thoroughly contemporary way. Trungpa Rinpoche was known for his fearless proclamation of the dharma: free from hesitation, true to the purity of the tradition, and utterly fresh. May these teachings take root and flourish for the benefit of all sentient beings.

BOOKS BY CHÖGYAM TRUNGPA

Born in Tibet (George Allen & Unwin, 1966; Shambhala Publications, 1977)

Chögyam Trungpa's account of his upbringing and education as an incarnate lama in Tibet and the powerful story of his escape to India. An epilogue added in 1976 details Trungpa Rinpoche's time in England in the 1960s and his early years in North America.

Meditation in Action (Shambhala Publications, 1969)

Using the life of the Buddha as a starting point, this classic on meditation and the practice of compassion explores the six paramitas, or enlightened actions on the Buddhist path. Its simplicity and directness make this an appealing book for beginners and seasoned meditators alike.

Mudra (Shambhala Publications, 1972)

This collection of poems mostly written in the 1960s in England also includes two short translations of Buddhist texts and a commentary on the Ox-Herding Pictures, well-known metaphors for the journey on the Buddhist path.

Cutting Through Spiritual Materialism (Shambhala Publications, 1973)

The first volume of Chögyam Trungpa's teaching in America is still fresh, outrageous, and up to date. It describes landmarks on the Buddhist path and focuses on the pitfalls of materialism that plague the modern age.

The Dawn of Tantra, by Herbert V. Guenther and Chögyam Trungpa (Shambhala Publications, 1975)

Jointly authored by Chögyam Trungpa and Buddhist scholar Herbert V. Guenther, this volume presents an introduction to the Buddhist teachings of tantra.

Glimpses of Abhidharma (Shambhala Publications, 1975)

An exploration of the five skandhas, or stages in the development of ego, based on an early seminar given by Chögyam Trungpa. The final chapter on auspicious coincidence is a penetrating explanation of karma and the true experience of spiritual freedom.

The Tibetan Book of the Dead: The Great Liberation through Hearing in the Bardo, translated with commentary by Francesca Fremantle and Chögyam Trungpa (Shambhala Publications, 1975)

Chögyam Trungpa and Francesca Fremantle collaborated on the translation of this important text by Guru Rinpoche, as discovered by Karma Lingpa, and are coauthors of this title. Trungpa Rinpoche provides a powerful commentary on death and dying and on the text itself, which allows modern readers to find the relevance of this ancient guide to the passage from life to death and back to life again.

The Myth of Freedom and the Way of Meditation (Shambhala Publications, 1976)

In short, pithy chapters that exemplify Chögyam Trungpa's hard-hitting and compelling teaching style, this book explores the meaning of freedom and genuine spirituality in the context of traveling the Buddhist path.

The Rain of Wisdom (Shambhala Publications, 1980)

An extraordinary collection of the poetry or songs of the teachers of the Kagyü lineage of Tibetan Buddhism, to which Chögyam Trungpa belonged. The text was translated by the Nālandā Translation Committee under the direction of Chögyam Trungpa. The volume includes an extensive glossary of Buddhist terms.

Journey without Goal: The Tantric Wisdom of the Buddha (Shambhala Publications, 1981)

Based on an early seminar at the Naropa Institute, this guide to the tantric teachings of Buddhism is provocative and profound, emphasizing both the dangers and the wisdom of the vajrayana, the diamond path of Buddhism.

The Life of Marpa the Translator (Shambhala Publications, 1982)
A renowned teacher of the Tibetan Buddhist tradition who combined scholarship and meditative realization, Marpa made three arduous journeys to India to collect the teachings of the Kagyü lineage and bring them to Tibet. Chögyam Trungpa and the Nālandā Translation Committee have produced an inspiring translation of his life's story.

First Thought Best Thought: 108 Poems (Shambhala Publications, 1983)
This collection consists mainly of poetry written during Chögyam Trungpa's first ten years in North America, showing his command of the American idiom, his understanding of American culture, as well as his playfulness and his passion. Some poems from earlier years were also included. Many of the poems from *First Thought Best Thought* were later reprinted in *Timely Rain*.

Shambhala: The Sacred Path of the Warrior (Shambhala Publications, 1984)
Chögyam Trungpa's classic work on the path of warriorship still offers timely advice. This book shows how an attitude of fearlessness and open heart provides the courage to meet the challenges of modern life.

Crazy Wisdom (Shambhala Publications, 1991)
Two seminars from the 1970s were edited for this volume on the life and teachings of Guru Rinpoche, or Padmasambhava, the founder of Buddhism in Tibet.

The Heart of the Buddha (Shambhala Publications, 1991)
This collection of essays, talks, and seminars presents the teachings of Budddhism as they relate to everyday life.

Orderly Chaos: The Mandala Principle (Shambhala Publications, 1991)
The mandala is often thought of as a Buddhist drawing representing tantric iconography. However, Chögyam Trungpa explores how both confusion and enlightenment are made up of patterns of orderly chaos

that are the basis for the principle of mandala. A difficult but rewarding discussion of the topic of chaos and its underlying structure.

Secret Beyond Thought: The Five Chakras and the Four Karmas (Vajradhatu Publications, 1991)

Two talks from an early seminar on the principles of the chakras and the karmas, teachings from the Buddhist tantric tradition.

The Lion's Roar: An Introduction to Tantra (Shambhala Publications, 1992)

An in-depth presentation of the nine yanas, or stages, of the path in the Tibetan Buddhist tradition. Particularly interesting are the chapters on visualization and the five buddha families.

Transcending Madness: The Experience of the Six Bardos (Shambhala Publications, 1992)

The editor of this volume, Judith L. Lief, calls it "a practical guide to Buddhist psychology." The book is based on two early seminars on the intertwined ideas of bardo (or the gap in experience and the gap between death and birth) and the six realms of being.

Training the Mind and Cultivating Loving-Kindness (Shambhala Publications, 1993)

This volume presents fifty-nine slogans, or aphorisms related to meditation practice, which show a practical path to making friends with oneself and developing compassion for others, through the practice of sacrificing self-centeredness for the welfare of others.

Glimpses of Shunyata (Vajradhatu Publications, 1993)

These four lectures on the principle of shunyata, or emptiness, are an experiential exploration of the ground, path, and fruition of realizing this basic principle of mahayana Buddhism.

The Art of Calligraphy: Joining Heaven and Earth (Shambhala Publications, 1994)

Chögyam Trungpa's extensive love affair with brush and ink is showcased in this book, which also includes an introduction to dharma art and a discussion of the Eastern principles of heaven, earth, and man as applied to the creative process. The beautiful reproductions of fifty-four calligraphies are accompanied by inspirational quotations from the author's works.

Illusion's Game: The Life and Teaching of Naropa (Shambhala Publications, 1994)

The great Indian teacher Naropa was a renowned master of the teachings of mahamudra, an advanced stage of realization in Tibetan Buddhism. This book presents Chögyam Trungpa's teachings on Naropa's life and arduous search for enlightenment.

The Path Is the Goal: A Basic Handbook of Buddhist Meditation (Shambhala Publications, 1995)

A simple and practical manual for the practice of meditation that evokes the author's penetrating insight and colorful language.

Dharma Art (Shambhala Publications, 1996)

Chögyam Trungpa was a calligrapher, painter, poet, designer, and photographer as well as a master of Buddhist meditation. Drawn from his many seminars and talks on the artistic process, this work presents his insights into art and the artist.

Timely Rain: Selected Poetry of Chögyam Trungpa (Shambhala Publications, 1998)

With a foreword by Allen Ginsberg, this collection of poems was organized thematically by editor David I. Rome to show the breadth of the poet's work. Core poems from *Mudra* and *First Thought Best Thought* are reprinted here, along with many poems and "sacred songs" published here for the first time.

Great Eastern Sun: The Wisdom of Shambhala (Shambhala Publications, 1999)

This sequel and complement to *Shambhala: The Sacred Path of the Warrior* offers more heartfelt wisdom on Shambhala warriorship.

Glimpses of Space: The Feminine Principle and Evam (Vajradhatu Publications, 1999)

Two seminars on the tantric understanding of the feminine and masculine principles, what they are and how they work together in vajrayana Buddhist practice as the nondual experience of wisdom and skillful means.

The Essential Chögyam Trungpa (Shambhala Publications, 2000)
This concise overview of Trungpa Rinpoche's teachings consists of forty selections from fourteen different books, articulating the secular path of the Shambhala warrior as well as the Buddhist path of meditation and awakening.

Glimpses of Mahayana (Vajradhatu Publications, 2001)
This little volume focuses on the attributes of buddha nature, the development of compassion, and the experience of being a practitioner on the bodhisattva path of selfless action to benefit others.

RESOURCES

FOR INFORMATION regarding meditation instruction or inquiries about a practice center near you, please contact one of the following:

SHAMBHALA INTERNATIONAL
1084 Tower Road
Halifax, NS
B3H 2Y5 Canada
Telephone: (902) 425-4275, ext. 10
Fax: (902) 423-2750
Website: www.shambhala.org (This website contains information about the more than 100 meditation centers affiliated with Shambhala, the international network of Buddhist practice centers established by Chögyam Trungpa.)

SHAMBHALA EUROPE
Annostrasse 27
50678 Cologne, Germany
Telephone: 49-0-700-108-000-00
E-mail: europe@shambhala.org
Website: www.shambhala-europe.org

DORJE DENMA LING
2280 Balmoral Road
Tatamagouche, NS
B0K 1V0 Canada
Telephone: (902) 657-9085
Fax: (902) 657-0462

E-mail: info@dorjedenmaling.com
Website: www.dorjedenmaling.com

KARMÊ CHÖLING
369 Patneaude Lane
Barnet, VT 05821
Telephone: (802) 633-2384
Fax: (802) 633-3012
E-mail: karmecholing@shambhala.org

SHAMBHALA MOUNTAIN CENTER
4921 Country Road 68C
Red Feather Lakes, CO 80545
Telephone: (970) 881-2184
Fax: (970) 881-2909
E-mail: shambhalamountain@shambhala.org

SKY LAKE LODGE
P.O. Box 408
Rosendale, NY 12472
Telephone: (845) 658-8556
E-mail: skylake@shambhala.org
Website: http://ny.shambhala.org/skylake

DECHEN CHÖLING
Mas Marvent
87700 St Yrieix sous Aixe
France
Telephone: 33 (0)5-55-03-55-52
Fax: 33 (0)5-55-03-91-74
E-mail: dechencholing@dechencholing.org

Audio and video tape recordings of talks and seminars by Chögyam Trungpa
are available from:

KALAPA RECORDINGS
1678 Barrington Street, 2nd Floor
Halifax, NS
B3J 2A2 Canada
Telephone: (902) 421-1550

Fax: (902) 423-2750
E-mail: shop@shambhala.org
Website: www.shambhalashop.com

For publications from Shambhala International, please contact:

VAJRADHATU PUBLICATIONS
1678 Barrington Street, 2nd Floor
Halifax, NS
B3J 2A2 Canada
Telephone: (902) 421-1550
E-mail: shop@shambhala.org
Website: www.shambhalashop.com

For information about the archive of the author's work—which includes
more than 5,000 audio recordings, 1,000 video recordings, original Tibetan
manuscripts, correspondence, and more than 30,000 photographs—please
contact:

THE SHAMBHALA ARCHIVES
1084 Tower Road
Halifax, NS
B3H 3S3 Canada
Telephone: (902) 421-1550
Website: www.shambhalashop.com/archives

The *Shambhala Sun* is a bimonthly Buddhist magazine founded by Chögyam
Trungpa. For a subscription or sample copy, contact:

SHAMBHALA SUN
P. O. Box 3377
Champlain, NY 12919-9871
Telephone: (877) 786-1950
Website: www.shambhalasun.com

Buddhadharma: The Practitioner's Quarterly is an in-depth, practice-oriented
journal offering teachings from all Buddhist traditions. For a subscription or
sample copy, contact:

BUDDHADHARMA
P. O. Box 3377
Champlain, NY 12919-9871

Telephone: (877) 786-1950
Website: www.thebuddhadharma.com

Naropa University is the only accredited, Buddhist-inspired university in North America. For more information, contact:

Naropa University
2130 Arapahoe Avenue
Boulder, CO 80302
Telephone: (303) 444-0202
Website: www.naropa.edu

INDEX

All books, articles, poems, and seminars are attributed to Chögyam Trungpa unless otherwise cited. Owing to the subtle content of the poems, only their titles have been indexed. Illustrations are indicated by italics and follow text entries. Books in translation are cited to translators; Nālandā Translation Committee appears as (NTC). Books and seminars contained within this volume are indicated by initial page number followed by ff.

Vidyadhara
  definition of, 39, 43
  eternity as first stage of, 40
Vikramanshila University, 370
Vipashyana meditation, 233, 382
Vision(s)
  panoramic, 180
  prajna, 339
  total, 289
  See also Naropa, trials/visions of
Visualization practice, 262, 266–267,
    331–332
  developing stage of meditation and,
    332
  shunyata and, 266
  theism and, 267
  training for, 332

Wakefulness, state of, 265
  as "blade of sword of prajna," 218
Wangchuk (Bhutan), King Jigme
    Singye, xxii
Warriorship, 349–350
  gentleness of dharmic, 349
  of Milarepa, 349–350
  nonaggression as essence of, 349
  Shambhala, 359
  training and fruition of, 349
Watcher
  ego as, 177–178
  enlightenment and, 177
  intellect without, 126–127
  as sense of continuity, 177
  tenth bhumi vs., 270
Watts, Alan, 177
Well-being, 208, 270–271
  appreciation and, 261
  sacredness and, 261
Western practitioners of Buddhism,
    training of, 266–267
Wisdom(s)
  coemergent, 249–249
  devotion and, 313
  ego as fuel for, 190
  five buddha family, 319
  hidden, treasures, 142–143

of phenomenal world, xxviii
  practicality of Milarepa, 375
  prajna vs., 212
  thought process as, of deities, 262
  as vajra reference point, 270
  See also Crazy wisdom
Words vs. sense, 161–162, 173, 230
  prajna and jnana and, 230
Workability of experience, 251
  compassion and, 271
World
  communication with, 238, 347
  of duality, 312
  magical aspect of, 234–235
  materialistic, 310
  offering geography of, 330–331
  penetration of, 110
  playfulness of, 29
  of projections, 268
  of qualities vs. size, 260, 261, 269
  of reference points, 312
  as teaching/scriptures, 374
  as trustworthy, 105
  up-to-date experience of, 99
  vajrayana, of form, 252
  wisdom of, xxviii
  working with, 20, 47

Yeshe Tsogyal, 139
  as pregnant tigress, 139, 140–141
Yeshen ("primordial ancestor"), 49–50,
    149n.1
Yidam deities, 261–262, 382
  sense perceptions as, 262
Yoga
  hatha, 265–268
  ultimate, 374
  See also Six dharmas/yogas of
    Naropa
"The Yogic Songs of Milarepa" (semi-
    nar), xxx
"Youthful prince in a vase," 98–99

Zen tradition, 229–230
  ox-herding pictures, 98
  practices, 42